THE
ANTE-BELLUM
CHARLESTON
THEATRE

THE ANTE-BELLUM CHARLESTON THEATRE

By W. STANLEY HOOLE

UNIVERSITY OF ALABAMA PRESS

MCMXLVI

To
Marcia Du Bose Hoole

FOREWORD

LOWLY, with great labor and the quiet devotion of many scholars, the history of the theatre in America is being written. It is instructive to compare the earlier accounts of the stage, by Ireland, Allston Brown, or Durang, with the present chronicles to which Dr. Hoole refers in his Introduction. It is not unfair to say that while both have been written by lovers of the theatre, the great distinction lies in the fact that the historians of today are scholars. The earlier histories are valuable, but the work had to be done over again. For to a scholar, the most essential quality is accuracy. A history of a theatre may be as charming, as gossipy, as it can be, but if the facts are not correct, it does more harm than good.

The writer of such a history as this volume presents has a choice between two courses. He may present a narrative including in his text every play that has been produced, and giving in that place all the information concerning it. When the book is well indexed, this is the ideal method, but unless an historian devotes his life to the task, as Dr. Odell has done in his *Annals of the New York Stage,* and unless he can find a publisher of unusual courage, this method is out of the question. The other alternative, which has been followed in the present volume, is to present a complete list of the productions upon the Charleston stage, and to preface this record with an historical account which dwells only upon the most important events and relates them to the cultural development of a city rich in theatrical tradition. An important feature of this form of history lies in the complete indices of plays, of players, and of playwrights which follow the chronological record. These establish the second important quality of such a history,—its completeness. Anyone who wishes to know when a play was produced in Charleston from 1800 to 1861 can find the information readily, and more important, he can be sure that if the name of the play or that of the actor does not appear, neither play nor actor belongs to Charleston history.

Through the history and through the chronicle and its related indices, Dr. Hoole has given a picture of a brave struggle on the part of managers, actors and lovers of the stage against evangelical intolerance, social prejudice, fire hazard and the other enemies of the theatre during three-fifths of a century. Perhaps to a student of the stage as a whole the most definite impression lies in the evidence of the rapid interchange of plays and actors between the North and the South. Notwithstanding the difficulties of travel, Cooper, Junius Brutus Booth, Forrest, Macready, Edmund and Charles Kean, Charlotte Cushman, Rachel, Edwin Booth and practically every other actor of note appeared upon the board in Charleston. Those who think that indices are dull reading do not realize how the very assembling of the records of production which makes *Hamlet, Richard III, Macbeth, Romeo and Juliet* stand out as the plays most often given, is itself a tribute to the discrimination of the city. At the other end of the scale, the appearance of the farce *Did You Ever Send Your Wife to Mt. Pleasant?* in 1846 is an amusing evidence that its prototype, *Did You Ever Send Your Wife to Newark?* took a very short time to be acclimated in Charleston. After all, there was never a question of states' rights in the theatre!

ARTHUR HOBSON QUINN

University of Pennsylvania

ACKNOWLEDGMENTS

URING the several years which have been devoted to this study I have become indebted to more people than I can mention here. But I wish particularly to record my gratitude to Mr. David H. Stevens, Mr. Jackson Davis, Mr. John Marshall, and other officials of the Rockefeller Foundation, whose generous grant-in-aid made possible the completion of the work.

I want also to thank Dr. Guy E. Snavely, erstwhile President of Birmingham-Southern College, and now Executive Secretary of the Association of American Colleges, for his friendly cooperation and interest.

Gratitude is due, also, to Professors Jay B. Hubbell and Paull Franklin Baum, of Duke University, and Professor Napier Wilt, of the University of Chicago, for their patient guidance and constructive criticism.

I wish also to make known my appreciation to Mr. Emmett Robinson, director of Charleston's Footlight Players, who, himself interested in Charleston's theatrical history, relinquished his claim on the work and put into my hands many memoranda. For all their painstaking assistance I am grateful to Misses Arabella Mazyck and Ellen Fitz Simons, of the Charleston Library Society.

And, finally, to Martha Sanders Hoole I owe more than I can here express. For months her patience in copying from newspapers, checking titles, names, and dates, and assembling data from more than two trunks full of memoranda exhibited a sincere faith in scholarship. Without her encouragement this work, I fear, would long ago have gone to the waste-basket.

W. STANLEY HOOLE

CONTENTS

ILLUSTRATIONS

INTRODUCTION

S ORIGINALLY PLANNED this work was to have been but a part of a larger, more inclusive study of ante-bellum Charleston's intellectual and artistic development. The scope of this larger study, as first conceived, was broadened so as to allow an interweaving of theatrical data with social, political, and industrial activities, the arts and sciences, and other forces generally accepted as outward evidences of an innate desire for cultural growth. By means of such a mosaic I had hoped to offer a better interpretation of the real Charleston, with its just claims for importance in matters literary, educational, artistic, and theatrical, against an all-governing background of commerce. But as the work on the theatres alone progressed, the materials gathered reached almost unmanageable proportions, finally obviating the possibility of treating more than the one subject in a single volume. Even then a most difficult task was the sorting and excluding of material.

Certainly one fact has been made manifest by such a procedure: Charleston's demand for cultural improvement (evidences of which may include the building of schools, churches, and art galleries, the organization of literary and scientific societies, the publication of books and magazines, the steady growth of a coterie of *literati,* and other indications, as well as the progress of the theatres) followed in direct ratio the rise and fall of business successes. Nor does this imply that culture is always a concomitant of wealth. An inborn propensity for refinement may have existed in the average citizen of this old Southern city as well in times of financial depression as in years of prosperity; but inasmuch as this tendency is always an imponderable, one is obliged to take external evidences as a guide. Indeed, it may be fallacious to bring the measuring stick of influence to so translucent and evasive a subject as "culture," but there can be little doubt that the drama, as one of its votaries, was an art of primary importance in indicating the striving for intellectual and cultural ennoblement. It must be remembered, however, that each of the Charleston theatres was a commercial enterprize operated by one man or a group of men mainly for financial profit. It necessarily follows that, as a criterion of the cultural standard of the community, the theatre must be considered only in so far as it indirectly reflected the public taste.

In attempting to compile this chronology the writer has been constantly reminded of the lack of attention paid to drama in the South by students of American literature. This failure to treat the theatre as a distinct factor in the moulding of public opinion and character has been a notable omission. Many have been the efforts to bring to light the novelists, poets, politicians, and pamphleteers, but there has been comparatively little effort to demonstrate the influence of the stage upon the literary and cultural reputation of the region. Perhaps this negligence may be accounted for in the rarity of published plays, the inaccessibility of general material, or the almost prohibitive task of compiling day-by-day lists of performances from newspapers, practically the only source of theatrical information. However, such work has been done for other cities. Philadelphia has been done by Reese Davis James, Thomas Clark Pollock, and Arthur Herman Wilson, under the direction and inspiration of Professor Arthur Hobson Quinn.[1] Work on the Chicago theatres is now going ahead under the direction of Professor Napier Wilt; New York has been eminently well studied in George C. D. Odell's *Annals of the New York Stage* (New York, 1927-); and the stage history of early St. Louis has been written by William G. B. Carson.[2] No doubt there are others. But so far as I have discovered no book dealing with theatricals in the South has appeared except Eola Willis' *The Charleston Stage in the Eighteenth Century* (Columbia, 1924), a volume which ends

---

[1] Thomas Clark Pollock, *The Philadelphia Theatre in the Eighteenth Century* (Philadelphia, 1933); Reese Davis James, *Old Drury of Philadelphia* (Philadelphia, 1932); and Arthur Herman Wilson, *A History of the Philadelphia Theatre, 1835-1855* (Philadelphia, 1935).

[2] *The Theatre on the Frontier* (Chicago, 1932).

where this one begins. Up to now complete theatrical histories of New Orleans, Savannah, Richmond, Mobile, Memphis, Augusta, and other important Southern centers, if they have been written, remain unpublished.[3]

Charleston in 1790 had a population of only 8,000 whites, yet its stage record shows that up to that time the city had had at least three different theatrical establishments, the first of which, the Dock Street Theatre, one of America's earliest, was opened in 1736. In 1793 a fourth was erected and in the prosperous days of 1837 a fifth—each with a seating capacity of 1200, yet the population until 1840 was never more than 13,000. Meanwhile, of course, each of the larger Northern cities supported three, four, or more theatres. Charleston could never support more than one at a time, but to these in succession came a steady stream of the best talent on the American stage. It is perhaps doubly creditable that this small, out-of-the-way Southern seaport, separated as it was from the larger metropolitan areas, can lay claim to so significant a theatrical history.

As Walter Hampden once remarked, people in these early days thought theatre, talked theatre, wrote theatre, and went to the theatre. Players were real personalities, not reflections on a silver screen. It was an event to be remembered when Edwin Booth, Charles Macready, Edmund Kean, or Jenny Lind came to town. Players were frequently feted, presented

[3] See, however, Harold F. Bogner, "Sir Walter Scott in New Orleans, 1818-1832," *Louisiana Historical Quarterly*, XXI, 420-517 (April, 1938); Martin Staples Shockley, "American Plays in the Richmond Theatre, 1819-1838," *Studies in Philology*, XXXVII, 101-119 (January, 1940); "The Proprietors of Richmond's New Theatre of 1819," *William and Mary College Quarterly*, Second Series, XIX, 1-7 (July, 1939); and "Shakspere's Plays in the Richmond Theatre, 1819-1838," *Shakespeare Association Bulletin*, XV, 88-94 (April, 1940); Douglas L. Hunt, "The Nashville Theatre, 1830-1840," *Birmingham-Southern College Bulletin*, XXVIII, 1-89 (May, 1935); Nellie Smithers, "A History of the English Theatre at New Orleans, 1806-1842," *Louisiana Historical Quarterly*, XXVIII, 85-276, 361-572 (January, April, 1945); Arthur H. Moehlenbrock, "The German Drama on the New Orleans Stage," *Louisiana Historical Quarterly*, XXVI, 361-627 (April, 1943); Lucile Gafford, *Material Conditions in the Theatres of New Orleans before the Civil War* (Master's Thesis, University of Chicago, 1925); and *A History of the St. Charles Theatre in New Orleans*, 1835-1843 (Doctor's Thesis, University of Chicago, 1932).

with gifts, invited to deliver addresses, and otherwise triumphantly received. Newspapers of Charleston for more than a
hundred and fifty years teemed with accounts of the activities
of the playhouses, and visitors trekked over almost impassable
roads to see Thomas Apthorpe Cooper, Junius Brutus Booth,
Tyrone Power, Anna Cora Mowatt, Lola Montez, James
Hackett, and other stage celebrities. Under such conditions it
is not difficult to understand the upspringing of a group of
local dramatists. Receiving impetus from the theatre, these
men sought to improve it by their enthusiasm and talent,
hoping, no doubt, that their contributions would aid in the
upbuilding of the local and ultimately the national drama.
As early as 1774 this resilience was being felt in two local
plays, *The Attack on Fort Moultrie* and *Young America in
London*, generally attributed to M. M. Pinckney; on April 16,
1796, Audin's *Apotheosis of Franklin* was presented in the
City Theatre; John Beete's *The Man of the Times* was first
played a year later; and the anonymous *Americana, or A Tale
of the Genii* was given in 1798. In the nineteenth century,
when theatrical seasons were more regular and of a genuinely
higher type, the list of plays written by Charlestonians grew
into larger proportions. James Workman's *Liberty in Louisiana* (1804), William Ioor's *Independence* (1805), John Blake
White's *Foscari* and *Mysteries of the Castle* (1806), and
Modern Honor (1812), Isaac Harby's *The Gordian Knot*
(1810) and *Alberti* (1819), Edwin C. Holland's *The Corsair*
(1818), William Craft's *The Sea Serpent* (1819), James W.
Simmons' *Manfredi* (1821), John A. Stone's *Fauntleroy*
(1825), William Gilmore Simms's *Michael Bonham* (1855),[4]
and many more, are indicative of this desire. Besides
these, several local playwrights saw their characters take
form on stages outside of their native city. William Henry
Hurlbert's *Americans in Paris* was first played at Wallack's
Theatre, New York, 1858; Ioor's *The Battle of Eutaw Springs
and the Evacuation of Charleston* was initially presented at
the Southwark Theatre, Philadelphia, in 1813, and J. B.

[4] See W. Stanley Hoole, "Simms's *Michael Bonham*: A 'Forgotten' Drama
of the Texas Revolution," *Southwestern Historical Quarterly*, XLVI, 255-
262 (January, 1943).

Williamson's *Preservation* was first staged at the Federal Street Theatre, Boston, in 1797. Furthermore, there were popular dramatizations of Simms's novels, particularly *The Partisan* (by H. H. Paul) and *The Yemassee*. And when one recalls that Henry T. Farmer's prize poem was read at the opening of the Bowery Theatre, New York, October 26, 1826,[5] that Simms's address dedicated the Charleston Theatre in 1837, and that Henry Timrod wrote the dedicating verses for the Richmond Theatre, February 9, 1863,[6] it is not difficult to believe that Charleston's interest in drama was far wider than local.[7]

[5] Odell, *op. cit.*, III, 256.

[6] Laurence Hutton and William Carey, *Occasional Addresses* (New York, 1890), pp. 82-86.

[7] Excerpts from this Introduction have previously appeared in "Charleston Theatres," *Southwest Review*, XXV, 193-204 (January, 1940), and in "The Charleston Stage, 1800-1861," *The Columbia* (S. C.) *Record*, November 29, 1945.

BIBLIOGRAPHY OF NEWSPAPERS

THIS LIST contains only those Charleston newspapers which served as source material for these records.

The Times, 1800-1813; 1816-1817; 1821.

The South Carolina Gazette, 1800-1801.

Carolina Gazette, 1801-1802; 1810-1828.

The City Gazette, 1800; 1802-1810; 1812-1833.

The Courier, 1803-1852.

The Charleston Daily Courier, 1853-1861.

The Charleston Mercury, 1829-1861.

The Southern Patriot, 1819-1820; 1823; 1825; 1827; 1829-1841; 1845-1848.

THE
ANTE-BELLUM
CHARLESTON
THEATRE

I: THE CITY THEATRE, 1800; THE CHARLESTON THEATRE, 1800-1813

O N OCTOBER 28, 1799, when Alexander Placide opened the City Theatre for the fall and winter seasons, he was beginning his fifth year as manager-player on the Charleston stages.[1] Having appeared in the city in 1791 as "the first Rope Dancer to the King of France and His Troop," he had returned in 1794 with a troupe of French players to open the French Theatre (later called the City or Church Street Theatre) in a renovated building known also as Sollee's Hall. Since that time he had made his home in Charleston.

In 1796 he had married Charlotte Sophia Wrighten, member of the Boston Theatre Company then playing in Charleston, had opened Vaux-Hall Gardens, a fashionable summer resort, and had in general established himself as a worthy citizen of the community. With John B. Williamson and Edward Jones as co-managers he had year by year alternated in presenting attractions between the French Theatre and the city's other playhouse, the Charleston Theatre; but upon Jones's death in 1799, he had continued as manager, with Williamson as acting manager, employing his own stock companies and presenting original pantomimes and interludes.[2] As the season of 1799-1800 began, therefore, Placide was familiarly known to Charlestonians as an active manager, pantomimist, rope dancer and actor.

For the opening performance of the new century, January 1, 1800, Placide selected David Garrick's *The Country Girl* and *Rosina,* a comic opera. News of the death of George Wash-

[1] The theatrical season referred to here and elsewhere in this work usually ran from September, October, or November until May, June, or July. There were rarely any attempts to present summer seasons.
[2] Most of the statements concerning the City Theatre are from Eola Willis, *op. cit.,* which tells the story of Charleston's various theatrical enterprises, 1734-1800.

ington, however, had put the city in mourning and Placide, with a keen eye for business, set aside the eighteenth as "commemoration day" in the theatre. *The Roman Father, or The Deliverer of His Country* was presented, a bust of the late General was exhibited; Williamson delivered an "occasional address," and the cast sang a "solemn dirge"—all of which so packed the theatre that a repetition of the performance had to be given four nights later to accommodate those "Ladies and Gentlemen who were disappointed of their places on Saturday last."

By March, however, the incommodious City Theatre had failed to justify its continuance as a playhouse, and Placide announced that he had been advised "by the most respected friends of the dramatic amusement of this city" to enter upon a lease of the Charleston Theatre, across town. Accordingly, on March 28 the doors of the City were permanently closed,[3] and three nights later the Charleston, "after having undergone the necessary repairs, a total interior redecoration, and the first five boxes enlarged,"[4] was re-opened with *Fountainville Forest* and a new farce, *Rinaldo and Armida,* for the benefit of the manager's wife.

The Charleston Theatre, to which the Placide Company of Comedians transferred and which for thirty-three more years was to be the city's chief center of amusement, had already in 1800 a short though worthy history. Built in 1792-93 with money raised by Thomas Wade West and John Bignall, theatrical managers well known in early American stage annals, the structure was situated on the triangular corner of Broad and Middleton (now New) streets, bordering on Savage's Green, a field used earlier as a drill ground. The theatre, 125′ x 56′ x 37′ over all, "with an handsome pediment, stone ornaments, a large flight of stone steps, and a courtyard palisaded," was modeled in general after London opera houses. The 56′ circular-front stage was illuminated by "three rows of patent lamps," and the three tiers of boxes, the pits and the gallery gave the building a seating capacity of twelve hundred. All mouldings and projections were painted silver

[3] The City Theatre, though used until December 31, 1800, for exhibitions of various sorts, was never after this date regularly used as a theatre.
[4] *City Gazette,* March 29, April 23, 1800.

against a background of French white. The building was advertised as a "combination of elegance and novelty," and Charlestonians believed that such a blend of "beauty and conveniency" rendered the structure "the first theatre on the continent."[5]

West and Bignall had officially opened the new playhouse February 11, 1793, with O'Keefe's *The Highland Reel* and Mrs. Inchbald's *The Adventures of a Shawl.* From that time until Placide leased it, however, the theatre had been only irregularly operated by West and Bignall and, later, by John J. L. Sollee. At one time it had been rented out as a seminary for boys. For some reason (perhaps a high rental) it had never been so popular as the less attractive City Theatre. But now, with the coming of Placide's Company, it was to continue without opposition for many years.

The season of 1799-1800 closed May 8, and immediately thereafter Placide and his wife and several of the cast members transferred their allegiance to Vaux-Hall Gardens where music and pantomimes were presented and ice cream and cold baths offered to the public.[6]

Placide's first year at the Charleston was evidently not profitable, for the following season, instead of beginning in the fall, he postponed the opening until January 23, 1801. The city's only amusements during the interim were Langley's Equestrian Circus in Church Street and Bellisariux's "Live Whale and Magics" at the outmoded City Theatre.[7] Even this latter did not last long, however, for on December 30, 1800, the *Gazette* announced that "the City Theatre has been con-

---

[5] For a full description of this theatre, the raising of the money, etc., see W. Stanley Hoole, "Two Famous Theatres of the Old South," *South Atlantic Quarterly*, XXXVI, 273-277 (July, 1937).

[6] Vaux-Hall Gardens, corner of Friend and Broad Streets, was a fashionable summer resort for many years. It was operated by Placide until his death, afterwards by his widow. In 1812 Pepin and Breschard, of the New York and Philadelphia Circus, erected an amphitheatre on the property. *Courier*, March 28, 1814, lists a Mr. Perez as intendant of the property, indicating that he may have by that time acquired the Gardens. It was, however, offered for sale at auction in 1818 and 1819 (see *ibid.*, December 7, 1819; *City Gazette*, May 9, 1800, June 8, 1801, June 6, 1804; and *The Times*, November 16, 1812).

[7] *City Gazette*, October 11, November 22, December 22, 1800.

verted, with very great expense, into elegant and roomy accommodations, for public balls and concerts."[8]

In 1801-02 Placide inaugurated a system of dividing his company's time between the Charleston and Savannah Theatres. Opening in Charleston in early November, the company would remain until Christmas, then move to Savannah where they would stay until late in January.[9] Upon returning, they would re-open the Charleston for a "winter season," usually running until late May or June. In this way the company managed always to be in Charleston during the famous Race Week which generally came in February.[10] Placide, ever an alert manager, tried novelty after novelty to win the public patronage. Now and then a cast member would "leap through a balloon of real fire" or "fly through a sun of brilliant fire from the gallery to the back of the stage" or do tumbling, bird calls or tight-rope walking. Season tickets were occasionally offered at reduced prices,[11] and benefit performances were frequently given for various public institutions of the city.[12] New cast members were added from year to year and Placide or his manager would always in late summer "journey to the northward" in search of talent or scenery to "render the theatre an object of worthy patronage of the audience of Charleston."[13]

[8] See also *The Times*, March 23, 1805.

[9] Typical of press announcements regarding the return from Savannah of the company is this, *Courier*, February 1, 1804: "The cloud of dulness with which the total dearth of news, or anything like a substitute for news, has for some time spread over Charleston will now be dispersed, and the sunshine of gaiety once more enliven and animate the hearts of our fellow citizens.—Our theatrical company has returned from a very successful trip to Savannah. Their houses were in general full, and the benefits were so profitable as to do great credit to the people of that town—to their taste and justice. . . Marshall and Sully, Hodgkinson and Placide had brimmers. . ."

[10] The races were held at the Washington Course, now Hampton Park, site of The Citadel, Military College of South Carolina. See John B. Irving, *History of the South Carolina Jockey Club* (Charleston, 1857).

[11] Regular prices were: box and pit, $1, gallery, 50c; season tickets were sold for $20 for 40 or 45 nights, exclusive of benefit performances.

[12] See *City Gazette*, March 26, April 28, May 7, 1802; March 3, 1809. The May 7, 1802, performance was given for the Charleston Orphan House; that of March 19, 1804, for the benefit of "the sufferers in the Norfolk, Virginia, fire."

[13] *Ibid.*, September 27, 1802; *Courier*, February 9, 1804. Among the many new players who arrived during Placide's management were the parents

ONLY KNOWN PICTURE OF THE "OLD" CHARLESTON
THEATRE, BUILT IN 1793, AFTER IT HAD BEEN
CONVERTED INTO A MEDICAL COLLEGE
Courtesy Charleston Library Society

In the summer of 1803 John Hodgkinson, Placide's beloved acting manager, died, and the first performance of the following season was given as a benefit for his orphans. Mrs. Whitlock delivered an original address in his memory,[14] and several days later *(Courier,* November 27) Placide announced that the night had been a successful one, $537.50 having been received. Of this amount $59.00 went for expenses and the balance was passed on to the Hodgkinson children.[15]

Although the *Gazette* had stated in November, 1804, that the famous English tragedian, Thomas Apthorpe Cooper, had arrived in New York, it was not until eighteen months later that Placide was able to secure his services for Charleston audiences. His appearance as a visiting player, April 14, 1806, inaugurated the "star system" in Charleston. He was engaged for twelve nights only, but remained until May 16, playing such favorite rôles as "Hamlet," "Macbeth," "Pendruddock" in *The Wheel of Fortune,* and the "Duke of Aranza" in *The Honeymoon.* Of his ability "Thespis," dramatic critic for the *Courier,* wrote: "We were at first disappointed in Cooper's first performance, and therefore conceived it to be our duty to wait 'til his performance in other characters should unfold his powers more fully." After Cooper had played several nights, "Thespis" confessed, however, that the actor had most certainly exhibited a "wonderful display of talent."[16] From the first Cooper was a favorite with Charleston audiences,

of Edgar Allan Poe. David Poe was a stock player in 1803-04, playing such parts as "Sebastian" in *Charlotte and Werter,* "Hortensio" in *Catherine and Petruchio,* and "The Lover" in *The Old Soldier.* Mrs. Poe was a cast member in 1810-11. She played "Jacintha" in *Suspicious Husband,* opposite John H. Dwyer's "Ranger," and "Little Pickle" opposite his "Vapid" in *The Spoiled Child,* and other leading rôles. On April 29 she had her benefit, playing in *The Wonder.*

14 Hodgkinson, whose real name was Meadowcraft, was once a favorite at the Southwark in Philadelphia. See *Courier,* November 15, December 7, 1805, for verses to his memory, and January 4, 1806, for notice of a benefit given for his children by the manager of the Boston Theatre.

15 This summary of receipts is given because it is one of the few instances when financial data on the theatre are available.

16 "Thespis," S. C. Carpenter, editor of the *Courier,* wrote full theatrical criticisms from April 4, 1803, to December 3, 1806, daily or weekly. On November 23, 1824, he began a second series which ran until the summer of 1825. Carpenter was well known in the city as a writer and publisher (see W. Stanley Hoole, *A Check-list and Finding-list of Charleston Periodicals,* Durham, 1936, pp. 19-20).

appearing frequently until the late thirties. Then, as an old
man, he returned with his daughter, Priscilla, a rising young
leading lady.

New plays were often presented during Placide's management to stimulate interest and keep the city abreast of
theatricals. *Speed the Plough,* given first on February 27,
1801, met with such favor as to be repeated three times before
the season closed. *Pizarro* was presented first on January 24,
1800; *A Winter's Tale,* given initially in 1811, was advertised
as its "first American performance;"[17] and *The Honeymoon,*
first played in Charleston December 28, 1805, was a favorite
until after the Civil War.[18]

Especially did Placide encourage local dramatists. White's
Mysteries of the Castle, Ioor's *The Battle of Eutaw Springs
and the Evacuation of Charleston,* Harby's *Gordian Knot,*
Williamson's *Preservation,* to mention but a few, were among
the local dramas produced under his management. He also
stimulated interest in his profession by giving over the theatre
now and then to local amateur companies.[19] And whenever
possible he would bring to the establishment such attractions
as war dances by real Indians, child actors—Master John
Howard Payne, for example, who starred during March, 1810
—acrobatic families, singers, and other "specialists." Frequent
newspaper notices indicate that he endeavored to keep the
theatre "respectable" by pleading against "smoking" during
performances, by constantly remodeling, redecorating, and acquiring new scenery, and by setting up various "Rules" for
patrons.[20]

Because the Placide Company was at the time playing an
engagement in Richmond, the Charleston Theatre did not
open in the fall of 1811. Philharmonic concerts at Fayolle's
Long Room (Charles Gilfert, later prominent in theatrical

[17] See W. Stanley Hoole, "Shakespeare on the Ante-Bellum Charleston
Stage," *Shakespeare Association Bulletin,* XX (October, 1945).

[18] First performances as advertised in the newspapers are marked by
asterisks in the Annual Chronological Records, Chapter VII, pp. 65-153.

[19] See *Courier,* April 6, May 1, 1805. When the theatre was closed for
Easter Week, Placide offered the theatre to various churches for musical
concerts *(City Gazette,* April 14, 1802, April 6, 1803).

[20] *Courier,* April 18, 1803; November 11, 1808. *Ibid.,* February 6, 1810,
outlines the "Rules." "No admittance for People of Colour in any part
of the House" was a fixed rule *(The Times,* February 19, 1802).

circles, was a member of this orchestra),[21] and Dawson and Pardee's Exhibition of Wax Figures at Jehu Jones's, Broad Street, next door to St. Michael's Church, were among the few entertainments in the city.

Upon the disastrous burning of the Richmond Theatre, December 26, 1811, Placide wrote a letter to the *Courier* (January 4, 1812), explaining that "more than *one hundred* bodies were taken from the flames . . . I saved nothing . . . my music, scenery, wardrobes, everything fell a prey to the flames." He hurried home, added more exits, changed the seating arrangement of the Charleston, and had the City Council to inspect and announce that the building was safe— "in case of fire, *thirteen doors* open into the street, by which the *House* can be emptied, almost in an instant."[22]

The winter season began January 31 (with *Adelgitha*, Robertson, a newly acquired leading man from New York and Richmond, playing the title rôle), but there were no visiting players. On April 20 the first Charleston presentation of *The Exile* was given as a benefit for Mrs. Placide, and on May 15 Placide himself portrayed "The Baron" in *Pavlo and Petrowna*—his last appearance on the Charleston stage—and in June he took his company to Augusta, Georgia, for a short summer season.[23]

On June 24, 1812, *The Times* announced the Senate's Declaration of War, and thereafter for months the papers were filled with news of combat. Sometime between June and September Alexander Placide died, soon to be followed by his second son,[24] and the bereaved widow strove in vain to carry on the theatre. In spite of the competition offered by Cayetaro's Charleston Circus, Broad Street, and Pepin and Breschard's amphitheatre in Vaux-Hall Gardens, and the embarkation of men to camps, Mrs. Placide announced that she would open the playhouse on December 7. The first performance, produced by the handful of faithful stock players as a benefit for "the late Manager Placide's children," was

21 *Ibid.*, November 18, 1811; *Courier*, May 12, 1812.

22 *Ibid.*, January 14, February 3, 1812.

23 *City Gazette*, June 8, 1812.

24 *Ibid.*, September 16, 1812, gives notice of the death of John A. Placide, "second son of Alexander Placide, *deceased*," but the exact date of the father's death was not located by this writer.

not successful, and in a few days Mrs. Placide reduced pit prices from $1 to 75c in hopes of a more numerous attendance. This failed also, and on the first day of the new year she closed the theatre. An anonymous writer in the *Courier* stated that "the present company are willing to make one more effort to awaken the dormant liberality of the Charleston public." The corps of players, he added, "however imperfect in numbers, do sincerely possess something that entitles them to be better rewarded. We have had the Charleston Theatre, heretofore, under the management of the husband of the Lady, who has now been left a widow with a young and numerous family, and with no other way under heaven for their support, but their exertion of their own talents . . ." Encouraged, Mrs. Placide re-opened the theatre, but after only two nights the curtain was rung down as an ignominious finale to the Placide family's control of Charleston's theatricals.[25]

However, the name was to be carried on, perhaps even more gloriously than the parents had dreamed, in the person of Henry, the eldest son. As a boy under his father's guidance he had gained the early training that was later to make him a leading American actor, known on two continents. Years later, when he returned to Charleston as star, he was billed with a "home-town-boy-made-good" sort of publicity, and always received the best at the hands of Charlestonians.[26] The other Placide children followed stage careers also. Thomas became a well-known player in New York and Philadelphia, and for several seasons managed the New Orleans Varieties. Jane left Charleston upon her father's death and was for ten years or more "the Queen of the Drama in New Orleans."[27] Elizabeth was playing on the Charleston stage as late as 1821-22; and Caroline, as Mrs. Leigh Waring and later as Mrs. William Rufus Blake, was a member of the Charleston stock until the 1830's.

25 *Courier*, February 8, 16, 1813, announces Mrs. Placide's musical concerts at Concert Hall, Church Street.

26 Henry Placide began his career in 1809 at the age of ten, as a member of his father's stock, playing children's rôles, dancing and fencing. He remained with the various local companies until the early 1820's. In December, 1840, he returned as a star.

27 T. Allston Brown, *History of the American Stage* (New York, 1870), pp. 291-292.

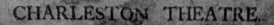

II: THE CHARLESTON THEATRE,
1813-1825

HE CLOUDS OF WAR hung heavily over Charleston during the two years following Mrs. Placide's closing of the theatre in January, 1813, and no brave soul came forward to open its doors. Musical concerts by the St. Cecelia Society, exhibitions of panoramas of the Battle of Lake Erie at Taslet's Long Room, or tumbling, tightrope walking and pantomimes at Langley's Charleston Circus (where some of the old Placide company sought employment) were the only amusements in the city. Vaux-Hall Gardens, with its new amphitheatre, was opened for short seasons each year, but legitimate drama was at a stand-still. Even Race Week, continued in spite of the war, was poorly attended.[1] After the newspapers carried the good tidings of peace in February, 1815, eight months were to pass before the theatre was again a center of attraction.

On October 25 the *City Gazette* announced gleefully that "our Theatre will shortly be opened," naming Joseph G. Holman as manager. Among the cast members were "several of our old favorites;" and the house had undergone a through repair. "From the rapid and prosperous increase of every kind of business, and the great number of visitors who will spend the season in our city, we presume the enterprize and labor of the manager and the company will be richly rewarded."[2] The City Council again examined the building and pronounced it safe "in event of fire or any other alarm," and

[1] *Courier*, December 10, 15, 30, 1813; February 23, March 28, November 12, 1814; February 22, 1815.

[2] "Among the alterations made in the theatre, due care has been taken to secure ladies of character from the possibility of being improperly associated; avenues completely distinct have therefore been made to lead to the separate divisions of the Boxes. . . the *first* Boxes, together with the Pit, are appropriated to the reception of Ladies of respectability exclusively" (*ibid.*, November 1, 1815).

Andrew Walton was granted a concession to open a bar in the lobby.[3]

Manager Holman, who had made his *debut* at Covent Garden Theatre, London, and who had played at the New York Park Theatre, engaged Thomas Hilson, a popular favorite with Northern audiences, as leading man. The season, which proved to be a long and profitable one, was opened November 1 with *The Road to Ruin* and *My Grandmother,* the curtain rising, as was the custom in these years, at 6:30 P.M. Hilson starred nightly during the first three weeks, but it was not until November 27 that Holman himself played.

On January 8, 1816, Mrs. Charles Gilfert *(nee* Agnes Holman and wife of the orchestra leader) joined the cast to play "Lady Townly" in *The Provoked Husband.* She proved immediately popular, and continued throughout the season to play leading parts opposite Hilson and her brother. She was for eight years (during her husband's managership of the theatre) a stock favorite, and later a visiting star. "As a performer, Mrs. Gilfert certainly ranks among the first now on the American boards," wrote the critic of the *Gazette* (January 29, 1816), and one admirer complained in a long letter that he was prevented from seeing her performances "by persons standing in front."[4] Manager Holman, recognizing the commercial value of so popular a player, kept his company continually studying new plays as vehicles for his sister,[5] himself and Hilson playing opposite her on special occasions.

Cooper returned to Charleston for his fifth starring engagement on March 20, opening in *Hamlet.* Mrs. Gilfert supported him and the combination filled Holman's coffers. Soon after the tragedian's departure the stock settled down to regular performances. April 29 was set aside for the benefit of Mrs. Leigh Waring *(nee* Caroline Placide) and an editorial writer "hoped that the citizens of Charleston" would "patronize the efforts of a Lady who was born among them."[6] Other benefit

3 *Ibid.,* November 1, 1815. This custom of having a barroom adjoining the theatre or in the lobby was practiced until after the Civil War.

4 *Ibid.,* February 9, 1816.

5 *Ibid.,* February 14, 1816. Holman's own play, *Votary of Wealth,* given first this night, was one of these.

6 See also *City Gazette,* May 15, 1818.

performances followed rapidly until Holman left the city for Richmond where (stated the *Richmond Enquirer,* May 11, 1816) he had purchased "an excellent lot on Schockoe Hill, for the purpose of erecting a theatre, with all possible expedition."[7] Hilson had left earlier with Cooper for the Savannah Theatre, and then travelled northward to Norfolk;[8] and the cast, stripped of its leading performers, dragged the season to a close on May 18.

Holman's second and last season, that of 1816-17, profitable financially, was marred by an ugly disagreement between himself and James H. Caldwell, his leading performer.

On October 30 Holman arrived in the city from Liverpool with his "Charleston Company of Comedians," among whom were Caldwell and Miss Lattimer, Holman's future wife.[9] The *Courier* praised "our indefatigable manager" and his new players, referring to Caldwell as "a gentleman, whose private character, and public talents as a comedian, have gained him the highest celebrity in England and Ireland." The actor had been "induced by liberal offers . . . to conclude an engagement abroad to perform in the United States, for twelve months."[10]

Promptly the theatre was opened,[11] Caldwell making his first American appearance in *The West Indian.* Congratulatory letters on his ability appeared in the papers,[12] and what with the appearance of Mrs. Gilfert and Holman, Miss Lattimer's singing and dancing, and the occasional production of new plays, the season gave promise of being a long one.[13] However, on March 8, without warning, Holman dismissed Caldwell, cancelled the shows and closed the theatre for a week. Play-goers were first informed of the cause of the rift

[7] *Ibid.,* May 17, 1816. In June he was back in Charleston from whence he embarked for England on the *Tea-Plant* "to engage performers, for the Theatre in this city" *(ibid.,* October 30, 1816).

[8] *The Norfolk Herald,* May 13; *City Gazette,* May 21, 1816.

[9] Holman married Miss Lattimer on August 17, 1817, only two days before his death at Rockaway, L. I. (Brown, *op. cit.,* p. 181).

[10] *Courier,* October 30, 1816.

[11] During this season the doors of the theatre were opened at 6 P. M., and the curtain was pulled at 7. Prices were: box and pit, $1, gallery, 50c.

[12] For instance, see *City Gazette,* November 16, 25, 1816.

[13] Race Week this year began on February 26. The purse of $1000 was won by Colonel J. B. Richardson's "Transport."

by Caldwell's "Letter to the Public" *(Gazette,* March 11). He had been induced, he wrote, to suffer "the expense and dangers attendant upon crossing the ocean" to come to Charleston. His verbal contract (Holman being a gentleman, there was no written one, he stated) specified that he should play only "light comedy," but if forced by necessity "to play in Tragedy," he should be given a "secondary character," and be allowed to play a farce part in the after-piece "to display myself more to my advantage." He had played "The Duke" and a farce rôle March 5, he added, but two nights later he had not been given a rôle in *The Agreeable Surprise,* though he had been billed as "Buckingham." He therefore refused to play in the tragedy unless he also played in a farce. The next day Holman sent him word that "he was no longer attached to the Theatre," discharging him "contrary to all justice and the law of customs of Theatres," without so much as a benefit performance.

Holman replied in both the *Courier* and the *Gazette* (March 15) by publishing the written contract in which Caldwell had agreed to perform "during the winter season, for the weekly sum of Thirty Dollars." He further stated that the actor had been "engaged equally for Tragedy as Comedy," and that "the very act of seceding from his duty was a positive violation of his contract." Caldwell retaliated by repeating that there had been no written contract; Holman restated his position, and Caldwell referred his case "to a liberal and just public, capable of deciding on all points of equity." Several days later a committee was appointed to decide the matter, and the case was finally brought before the Court of Common Pleas. The result was a draw. Caldwell was granted the right to play a benefit. Holman was given the legal authority to dismiss the recalcitrant player.[14] Caldwell chose the title rôle in *Hamlet* and three parts in *Three and Deuce* for his benefit, but Holman refused to assist in the presentation. The comedian left the city the next day and did not return until 1820, at which time he brought his own cast.[15]

[14] *Courier,* March 17-21; *City Gazette,* March 17-18, 1817.

[15] In the fall of 1817 Caldwell became manager of the Columbus (Ky.) Theatre. In 1827 he was managing the American Theatre in New Orleans, and in 1827-1828 he was at the St. Louis (Mo.) Theatre (Carson, *op. cit.,* pp. 84ff.). In 1835 he was back in New Orleans at the St. Charles Theatre (Brown, *op. cit.,* p. 61).

The remainder of the season continued without interruption, Holman acting more frequently than had been his custom. The final performance was presented May 2—a "grand chorus" sang "God Save the United States" and an "American Eagle descended and hovered over the head of the Immortal Washington."

Charles Gilfert, Holman's successor, was born in Germany in 1787. As a young man he had come to Charleston, opened a "musical establishment" at 40 Broad Street, joined the Philharmonic Society Orchestra, directed the theatre orchestra, and otherwise identified himself with the music-lovers of the city. His original medleys, composed for the Philharmonic (particularly the "Maid of Lodi, with Six Variations for the Piano Forte," and "Serenading Waltz"), coupled with his ability as a critic, won for him more than local fame.[16] Late in 1815 he had married Agnes Holman, and for ten years thereafter their names were indelibly written in Charleston's theatrical annals.

Having been connected with the theatre business for several years, and being fully aware of its handicaps, Gilfert assumed the managership of the Charleston with recognizable fears and misgivings. In the *Courier* (December 9, 1817) he stated that he had exerted every effort in "procuring the highest Theatrical Talents" for the pleasure of the public. Several old names were among the announced list of players,[17] and Cooper, Benjamin Charles Incledon, and Hilson were engaged as stars.[18]

In a completely redecorated building *Speed the Plough* and *No Song, No Supper* were presented as opening attractions, December 12, 1817. Hilson came within a few days, followed by John H. Dwyer, the comedian, who had not been in Charles-

[16] *Appleton's Cyclopedia*, II, 649-650; *Courier*, December 29, 1810, January 16, 1811, December 26, 1815; *The Times*, November 18, 1811, May 12, 1812. Abraham Motte, *Charleston Directory, and Strangers' Guide for the Year 1816* (Charleston, 1816), p. 35.

[17] Mr. and Mrs. Thomas Faulkner came this year as new players. Because they were for so long identified with Charleston theatricals (Faulkner was manager in 1829-31) their names are pointed out here.

[18] The status of Thomas Hilson remains more or less a puzzle. Billed as a star, he would come and remain all season. In 1819-20, for example, he did not appear until January and left in March. In May he was "re-engaged;" yet during the season he was listed as "acting manager."

ton since 1810-11, and these, assisted by Mrs. Gilfert, played
frequently until after Race Week.[19] Neither they nor the
tragedian Williams could revive interest in the drama, however, and on February 18 Gilfert staged Edwin C.
Holland's *The Corsair*, for the "first time in America, with special music
by Mr. Gilfert," in the hopes that a local author's play might
stimulate attendance.

Incledon, scheduled to arrive March 2, was delayed. Gilfert
apologized publicly,[20] "re-engaged" Hilson, and retained Dwyer
until the eleventh, "his last night on the American Stage."
Cooper arrived towards the end of the month, was "re-
engaged because of his great success;" and, finally, when
Incledon did arrive, patrons were offered the rare treat of
seeing him, Cooper, and Mrs. Gilfert in the same week.
Incledon's only visit to Charleston was very successful. His
singing of such songs as "When First this Humble Roof I
Knew" and "Scots Wha Ha'e wi' Wallace Bled" were long
remembered.[21]

Gilfert's second year was not so successful although it was
stated as "a very generally received opinion, that the Charleston Company, is the best in the Union." In spite of the fact
that Cooper and Henry Wallack were announced as stars,[22] the
season of 1818-19 got off to a poor start, and late in November
Gilfert, following the custom of Alexander Placide, took his
company to the Savannah Theatre for "some weeks."[23] On
February 1 the company returned and played to "full and
fashionable houses" for a short time, but were unprofitably
rewarded.[24] Not to be outdone, Gilfert packed his wardrobes
and returned to Savannah, stating that he was "under obliga-

---

19 "The Races, this year, have been uncommonly meagre and uninterest-
ing—offering little to excite or reward. Not one handsome race—not
many handsome ladies—and very few handsome equipages have been
exhibited on the course" *(Courier,* February 9, 1818).

20 *Ibid.,* March 17, 1818.

21 *Ibid.,* April 24, 1818.

22 *City Gazette,* October 21, 1818. Wallack did not appear this season,
however.

23 *Ibid.,* November 30, 1818. In their absence "The Museum," corner of
Market and Meeting streets, exhibited "for 30c" a live elephant, "the
largest and most sagacious animal in the world. . . and weighs more than
3000 pounds!" *(ibid.,* January 1, 1819).

24 *Ibid.,* February 8, 1819.

tion" to the Georgians "to perform a certain extent this season," and was therefore obliged unwillingly to "compress his performances in Charleston."[25] More than a month later he returned, bringing Cooper with him.

Early in April it was made known that General Gaines, hero of the Battle of Lake Erie, and a man "whose valour has maintained the honour, dignity and independence of America," would attend the theatre on the nineteenth. For him Gilfert decorated a box with "evergreen and roses" and the word *ERIE*, and presented *Alexander*, starring Cooper, who "drew forth repeated rounds of applause."[26]

Enthusiasm did not run highest, however, until it was announced that James Monroe, President of the United States, was on his way to the city. After a week of expectant waiting, crowds gathered at high noon, April 26, at Gordon and Springs's Ferry "where the elegant Barge, prepared by the City Council, manned by twenty-one Masters of Vessels and Members of the Marine Society, was in waiting for his reception." Upon landing, the President was greeted by cheers. He jumped in the Governor's barouche, and, escorted by mounted riflemen and a troop of cavalry, rode away. Later he triumphantly rode on horseback to the junction of Meeting and Boundary (now Calhoun) streets where he was met by the Intendant who welcomed him to the city.

Two days later the President visited the theatre, accompanied by the Governor and his Staff. When he entered, "the orchestra struck up *Hail Columbia* and the audience rose and gave him nine hearty cheers." Seated in a box decorated with wreaths of roses, an American eagle and a scroll "on which was inscribed in letters of gold, *'The People's Choice,'*" the President watched Cooper and Cleary interpret "Mark Antony" and "Brutus" before the largest crowd, eighteen hundred people, ever assembled in the theatre. After having been feted by the St. Cecelia Society, the Museum of Natural History, the Cincinnati Society, and Joel R. Poinsett, the President again attended the Charleston. This time he witnessed Cleary play the title rôle in *Alberti*, by the local

[25] *Courier*, March 3, 1819.
[6] *Ibid.*, April 19, 21, 1819.

journalist, Isaac Harby. On May 3, after paying respects to several of the city's public institutions, President Monroe continued on his journey to Savannah.[27]

Meanwhile, the *Courier* had complained that Gilfert was not making expenses, scarcely finding it "to his advantage to engage an actor of such splendid powers as Mr. Cooper." Even the two "bumper nights" when the President had visited the theatre had not given the manager "adequate remuneration" for his previous losses—and on May 12 he brought the unprofitable season to a close with *The Sea Serpent,* from the pen of a Charleston lawyer, William Crafts. "The dulness of the times, and the almost entire annihilation of commercial prosperity" were given as reasons for the financial failure, and one despondent writer added that those who could have afforded tickets "were kept from the Theatre by the melancholy reflections occasioned by dwelling on the misery and misfortunes of others."[28]

The next four years, though somewhat better financially, were not what Gilfert had expected, and he resorted once more to trips to Savannah. In January, 1820, a mathematical-minded writer in the *Courier* took occasion to flay the theatrical profession by stating that each night's performance extracted from the pockets of Charlestonians more than $300 —that in four months the amount grew to $19,200, and in ten years to $192,000. If this money, along with similar funds from other cities, "were loaned systematically," he added, it would "support about seventy students annually in any one of our colleges," endow "all the professorships in a National University," purchase "an immense library," or keep the poor and "bind up many a broken heart and heal many a bleeding wound."[29] His attack was answered under the caption "Defense of the Theatre" in which the writer replied that the "manager pays annually to the city, a tax equal to that of the owner of five hundred negroes, or $100,000 in real estate," that the profession "supports numerous men and women, imparts information, corrects taste, tends to produce proper pronunciation, inculcates politeness, ease and grace, and

[27] *Ibid.* and *City Gazette,* April 19-May 4, 1819.
[28] *Courier,* May 12, 1819.
[29] *Ibid.,* January 29, 1820.

teaches society how to mingle together without jarring and collision."[30]

Gilfert passed the argument by without comment, announcing quietly that he had appropriately engaged the West Horse Troupe, "exhibiting various surprising displays of training and sagacity," to appear during Race Week.[31] Henry Wallack came for his first Charleston visit in March, and Cooper reappeared soon after. After a few weeks Gilfert closed the season with *Steward,* at which time a *Monody on the Death of General Stephen Decatur,* by a local writer, was read to the audience by Mrs. Gilfert.[32]

In the fall of 1820 James H. Caldwell, manager of the New Orleans and Petersburg, Virginia, theatres, rented the Charleston from Gilfert for six weeks and opened it with his own company. Presenting a number of brilliant new plays and operas,[33] he more than atoned for his misbehaviour of a few seasons previous. Towards the end of December, however, he took his cast on to New Orleans, and Gilfert, reluctant to start a late season, made a trip north in an unsuccessful attempt to bring Edmund Kean to Charleston.[34] In his absence the season began under his wife's direction. Master Smith, "age 9, the American Young Roscius from New York, Boston, and other Theatres," played a short engagement in April, and Cooper came for five nights in May to bring to an end the short and unsuccessful year.

If Gilfert had been unsuccessful in securing Kean, he was more fortunate in persuading Junius Brutus Booth to make a Charleston appearance. Advertised from "Theatre Royal, Drury Lane, and Covent Garden," on November 29, 1821, Booth played his first rôle before a Carolina audience in *Richard III;* a week later he left (with the Gilfert Company) for a season in Savannah.

But the closing of the theatre was no cause for worry this

30 *Ibid.,* February 2, 1820.

31 The competition offered by a daily showing of horses, camels, bears, and other animals at the circus ground and at the corner of Market and Meeting streets perhaps forced Gilfert to this type of entertainment.

32 *Ibid.,* April 28, 1820, contains the *Monody* in full.

33 *Ibid.,* November 28, December 16, 18, 1820.

34 *Ibid.,* March 19-20, 1821. Gilfert discovered that Kean had been induced to return to England to play at Drury Lane.

year. In January the city was filled with entertainments:
Signor Juan Brosa and his daughter, Josephine, with Monsieur
Le Fevre "of the Opera in Paris" were dancing and giving
pantomimes at Fayolle's Long Room; the Union Harmonic
Society was giving concerts of sacred music; W. Blanchard's
exhibitions of "balancing" and slack-wire walking were to
be seen at Lege's Long Room, Queen Street; and various
panoramas were on display throughout the city. "For the
fanciers of great things" there was an elephant and "two
Mammoth Hogs. . . for the fanciers of little things, a White
Rat, for those who are tired of reason, *Exhilirating Gas!*"
But the most interesting, "because the most useful" was a
model of a steam railway—"a real waggon loaded with
cotton . . . and a coach which any person can ride himself in
for 50c."[35]

Not until February did the Gilfert Company return from
Savannah. Success was not theirs, however, and in less than
three weeks they returned to the Georgia seaport.[36] The
manager was in town only long enough to decide that his
failures in Charleston were caused by the dilapidated con-
dition of the 29-year-old theatre. Promptly, he made known
his proposal to build a new one better suited to present
"certain beauties and novelties of scenery." The rent at the
Charleston was too high, he declared, and the "deranged and
decayed state of the interior" prohibited the presentation of
first-class performances. It was the opinion of others, however, that "the population of this city is too slender to
[support] two theatrical establishments; in a contest *both*
would sink, and the public must be the last and greatest suf-
ferer."[37] The whole project was finally put aside, and the
theatre-goers of Charleston, though they did not at the time
know it, were to wait another fifteen years for a new playhouse.

In the fall and winter of 1822-23 the company did not
appear in Charleston. Savannah had proved a more lucrative

---

[35] *Ibid.*, December 12, 1821, January 3, 8, 15, 19, 21, 29, 1822.

[36] In April the company returned to Charleston to play regularly until
May 17, at which time Gilfert and all the players went to the Richmond
Theatre for a summer season (*ibid.*, May 17, 1822).

[37] *Ibid.*, March 1, 1822.

city, and there Gilfert decided to stay, at least temporarily. The Proprietors of the Charleston Theatre, feeling keenly the loss of so estimable a manager,[38] called an urgent meeting,[39] but nothing was done; and it was not until May 22 that the Gilfert Company returned to the city.[40] The Governor and other notables attended the re-opening,[41] but by the end of June the hot weather had begun "to weaken the beauties of the best acted plays,"[42] and Gilfert closed the doors early in July.

Gilfert's last two seasons as manager of the Charleston was deservedly his most successful. Perhaps no man did more for the advancement of the theatrical art in the city than he, and his ten years' connection with the drama stand out notably in its history. Indeed, with theatrical interests in Charleston, Savannah, Richmond, and elsewhere, he did much to further the profession in the South.

The proprietors of the Charleston Theatre, spurred on by Gilfert's recent threat to build a competitive institution, erected during the summer of 1823 "an entirely new stage, with improved proscenium," bought new scenery, and generally redecorated the old building.[43] Delighted with the new arrangements, the manager selected "a company inferior to none in the United States" and "several auxiliaries of eminence" and began the season late in November. The first star was Vincent De Camp, who opened as "Gossamer" in *Laugh When You Can* to a "full and fashionable audience," the supporting cast "animated by his fine playing."[44] After his last appearance, January 12, 1824, which alone brought more than $1000 into the box-office, he was given several curtain calls, and finally forced to address the audience.[45]

[38] Frequent newspaper comments refer at this time to the "dearth of amusement in our City" (*ibid.*, February 8, March 7, 1823, for examples).
[39] *Ibid.*, January 30, 1823.
[40] *City Gazette*, May 21, 1823.
[41] *Courier*, June 3, 1823.
[42] *Ibid.*, June 23, 1823.
[43] *Ibid.*, November 26, 1823.
[44] *City Gazette*, January 5, 1824.
[45] *Ibid.*, January 14, 1824. Gilfert opened this season with reduced prices: box and pit, $1, second tier of boxes, 50c, gallery, 25c; three tickets for $2, five for $3; season tickets, $30. This no doubt aided attendance (*ibid.*, December 4, 1823).

Keene, a stock player, was allowed, after De Camp had gone, to direct several operas, and early in February Gilfert sought the good will of the community by giving three benefit performances for "the Greek Fund." The last two of these raised $500 and $550, respectively, for the local organization.

Henry Wallack came in February. De Camp reappeared immediately after, and both of them remained until the latter part of March, filling the theatre almost nightly.[46] De Camp's interpretation of "Tom" in the new *Tom and Jerry* met with hearty acclaim, and the play was repeated no less than thirteen times before the season ended. Wallack's "Rolla" was, as always, his most popular rôle. On March 12 De Camp, Wallack and Mrs. Gilfert united to present *Henry IV*, "a treat," stated one writer, "very seldom enjoyed on any American stage."[47] De Camp sailed for England in March, but Wallack played a short "re-engagement" before leaving "for the North." The first American performance of James W. Simmons' *Ravenwood*, with a special prologue written by his fellow-townsman, Henry T. Farmer, was well patronized on April 12.[48] Benefits began with Hyatt's presentation of his own *Youthful Days of Mr. Hyatt*, and ended May 24 with an exhibition of fire works and Gilfert's "own arrangement," sung by the cast, of "God Save the United States."[49]

A revival of interest in the drama during these years is evidenced by the recommencement of a series of articles in the *Courier* by S. C. Carpenter, the "Thespis" of 1803. His observations began anew in November, 1824, and continued throughout the season.[50] Carpenter had highest regards for Gilfert's ability, writing, for example, after the opening performance of *Town and Country*, "How Elegant! How Superb!"[51] When William A. Conway appeared, Carpenter commented at length on "his immensity of power, and magnificent flexibility of countenance," a criticism heartily agreed

[46] *Ibid.*, February 23-25, 1824.
[47] *Ibid.*, March 12, 1824.
[48] See *ante*, p. xix.
[49] The theatre was "re-opened by request" on May 26 for a presentation of *The Bride of Abydos* and *Tom and Jerry*.
[50] See especially November 25, December 3, 9, 13, 18, 25, 1824, January 25, February 25, March 12, April 28, 1825.
[51] *Courier*, November 26, 1824.

to by Charlestonians, for on one night alone (December 27) Conway's rendition of *The Apostate* brought "upwards of $1000" to the box-office.[52]

Aladdin, or The Wonderful Lamp, with its "splendour, variety, beauty and brilliance of scenery and machinery," was presented in Charleston for the first time on January 10, 1825. Received with "continuous bursts of admiration, and rapturous applause," it did not "fail of remunerating, most amply, the increasing and indefatigable exertions of our judicious, enterprizing, and tasteful manager."[53] During the season it was given ten times, and for many years remained a popular spectacle with Charleston audiences.

In February newspaper stories concerning the proposed visit of General Lafayette, "the Nation's Guest," began to appear, and almost daily thereafter accounts of his itinerary and poems praising him were printed. He arrived in the city on March 14, 1825, was met by a grand military procession, and that night was escorted to the theatre by "the City Council and the United States Government Officials." Gilfert had prepared his patrons for the arrival by presenting *Lafayette, or The Castle of Olmutz*, exhibiting portraits of the General, and decorating the theatre in his honor. All performances were cancelled March 16 so that the theatre could be used for a "Grand Ball" complimenting the Frenchman, a "Grand Concert composed by Mr. Gilfert" opening the dances.[54]

While all decorations were still left intact, Booth began an eight nights' engagement on March 18; and after his departure the first American production of *Fauntleroy*, by J. A. Stone, a stock player, was presented. Mrs. Gilfert's benefit, the last night of the season, drew from the pen of "Carioliensis" a long congratulatory letter.[55]

Almost a month before the season closed Gilfert had gone to Albany, New York, where, as one writer put it, "better auspices and more genial spirits are likely to await him."[56]

[52] *Ibid.*, December 29, 1824.
[53] *Ibid.*, January 12, February 25, 1825.
[54] *Ibid.*, March 14-18, 1825.
[55] *Ibid.*, April 22, 1825. He appealed for Mrs. Gilfert's benefit by saying that she was "one of the most distinguished actresses in America."
[56] *Ibid.*, February 28, 1825.

However, in the fall it was reported that conditions there were not at all favorable for him.[57] Though his wife returned as a special player in March, 1827, Gilfert was not in any way again connected with the Charleston Theatre. After leaving the South he met with misfortune, finally terminating his career in "pecuniary ruin" and an untimely death. Mrs. Gilfert quit the stage in 1829, taught school for a short time, and finally died in Philadelphia, April 19, 1833, "in abject poverty, and was buried by subscription."[58]

Gilfert's ability as a manager and musician in Charleston cannot be too highly commended. For years he kept the drama on a high and respectable plane and brought leading American actors to the small, isolated Southern city. That his departure was keenly felt can best be proved by an examination of theatrical activities during the ten or twelve years that followed.

[57] *City Gazette*, December 10, 1825, as copied from *The Albany Patriot*.
[58] Brown, *op. cit.*, p. 145.

III: THE CHARLESTON THEATRE,
1825-1833

GILFERT'S resignation had a deadening effect on Charleston's theatricals, for it was not until February, 1826, that his successor, Joe Cowell, an actor who had never appeared on a Charleston stage, came forward to undertake the work. And he, as it will be seen, did not rely solely on legitimate drama for a livelihood.

Cowell, who has left a complete record of his threatrical endeavors,[1] came to the city under disadvantageous circumstances. A storm at sea on his voyage south from Washington caused him severe losses; and when he arrived, he found the Southern seaport quite disturbed over an announcement that the unpopular Edmund Kean had been invited to play in the local theatre.[2] Nevertheless, with a cast "of 55 souls, including musicians, artists, and carpenters," he set about to open "the exhibitions of the Drama." His first gesture for conciliation was a benefit performance for Mrs. Gilfert (who was not in the cast) ; and immediately thereafter he made known his intention to operate, in connection with the theatre, a "circus with equestrian department," the two enterprises alternating nightly.[3] This system was begun at once, but within a few days the circus, more profitable doubtless than the drama, was showing nightly—and the theatre, now of secondary interest to the manager, was neglected.

Kean's arrival provided the needed stimulus, however. The

[1] Joe Cowell, *Thirty Years Passed Among the Players in England and America; Interspersed with Anecdotes and Reminiscences* (New York, 1844).

[2] Kean had made himself very unpopular in Boston by refusing to play to small houses and by making uncomplimentary statements concerning America. He was hissed off the stage. Later, rotten apples, eggs, and sand were thrown at him as he appeared on the stage (Brown, *op. cit.*, p. 200).

[3] The theatre-players appeared at both places. Stoker was in charge of the circus, and Wilkinson "from the Royal Amphitheatre in London" managed the "equestrian department" (*Courier*, February 23, 1826).

Courier had warned its readers of his coming by "fearing" that his appearance would "be attended with unpleasant and alloying circumstances." Kean's ability as an actor of merit was of course acknowledged, but the trouble in which he had recently become involved in the North gave the paper reason to suspect that he would meet with violence in the South. "The good sense and discretion of our city will govern itself on this occasion," but measures "to prevent breaches of the peace . . . and to hinder public disturbances," the writer added, should be taken. He recommended that those who were hostile "to the appearance of Mr. Kean on the Charleston stage . . . absent themselves from his performances." In this way only could "public peace and tranquility as well as the property of the innocent owners of the theatre" be preserved.[4]

Kean too felt the tension. In spite of Cowell's attempt to "smooth the path," he feared the Charleston audience. " 'For God's sake,' " he said to Cowell, " 'by the ties of old fellowship and countrymen—I entreat you not to let me play, if you think the audience will not receive me.' " Cowell sought the advice of fifty friends who gave him "fifty opinions."

On the night of Kean's opening, not a single seat had been sold in advance—but the "house was filled soon after the doors were opened." Cowell peeped from behind the curtain. Amid the twelve hundred men who composed the audience *"there was but one lady,* the wife of the district attorney, and a warm friend of the drama." But she saved the night. According to Cowell, she "acted like a charm," awing to "respectful silence the predetermined turbulence of 1200 men!" And Kean, before an audience "hushed as midnight," played *Richard III* better than he ever had before.[5]

For almost a month thereafter he continued to "charm" the play-goers, and on April 24, the last night of the season, volunteered his services as "Bertram" for the benefit of Cowell. This time the *Courier,* having changed its tone completely, begged for the actor "a crowded house," and praised him in superlative terms.[6]

4 *Ibid.,* January 24, 1826.
5 Cowell, *op. cit.,* II, 67-72.
6 *Courier,* April 24, 1826. Kean returned to England shortly after his Charleston appearance *(ibid.,* December 11, 1826).

When Cowell did not apply for the lease the following season (1826-27), it was believed that there would be no performances. Frequent newspaper comments made it well known that Charleston was not a lucrative theatre town. But the city wanted badly "a first-class Drama," and Dr. John Dyott, a local druggist at "the corner of King and Market Streets,"[7] was prevailed upon to try his hand as show-man.

Unfamiliar with the stage, Dyott employed Frederick Brown, who had appeared in the city two years previous, to return as acting and stage manager, and the season got under way promptly. The cast which Brown selected came mostly from the Royal Theatre, Montreal, where Brown himself had been extremely popular.[8] Most of the serious rôles were played by Brown, Mrs. Riddle and her daughters; Kent led in comedy, and Lamb was the singer. Thomas S. Hamblin, the first visiting performer, came in January, to be followed by Cooper, and both remained to play together through Race Week at advanced prices.[9] On March 22 the schooner *Niagara* brought the old favorite, Mrs. Charles Gilfert, to the city from New York, and for the first time in two years she played before a Southern audience. This lady, however, had lost some of her former appeal, and her engagement was not so profitable as Dyott and Brown had hoped.[10]

Dyott had succeeded in bringing one or two meritorious players to Charleston, but the season was nevertheless proving unprofitable. One member of the cast, Mrs. Mary Riddle, complained publicly that she had not been given her salary and could not leave town until Dyott paid her. The lessee replied that "the temporary embarrassment of the Theatre, is too apparent to need illustration." The actress had already received $800 "for a season of less than twenty weeks," he said, and the balance of $300 would be sent to her as soon as

[7] *Directory and Strangers' Guide for the City of Charleston* (Charleston, 1822), p. 37.

[8] Brown, upon leaving Montreal, had been presented with a ring by the citizens "as a slight testimony of the esteem in which his talent is held by them" *(Courier*, November 11, 1827).

[9] *Ibid.*, January 31, February 23, 27, March 1, 1827.

[10] *Ibid.*, April 9, May 7, 1827. There were complaints that Mrs. Gilfert had "intentionally shown a disrespect for the community of Charleston" by not returning sooner, but she denied them *(ibid.*, May 9, 1827).

possible. Mrs. Riddle replied by printing an itemized state-
ment of their business relationship, and demanded an amount
in cash and the balance on a promissory note. An anonymous
writer joined the controversy to suggest that Dyott lend Mrs.
Riddle the theatre for a benefit night, but the unhappy lady
refused the offer and moved over to St. Andrews' Hall where
she advertised a "concert for $1."[11]

Undaunted by Dyott's failure,[12] another local man, Dr. John
B. Irving, who was well known in the city as "an enterprizing
young gentleman" in literary and professional circles,[13] assumed the managerial duties for the 1827-28 season. Arrang-
ing his policies to appeal especially to the ladies,[14] he
commenced the season in November with several new stock
players. Hamblin, who had proved more popular than Cooper
the previous spring, came early in December, and Vincent
De Camp arrived a month later, but profits for Irving were
far from plentiful,[15] and in February he rented the building
to the Villalave Family of acrobats and gymnasts.[16] Before
they left, John Barnes came for a special engagement, but
without proper supporting cast he could not attract large
audiences.[17] It was not until the arrival of Mrs. Eliza Povey
Knight from Drury Lane who, with Barnes and Keene, presented operettas, that the season reached its climax.[18] As Mrs.

[11] *Ibid.*, May 19-25, 1827. Mrs. Riddle claimed that, counting tickets sold
by herself and her salary of $45 per week, Dyott owed her $340.25. Of
this she demanded $193.25 in cash.

[12] *Ibid.*, October 20, 1827, contains a proposal for the publishing of a
Theatrical Budget, a weekly magazine devoted to local and general
theatrical news. The project did not materialize; but the idea shows the
interest in the drama in spite of the fact that in these days it was on
the down hill.

[13] See Hoole, *A Check-list and Finding-list of Charleston Periodicals*, pp.
7, 47; *Courier*, November 9, 1827, copied from *The Philadelphia Stage
Advocate;* John B. Irving, *History of the South Carolina Jockey Club*,
and *A Day on Cooper River* (Charleston, 1842).

[14] *Courier*, November 9-11, 1827.

[15] *Ibid.*, December 8, 1827; *City Gazette*, January 21, February 16, 1828.

[16] The first picture used in theatrical advertising in Charleston appeared
as a sketch of the Villalave Family, *City Gazette*, February 2, 1828.

[17] *Ibid.*, February 19, 1828, states that "with the exception of Barnes,
there was scarcely an individual who knew a line of his part [in *The
Soldier's Daughter*, February 15], the Stage was frequently kept waiting,
and a want of attention and application were palpably manifested
throughout."

[18] *Ibid.*, March 4, 8, 1828.

Knight left for Augusta, a trio composed of John Mills Brown, Watkins Burroughs, and Mrs. Robertson came to play *The Iron Chest, Matrimony,* and other dramas, but even they could not make Irving's venture lucrative, and he abruptly announced that "from circumstances, and from the severe loss he has sustained during the present season," he was compelled to "close the concern." A sympathetic editorialist, emphasizing the doctor-manager's "severe pecuniary loss," appealed for his "special benefit"—but it too was only meagerly attended.[19]

On April 25, 1827, a young actor named John Jay Adams had made his *debut* in Charleston as a minor performer, and had returned to New York to become fairly well known as "our only tragedian—in those days—of American birth." It was he who decided to try his fortune as manager of the Charleston in 1828-29.[20] The *Gazette* hoped that he would "meet with that encouragement" he deserved in bringing "so strong a cast" to the city, but the suspicious Adams announced in advance that he had no intentions of staying in Charleston more than twelve nights before proceeding to Augusta and Savannah. In his cast was Vincent De Camp who, as usual, delighted his audiences, and in December the corps was augmented by the arrival of Cooper and George Holland from the London Theatre. Adams, by continually reminding his patrons that "the season is a short one," managed to keep the house well filled, but he left for Savannah December 20.[21]

He returned in February with several new players, in cluding Lydia Kelly,[22] but the competition of the "grand menagerie" in Queen Street, a circus and a museum, all of which had opened in his absence, was keenly felt. Clara Fisher's arrival in March was of some help, however. She was greeted "with very strong applause,"[23] and won the public's good favor by contributing $100 of her share of one night's receipts to the "Friends of Ireland."[24] As the year ended, one

[19] *Ibid.*, April 22, 28, 1828.
[20] Odell, *op. cit.*, III, 20, 103, 413; IV, 167ff.
[21] *City Gazette,* November 20, December 24, 1828. The Villalave Family rented the theatre during Adams' absence.
[22] *Ibid.*, February 26, 1829.
[23] *Ibid.*, March 13, 1829.
[24] *Ibid.*, April 11, 1829. On the night of the benefit for the "Friends of Ireland" an address written for the occasion by William Gilmore Simms was spoken.

critic stated that "in the face of disadvantages and interruptions Adams has succeeded in giving to our boards a variety of splendour of exhibition, and now he is about to leave us, not only without remuneration, but even impoverished."[25] Adams at once threw himself "upon the generous feeling of the community" by offering *The Manager in Distress* as a benefit, and left at once for New York.

He returned in the fall of 1829 for a second attempt, but on December 22 "circumstances beyond control compelled him to abandon the management," and a committee of local men, believing that "confidence should be restored to the Theatre at home as well as abroad," engaged John B. Irving, Thomas Faulkner, a member of the stock for eight or nine years, and Charles L. Green to carry on the work.[26] Immediately these men showed their aggressiveness: on January 13 they reduced prices, announced an engagement with Cooper, and opened the theatre to the public for "masquerades in imitation of those in Europe." Mr. and Mrs. John Sloman appeared in February,[27] and Clara Fisher, whose generosity had not been forgotten, began an engagement on March 10. But exhibitions of the "Grand Anaconda, Terror of Ceylon," banded armadillos, silver pheasants and singing birds, together with a display of "the celebrated painting of Cain, meditating the murder of his brother, Abel," drew too many people away from the theatre,[28] and the committee was forced to stop production in April.[29] Perhaps this was best, for quarrels over salaries among the cast, some of whom had already been "discharged," had become known,[30] and a continuance of plays might have meant further disruptions as well as financial losses.

Faulkner alone accepted the control of the playhouse in the

25 *Ibid.*, May 8, 1829.
26 *Courier*, December 22, 1829, March 18, 1830; *Southern Patriot*, January 23, 1830.
27 *Courier*, March 1, 1830.
28 *Ibid.*, February 4, March 15, 1830.
29 Faulkner, Chairman of the Committee, advertised his benefit (April 19) in boldest type, asking that he be not forgotten "for old lang syne," and engaged a troop of United States soldiers from Fort Moultrie to appear on the program in the "ceremony of shooting a deserter."
30 *Ibid.*, March 18-19, *Southern Patriot*, March 19, 1830.

fall of 1830, had the building renovated, and acquired a new drop curtain representing "a view of the City of Charleston taken from the Southern extremity of the Battery."[31] He begged the public to patronize him because of his long attachment to the theatre.[32] His first visiting performers were Mary Rock and Mary Duff, but Faulkner realized that female celebrities without proper male support were tiring his attendants, and he closed the establishment until more profitable plans could be made. As a consequence, there were no performances for two months. When the doors were re-opened, however, Edwin Forrest was on hand to play before his first Charleston audience,[33] and as his contract ended, Cooper, who by now was better known in the city than any other American actor, came for six nights. No other visitors played during the spring, and the curtain was rung down April 4 to end Faulkner's long career on the Charleston stage.[34]

Vincent De Camp, who had first appeared in the city in 1823-24, and who had later become famous at the old Park Theatre, New York,[35] had applied for but failed to get the management of the Charleston in 1830.[36] After Faulkner relinquished his claim, however, he was more successful, and for two seasons—the last two years of the "Old" Charleston Theatre—De Camp conducted the affairs of this important Southern playhouse.

De Camp did not attempt a fall season in 1831 and when he announced a "winter" opening, he was frank to state, as had Adams before him, that it would be "a short season only."

[31] *Southern Patriot*, April 3, 1830.
[32] Faulkner, known generally as "Old Faulkner" and "Tam O'Shanter," was for years "an especial favorite . . . popular with all classes" *(Courier*, January 19, 1858). This article is one of a series entitled "The Theatre, As It Has Been, and As It Is in Charleston" (perhaps by John B. Irving), which appeared October 24, 28, 30-31, 1857, January 6, 12, 19, 21, 26, 30, February 20, 25, March 2, 9, April 15, November 25, December 14, 28, 1858, and January 5, 15, 1859.
[33] *Ibid.*, February 28, 1831. Forrest was "powerful, superior, and elevated." It was thought that he was amply qualified "to supply the place of Cooper, whenever that favorite performer shall have quit the stage."
[34] *Ibid.*, April 4, 1831.
[35] Odell, *op. cit.*, III, 98-99; James E. Murdoch, *The Stage, or Recollections of Actors and Acting* (Philadelphia, 1880), pp. 201-202; *Southern Patriot*, January 30, 1830.
[36] *Courier*, January 30, 1830.

"The celebrated Mr. James Hackett" was his first outstanding performer. In *Jonathan* he was "inimitable,"[37] winning such applause that he had no trouble in filling the house every night of his engagement; and when Charles Kean joined him to play "Othello" opposite his "Iago," the theatre "was packed in every corner."[38] With their departure came Clara Fisher and, again, Cooper,[39] but the manager was not being sufficiently well remunerated for his exertions in bringing such internationally known players to Charleston, and, March 30, after a season of only two months, he ceased production.

Notices appeared immediately that the proprietors were anxious to rent the Charleston Theatre for the coming fall and winter, "for one thousand dollars, with approved security for its payment,"[40] but no one came during the summer to accept the terms. In November, 1832, De Camp gave notice that he would make a second attempt, now that "the necessary repairs" had been completed; and, as he had done before, he began the season with a star—Josephine Clifton, "a tragic actress," as "Belvidera" in *Venice Preserved*. For variety De Camp rented " real horses" from Harrington's Circus to aid his production of *Timour the Tartar,* but nothing seemed to "awaken the dormant public," and the manager "in consequence of severe losses" closed the theatre for two weeks. James Wallack was engaged to re-open it a few weeks later, and Master Joseph Burke, "the Irish Roscius," came for fourteen nights thereafter, but the curtain was dropped finally on April 1, 1833. The last night's show was given as a benefit for Mr. and Mrs. Hilson who had joined the stock in March. Although it was perhaps not realized at the moment, this presentation proved to be the last regular performance ever to be given in the "Old" Charleston Theatre on Savage's Green.[41]

[37] *Ibid.*, February 2, 1832.
[38] *Ibid.*, February 13, 1832. Kean, "from Theatre Royal, London, and Park Theatre, New York," remained ten nights, winning the "enthusiastic applause of well-filled houses."
[39] *Ibid.*, February 25, 1832.
[40] *Ibid.*, March 21, 1832ff.
[41] The theatre was opened, however, for one night, May 10, 1833, for a presentation of *Marion, or The Carolina Swamp Fox,* by Laurent Drusse's Company (see Hoole, "Two Famous Theatres of the Old South," pp. 274-275).

Within a few days after De Camp's season ended, notices appeared advertising the theatre and scenery for rent for the remainder of the year or for the next fall, but they went unanswered.[42] Late in the summer, when the newly organized Medical College of the State of South Carolina[43] set about to acquire a building for classroom use,[44] the Proprietors of the Charleston Theatre,[45] aware of the difficulties they had experienced with the old playhouse, were glad to accept $12,000 for it and the two small adjoining lots.[46] The interior was soon remodeled to fit the needs of the college, but no changes were made in the exterior. And, on November 10, 1834, the building which for forty years had been used as a theatre, was formally opened as an institution of higher learning. As Tyrone Power later wrote: "The building originally erected [for a theatre has been] changed into a school of anatomy; so *cutting up* is still the order of the day; only this practice is no longer confined to the poets, but extends to subjects generally."[47]

[42] *Ibid.*, April 9-13, 20-May 3, 1833. Philadelphia, Boston and New York papers were asked to copy.

[43] The Medical College of the State of South Carolina was organized December 20, 1832, by a group of disgruntled professors who had withdrawn from the faculty of the older Medical College of South Carolina. See *The Centennial Memorial of the Medical College of the State of South Carolina, 1824-1924* (Charleston, 1924), p. 16; *The Catalogue of the Trustees, Faculty and Students of the Medical College of the State of South Carolina* (Charleston, 1835), p. 5; and *Introductory Address Delivered at the Opening of the Medical College of the State of South Carolina, November 10, 1834* (Charleston, 1834).

[44] *Courier*, August 8, 1833, January 26, 1858.

[45] Benjamin F. Pepoon and R. Witherspoon were President and Secretary-Treasurer of the Proprietors. This transfer was made through their agency.

[46] For a record of the transfer (with names of Proprietors) see *Mesne Conveyance Records*, Charleston, Books E 10, pp. 350-356; E 7, pp. 443-445; W 7, pp. 277-278; L 6, pp. 245-248.

[47] Tyrone Power, *Impressions of America During the Years 1833-1836* (London, 1836), II, 93.

IV: THE QUEEN STREET THEATRE, 1833-1837; SEYLE'S "NEW" THEATRE, 1836

ESPITE the selling of the "Old" Charleston Theatre, the city was not to be deprived of theatricals. Within twenty-four hours after its closing, announcements were made by Mr. Hart, erstwhile member of Vincent De Camp's Company, that he would open the Queen Street Theatre to finish out the season. It was not an admirable building, he inferred, but he had incurred "great expense" in providing "for the citizens a delightful and cheap" place of amusement, and it was hoped that they would "not fail in bringing him a bumper."[1]

Manager Hart had been with De Camp for two seasons and was well known in the city. He employed W. C. Forbes of the Bowery Theatre, New York, to take leading rôles,[2] engaged a handful of stock players and opened the "new" theatre on April 2, 1833, with *Pizarro*. Conditions were unfavorable, however, and even Hart's presentation at "great expense" of the "celebrated pantomime, *Mother Goose, or The Golden Egg*," did not justify the continuance of the season, and the attempt to offer substitute theatricals ended ignominiously on June 19 with a benefit for one of the officials.

The move from the Charleston to the less pretentious Queen had been unsuccessful. Patrons, accustomed to comfortable seats in a well-lighted, spaciously arranged building with excellent stage accommodations, were not enthusiastic over a "make-shift barn" better suited for a circus than for the presentation of legitimate plays. As a result, the show business

[1] The Queen Street Theatre was situated on the corner of Queen and Friend (now Legaré) streets. The building, evidently a wooden, barnlike structure, was in no way comparable to the Charleston Theatre. Tyrone Power, who visited the playhouse in November, 1834, called it a "barn" and generally expressed his dissatisfaction (Tyrone Power, *op. cit.*, II, 93). See also *Courier*, April 27, 1833.

[2] Forbes thereafter became an irregular player in the city. From 1842-47 he was the active manager of the "New" Charleston Theatre.

of Charleston, if it had been on a slow decline for ten years, was destined now for a precipitous fall. Indeed, 1833-37 were, perhaps, the poorest years in six decades of the city's theatrical history.

Hart and W. Hardy, his co-manager, accepted the terms of Abram Miller, owner of the Queen Street Theatre,[3] and "respectfully announced" their desire to make a second attempt in the fall of 1833. T. D. "Jim Crow" Rice was engaged for the latter half of December to sing comic songs and play light comedy rôles, and Zip Coon followed for a week of similar performances. In January the Ravel Family, famous on both continents for their "astonishing exhibitions of gymnastics,"[4] proved very popular on their first Charleston visit and remained, playing irregularly, until late in April. Meanwhile, Palmer and Harrington's Circus, operating in Clifford Street and featuring *Timour the Tartar* and *Cataract of the Ganges*, was giving competition too strong to be overlooked. Hart and Hardy soon made a deal with them to appear at the theatre in conjunction with the stock company. Under the caption "Circus and Theatre—Queen Street" the two establishments joined forces for a month, beginning March 10. G. H. "Yankee" Hill played one night under this combined management, but when the circus moved back to its original site, the theatre, failing financially, was closed.

The year 1834-35 was slightly more successful. Many improvements had been made during the summer months,[5] and with an enlarged cast the same courageous managers opened the playhouse much earlier than usual in their effort to "rejuvenate the drama." "Yankee" Hill, whose single performance the previous season had been well received, came again this year, and in December Tyrone Power, from Theatre Royal, Drury Lane, joined the corps for four nights. The scheme of enlisting the help of a circus the season previous appealed too strongly to Hart and Hardy, however, and they could not refuse G. Sweet and Hough's offer to join them. Whatever merits could be placed at the feet of legitimate

---

[3] *Courier*, September 9, 1833.
[4] *Ibid.*, January 7, 11-19, 1834. The Ravel Family was popular throughout the South for thirty years prior to the Civil War. See Odell, *op. cit.*, III, index.
[5] *Courier*, October 11, 1834.

drama, it was certainly not so lucrative as horsemanship, tumbling, and gymnastics—at least not in these depressing years of the theatre. Accordingly, the circus with "eight beautiful horses" moved over to the Queen in January, and rope-dancing, pantomimes, acrobatic stunts, and equestrian exhibits were all that patrons were offered until the end of the next month.

By March 4 rumors began to circulate that the old actor-gentleman, Thomas A. Cooper, accompanied by his accomplished daughter, Priscilla, were on their way South. Hart and Hardy were encouraged to invite them to the Queen, and in the middle of the month the oldest visiting star in Charleston theatricals, played "Virginius," "Benedict," and "Mercutio" opposite his daughter's "Virginia," "Beatrice," and "Juliet" to audiences that fairly shook the frame building with applause. The theatre was time after time "filled in every quarter" during their entire engagement—and for once the managers were earning a deserved profit. They had brought to the Queen within twelve months such outstanding players as Tyrone Power, "Jim Crow" Rice, "Yankee" Hill, the famous Ravel Family, and the Coopers—surely they were due patronage. And as if these were not enough, they added James Hackett. Arriving the last of March, Hackett played *The Kentuckian, Jonathan Doubikins,* and other favorite pieces during his five nights' stay,[6] but would not accept a re-engagement. When he left, the patrons, now accustomed to outstanding performers, would not patronize the regular stock, and Hart and Hardy were forced to close their doors. Evidently the antics of Monsieur Gouffe at Sweet and Hough's Circus were more pleasing than legitimate drama, for that concern ran until late in May, long after the theatre had closed.[7]

Throughout the summer of 1835 Hart and Hardy made preparations for the beginning of their fourth consecutive season. What with a thrice-a-week showing of "Noble and Elegant French Soirees" at Saubert's hall in Fayolle's Long Room and rumors that another theatre would be opened shortly, they faced a year that must have seemed none too inviting. But the arrival of Emanuel Judah from New York, who

[6] Hackett was even more popular this season than he had been in 1831-32 (*ibid.,* April 8, 1835).
[7] *Ibid.,* May 14, 1835.

played seven tragedies at the commencement of the season, and the announcement that Il Diavolo Antonio and Family would soon join the cast, suggested a combination that would meet all competition. However, such was not the case, for on December 10 the Queen was again closed. It re-opened early in February, at which time a misunderstanding caused Mr. and Mrs. T. Preston and several other stock players to withdraw and go into business for themselves at Seyle's "Theatre."

In Seyle's Long Room, Meeting Street, Preston, who was elected manager of the new company, fitted up a "new theatre capable of containing six or seven hundred persons." He bought "handsomely cushioned" seats, new scenery, employed Schmidt, "a pupil of the celebrated Pagininni," as orchestra leader, and promised his patrons "pleasure combined with comfort"—things, doubtless, not to be found at the Queen Street.[8] The new playhouse was formally opened March 2 with a presentation of the ever-popular *The Hunchback.*

The Queen Street Theatre, ignoring the competition, continued as usual, and from March 2 to 23 Charlestonians were given the choice of patronizing the Barneses at the Queen or the Prestons at Seyle's. Consequently, neither place prospered. Rather than fight losing games, the two companies came finally to amicable terms, appointed W. M. Lanning, a cast-member, as manager, and went back *en masse* to the older playhouse where the season wore itself to a close in April.[9]

During the last season of the Queen Street, 1836-37, the drama of Charleston reached its lowest ebb. There were no fall engagements. W. Keyser's "soiree musicale" at St. Andrews' Hall, a "mammoth exhibition of animals" on the lot next to Seyle's, Professor Kenworthy's feats of ventriloquism at Lege's Long Room, balloon ascensions by Herr Staebler and Monsieur Louis, Signor Blitz, the "Great Magician," and Signor Vivalla, dancer—these and other similar entertainments constituted the amusements of the fall. In March of the next year the Ravel Family rented the Queen Street Theatre to present pantomimes and gymnastic exhibitions for more than a month, but there were no legitimate plays.[10] The low-tide in theatricals had been reached.

8 *Ibid.*, February 26-27, 1836.
9 *Ibid.*, December 3, 7, 26, 1836, January 2, 13, 23, March 17, 1837.
10 *Ibid.*, March 9-10, 17, 1837.

V: THE "NEW" CHARLESTON THEATRE, 1837-1847; THE OLYMPIC THEATRE, 1843

HAT 1837 should have been selected for the erection of a new theatre is not surprising: five years had passed since the converting of the "Old" Charleston into a medical college, and 1837 was commercially one of the most prosperous years the city enjoyed between the Second War with England and the Secession of the Southern States.

In 1837-39 the Bank of Charleston, organized in 1835 with a capital of $3,160,800, was paying annual dividends of 10%, and the Charleston Insurance and Trust Company and the South Western Rail Road Bank were chartered with capitals of $500,000 and $869,425, respectively. Slave prices reached in 1837 the highest level prior to 1861—$1200 for a prime field hand. Imports of the state increased from $1,891,805 (1835) to $3,086,077 (1839), and exports from $11,207,778 in 1834 to $13,684,376 in 1836. Meanwhile, between 1835-39 more than 16,000 vessels were registered in the city's harbor.[1] Whereas cotton receipts at the local port had been 175,319 bales in 1833, the total rose to 286,866 in 1838, and exports of this commodity jumped from 257,571 bales in 1834 to 303,737 in 1838. Likewise, rice exports increased from only 196,881 bushels in 1831 to 493,262 in 1839.

The South Carolina Rail Road, opened officially in 1833, handled 53,000 bales of cotton and 38,000 passengers in 1839, and paid 7% dividends. Prices for rice which had averaged 2.75c per pound at the beginning of the decade, rose to 4.37c in 1839, while cotton, always the chief commodity, rose from 9.9c per pound to 16.8c between 1830-36. Meanwhile, the city's retail merchandise sales were averaging more than $15,000,000

---

[1] In travel books during this era it is not uncommon to find the masts of ships in the harbor compared to trees in a forest. See, for example, the picture of Charleston Harbor in J. Silk Buckingham, *The Slave States of America* (London, 1842), I, 47.

THE "NEW" CHARLESTON THEATRE, OPENED
DECEMBER 15, 1837

Courtesy Charleston Library Society

annually. New enterprizes were dotting King, Meeting, and Broad streets; new paving, a new high school, an improved fire department, new drainage systems, churches, homes, civic organizations, and many other municipal improvements attested to Charleston's commercial rejuvenation.[2]

Encouraged by these many indications of prosperity, Robert Witherspoon, Samuel Rose, Henry Gourdin, Richard Cogdell, and William A. Carson, local business men, had earlier, while Hart and Hardy were yet struggling with the establishment in Queen Street, forseen the possibility of a new theatre. On July 10, 1835, they had bought a 99' x 253' lot of the west side of Meeting Street (between Market and Horlbeck Alley) from the Grand Lodge of Ancient Freemasonry of South Carolina, for $12,500.[3] Shortly thereafter they had organized "The Charleston New Theatre Company," with Witherspoon as Chairman and G. W. Logan as Secretary-Treasurer, and begun the sale of stock. By March 15, 1837, Herr Reichardt, architect, and Curtis, Fogartie & Sutton, builders, had the work of the new building "going on with despatch, to be completed by November next;" and a month later the trustees were ready to "receive proposals for leasing the same for one or more years."[4] State authorities had meanwhile granted the company an act of incorporation with a capital of $60,000, to be increased to $100,000, if desired.

As contracted, the building, which was 121' x 73', "comprehended in two stories on a high basement," was completed in November in spite of such anathemas as this one in *The Southern Baptist:* "A new theatre is about to be erected in

[2] These figures are summarized from the *Semi-Annual Report of the South Carolina Canal and Rail Road Company, July, 1843* (Charleston, 1843); J. L. Dawson and H. W. De Saussure, *Census of the City of Charleston for the Year 1848* (Charleston, 1849); Henry Pinckney, *Oration on the Fourth of July, 1833* (Charleston, 1833); *Niles Register*, LI, 46 (September 17, 1836); *De Bow's Review*, I, 325, 332 (April, 1846); George R. Taylor, "Wholesale Commodity Prices at Charleston, S. C., 1796-1861," *The Journal of Economic and Business History*, IV, 848-876 (August, 1932); J. G. Van Deusen, *Economic Basis of Disunion in South Carolina* (New York, 1928); and contemporary newspapers.

[3] See *Mesne Conveyance Records*, Charleston, Books K 10, pp. 284-286; D 11, pp. 209-212. F. A. Ford, *Census of the City of Charleston, 1860* (Charleston, 1861), p. 143, gives the address as 115 Meeting Street. It is now approximately 169.

[4] *Courier*, March 15, April 20, 1837.

this city. . . *What a pity.*"[5] In Grecian style the upper story of the new edifice showed "a portico of four Ionic columns *tetrastulos,* supporting an entablature and pediment," and a porch "protected by large abutments at either end." Three front doors opened into a "spacious vestibule" which led through a corridor into the boxes. These formed "a sort of segment of about two-thirds of a circle, receding as they approach the stage, something in the shape of a horseshoe." Like French theatres, the pit was connected with the dress circle, and pillars "only two and one-half inches thick" supported the upper tiers. The interior decorating consisted of ornamental relief work, appropriate dramatic designs, medallions, and a large dome "of commingled splendour, ornamented with arabesque and emblematic figures." At the summit there was a forty-eight lamp chandelier with strong reflectors, capable of throwing light into every one of the twelve hundred seats.[6] In short, there was nothing in the South at the time that could have been compared favorably with the New Charleston, it having even "surpassed the expectations" of those "most familiar with theatrical architecture."[7]

On November 22 it was announced that William Abbott, formerly of the Haymarket Theatre and long an English favorite,[8] had contracted with the proprietors for the management of the new playhouse. "It is hoped," stated the *Courier,* "that the effort now to be made by Mr. Abbott to restore legitimate drama to its original purity and usefulness may be seconded with energy by our play-going community."

On Friday evening, December 15, 1837, the grand opening night of the "New" Charleston, the auditorium was "literally crammed in every part; many had to go away from the doors, unable to get in." Procedures began formally: Latham, the stage manager, "came forward under the most deafening applause. . . and delivered a poetical address, written for the

[5] I, 331 (May 22, 1835).

[6] *Courier,* December 18, 1837, January 30, 1858. A full description of the building may be seen in Hoole, "Two Famous Theatres of the Old South," pp. 273-277.

[7] The original of the heretofore unpublished picture of the "New" Charleston Theatre (1837) facing page 38, is in possession of the Charleston Library Society.

[8] Brown, *op. cit.,* p. 5; Odell, *op. cit.,* IV, 52.

occasion by our highly distinguished fellow citizen, William
Gilmore Simms." Round after round of applause greeted the
actors and actresses as they played *The Honeymoon* and *The
Waterman*—Charleston had never experienced a night of such
splendor and magnificence in all her history of lights and
shadows.[9] One editor wrote: "After a long sleep, Rip Van
Winkle like, the drama has again lifted her head among us
under the most favorable auspices. She is again wide awake
with renovated beauty and attractions."[10] Abbott was con-
gratulated also: he had refused to grant concessions to bar-
keepers and prohibited *"dram drinking* in the body of the
house to create an uproar and confusion."[11]

There were other opinions, however, concerning the re-birth
of the drama. The Reverend Doctor Thomas Smyth, for
example, lamented the erection of a new theatre as a "corrupt-
ing influence," warned the community against pickpockets and
other undesirable characters who frequented such establishments,[12] and oratorically begged Charlestonians not to
patronize the place, especially "after one theatre has so
signally failed" in the city.[13] *The Southern Literary Journal,*
nevertheless, greeted "the return of the Muses, after so long
an estrangement,"[14] and patrons, anxious to see "the new stars
falling thick and fast around us," packed the house nightly
throughout the season to see Ellen Tree, Thomas A. Cooper,
Priscilla Cooper, Josephine Clifton, John M. Vandenhoff,
Charles K. Mason, James Hackett, and Junius Brutus Booth,
each of whom played a profitable engagement.[15] The season
would probably have been the longest in Charleston's theatrical history had not a most disastrous fire abruptly stopped

[9] *Courier,* December 18, 1837, January 30, 1858.

[10] *Ibid.,* December 21, 1837.

[11] *Ibid.,* December 27, 1837.

[12] *The Southern Patriot,* December 16-21, 1838, *Courier,* December 19,
and *Mercury,* December 21, 1838, also make complaints against pickpockets, yelling, talking, smoking, and spitting in the theatre.

[13] Thomas Smyth, *The Theatre, A School of Religion, Manners, and
Morals!* (Charleston, 1838), pp. 12ff.

[14] III, n. s., 77 (January, 1838).

[15] On one night Abbott engaged Osceola and other Indian chiefs to appear
on the stage, and more than $1200 were taken in *(Courier,* January
30, 1858).

production on April 28.[16] As it was, the year amply repaid
Abbott for his exertions and helped "raise high the head of
the Drama." Had it not been for the fire and a shameful
drunken fight between Booth and Tom Flynn, Abbott's first
year as *"entrepreneur"* of the Charleston Theatre would
have been a perfect one.[17]

This season and the three that followed, all of which were
under Abbott's guidance, constitute one of the gala periods
in Charleston's dramatic history. In February, 1839, he succeeded in bringing to the city the Madame Otto Opera
Company, a group which proved extremely popular in its
presentations of *Amilie, La Somnambula,* and *Fra Diavolo,* and
began the regular "opera seasons" so numerous until the Civil
War. The Seguin Opera Company, which also made its first
appearance during Abbott's management, made frequent visits
to the city until 1849.[19] But Abbott did not rely solely upon
opera to please his audiences.[20] He brought the famous Ravel
Family to the theatre twice between April and November
(1839), William E. Burton, the comedian,[21] and Charles Kean,
the tragedian.[22] John Sloman and C. T. Parsloe were also
received with highest commendations.

[16] *Ibid.,* May 1, 1838, January 30, 1858. The first of these accounts
contains a diagram of the burned area, about one-third of the city. The
theatre was saved from destruction by the efforts of the actor, C. K.
Mason, who twice extinguished flames by "his timely aid and watch-
fulness."

[17] Various accounts of this incident are to be found. Booth, suffering
from an "aberration of mind" brought on by excessive drinking, attacked
Flynn, his roommate at the Planter's Hotel, about two o'clock one night,
and severely wounded him. Flynn hit his opponent with a fire-poker,
breaking his nose and "marring his noble countenance forever." Booth
chased the other man down the hall and into the lobby where calls
brought help. Flynn would later "actually shed tears whenever allusion
was made to the affair, for he idolized Booth." Booth did not play for a
week after the incident occurred. See *ibid.,* March 14, 1833; Henry D.
Stone, *Personal Recollections of the Drama* (Albany, 1873), pp. 175-176;
and H. P. Phelps, *Players of a Century* (Albany, 1880), p. 72.

[18] *Courier,* February 11, 16, March 20-21, April 1, 1839.

[19] *Ibid.,* December 24, 1839, March 14, 1830.

[20] *Ibid.,* March 26, 1840, contains an article entitled "The Stage" and
signed "Dramatic Justice," which praises Abbott for his ability to make
money, but begs that legitimate drama be presented more frequently.

[21] *Ibid.,* November 28, December 2, 1839.

[22] *Ibid.,* February 13, 1840.

NEW THEATRE.

Two New Pieces!

First Night of a New Drama, entitled

FAITH and FALSEHOOD.

In which will be introduced

A GRAND MASQUERADE,

AND

NEW QUADRILLES.

The Music arranged by - Mr. TIMM.

This Evening, Monday, Dec. 24,

Will be produced a New and highly interesting Drama, entitled

FAITH & FALSEHOOD.

The HON. ALGERNON PERREAU, (afterwards Lord Stainford,)	Mr. REED.
CAPTAIN GARTON,	CONUALLE.
SIR JAMES JUKES,	STEWART.
CHARLES GRAVES,	HENKINS.
LYSIMACHUS DOBBS,	H. EBERLE.
BENJAMIN	CLIFFORD.
HARRY BRUNT,	A'BECKET.
BILLY BUCKRIDGE,	BENSON.
CONSTABLE,	BARBER.
MAN,	CLIFFORD.

Characters in Masquerade—Italian Brigands, Turks, Chinese Knights, Pages, Queens, &c. &c. &c.

JANE MARSDEN,	Mrs. TIMM.
LOUISA,	Miss HORN.
ARABELLA SHAW, (afterwards Mrs. Slammerky,)	Mrs. EBERLE.

In the course of the Evening two Overtures.

To Conclude with, first time in this City, the Farce of

The Bengal Tiger.

SIR PAUL PAGODA,	Mr. McCLURE.
EDWARD HENDERSON,	REED.
DAVID,	H. EBERLE.
ARTHUR ONSLOW,	STEWART.
BLACK ATTENDANTS,	CLIFFORD. BARBER.
MISS YELLOW LEAF,	Mrs. EBERLE.
CHARLOTTE HENDERSON	Miss HORN.

To-morrow, (Christmas Evening,) No Performance.

The Manager has the pleasure of announcing the arrival of the

BEDOUIN ARABS,

THEY WILL APPEAR IMMEDIATELY.

In Preparation, the New Fairy Operatic Drama of

KATE KEARNEY.

Places for the BOXES and PARQUET to be had of Mr. Malton at the office of the Theatre only, from 10 till 3 o'clock.
Boxes and Parquet $1; Third Tier 50 cents; entrance at the north side door. Doors to be opened at half past 6, and the performance to commence at 7 o'clock precisely.

Printed at the Office of Burger & James, Charleston.

OLDEST KNOWN HANDBILL OF THE "NEW" CHARLESTON
THEATRE, DECEMBER 24, 1838 (ONE-HALF ACTUAL SIZE)
Courtesy Harvard College Library

Though the second and third of Abbott's four years were perhaps his most fruitful financially,[23] it was not until the last, 1840-41, that he was able to secure the largest group of internationally known players. In a theatre which had recently undergone "magnificent embellishments," James F. Browne, Theatre Royal, began the season.[24] He was followed by Henry Placide, "a native of Charleston, and withal one of the best actors living." Because he was held in such "high respect" in the North, "he should, for the honor of Charleston, be warmly greeted here," one paper stated.[25] Indeed, Charlestonians had not forgotten Alexander Placide and his little band of players at the "Old" Charleston thirty years before, and this son, who had played in the city as a child in 1809, was given a memorable reception. So popular did he become that he was re-engaged in January, and came back for longer engagements in 1844, 1845, and 1847.

The climax of Abbott's last season, however, came toward the end of the year when in succession came Fanny Ellsler, Edwin Forrest, Henry Placide, and Tyrone Power. Ellsler had made her American *debut* at the Park Theatre in New York the preceding May, and Abbott was considered fortunate in getting so distinguished a personality to include Charleston on her Southern tour. She "captivated all hearts by her grace and agility," won all "the Southern beauxs" by her "fascinations of beauty" and caused "such a feeling" as had never before gripped a Carolina audience.[26] Tyrone Power was perhaps the most enjoyed comedian of the decade. The *Courier* greeted his arrival in these terms: "Tonight—Power! the inimitable Power!! the laughter-moving, side-splitting Power!!! he who is so decided and invincible an enemy to the Blue Devils." "Oh, Paddy Power, you comical rogue," the article continued, "with your handsome phiz, and your wicked eye, you have much to answer for."[27]

Needless to say, the Irishman's comic portrayals were hilariously received. After Power's departure the season

23 *Ibid.*, May 28, November 19, 1839, May 18, 1840.
24 *Ibid.*, December 3, 1840, praises Browne.
25 *Ibid.*, December 7, 12, 18, 1840.
26 *Ibid.*, December 28, 1840, January 30, 1858.
27 February 8, 1841; see also *ibid.*, January 30, 1858.

reached a *denouement,* and Abbott began his benefits. His
friends stated that he had "not personally derived any advantage" from the season's activities, and that "the only
recompense [he] has received for his time and labor, is the
inward satisfaction of having labored to please the public."[28]
Others wrote that he had received "every attention that a
generous hospitality could offer;"[29] so whether the financial
rewards of his four years as manager were good or bad
remains an uncertainty. It seems doubtful that he lost money,
judging from the many evidences of "full houses." Suffice
it to say that when he left the city "the regret was universal"
—for he had without doubt done much to restore the drama as
a definite part of the city's cultural and literary background.
His régime made Charleston an important theatrical center
in the South. Those who came after him to direct the affairs
of the "New" Charleston were considered fortunate if they
maintained the standards William Abbott had set.

W. H. Latham, who assumed the management of the theatre
after Abbott gave it up, had been a stock player in the city for
three years. He was an Englishman by birth, his American
debut having been made in 1834 at the New York Park.
Possessing a fairly good voice, he had gone into the profession
as a singer; now, as manager, he was to emphasize perhaps
more than was necessary the musical side of theatricals. With
Miss Melton, Stephens, Dennison, and others of the cast he
frequently presented "vocal and instrumental concerts," and
twice during his short season he brought the Seguin Opera
Company to the Charleston. He employed a stock chorus
"never before equalled in our Theatre," an orchestra that
was "the best, by far the best," ever heard in the city, and
began his season November 15, 1841. As he doubtless wished,
the Seguins came first with a "galaxy of brilliant stars in
their profession," and presented all the favorite operas to
patrons who "could not speak too highly of the splendid performances."[30] By the middle of December Latham was recognized as the man "of indefatigable exertions" who had brought
opera of "such superior manner as to preclude the likelihood

28 *Ibid.,* March 15, May 15, 1841.
29 *Ibid.,* January 30, 1858.
30 *Ibid.,* December 7-9, 11, 1841.

of our ever seeing or rather hearing it equalled." But the esteemed manager was losing money.[31] In the hopes that variety would help matters, he engaged the comedian-singer "Jim Crow" Rice and "the greatest comic actress in the country," Fanny Fitzwilliam, the tragedian Samuel W. Butler from Theatre Royal, Covent Garden, and the old favorite, James Hackett, to appear in rapid succession in January and February. In spite of complimentary newspaper comments, the theatre still failed financially.[32] *London Assurance*, a new play first given on January 9, 1842, was continually repeated,[33] but still Latham lost money. Unable to determine the varying tastes of his audiences,[34] he fell back upon opera to close the season, and the Seguins again came to play *La Somnambula, La Gazza Ladra,* and *Norma*. With this engagement the manager ended his only year.

During the next five years (1842-47) the Charleston was under the control of William C. Forbes. He had made his first Charleston appearance at the Queen Street Theatre, but had not played in that city since 1835. In the interim he had been at the Park and the Philadelphia Walnut Street, and had married Fannie Marie Gee, an actress well known in both England and America.[35] Forbes had interests in both the Savannah and Augusta theatres, and this connection enabled him to engage a more numerous selection of stars than he would otherwise have been able to get.[36]

A poetical address "written expressly for the occasion by a Gentleman of our City" and delivered by the manager's wife opened Forbes's first season.[37] One writer prophesied that the season ahead would surely be "the most satisfactory since the erection of the building." His prediction seemed correct, for another correspondent added that "the good ship com-

[31] *Ibid.*, December 16, 1841.
[32] *Ibid.*, January 4, 17, February 1, 14, 1842.
[33] *London Assurance* was eleven times repeated before this season ended, and remained one of the most popular plays on the ante-bellum Charleston stage.
[34] *Ibid.*, March 4, 1842, has an editorial defending the drama, intimating that Latham was too opera-minded to suit the general public's taste.
[35] Brown, *op. cit.*, p. 129.
[36] *Courier*, December 13, 1842.
[37] *Ibid.*, December 19, 1842.

manded by Capt. Forbes, is now under weigh, and the present
aspect promises a prosperous and profitable voyage."[38] Forbes
was himself a favorite in tragic rôles,[39] on all sides winning
"fastidious" and "indefatigable" praise.[40] Monsieur Paul, "the
strongest man of the age," was engaged for January, and the
inevitable Seguins came in March and April. Both swelled
the manager's pocketbook[41] and helped to make this season
one of the theatre's most lucrative.[42] In March, satisfied with
his efforts, Forbes closed the theatre; but in less than a month
he re-opened it to present "a season of opera." The house was
crowded nightly, for the opera was "again in Charleston, as
in brighter, happier days, the habitual amusement of fashion
and beauty of the city."[43]

By the fall of 1843 Forbes's prosperity had attracted another stock company to the city—that of H. B. Phillips, a
former Forbes's player. He rented Lege's Long Room,
converted it into "The Olympic Theatre" and began perform-
ing "with an entirely new cast" a night before the Charleston
opened. But the project was not successful and in less than
a week the Olympic was closed, and the company moved on to
Augusta.

To the Charleston in December Forbes brought John R.
Scott and James Hackett,[44] both of whom were well received,[45]
but the engagement of William Charles Macready, of Drury

---

[38] *Ibid.*, December 23-29, 1842. One reason for this prediction was
Forbes's reduction in prices.

[39] *Ibid.*, December 29, 1842. This writer declared Forbes's "Hamlet" better
than that of "Algergsson in Stockholm, Nelson in Copenhagen, the
lamented Jacobi in Hamburgh, Esnil Devrient in Berlin, Lowe in
Vienna," or practically any other.

[40] *Ibid.*, December 31, 1842.

[41] *Ibid.*, January 19, 1843. "Every week's receipts since the opening night
have considerably exceeded the expenditures, and the amount taken last
week with an exception or two equaled that of any week since the
Theatre was built."

[42] *Ibid.*, January 21-30, February 21-24, 1843.

[43] *Ibid.*, March 10, 1843.

[44] Scott was without doubt a visiting player this season, though in 1842-
43 he was listed as a stock-member.

[45] *Ibid.*, December 18, 1843, states that Scott gave "real satisfaction,"
particularly because "it is gratifying to national pride to see *American
actors* treading the *American Stage*, with powers and merits equal, if
not already superior to those whose fame comes heralded to us across
the Atlantic."

Lane, Covent Garden, was without question the high spot of this, Forbes's second season.

Macready's first act upon reaching the city on January 1, 1844, was to pay his respects to an old connoisseur of the theatre, Dr. John B. Irving; later he took walks about the city, enjoying its quaintness. Not until the eighth did he appear at the theatre. Of this performance the English tragedian later wrote: "Acted Hamlet, I scarcely know how. I strove and fought up against what I thought the immobility of the audience; I would not be beaten cravenly, but such a performance is never satisfactory. . . I died game, for I tried to sustain myself to the end. Called for."[46] *Macbeth, Richelieu, Othello,* and others of his repertoire followed, but he could not please himself "in the performance of Hamlet with all the pains I could take." Ryder, the Ghost, got caught in the trap, fell and disappeared, and things generally went awry, but Macready was again "called for, and got very well through an address of about half-a-dozen lines."[47]

From January 19 to February 8 Forbes's company was in Savannah, and Charleston's theatre was closed. Falvy Williams and Mrs. John Brougham, Edwin Forrest, J. B. Booth, and James W. Wallack came in February to compensate for the lost time,[48] and in March exclamations of *"Opera! Opera!! Opera!!!"* welcomed the Seguin Company for its fourth annual visit. Wallack then played a short return engagement, and the season closed as J. S. Silsbee, comedian, asked for a benefit.

Forbes had given the city a gala season: more than ten internationally known artists in the short space of five months.

In a redecorated building the Ellsler Brothers inaugurated Forbes's third season. Greeted by "large and respectable"

[46] *Macready's Reminiscences and Selections from His Diaries and Letters,* edited by Frederick Pollock (New York, 1875), p. 539.

[47] *Ibid.,* pp. 541-542. Macready stated that "there is quite an excitement about the theatre; the house tonight overflowed." Charleston's enthusiasm for Macready was greater than he here intimates *(Courier,* February 25, 1859).

[48] For comments regarding these various players, see *ibid.,* February 8, 15, 19, 26, 1844.

audiences,[49] they were followed by "Charleston's own" Henry
Placide, an actor whose appearance indicated that "Forbes
seems in earnest, to make the present theatrical season a
brilliant one." It was the general wish that "a fashionable
house attest the high admiration" in which this native son
was held.[50] He was followed by Booth who played more
serious rôles;[51] and toward the end of January Josephine Clifton alternated nights with the Seguin Company.[52] The Robinson Equestrians, presenting *Mazeppa* and *Timour the Tartar*
(with live horses!) brought an end to the uneventful season.

If Forbes had failed to maintain high standards of production in 1844-45, he more than repaid the public for his
deficiencies in the two years that followed. With renewed
energy he set about to make 1845-47 the noteworthy years of
his managership. He arranged contracts with several leading
players of the American stage, engaged excellent stocks,
enlarged his orchestra, and had the entire building repainted.
Clara Ellis began the 1845-46 season; Dan Marble appeared
immediately after, and on December 4 Anna Cora Mowatt,
accompanied by W. H. Crisp, played her first rôle on a
Charleston stage. *The Lady of Lyons, The Honeymoon, Romeo
and Juliet, The School for Scandal,* and *Jane Shore,* constituted in part the repertoire of this accomplished actress, each
of which was played to "houses filled in every part." *Fashion,*
Mrs. Mowatt's own play, won special favor in the city, having
been produced, as the actress modestly recorded later,[53] "with
its usual good fortune." No player was ever more generously
applauded in Charleston than Mrs. Mowatt, and she became
"very much attached to this warm, southern audience." During the presentation of *The Stranger,* she later wrote, one

49 *Ibid.*, November 23, 1844.
50 *Ibid.*, December 16, 1844.
51 *Ibid.*, December 23, 1844. Booth's "Richard" is called "the best repre-
sentative of the Hump-backed Tyrant" alive.
52 *Ibid.*, February 3, 1845. "Charleston *will* continue generously to support the opera in its strength and glory," stated this writer. "The expense
of travelling, costumes, increase in numbers of choruses, etc., are heavy
and the manager *will* be rewarded for his efforts to please. In other
cities of the Union the *Opera* has increased in popularity. . . Charleston
will be the *first* to *welcome*, and the *last* to *part* with its votaries."
53 Anna Cora Mowatt, *Autobiography of an Actress, or Eight Years on
the Stage* (Boston, 1854), p. 250.

lady in the dress circle fainted and was carried out "bordering on frenzy." This auditor, who "had been on the eve of bringing upon herself the lifelong miseries endured by 'Mrs. Haller,' " changed her plans after having seen Mrs. Mowatt's interpretation of the part—and the actress claimed that she had been "instrumental in saving at least one frail being from becoming 'Like stars that fall to rise no more.' "[54]

Henry Placide joined the cast before Mrs. Mowatt left, and played opposite her for five performances late in December, 1845. Julia Turnbull and James Hackett came next, and then Mrs. Mowatt was recalled for ten nights in January.[55] Mr. and Mrs. Charles Kean filled an engagement during Race Week, the former "wearing with dignity and honor the mantle of his distinguished father," and the latter "unsurpassed for fidelity of conception, or power in execution."[56]

In the fall of 1846 Forbes leased the Charleston for his fifth and last season. He re-engaged John Oxley as leading man of the stock, and added Mary Anne Lee, "our own American *danseuse*, an artist second to a choice few, only, in her profession." Forbes himself played frequently, and with Oxley shared the honors of the local cast.

Beginning November 18 with Clara Ellis and ending in March with the Seguin Company, there was scarcely a night during the entire season that a visiting player of national prominence did not appear on Forbes's boards. Clara Ellis, J. W. Wallack, Anna Cora Mowatt, Edward L. Davenport, John Collins, John Sloman, Henry Placide, James R. Anderson, Edwin Forrest, Dan Marble, and the Seguins followed each other in rapid succession. This group not only climaxed Forbes's career as manager, but also made the season of 1846-47 stand out noticeably in Charleston's stage history.

Ellis and Wallack were as usual welcomed by good houses, but it was Mrs. Mowatt, "the bright particular star" of the previous year, who again captured the city's heart.[57] John

[54] *Courier*, December 30, 1845, March 9, 1858. During Mrs. Mowatt's visit she was invited to deliver a farewell address to the Charleston Volunteers (Mowatt, *op. cit.*, p. 248).
[55] *Courier*, January 21, 1846.
[56] *Ibid.*, February 12, 1846.
[57] Mowatt, *op. cit.*, p. 254.

Collins, the Irish, and Henry Placide, the American comedian, were highly complimented in the press. Placide, now familiarly known as "Old Harry," merited full houses and again won such praise as "sterling actor," "unequalled in his line," and "deserving of much success." Anderson's and Forrest's heavy rôles were lightened by Marble's interpretation of *Sam Patch* and *Animal Magnetism,* and other "laughter-provoking" pieces, and, as the season neared its end, the Seguin Company, this time augmented by a full chorus from the New York Park Theatre, came to present the usual "opera season."

On March 6 Forbes rang down the curtain on the tenth year of the Charleston Theatre. For five of these the arduous task of pleasing a fastidious public had been his responsibility. He had given his patrons longer and more varied programs than they had ever had before; and he had brought to the stage an enviable number of celebrities. He had also managed the new playhouse longer than any other lessee, and had won general favor by his own acting. As a playing manager he was not equalled by any man who guided the affairs of the "New" Charleston. One who knew him intimately wrote of him: "Mr. Forbes was an upright, good man—faithful and just in all his dealings—he was a very meritorious and painstaking actor, perfect to the letter." And this critic joined the many friends of the actor-manager in wishing him "success and happiness in the future."[58]

58 *Courier,* April 15, 1858.

VI: THE "NEW" CHARLESTON THEATRE, 1847-1861

ORBES'S relinquishing of the management of the Charleston Theatre seems to have served as a signal for the relapse of histrionic art in the city. As if possessed of an actor's sixth sense, he probably foresaw the approaching local theatrical dilemma and withdrew into new fields, leaving behind him an enviable record.[1] For the next six years the Charleston was to have at its helm six different managers, not one of whom equaled Forbes in either production or the acquiring of talent.

Long before the season of 1847-48 was commenced, the proprietors of the ten-year-old structure became dissatisfied with their investment. Sufficient interest from their outlay of $60,000 was not forthcoming, and rumors went about that the structure would be converted into other uses. However, a "private association of gentlemen friendly to the drama, desirous of perpetuating the building as a Theatre," bought the playhouse from the original owners, and advertised that they "would carry on the show."[2]

The Lehman Family of acrobats and dancers rented the building for two weeks in November, 1847, and immediately after Henry W. Preston leased it for the fall season.[3] Charles Dibden Pitt (Theatre Royal) came in December for a short but fairly successful series as "an artist of the highest order of excellence,"[4] but was not so popular as George Vandenhoff, who, with John Collins and Mrs. W. H. Crisp of the stock, filled the theatre for an entire week.

"We have at length *an opera* in Charleston!" was the en-

[1] In 1852 Forbes was managing the Providence, R. I., Theatre (Brown, *op. cit.*, p. 129).

[2] *Courier*, April 15, 1858.

[3] Preston "indulged in drink to excess," wrote Brown, *op. cit.*, p. 297, and died April 3, 1859, in poverty.

[4] *Courier*, December 13, 25, 1847.

thusiastic greeting extended Anna Bishop's Opera Company
as they arrived January 12 to open with *Norma*.[5] Madame
Bishop, who, says Odell,[6] "created a sensation" because "few
who preceded her on the American stage had been her equal,"
attracted "full and fashionable audiences" in Charleston. "We
scarcely know," wrote a critic, "which to admire most, her
singing or her acting."[7] But "something suddenly went wrong"
when the Bishop cast left, and the playhouse was "kept open
from night to night as a commonwealth, upon a precarious
footing," to close finally on March 28 with dances by Madame
Augusta's Ballet Troupe.[8]

During the summer of 1848 "gas lighting appliances" were
installed in the theatre, the backstage was rebuilt so as to
adapt it to "spectacle pieces" and the wardrobe was re-
plenished,[9] but no experienced manager dared lease the
establishment. However, on the first day of October Alexander
Robinson and G. N. Eldred, "Conductors of the Circus Company," announced their interest in "theatricals" and rented
the establishment for a year for $2200.[10] With James E.
Murdoch and a "notable stock" the lessees began their 1848-49
season on October 25. Murdoch was well patronized,[11] but the
Viennoise Children who followed him so pleased the public
that they were re-engaged twice during the season. By dress-
ing and dancing like grown-ups, the children, who were from
ten to fourteen years of age, produced "astonishing and
pleasing effects by their well-drilled combinations," executing
"with an ease and one-mindedness wonderful, and with an
expression of countenance on their part indicative of deserving as much happiness and enjoyment from the pastime, as
they afforded to others! It was certainly a pretty display."[12]

[5] *Ibid.*, January 13, 1848.
[6] *Op. cit.*, V, 321.
[7] *Courier*, January 21, 1848.
[8] *Ibid.*, April 15, 1858.
[9] *Ibid.*, October 24, 1848, April 15, 1858.
[10] *The Mesne Conveyance Records*, Charleston, Book B 12, pp. 7-9. The
officials of the theatre company at this time were: James Rose, Henry
Gourdin, Charles Maywood, and William C. Gatewood. The $2200 was to
be paid in four $550 installments, October, 1848-January, 1849.
[11] *Courier*, October 28-30, 1848.
[12] *Ibid.*, April 15, 1858.

After the Seguin Company and the Ravel Family had played short engagements, William Charles Macready returned to the city for the first time in five years. As usual, he filled the theatre with his representations of "Macbeth," "Richelieu," "The Stranger," "Shylock," and "Werner," and then remained in town visiting friends.[13]

Infrequently during the season Robinson and Eldred would close the Charleston for a week or more and devote their entire time to the circus which was running on "the vacant lot at the rear of the theatre." After such an interim the Charleston was re-opened in February to accommodate the Kilmeste Family in "songs, dances, and comics." They were followed by the Tedesco Opera Company, and then the theatre, which had been on the down grade since Macready left, degenerated into nothing more than a circus side-show. The Bedouin Arabs Company,[14] Herr Alexander, a magician, and the Heron Family of actors, dancers, and gymnasts closed the season in May, 1849.[15]

Charleston enjoyed little dramatic success under the circus-theatre management of Robinson and Eldred. Older citizens doubtless remembered the failure of another such combination at the Queen Street Theatre some sixteen or seventeen years before. Except for one or two sterling performances the lessees deserved no credit for their selection of players.[16]

On January 22, 1850, after an interval of ten months, it

[13] Macready was to have appeared at the St. Charles Theatre, New Orleans, under the management of Sol Smith, in January. He refused to go on account of an epidemic of cholera in that city. Letters from Macready to Smith concerning this may be seen in Sol Smith, *Theatrical Management in the West and South for Thirty Years* (New York, 1868), pp. 213-218.

[14] See Odell, *op. cit.*, V, 346, 390, 410; VII, 578, 602, for discussions of the Bedouin Arabs.

[15] Robinson and Eldred evidently subleased the theatre to these various companies after their efforts at legitimate drama had proved unsuccessful. Meanwhile the circus continued nightly.

[16] Charlestonians showed a "greater inclination for light amusement than for anything serious" at this time, wrote an eyewitness to Macallister's shows *(Courier,* November 25, 1858). Eliza Brienti's Opera Troupe was at the Hibernian, panoramic exhibitions were on display at the Apprentice Library Society, and lectures by "the Great Psychologist, Williams," were offered at the Temperance Society Hall during Macallister's stay at the theatre. Early in January Stone and McCollum's Circus opened on the lot formerly used by Robinson and Eldred.

was announced that F. C. Adams with a stock "equal to any
in America" would bring legitimate drama back to town.
"It will be gratifying to the lovers of the legitimate drama,"
wrote a critic, "to learn that the Charleston Theatre is to be
again opened" by a manager who will "diversify the performances by making engagements with the popular Operatic
Corps of the country... but to have the distinct object in view
of preserving the legitimate Drama."[17] Two nights later H.
V. Lovell, Adams' acting manager, opened the season in *The
Stranger*. The stock played without visiting support until
the first week in February, giving one performance in honor
of the South Carolina Jockey Club which attended the theatre
in a body. "By his judicious arrangements," stated the *Courier*
(January 31), Adams "is acquiring a reputation," and a week
later added in a lengthy editorial that the stock was "equal
to, and in some respects superior to any we have had in
Charleston for many years." However, it was added, the
entertainments offered lately were "so different" that "our
play going people have got out of the habit of going to the
theatre." It was obvious that Adams was losing money.

The elder Booth's engagement in February, 1850, was made
memorable by the appearance of his son Edwin, who as
"Wilford," played opposite his father's "Sir Edward" in *The
Iron Chest*. Their performance was "admirably sustained,"
but this, it was hinted, was due largely to the excellent supporting cast which was in some respects better than the visiting players.[18] Andrew Jackson Neafie, who was said "to have
thrown up his trade as carpenter to become a tragedian,"[19]
and Fanny Davenport (London Theatre) played a brief engagement in March.[20] They were followed by James Hudson,
the comedian, who drew "the best house of the season."[21] But

[17] *Ibid.*, January 22, 1850.
[18] *Ibid.*, February 19, 1850.
[19] Phelps, *op. cit.*, p. 269.
[20] *Courier*, March 6, 1850, gave these players only half-hearted praise,
a fact which caused another writer to reply (May 4) that their engagement had been very successful.
[21] *Ibid.*, March 2-23, 1850. Hudson's performances were "unrivalled. . .
His rich humor and gentlemanly bearing, and his fine vocal powers bring
down rounds of well merited applause, and none should miss the oppor-
tunity of seeing him."

the Havana Italian Opera Company of more than ninety artists, which stopped off *en route* to Niblo's Garden, New York City,[22] was far better received. From March 22 to April 2 they played to houses that "overflowed" even though prices had been doubled for the occasion.[23] This company, said the *Courier* (March 28, 1850) "has proved itself equal to what the most critical taste could demand, and its visit to our city will be long remembered in the future as an era." Never had a Charleston audience "enjoyed anything that approached the rich musical treat which this magnificent Company" gave them, and it was hoped that the singers would favor the city with a reappearance.[24]

From April 2-15 the theatre was closed, but prospects for a "bright spring season" lay in the announcement that the "greatest actress produced on the American stage," Charlotte Cushman, had been engaged for Charleston. Literally, there were fights for tickets to see her initial performance of "Mrs. Haller," and she answered every request by presenting *Macbeth, As You Like It,* and other popular dramas before her visit ended in April.[25]

Commenting on "the admirable manner" in which the Charleston had been managed during the season of 1849-50, the *Courier* asked that Adams' benefit be a "bumper one." But it must not have been—the manager did not return the following fall. For an unknown reason he omitted a season, and then, in 1851-52, again took over the playhouse. During his one year's absence the theatre was managed by H. S. Smith and C. K. Mason whose season was made memorable by the visit of Jenny Lind.

Early in December, 1850, the newspapers had announced Miss Lind's desire to sing before a Charleston audience,[26] and daily thereafter followed her every move. Two days before Christmas when the "inimitable songstress" arrived, curious crowds gathered at the wharf to see her boat come in. As she landed, hundreds of enthusiastic citizens jammed sidewalks

[22] Brown, *op. cit.,* p. 157.
[23] Prices were $1, $2; and $20 for private boxes.
[24] *Courier,* April 3, 1850, December 14, 1858.
[25] *Ibid.,* April 3, 1850.
[26] *Ibid.,* December 18, 1850.

and streets to see her ushered triumphantly to the Charleston Hotel where the ladies of the town had erected a brilliant Christmas tree in front of her window.[27]

Pandemonium is perhaps the only word to describe the mad rush for tickets to Miss Lind's performances. Several arrests were made and one unfortunate victim's pocket was picked of $124.[28] On December 26 her first concert, the forty-sixth in America under the direction of Phineas T. Barnum, was given to a house "filled to capacity"—many people having been refused admittance. Accompanied by a special orchestra of thirty-five people, the Swedish nightingale was recalled time after time,[29] and the next day's *Courier* stated that her appearance had "excited much curiosity," but that "the most sanguine expectations of all were realized." Since the Charleston had been built "a more brilliant, attentive, and orderly assemblage has never graced it, than that which greeted this fair votaress of melody, whose visit will form an era in the annals of our music-loving community." In her second concert Miss Lind "afforded a specimen of her powers that exalted . . . her genius and classic spirit as a musician."[30] One enthusiastic admirer, the daughter of a planter, was so determined to see the singer in private that she bribed the servants, put on a cap and white apron and carried in Miss Lind's tea tray. Later, when the actress was told of the incident, she was tempted to give the lady an interview, but finally dismissed the matter as curiosity, not admiration, and refused to "encourage such folly."[31]

Miss Lind did not enter into the holiday celebrations, but remained quietly at her hotel distributing Christmas gifts to her cast-members. When she departed for Havana, well-wishers again lined the wharf to "wave *bon voyage*"—then

[27] *Ibid.*, December 25, 1850 (No. 1).

[28] *Ibid.*, December 25, 1850 (No. 2).

[29] Miss Lind's program included "Overture, La Dame Blanche" (Boielieu), two songs from "Aria" (Rosini), "Overture from Fra Diavolo" (Auber), and "Cavatina" (Rosini).

[30] *Ibid.*, December 14, 1858.

[31] *The Life of Phineas T. Barnum, Written by Himself* (New York, 1855), pp. 323-324. Miss Lind's third concert, the proceeds of which she donated to local charity, netted $3,440 (see C. G. Rosenberg, *Jenny Lind in America*, New York, 1851, pp. 100-103).

settled down to what was destined to be an otherwise dull theatrical season.

Mason, in the absence of visiting stars, played many of the principal rôles. He was rewarded "by a succession of crowded houses;"[32] and Smith, by a "determination not to submit to dictation on the part of employees," maintained "the respectability of the establishment."[33] In March the Italian Opera Company presented favorite operas to "enthusiastic plaudits,"[34] but misleading advertisements which stated that "Tonight Is Positively the Last Night of the Season" perplexed attendants and hurt business.[35]

It must be said, regardless of whether the 1850-51 season was profitable, that Smith had done much to raise the standard of the theatre in the city. Only two years had passed, it will be remembered, since Robinson and Eldred's circus had almost snuffed out the life of legitimate drama. Had it not been for the competition of Mlle. Teresa's Concert Company, Mlle. Tedesco's Opera Troupe, and Bishop's Opera Company at the Hibernian Hall during April and May, Smith's only season might have been longer and more lucrative.[36]

As has been stated, F. C. Adams returned to take charge of the theatre in 1851-52. Two ballet troupes and three opera companies came within his first two months,[37] but Adams was not satisfied with the proceeds and without warning resigned the last day of the year. In January J. J. Jefferson

[32] *Courier*, February 6, 1851.

[33] *Ibid.*, March 5, 1851.

[34] *Ibid.*, March 24, 1851.

[35] *Ibid.*, May 14, 1851. "Our commodious and well arranged little temple will not for several months be adorned with the smiling faces and graceful forms of the fair, nor the moustachoed lips or the bearded chins of the rougher lover. . . The mimic representations of Kings and Nobles, of love-sick youths and coy maidens, of stern patriots and country bumpkins are to migrate to other climes—to return, we hope, to enliven, amuse, and instruct us at an early period of the ensuing season."

[36] The Hibernian Hall, Meeting Street, erected in the early 1840's, was frequently used by visiting and local companies for performances of nearly every kind.

[37] Of these casts the Max Maretzek Opera Troupe was by far the most popular. Maretzek was "an admirable conductor, a superior timist, a great tactician, and a general favorite" (Brown, *op. cit.*, p. 234; Odell, *op. cit.*, VI, VII, indexes).

and John Ellsler leased the playhouse and offered such a diversity of performances that the *Courier* (January 29) remarked that "variety is the order of the day at the theatre. Novelty succeeds novelty in rapid succession."

On February 2, 1852, the managers introduced Julia Dean in *The Hunchback,* a performance which began a series of star engagements that lasted many seasons. Without doubt, Miss Dean, who later married a Charlestonian, Arthur Hayne, son of Senator Hayne of the famous Hayne-Webster debate, was the most popular actress who appeared in Charleston prior to the Civil War.[38] After playing "Juliet," "Pauline" and other rôles, Miss Hayne was re-engaged for two weeks, and the *Courier* praised her in these words: "Crowded houses have testified the appreciation by our citizens of the rare talent exhibited by Miss Julia Dean. She is indeed one of the most accomplished actresses that has ever visited our city." Four days later the paper added that she had done much "to create a disposition on the part of our citizens to foster the drama, by her brilliant and artistic delineations."[39]

After Miss Dean left, Charles Burke, comedian, and the ever-popular Booth came to round out the season. Adams, Jefferson, and Eldred had succeeded, at least in part, in restoring Charleston to its former high position in the realm of Southern theatricals.

The fifth decade of the nineteenth century brought to Charleston an era of prosperity as great in many respects as the halcyon days of the late 1830's. This period, which had a marked bearing on the Secession Movement, came about rather suddenly as a result of a combination of forces. The reduction in tariff rates aided materially.[40] Cotton prices, which during the previous decade had led to frantic attempts at diversification of crops and industry, grew gradually better

[38] Miss Dean married Hayne in January, 1855. She divorced him eleven years later to marry James Cooper of New York City. From the day of her marriage to Hayne, states the *Dictionary of National Biography,* V, 171, "her fortunes declined."
[39] February 10, 14, 1852. See also *The Autobiography of Joseph Jefferson* (New York, 1897), pp. 148-149. Jefferson and Ellsler cleared more than $900 each from Miss Dean's first week of performances.
[40] *De Bow's Review,* XXV, 703-705 (December, 1858); XXII, 655 ff. (June, 1857). The former contains an article, "Effects of the Tariff Upon the Prices of Cotton."

after 1850 and this crop became recognized as "the all-com-
pelling force of southern economic, social, and political
activity."[41] Whereas a pound of short staple had brought 6.6c
in 1845, the price in 1850 was 12.6c and sea-island cotton
rose to more than 36c during the five years before the Civil
War.[42]

By 1860 imports and exports of all commodities reached
figures previously undreamt of. Coast-wise and foreign shipping, augmented by the spreading network of railroads in the
southern and western states,[43] doubled commercial activities
and increased markets, direct trade with Europe, vessels,
shipyards and harbor improvements. In an article entitled
"The Maritime Prosperity of Charleston" one writer pointed
out that the city had recently enjoyed a 40% increase in
shipping and that all manner of commerce would soon "pour
into the lap of Charleston."[44] Another stated that had Charlestonians been told a half century before that "the proud waters
of our capacious harbor would bear on their bosoms no less
than some two dozen large and minor class steamers" they
would not have believed;[45] and many people felt that Charleston would soon vie with New York as the chief shipping
center on the Atlantic seabord. As in the 1830's new banks,
loan companies and industries were rising on all sides. The
city contained eleven fire departments, a new water supply
system, a City Railway which in 1860 furnished horse-car
transportation, and two new gas companies. Forty-six manu-
facturing establishments within the city limits employed more
than a thousand workers on an annual payroll of nearly
$300,000.[46] Everyone indeed spoke of the "improved time."[47]

[41] *Atlas of America Agriculture,* edited by O. C. Stine and O. W. Baker
(Washington, 1918), p. 20.

[42] Taylor, *op. cit.,* p. 866.

[43] *De Bow's Review,* XIV, 184 (February, 1853); XIV, 405 (April, 1853);
XVII, 538 (November, 1854); XIX, 460 (October, 1855); XXIX, 526-
527 (October, 1860).

[44] *Ibid.,* XVII, 82-83 (July, 1854).

[45] *Ibid.,* XXV, 100-101 (July, 1858).

[46] *Charleston Directory for 1859,* edited by Mears and Turnbull (Charleston, 1859), pp. 252-254; *United States Census,* 1860, pp. 553, 558-559;
and *De Bow's Review,* XVI, 633 (May, 1854); XXVIII, 122 (January,
1860).

[47] See J. N. Cardozo, *Reminiscences of Charleston* (Charleston, 1866).

Louis Agassiz, Professor of Sciences at the College of Charleston, organized the Museum of Natural History early in the fifties; the South Carolina Historical Society was begun in 1855, and the Elliot Historical Society, the Charleston Library Society, the Medical Society Library, and the College Library were growing rapidly. Three colleges, a high school, and ten grammar schools were flourishing. The building of such edifices as the Unitarian, Bethel, Westminster, and St. Luke's churches, the Roper Hospital, and numerous other institutions during this period indicates the general prosperity. Twenty-eight benevolent societies, not including the Deutschen Breuderlicher Bund, the Turn Verein Club, and many other "societies" were at the height of their prosperity. Three dailies and one weekly newspaper and twenty locally published periodicals were issued between 1845-1861.[48] And all of these activities came to pass in a town that contained between 1850-1860 a population of only 23,000 whites.

Evidences of cultural improvements increased as the decade went on. Out of this commercial boom there grew a feeling of complacent satisfaction with existing customs, manners, attainments, economic systems, and general life. It was to some degree this feeling of self-sufficiency and, perhaps, of superiority that urged the South to build a separate nation. Out of it grew a defiant independence that was to play a major part in the Secession Movement of 1860.

During the prosperous era between 1852 and 1861 three managers directed the policies of the Charleston Theatre. John Sloman, the first, served only one year; his successor, John Sloan, four; and G. F. Marchant, five, though two of his years were fraught with anxieties and uncertainties, results of the impending crisis.

"Funny John" Sloman had appeared infrequently in Charleston for more than twenty years. His humorous interpretations of "Sam Savory" and "Sir Harcourt" had made him a well-loved figure, indeed a "favorite."[49] Sloan, on the contrary, was a new-comer. When he assumed the managership in 1853-54, he had played in the city but one season. G.

[48] See Hoole, *A Check-list and Finding-list of Charleston Periodicals, 1732-1865*, pp. 48-65.
[49] Odell, *op. cit.*, III, 312 ff.; IV, 285-362, 379, 387, 479, 526.

F. Marchant, who was a stock player during Sloan's *regime*, succeeded his employer and guided the theatre through its most prosperous seasons.[50] The sagacity these three men exercised in securing first-class stage celebrities during the decade was of much help in establishing the city's claim to theatrical importance in the South. As if they had worked on some pre-established agreement, they presented season after season many of America's outstanding actors, actresses and opera companies.

But as always the stars of first magnitude attracted the largest audiences and earned the greatest approbriums. Among these it was perhaps Julia Dean [Hayne] who stood foremost. Her delineations of "Evadne," "Julia," "Pauline," and "Mrs. Haller" were ever popular, and she was recognized throughout the Carolinas as "a most accomplished actress and a sincere and true-hearted woman," with "a great power of abandonment to the character." Her arrivals were always cheered, her departures regretful.[51]

Lola Montez, Countess of Bavaria, who played during Sloan's management, "filled the Theatre from Parquette to Gallery,"[52] and F. S. Chanfrau's portrayals of "Ollapod," and "William" in *Black Eyed Susan* were well patronized.[53] Agnes Robertson and Dion Boucicault came twice during the decade, to play principally in Boucicault's own dramas.[54] Mlle. Rachel and Her French Dramatic Corps, including her sisters Sarah, Lia, and Dinah, played a short series during Sloan's last year, the engagement being cut short by the illness of Mlle. Rachel. On December 17, 1856, at the Charleston, she played her last rôle on any stage.[55]

J. Wallack Lester came in November, 1856, for twelve nights, to be followed immediately by James W. Wallack who

[50] John Sloman, John Sloan, and G. F. Marchant are each discussed by Brown, *op. cit.*, pp. 233, 237. For a number of years after 1853 the theatre was governed by "The Charleston Theatre Association" (see *Courier*, April 17, 1854, December 29, 1855).

[51] *Ibid.*, November 24, 1852, February 14-26, December 13-15, 1853, December 6-16, 1854, February 27, 1856, January 24-February 5, 1859, and April 2, 9-21, 1860.

[52] *Ibid.*, December 6-10, 1852.

[53] *Ibid.*, January 14, 1854, April 7-21, 1856.

[54] *Ibid.*, March 13-29, 1856, December 15-27, 1857.

[55] Brown, *op. cit.*, pp. 302-303.

performed to "enthusiastic audiences" and "houses filled in
every part."[56] John Drew of the New York Bowery played a
"Dromio" opposite his brother Frank in 1857,[57] the latter
player remaining in Charleston as a member of the stock. In
October, 1859, E. A. Sothern made his first bow to a Charleston audience in *Our American Cousin,* a play which was offered six nights consecutively before the actor left the city.[58]
Campbell's Minstrels and the Ravel Family played three times
each, and Annette Ince appeared during both the 1854-55 and
1856-57 seasons.[59]

It was Edwin Booth, however, more than any other male
performer, who won the hearts of the theatre-goers. As a
young man he had played one night in the city in 1850, and
now as a leading American actor, he returned for three consecutive seasons. His first appearance, February 17, 1858,
as "Cardinal Richelieu" was so generously applauded that he
was asked to repeat it the next night; and he was compelled
to accept several curtain-calls before his engagement was
over.[60] The following year he lengthened his stay from four
to eighteen nights, giving as fine a "specimen of pure acting
as the boards of our Theatre have presented this season;"[61]
and in 1859-60 he came again, remaining after his contract
expired to play opposite Julia Dean in *Romeo and Juliet* as a
benefit for Marchant.[62]

Throughout the decade the newspapers complimented the
wisdom and exertions of Sloman, Sloan, and Marchant. The
"enterprizing managers deserve success by their untiring
efforts to cater for the amusement of the play-going portion
of our population," stated a writer in 1854, indicating the
general tone of the many criticisms that came during the
period.[63]

56 *Courier,* November 17, 29, December 2-8, 1856.
57 *Ibid.,* March 2, 1857.
58 *Ibid.,* October 24-29, 1859.
59 *Ibid.,* March 21, 1854, January 10, 1859, January 25, 1860.
60 *Ibid.,* February 14-24, 1858.
61 *Mercury,* April 2, 1859.
62 *Ibid.,* April 2, 1860.
63 *Courier,* February 2, December 17, 1852, March 2, 1853, February 13-
17, 21-22, March 21, April 17, October 20, December 5, 1854, January 29,
November 25, 1858; *Mercury,* March 21, 1860.

On October 16, 1860, Marchant announced the opening of the Charleston for his fourth season. The bill was a "whimsical, farcical, fanciful, laughable oddity in one act," played by Mr. and Mrs. Henry Drayton of "the Paris and London Opera Houses."[64] Five nights later the theatre was closed, not to reopen until Adelina Patti's company presented a series of "grand concerts" which began November 5. From the middle to the end of the month Cooper's English Opera Troupe offered *La Somnambula, Il Trovatore,* and other favorites to small, disinterested audiences, and Marchant curtailed the engagement.

Too many were the pressures and excitements of real life in these stirring days for Charlestonians to be much interested in "the mimic scene." *Leslie's Weekly* (November 28, 1860) contained full-page illustrations of Charleston, Forts Sumter and Moultrie and other fortifications. At the Institute Hall a thrilling "Celebration of the British Evacuation of Charleston" indicated the trend of the public mind; and at the theatre George Christy's Minstrels tried feebly to combat the trend of events with jokes and songs. On December 20, 1860, the storm broke; South Carolina seceded from the Union.

At every hour of the day and night crowds thronged the Battery, eager for the slightest turn of events. On December 28 Major Anderson evacuated Fort Moultrie and moved to the more advantageous Fort Sumter in the center of the harbor. Every day's *Courier* was filled with news of a new Congress, a new Confederacy, a new flag; but most important was the news of the firing on *The Star of the West,* Anderson's supply ship, which had tried in vain to gain access to the Northern troops in Fort Sumter.[65]

Marchant tried desperately to carry on the show. Duprez and Green's New Orleans and Metropolitan Burlesque Company made appearances in January and February, 1861, but failed. The arrival of General Beauregard to take charge of the military of the city, and the daily arrival of troops from up-state; the attack on Fort Sumter, the embarkation of troops to Virginia—these and other matters more weighty

64 Odell, *op. cit.,* VII, 212, 264-265, 292, 299-300, 302, 372.
65 *Courier,* January 16, 1861.

than make-believe tragedy filled the hearts of Charlestonians. Throughout the summer soldiers continued to leave the city by the hundreds. Ladies knitted, sewed, cared for wounded. There was little thought for the closed theatre on Meeting Street. On October 15-16 the "Savannah Quartette Club" were presented "in aid of the sick and wounded soldiers;" and a week later the "Thespian Family" played for the "benefit of the Irish Volunteers." But they were meagerly patronized.

In the middle of November the besieged city received word that Port Royal, fifty miles down the seacoast, had been captured, and that an invasion of South Carolina was imminent. Calls for volunteers were issued; troops were rushed here and there; fortifications were thrown up; excitement ran high. Quietly Marchant announced the opening of his theatre: the Zouaves, French Soldiers of the Crimea, were to be presented in *The Troubadour Soldier*. The *Courier* stated that the "Zouave Corps will afford a novel and instructive exhibition,"[66] and urged attendance. On November 27 the Zouaves announced "A Grand Apotheosis to the Confederate States, *The Past! The Present!! The Future!!!*," and three nights later presented the *Battalion of Forlorn Hope*. Appropriately augmented by drills by the Charleston Volunteers this was the last performance ever to be given in the proud old playhouse.

On the night of December 11, 1861, almost twenty-four years to the day and hour of its auspicious opening, the Charleston Theatre was consumed by a fire (not caused by the war) which destroyed more than one-third of the city.[67] Of the establishment the next morning nothing was to be seen through the smoke of smoldering ruins but "a flight of steps, protected by a large abutment on either side."[68]

[66] *Ibid.*, November 25, 1861.
[67] For an account of the theatre during the next few years see W. Stanley Hoole, "Charleston Theatricals During the Tragic Decade, 1860-1869," *Journal of Southern History*, XI, 538-547 (November, 1945).
[68] *Ibid.*, December 12, 1861. The ruins of the Charleston Theatre may be seen in the foreground of a picture of the burned area in *A Photographic History of the Civil War*, edited by F. T. Miller (New York, 1911), III, 329.

VII: ANNUAL CHRONOLOGICAL RECORDS, 1800-1861

THE FOLLOWING PAGES contain the day-by-day records of the plays presented in the Charleston theatres, the names of managers and officials, members of stock companies, and players on special engagements *(SE)* for each season from 1800 to 1861. The title of a play is marked with an asterisk (*) whenever the newspapers advertise that performance as the first in Charleston. When the regularly employed stock company performed, no cast is listed; only when a player on special engagement appeared is the rôle given. It is to be understood that this player was supported by the stock company.

Semicolons are used to separate the two or more pieces played in one evening; the word "farce" is used when the after-piece is advertised as such, with no specified title.

[1799]-1800
City Theatre

Mgr.: Alexander Placide; *scenist:* Jones; *treas.:* Mayberry. *Stock:* Boree, Chambers, Chalmers, Hughes, Jackson, Latte, Lege, Leoval, Marshall, G., Mauroi, Prigmore, Ryder, Solomon, Taylor, Turnbull, J., Williamson, J. B.; *Mrs.* Chambers, Hughes, Jones, Marshall, G., Placide, A., Prigmore, Ryder, Spencer, Turnbull, J.; *Misses* Grayham, Sully, E.; The Cooper Ballet Team.

Ja (1) Country Girl; Rosina (4) Belle's Stratagem; Romp (6) Mountaineers; Spoil'd Child (8) Heir at Law*; Jew and the Doctor (9) Stranger; farce (11, 13) Heir at Law; Miss in Her Teens (16) Merchant of Venice; My Grandmother (18) Roman Father; musical program in commemoration of the death of George Washington (20) Child of Nature; Agreeable Surprise (22) Highland Reel; musical program in commemoration of the death of George Washington (24) Pizarro*; No Song, No Supper (27) Pizarro; Spoil'd Child (28) Pizarro; Purse (29) Pizarro; No Song, No Supper (31) Richard III; Padlock

F (3) Laugh when You Can*; Village Sports (4) Laugh when You Can; Village Sports; Romp (5-6) Pizarro; Love a la Mode (7) Laugh when You Can; Harlequin Skeleton (10) Columbus; Farmer (11-12) Lovers' Vows; Purse (13) Pizarro; Jew and the Doctor (14) Heir at Law; Padlock (15) Pizarro; Rosina (17) Columbus; Virgin Unmasked (19) Will; Poor Soldier (21) Pizarro; Village Lawyer (24) Distressed

Mother; Adopted Child (27) Count of Narbonne*; Thelypthora; Preparation for Privateering; Chit Chat; Monsieur Tonson (28) Count of Narbonne; Thelypthora; Preparations for Privateering; Chit Chat

Mr (3) Virgin of the Sun*; Spoil'd Child (5) School for Citizens*; Highland Reel (7-8) Rivals; Strange Adventure; Flitch of Bacon (10-12) Deserted Daughter; Jew and the Doctor (14) School for Wives; St. Patrick's Day (17) Heir at Law; Poor Soldier (19) False Shame*; Mountaineers (22) Deserted Daughter; Adopted Child (24) Robin Hood; Critic (26) Secrets Worth Knowing; Spoil'd Child (28) Wives as They Were and Maids as They Are; Iron Mask

Charleston Theatre

Mr (31) Fountainville Forest; Rinaldo and Armida*

Ap (2) Pizarro; Flitch of Bacon (4) Virgin of the Sun; American True Blue; Milliners (14) Preservation*; Man and Wife*; Homeward Bound (16-17) Natural Son; Rosina (21) Preservation; Rinaldo and Armida (23) Douglas; Rinaldo and Armida (25) False Shame; Liar (30) Country Girl; Mountaineers

My (2) False Shame; Genevieve of Brabant (5) Man of Fortitude*; Village Lawyer (8) Laugh when You Can; Children in the Wood

1800-1801

Charleston Theatre

Mgr.: Alexander Placide; *scenist:* Jones; *treas.:* Mayberry. *Stock:* Barrett, G. L., Chalmers, Hamilton, Jackson, Lege, Lewis, Marshall, G., Nugent, Perkins, Seymour, Taylor, Turnbull, J., Western, H., Williamson, J.B.; *Mrs.* Barrett, G. L., Hamilton, Jones, Marshall, G., Perkins, Placide, A., Seymour, Turnbull, J.; *Miss* Miller.

(No Fall Season)

Ja (23) Wonder; Adopted Child (24) Birthday*; Irish Widow (26) Roman Father; Quaker (28) Suspicious Husband; Horse and the Widow; Two Hunters (30) Earl of Essex; Rosina

F (2) Self Immolation; Critic (4, 6) Castle Spectre; Jew and the Doctor (9) Venice Preserved; Purse; Poacher (10) Wives as They Were and Maids as They Are; No Song, No Supper (11) Lovers' Vows; Horse and the Widow (12) Castle Spectre; Love a la Mode (13) School for Wives; Don Juan (14) Birthday; Mountaineers (16) Castle Spectre; Romp (18) Everyone Has His Fault; Poor Soldier (20) Pizarro; Waterman (23) Castle Spectre; Village Lawyer (25) West Indian; Harlequin Invasion (27) Speed the Plough*

Mr (2) Macbeth; Horse and the Widow (4) Speed the Plough; Catherine and Petruchio (6) Speed the Plough; Liar (9) Pizarro; Lying Valet (11) Stranger; Deserter (13) Speed the Plough; Critic (16) Fair Penitent; Fortune's Frolic; Castle Besieged (20) Bluebeard*; High Life below Stairs (23) Castle Spectre; Padlock (25) Bluebeard; Three Weeks after Marriage (27) Bluebeard; Catherine and Petruchio (30) Follies of a Day; Charleston Sailor

Ap (6) Count of Narbonne; Castle Besieged (8) As You Like It; Don Juan (11) Rivals; Cymon; Generous Cottager (13) Jealous Wife; Shipwreck (15) Count Benyowski; Death of Captain Cook (18) Stranger; Midnight Hour (22) Battle of Bunker Hill; Gentle Shepherd; Bluebeard (24) School for Scandal; Adopted Child (25) George Barnwell; Inkle and Yarico (27) Hamlet; Pedlar; Agreeable Surprise (29) Surrender of Calais*; Irishman in London

My (1) Wonder; Highland Reel (4) Alexander the Great; Siege of Quebec (6) Jealous Wife; Irishman in London (11) Know Your Own Mind*; Richard Coeur de Lion (13) School for Wives; Telemachus (15) Days of Old; Richard Coeur de Lion (18) Everyone Has His Fault; Poor Soldier (20) Venice Preserved; Merchant of Smyrna (22) Provoked Husband; Quaker

1 8 0 1 - 1 8 0 2

Mgr.: Alexander Placide; *scenist:* Jones. *Stock:* Barrett, G. L., Branthwaite, Collins, Darley, J., Jr., Darley, J., Sr., Hamilton, Marshall, G., Rickets, Robertson, Solomon, Stervill, Story, Stowell, Swain, Turnbull, J., Villiers, Williamson, J. B.; *Mrs.* Barrett, G. L., Darley, J., Jr., Darley, J., Sr., Marshall, G., Placide, A., Seymour, Story, Turnbull, J., Williamson, J. B., Winson; *Misses* Broadhurst, Miller.

N (7) Child of Nature; Purse (11) Provoked Husband; Rosina (13) Mountaineers; Village Lawyer (16, 18) Lovers' Vows; No Song, No Supper (20) Robin Hood; Jew and the Doctor (21) Love in a Village; Child of Nature (23) Speed the Plough; Agreeable Surprise (25) Spectre Bridegroom; Jew and the Doctor (27) Bluebeard; Irish Widow (Company moves to Savannah)

Ja (20) Highland Reel; Jew and the Doctor (21) Speed the Plough; Romp (22) Alexander the Great; Quaker (23, 25) Deaf and Dumb; Rosina (27) Pizarro; Spoil'd Child (29) Deaf and Dumb; Poor Soldier

F (1) Castle of Andalusia; Fortune's Frolic (3) Highland Reel; High Life below Stairs (5) Count Benyowski; Farmer (8) Abaellino; Padlock (9) Macbeth; Fortune's Frolic (10) Castle of Andalusia; Village Lawyer (11) Pizarro; Agreeable Surprise (12) Lovers' Vows; Bluebeard (13) Count Benyowski; Poor Soldier (15) Abaellino; Jew and the Doctor (16) School for Scandal; Jew and the Doctor (17) Robin Hood; Don Juan (19) Lucid Interval; My Grandmother (22) Inkle and Yarico; Adopted Child (24) Douglas; No Song, No Supper (26) She Stoops to Conquer; Roly Poly; Quaker

Mr (1) Abaellino; My Grandmother (3) Poor Gentleman*; Romp (5) West Indian; All the World's a Stage (8) Haunted Tower; Citizen (10) Poor Gentleman; Irishman in London (12) Stranger; Poor Soldier (15) Poor Gentleman; Inkle and Yarico (17) Wise Man of the East; Lock and Key (19) Siege of Belgrade; Fortune's Frolic (23) Heir at Law; All the World's a Stage (24) Siege of Belgrade; Irishman in London (26) Castle Spectre; Roly Poly; Clown's Triumph (29, 31) Pizarro; Poor Soldier

Ap (2) Poor Gentleman; Bluebeard (5) Happy Family*; Alonzo and Imogene (7) Castle of Andalusia; Honest Thieves* (9) Siege of Belgrade; Honest Thieves (12) Henry VIII; Charleston Sailor; Maid of the Oaks; Monsieur Tonson (19) Sighs*; Blue Devils; Mayor of Garratt (21) Way to Get Married; Village Lawyer (23) Beaux's Stratagem; Recruit; Old Maid (26) West Point Preserved; Maid of the Mill (28) Merchant of Venice; My Grandmother; Generous Cottager

My (1) Point of Honor*; Farmer (3) Life*; Turnpike Gate (5) Stranger; Examination of Dr. Lost; Death of Captain Cook (7) Lovers' Vows; Unhappy Family; Lock and Key (10) Folly as It Flies; Battle of Bunker Hill (12) Tempest; Care and Mirth (14) Poor Gentleman; Alonzo and Imogene; Thomas and Sally (17) Life; Care and Mirth

1802-1803

Mgr.: Alexander Placide; *acting mgr.:* Villiers; *scenist:* Jones. *Stock:*
Burke, T., Chalmers, Charnock, Church, Cromwell, Dickenson, Dykes,
Marshall, G., Morden, Rickets, Rutley, Seymour, Solomon, Story, Turn-
bull, J.; *Mrs.* Dykes, Marshall, G., Melmoth, Placide, A., Rutley, Simpson,
Story, Stuart, Turnbull, J.; *Misses* Broadhurst, Placide, E., Solomon,
Westray, E. A.

N (5) Dramatist; Spoil'd Child (8) West Indian; Rosina (12) Wonder; Agreeable Surprise (13) Castle Spectre; Village Lawyer (15)
Mountaineers; Liar (17) Douglas; Highland Reel (19) Way to Get
Married; Quaker (22) Pizarro; Purse (24) Poor Gentleman; My Grandmother (26) Carmelite*; Fortune's Frolic (29) Carmelite; Liar

D (3) Pizarro; Jew and the Doctor (6) Cure for the Heartache;
No Song, No Supper (8) Macbeth; Poor Soldier (10-11) Inkle and
Yarico; Critic (13) Sighs; Catherine and Petruchio (15-16) Grecian
Daughter; Lock and Key (18) Heir at Law; Rosina (20) Heir at
Law; My Grandmother (22) Sighs; All the World's a Stage (24)
Lovers' Vows; Rosina
(Company moves to Savannah)

Ja (31) Earl of Essex; Village Lawyer

F (2) School for Prejudice; Waterman (4) Notoriety; Purse (7)
Belle's Stratagem; Adopted Child (8) Carmelite; Liar (9) School for
Prejudice; Quaker (11) Poor Gentleman; Three Weeks after Marriage
(12, 14) Life; Mock Doctor (17) Everyone Has His Fault; Highland
Reel (18) Isabella; Padlock (21) All in the Wrong; Lame Lover;
Notoriety (23) School for Prejudice; Siege of Belgrade (26) Suspicious
Husband; Lock and Key

Mr (2) Cure for the Heartache; Jupiter and Europa (4) Italian
Monk*; Critic (5) All in the Wrong; Mock Doctor (7) Speed the
Plough; Jupiter and Europa (9) Italian Monk; She Stoops to Conquer
(11) Will; Jupiter and Europa (14) Grecian Daughter; La Forêt
Noire (16) Italian Monk; Ways and Means; Pedlar (18) Self Immo-
lation; Bluebeard (21) Adelmorn*; Jew and the Doctor (23) Sighs;
Jupiter and Europa (24) Life; Jupiter and Europa (25) Adelmorn;
Ways and Means (28) Countess of Salisbury*; Generous Farmer (31)
School for Greybeards; Oscar and Malvina

Ap (4) Self Immolation; farce (12) Il Bondocane*; Two Strings to
Your Bow (14) Next Door Neighbors; Children in the Wood; Don
Juan (18) Adelmorn; Oscar and Malvina (21) Jew; Mountaineers;
Union Oath (25) Delays and Blunders; Robinson Crusoe (28) Will;
Jupiter and Europa

My (3) Hear Both Sides; Tale of Mystery (6) Romeo and Juliet;
Tale of Mystery (10) Young Quaker; La Perouse

1803-1804

Mgr.: Alexander Placide; *acting mgr.:* John Hodgkinson; *scenist:*
West. *Stock:* Charnock, Cromwell, Douglas, Dykes, Fournier, Hughes,
Labotierre, J. K., Marshall, G., Perkins, Poe, D., Sully, M., Sr., Turnbull,
J., West, J., Whitlock; *Mrs.* Brett, Douglas, Dykes, Marshall, G., Placide,
A., Simpson, Stuart, Turnbull, J., Villiers, Whitlock; *Misses* Field,
Hodgkinson, Placide, E.

N (9) Suspicious Husband; Agreeable Surprise (11) Pizarro; Farmer
(14) Merchant of Venice; Care and Mirth (17) West Indian; Children

in the Wood (19) Jane Shore; Don Juan (21) Wonder; Modern
Antiques (23) John Bull; Rosina (26) Poor Gentleman; Liar (28)
John Bull; Fortune's Frolic

D (1) Jealous Wife; La Perouse (3) John Bull; Children in the
Wood (5) Gustavus Vasa*; Jupiter and Europa (7) Wild Oats; Poor
Soldier (9) Macbeth; All the World's a Stage (12) Provoked Husband;
Highland Reel (14) Wonder; address in celebration of the evacuation
of Charleston (16) Robbers*; Robinson Crusoe (19) Jealous Wife;
Tale of Mystery (20) Wild Oats; Two Strings to Your Bow (21)
Stranger; Agreeable Surprise (22) Castle Spectre; Waterman
(Company moves to Savannah)

Ja (31) Abaellino; Farmer

F (2) Undescribable Something*; Tale of Mystery (4) Jew; Farmhouse* (6) Undescribable Something; Highland Reel (8) John Bull;
Whim upon Whim (10) Richard III; Midnight Hour (11) Useless
Resolution; Two Hunters (13) Abaellino; Jupiter and Europa (14)
Voice of Nature*; Tale of Mystery (15) Robbers; Whim upon Whim
(16) Cheap Living; Children in the Wood (17) Pizarro; Farmhouse
(18) John Bull; Ladies' Race* (20) Cheap Living; Purse (21) Voice
of Nature; Robin Hood (25) Much Ado about Nothing*; Cosmetique
Doctor; La Perouse (29) Richard III; Fortune's Frolic

Mr (2) Voice of Nature; Wild Goose Chase (3) Fair Penitent; Robin
Hood (5) Marriage Promise*; Two Strings to Your Bow (7) George
Barnwell; Wild Goose Chase (9) Marriage Promise; Telemachus (13)
Julia; Maid of the Oaks (15) Rivers*; Robin Hood (19) Undescribable
Something; St. Patrick's Day (21) Rivers; Telemachus (23) Wild
Oats; Quaker (26) Hampton Court Frolics*; Poor Soldier

Ap (2) Bold Stroke for a Husband; Touchstone of Truth* (4)
Liberty in Louisiana*; Spoil'd Child (6) Liberty in Louisiana; Ways
and Means (9) Rivers; Adopted Child; Fatherless Children (12) Maid
of Bristol*; Milliners; Catherine and Petruchio (16) Busy Body;
Children in the Wood; Bird Catcher (19) Charlotte and Werter*; Ship-
wreck; Old Soldier (23) Chapter of Accidents; Vulcan's Gift (26)
Dramatist; Love a la Mode (30) Charlotte Corday*; Shakespeare's
Jubilee; Bird Catcher

My (3) Cure for the Heartache; No Song, No Supper; La Bonne
Fille (7) Which Is the Man?*; Midas (11) Wives as They Were and
Maids as They Are; Critic; Pedlar (14) Speed the Plough; Cosmetique
Doctor; Shipwreck (17) New Ways to Win Hearts*; Vulcan's Gift
(21) Liberty in Louisiana; Midas (25) Hamlet; Care and Mirth; Love's
Offering (28) John Bull; Robin Hood (31) Everyone Has His Fault;
Mahmoud the Robber

Ju (7) Liar; Love's Orphan; Miller (12) Busy Body; Adopted Child

1804-1805

Mgr.: Alexander Placide; *acting mgr.*: John Hodgkinson; *box-keeper*:
C. G. Bailey; *scenist*: J. West; *orch. leader*: Leaumont. *Stock*: Barrett,
G. L., Barrymore, Charnock, Dykes, Hayman, Hughes, Lindsey, Ruther-
ford, Story, Sully, M., Sr., Turnbull, J., Whitlock, Wilmot; *Mrs.* Barrett,
G. L., Douglas, Dykes, Marshall, Marshall, G., Placide, A., Simpson,
Story, Turnbull, J., Villiers, Whitlock, Woodville; *Misses* Field, Placide,
E., Sully, E., Sully, S.

N (12) Venice Preserved; Adopted Child (14) Suspicious Husband; Rosina (16) West Indian; Raising the Wind (19) Romeo and Juliet; Padlock (21) Mountaineers; Vulcan's Gift (23) Wonder; Raising the Wind (26) Rivers; Irish Widow (28) John Bull; Romp

D (1) Alfonso of Castile*; Spoil'd Child (3) Alfonso of Castile; Raising the Wind (5) Busy Body; Review* (7) Alfonso of Castile; Farmer (10) Everyone Has His Fault; Jupiter and Europa (12) Rule a Wife and Have a Wife; No Song, No Supper (14) John Bull; Raising the Wind (15) Macbeth; High Life below Stairs (17) Fraternal Discord*; Midas (20) Lovers' Vows; Review (21) Fraternal Discord; Children in the Wood (22) Jane Shore; Robin Hood (24) Soldier's Daughter; Don Juan (26) George Barnwell; Bluebeard (27) Fraternal Discord; Highland Reel (28) Battle of Bunker Hill; Bluebeard

(Company moves to Savannah)

F (7) Wheel of Fortune*; Children in the Wood (8) Abaellino; Adopted Child (9) Alexander the Great; La Perouse (11) New Ways to Win Hearts; Spoil'd Child (15) Soldier's Daughter; Wild Goose Chase (16) School for Wives; Review (18) Cheap Living; Robin Hood (19) Pizarro; Jupiter and Europa (20) Fraternal Discord; Cymon and Sylvia (21) Rule a Wife and Have a Wife; Vulcan's Gift; Raising the Wind (22) Suspicious Husband; Vulcan's Gift (23) Mountaineers; Bluebeard (26) School for Scandal; Tale of Mystery (27) Fraternal Discord; Review

Mr (1) Much Ado about Nothing; Critic (4) Elder Brother; Lie of the Day (8) Alfonso of Castile; Zemire and Azor* (9) Castle Spectre; Catherine and Petruchio (11) Wheel of Fortune; Cymon and Sylvia (13) Robbers; Romp (15) Which Is the Man?; Milliners; Love in a Village (19) Guilty or Not Guilty*; La Belle Dorothe; Bombardment of Tripoli by the American Fleet (21) Hamlet; Prize, Ten Thousand Pounds (23) Sailor's Daughter*; Quaker (25) Soldier's Daughter; Zemire and Azor (27) Sailor's Daughter; Critic (30) Independence*; Prize, Ten Thousand Pounds

Ap (3) Rivers; Nina* (6) Visitandines; Hussard's Daughter (8) Glory of Columbia*; Care and Mirth (15) Tale of Terror*; Comet*; Easter Frolics (17) Glory of Columbia; Agreeable Surprise (19) Notoriety; Shipwreck; Fête (22) Inconstant*; Comus; Two Quakers and the Merry Girl (25) Paul and Virginia*; Tale of Terror; Care and Mirth (29) Douglas; Follies of a Day

My (1) Chaste Susanna; Rose and Colas (2) She Would and She Would Not; Paul and Virginia; Devil Among the Taylors (6) Hearts of Oak*; Flitch of Bacon (9) Management*; Birth, Death, and Renovation of Harlequin (14) Voice of Nature; Nina; Tom Thumb the Great (17) Douglas; Love a la Mode; Family Picture* (20) Miss in Her Teens; Tom Thumb the Great; Birth, Death, and Renovation of Harlequin (23) Force of Calumny; Tomar, the Corsair (27) Poor Gentleman; Devil to Pay (31) King John; Love Laughs at Locksmiths; Medley Olio

1 8 0 5 - 1 8 0 6

Mgr.: Alexander Placide; *acting mgr.:* William Bates; *box-keeper:* C. G. Bailey; *scenist:* Jones; *orch. leader:* J. Eckhardt. *Stock:* Bachelier, Berry, Clarke, Claude, J., Dykes, Hardinge, Jones, Sierson, Story, Sully, M., Sr., Turnbull, J., Whitlock, Wilson; *Mrs.* Claude, J., Dykes, Hogg, J., Oldmixon, Placide, A., Story, Turnbull, J., Whitlock; *Miss* Placide, E.

SE: T. A. Cooper: Ap 14-My 16.

N (13) Cure for the Heartache; My Grandmother (15) Jew; Irishman in London (16) Poor Gentleman; Rosina (18) Everyone Has His Fault; Farmer (20) Wife of Two Husbands*; Padlock (22) Grecian Daughter; Spoil'd Child (25) Wife of Two Husbands; Lock and Key (27) Who Wants a Guinea?*; Quaker (28) Hamlet; Purse

D (2) Road to Ruin; No Song, No Supper (4) John Bull; Rosina (6) Blind Bargain*; Tale of Mystery (9) School for Scandal; Love Laughs at Locksmiths (11) Isabella; Village Lawyer (13) Blind Bargain; Romp (14) Jew; Love Laughs at Locksmiths (16) Who Wants a Guinea?; Sprigs of Laurel* (18) Grandfather's Will; Poor Soldier (20) Hamlet; Prize, Ten Thousand Pounds (23) Miser; Don Juan (24) Hamlet; Irishman in London (26) George Barnwell; Whim upon Whim (28) Honeymoon*; Padlock (30) She Stoops to Conquer; Turnpike Gate

Ja (1) Wives as They Were and Maids as They Are; Gil Blas* (3) Duenna*; All the World's a Stage (6) Gil Blas; Mountaineers (8) Grandfather's Will; Jupiter and Europa (10) Foscari*; Jew and the Doctor (11) Grandfather's Will; Jupiter and Europa (13) Foscari; Harlequin Skeleton (15) Way to Get Married; Bluebeard (17) As You Like It; Review (20) George Barnwell; Tom Thumb the Great (22) Honeymoon; Hunt the Slipper (24) Macbeth; Sailor's Landlady (27) Castle of Andalusia; Sailor's Landlady; Who's the Dupe? (29) Richard III; Harlequin Skeleton (31) Chapter of Accidents; Review

F (3) School of Reform*; Prize, Ten Thousand Pounds (5) Speed the Plough; Shipwreck (7) Henry IV; Birth, Death, and Renovation of Harlequin (10) School of Reform; Inkle and Yorica (12) Adelmorn; Catherine and Petruchio (14) Love in a Village; Vulcan's Gift (17) Who Wants a Guinea?; Sailor's Landlady; Family Picture (18) Blind Bargain; Bluebeard (20) Wife of Two Husbands; Love Laughs at Locksmiths (21) Duenna; Gil Blas; Spanish Fair (22) School of Reform; Sailor's Landlady; Poor Soldier (24) Foscari; Lock and Key (26) Independence; Tom Thumb the Great (28) Castle of Andalusia; Who's the Dupe?

Mr (3) Secret*; Highland Reel; Mad Bess (5) Clandestine Marriage; Flora* (7) Robin Hood; Lying Valet (10) What Is She?*; Children in the Wood; Milliners (12) Secrets Worth Knowing; Mogul Tale; Mirza and Lindar (14) Busy Body; Agreeable Surprise; Old and Young (17) Country Girl; Death of Captain Cook (21) Deserted Daughter; Valentine and Orson*; Petite Savoyards (24) To Marry or Not to Marry; Castle of Sorento*; Cooper (26) Barbarossa*; Maid of Hungary; Burning of the Frigate Philadelphia in the Harbor of Tripoli (31) Tempest; Harlequin Free Mason

Ap (11) Barbarossa; Dermot and Kathleen; American Heroine (14) Hamlet: *Hamlet*–Cooper; My Grandmother (16) Macbeth: *Macbeth*–Cooper; Mock Doctor (18) Wheel of Fortune: *Pendruddock*–Cooper; Highland Reel (21) Richard III: *Richard*–Cooper; Dermot and Kathleen; Harlequin Skeleton (23) Douglas: *Glenalvon*–Cooper; Purse; Cooper (25) Honeymoon: *Duke of Aranza*–Cooper; Love Laughs at Locksmiths (28) Romeo and Juliet: *Romeo*–Cooper; Mirza and Lindar (30) Rule a Wife and Have a Wife: *Leon*–Cooper; Farmer

My (2) Gamester: *Beverly*–Cooper; Sailor's Landlady; Catherine and Petruchio (5) Pizarro: *Rolla*–Cooper; Don Juan (7) Fair Penitent:

Horatio–Cooper; Tale of Mystery (9) Castle Spectre: *Osmond*–Cooper; Rosina (10) Alexander the Great: *Alexander*–Cooper; Review (12) Mountaineers: *Octavian*–Cooper; Death of Captain Cook (13) Macbeth: *Macbeth*–Cooper; Bluebeard (14) Abaellino: *Abaellino*–Cooper; Spanish Fair; Gil Blas (15) Macbeth: *Macbeth*–Cooper; Bluebeard (16) Stranger: *Stranger*–Cooper; La Perouse (22) World as It Goes; Harlequin Free Mason; Sultan (27) Point of Honor; Purse

1806-1807

Mgr.: Alexander Placide; *acting mgr.:* William Bates; *box-keeper:* C. G. Bailey; *scenists:* J. West, Holmes; *orch. leader:* Leaumont. *Stock:* Burd, Clarke, Claude, J., Harper, Hatton, Hayman, McDonald, Morse, Rice, Ringwood, Santford, Stockwell, Sully, M., Sr., Taylor, Turnbull, J., Young; *Mrs.* Clarke, Claude, J., Darley, J., Sr., Harper, Hatton, Hogg, J., Marshall, G., Movray, Placide, A., Turnbull, J., Turner, Young; *Misses* Placide, E., Sully, E., Sully, S.

SE: T. A. Cooper: Ap 9-My 27.

N (10) Mountaineers; Weathercock* (12) Chapter of Accidents; Tale of Mystery (14) School of Reform; Raising the Wind (17) Richard III; Quaker (18) Country Girl; Weathercock (21) John Bull; Children in the Wood (24) Poor Gentleman; Tom Thumb the Great (26) Honeymoon; Village Lawyer (28) Pizarro; Lying Valet

D (1) Blind Bargain; Adopted Child (5) Castle Spectre; Care and Mirth (6) Speed the Plough; Highland Reel (8) Pizarro; Romp (10) Finger Post*; Highland Reel (12) Henry IV; Don Juan (15) Point of Honor; Finger Post; Camp (17) Romeo and Juliet; Whim upon Whim (19) School for Scandal; Prize, Ten Thousand Pounds (20) Richard III; No Song, No Supper (22) Country Girl; Camp; Finger Post (23) Mock Doctor; Will for The Deed (26) Mysteries of the Castle*; Gil Blas (27) Castle Spectre; Love Laughs at Locksmiths (29) Mysteries of the Castle; Rosina (31) Grandfather's Will; Jew and the Doctor

Ja (1) George Barnwell; Vulcan's Gift (6) Macbeth; Weathercock (8) School of Reform; Hunter of the Alps* (10) Battle of Eutaw Springs and the Evacuation of Charleston*; Village Lawyer (12) John Bull; Hunter of the Alps (14) Battle of Eutaw Springs and the Evacuation of Charleston; Jew and the Doctor (16) Poor Gentleman; Will for the Deed (19) School for Friends; Whim upon Whim (21) Jane Shore; Sailor's Landlady; Review (23) School for Friends; Alonzo and Imogene; Highland Reel (26) Lovers' Vows; Death of Captain Cook (28) Delinquent; Sprigs of Laurel (30) Marriage Promise; Who's the Dupe?

F (2) Speed the Plough; House to Be Sold* (4) Soldier's Daughter; Love Laughs at Locksmiths (6) Young Quaker; House to Be Sold (9) Folly as It Flies; Children in the Wood (13) Dramatist; Cinderella* (14) Marriage Promise; Cinderella (16) School for Friends; Cinderella (17) Folly as It Flies; Cinderella (18) Soldier's Daughter; Cinderella (19) Mysteries of the Castle; Poor Soldier (20) Finger Post; Will for the Deed; Hunter of the Alps (21) School of Reform; Don Juan (23) Battle of Eutaw Springs and the Evacuation of Charleston; Review (25) Honeymoon; Cinderella (27) Clemence and Waldemar*; Bluebeard (28) Clemence and Waldemar; Bluebeard

Mr (2) Merry Wives of Windsor; Soldier's Landlady; Paul and Virginia (4) Robbers; Ugly Club; Robin Hood (6) Cinderella; Clemence and Waldemar; Sylvester Daggerwood* (9) Belle's Stratagem; Matrimony; Medea and Jason (12) Virgin of the Sun; Bluebeard (14) Stranger; American Brothers; Hunter of the Alps (16) Iron Chest*; Lady of the Rock (18) Abaellino; Honest Thieves; Chrononhotonthologos (20) Lodoiska*; Veteran Tar (23) Lodoiska; Harlequin Doctor Faustus (30) Such Things Are; Dominion of Fancy

Ap (1) Fraternal Discord; Lady of the Rock (3) King Charles I*; Oscar and Malvina (6) Columbus; Robinson Crusoe (9) Hamlet: *Hamlet*–Cooper; Weathercock (11) Gamester: *Beverly*–Cooper; Veteran Tar (13) Venice Preserved: *Jaffier*–Cooper; Will for the Deed (15) Wheel of Fortune: *Pendruddock*–Cooper; Cinderella (17) Richard III: *Richard*–Cooper; Hunter of the Alps (20) Rule a Wife and Have a Wife: *Leon*–Cooper; Purse; Village Lawyer (22) Coriolanus*: *Coriolanus*–Cooper; House to Be Sold (24) Honeymoon: *Duke of Aranza*–Cooper; Oscar and Malvina (28) Macbeth: *Macbeth*–Cooper; Sailor's Landlady; Catherine and Petruchio (30) Douglas: *Douglas*–Cooper; Tale of Mystery

My (2) Romeo and Juliet: *Romeo*–Cooper; Agreeable Surprise (4) Venice Preserved: *Jaffier*–Cooper; Wedding Day (6) Wonder: *Don Felix*–Cooper; Prize, Ten Thousand Pounds (8) Abaellino: *Abaellino*–Cooper; Inkle and Yarico (13) King Lear: *King Lear*–Cooper; Agreeable Surprise (15) Stranger: *Stranger*–Cooper; Cinderella (16) King Lear: *King Lear*–Cooper; Poor Soldier (18) Pizarro: *Rolla*–Cooper; Children in the Wood (20) Henry IV: *Henry*–Cooper; Lock and Key (22) West Indian: *Belcour*–Cooper; Padlock (25) Count Benyowski; No Song, No Supper (27) Much Ado about Nothing: *Benedict*–Cooper; La Forêt Noire (30) Cure for the Heartache; Farmer; Recruit

Ju (1) Family Picture; We Fly by Night; Dominion of Fancy; Bird Catcher (3) Jew; Mr. H! (5) Way to Get Married; We Fly by Night

1807-1808

Mgr.: Alexander Placide; *scenist:* J. West; *orch. leader:* Leaumont. *Stock:* Bailey, Barrett, G. L., Bernard, J., Clarke, Downie, Harper, Hayman, Huntingdon, Jacobs, Jones, Mayberry, McDonald, M'Kenzie, D., Morse, Ringwood, Santford, Spear, Spinicuta, Stockwell, Sully, M., Sr., Utt, Young; *Mrs.* Barrett, G. L., Clarke, Downie, Hatton, Placide, A., Spinicuta, Turnbull, J., Utt, Woodham, Young; *Misses* Placide, C., Sully, E., Sully, S., Thomas; *Masters* Barrett, Downie.

SE: Manfredi Family, with Mr. Victorian and Misses Minnigin and Catherine: F 15-Mr 25.

N (11) Stranger; Weathercock (13) Mountaineers; Village Lawyer (16) Poor Gentleman; Poor Soldier (18) Lovers' Vows; Farmer; Sylvester Daggerwood (23) Abaellino; Adopted Child (24) Castle Spectre; Spoil'd Child (25) Pizarro; Romp (27) School for Scandal; No Song, No Supper (28) Castle Spectre; Purse (30) Marriage Promise; Review

D (2) George Barnwell; Highland Reel (5) Grandfather's Will; La Perouse (7) Adrian and Orrilla*; Romp (9) Soldier's Daughter; Spoil'd Child (12) Adrian and Orrilla; Children in the Wood (14) Belle's Stratagem; La Perouse (16) School of Reform; Soldier's Landlady; Love Laughs at Locksmiths (18) Marriage Promise; Forty

Thieves (19) Forty Thieves; Catherine and Petruchio (22) Glory of
Columbia; Whim upon Whim (23) Jane Shore; Too Many Cooks*
(26) Irish Widow; Cinderella; Too Many Cooks (28) Henry IV; Highland Reel (30) Town and Country*; Whim upon Whim

Ja (1) Adrian and Orrilla; Vulcan's Gift (2) Jane Shore; Adopted
Child (4) Town and Country; Tale of Mystery (6) Speed the Plough;
Cinderella (8) Curfew*; Farmer (9) School for Scandal; Love Laughs
at Locksmiths (11) Curfew; Care and Mirth (14) Honeymoon; Love
a la Mode (16) Adrian and Orrilla; Weathercock (18) To Marry or
Not to Marry; Camp; Sprigs of Laurel (20) John Bull; Vulcan's
Gift (21) Point of Honor; Camp; Romp (23) Tekeli*; Review (25)
Venice Preserved; Love a la Mode (27) Man of the World; Bluebeard
(29) Tekeli; Midnight Hour

F (1) Road to Ruin; Brazen Mask* (3) Forty Thieves; Midnight
Hour (6) Man of the World; We Fly by Night (8) Lovers' Vows;
Valentine and Orson (10) Man of the World; We Fly by Night (13)
Castle Spectre; farce (15) To Marry or Not to Marry; Manfredi Family
(16) Town and Country; Manfredi Family (17) Tekeli; We Fly by
Night; Manfredi Family (18) Cinderella; Spoil'd Child; Manfredi
Family (19) Forty Thieves; Care and Mirth; Manfredi Family (20)
Ways and Means; Romp; Manfredi Family (22) Honeymoon; Children
in the Wood; Manfredi Family (24) Soldier's Daughter; Whim upon
Whim; Manfredi Family (26) John Bull; Hunter of the Alps; Manfredi
Family (29) Speed the Plough; Who's the Dupe?; Manfredi Family

Mr (2) Prior Claim*; High Life below Stairs; Manfredi Family
(4) Wonder; Agreeable Surprise; Manfredi Family (7) Who Wants
a Guinea?; Death of Captain Cook; Manfredi Family (9) Mountaineers; We Fly by Night; Manfredi Family (11) Town and Country;
High Life below Stairs; Manfredi Family (14) Travellers*; Abritra-
tion*; Manfredi Family (16) Tekeli; Arbitration; Manfredi Family
(18) Travellers; Too Many Cooks; Manfredi Family (21) Next Door
Neighbors; Arbitration; Manfredi Family (23) Travellers; Jew and
the Doctor; Manfredi Family (25) She Stoops to Conquer; Love a la
Mode; Manfredi Family (28) Rivers; Robin Hood (30) Everyone Has
His Fault; Oscar and Melvina; Scot's Pastoral

Ap (1) Way to Get Married; Shipwreck; Chrononhotonthologos (4)
Hamlet; La Perouse (6) Clemence and Waldemar; Matrimony; Jupiter
and Europa (8) Adrian and Orrilla; Thomas and Sally; Bluebeard
(13) Douglas; Release of the Captives of Tripoli (18) Rivals; Fusilier;
Columbine's Choice (21) Fraternal Discord; Thomas and Sally; Ship-
wreck (22) Wheel of Fortune; Paul and Virginia (25) Curfew; Sailor's
Joy; Forest of Rosenwald (27) Fashionable Lover*; Wedding Day;
Embargo (29) Deserted Daughter; Prisoner at Large

My (2) Child of Nature; Lock and Key; Deserter of Naples (4)
Battle of Bunker Hill; Youth, Love, and Matrimony; Prisoner at Large
(6) Adelmorn; La Bonne Fille; Rosina (9) Pizarro; Battle of Eutaw
Springs and the Evacuation of Charleston (11) Surrender of Calais;
Wedding Day; Tom Thumb the Great (13) Man of the World; Two
Strings to Your Bow (17) Zorinski*; Cure for Care (19) Forest of
Rosenwald; Everyone Has His Fault (21) Barbarossa; Telemachus (23)
Richard III; Highland Reel; Donald M'Intosh's Travels (25) Fountain-
bleau Races; Thomas and Sally; Maid of Lodi (28) Child of Nature;
Sprigs of Laurel

1808-1809

Mgr.: Alexander Placide; *acting mgr.:* J. William Green; *scenists:* J. West, Holmes; *orch. leader:* Remoussin. *Stock:* Bailey, C. G., Clarke, Claude, J., Fox, Hayman, Holland, Rice, Ringwood, Spear, Sully, M., Sr., Utt, Webster, Young; *Mrs.* Clarke, Claude, J., Green, J. W., Placide, A., Simpson, Young; *Misses* Field, Placide, E.. Placide, J., Sully, E., Sully, S.; *Master* Sully, M., Jr.

SE: T. A. Cooper: Ja 27-F 27.

N (11) Love in a Village; Irishman in London (14) Mountaineers; Raising the Wind (16) Pizarro; Padlock (18) Dramatist; Rosina (21) Macbeth; Review (23) Love in a Village; Raising the Wind (25) Time's a Tell-Tale*; Rosina (28) Duenna; Irishman in London (30) Time's a Tell-Tale; Tale of Mystery

D (2) Richard III; We Fly by Night (5) Travellers; Fortune's Frolic (7) Duenna; Critic (9) World*; Poor Soldier (10) Douglas; Love Laughs at Locksmiths (12) John Bull; No Song, No Supper (14) Abaellino; Camp (16) Wanderer; Highland Reel (17) Douglas; Lock and Key (19) Honeymoon; Hunter of the Alps (21) Tekeli; Love Laughs at Locksmiths (23) Castle of Andalusia; Prisoner at Large (24) George Barnwell; Review (26) She Stoops to Conquer; Vulcan's Gift (28) George Barnwell; Castle of Andalusia (30) Tekeli; Soldier's Landlady; Quaker

Ja (2) Wheel of Fortune; Cinderella (6) Wanderer; Tekeli (7) Suspicious Husband; Robin Hood (9) Heir at Law; Quaker (12) Haunted Tower; False and True (14) Fortress*; Catherine and Petruchio (16) Heir at Law; Woodcutters; Farmer (19) Fortress; Prize, Ten Thousand Pounds; Manager in Distress* (20) Foscari; Robin Hood (21) Will; Review (23) Suspicious Husband; Don Juan; Manager in Distress (25) Forty Thieves; Son-in-Law; Views in Tripoli (27) Venice Preserved: *Pierre*–Cooper; Jack in Distress; Weathercock (30) Othello: *Othello*–Cooper; Purse

F (1) Haunted Tower; Spoil'd Child (3) Hamlet: *Hamlet*–Cooper; Quaker (6) Revenge: *Zanga*–Cooper; Romp (8) Duenna; Liar (10) Macbeth: *Macbeth*–Cooper; Sprigs of Laurel (13) Adelgitha*: *Guiscard*–Cooper; Irishman in London (14) Travellers in Turkey; Prisoner at Large (15) Richard III: *Richard*–Cooper; Son-in-Law (16) Gamester: *Beverly*–Cooper; Forty Thieves (17) Othello: *Othello*–Cooper; Arbitration (18) Rule a Wife and Have a Wife: *Leon*–Cooper; Cinderella (20) Romeo and Juliet: *Romeo*–Cooper; Catherine and Petruchio: *Petruchio*–Cooper (22) Wheel of Fortune: *Pendruddock*–Cooper; Rosina; Woodcutters (25) Honeymoon: *Duke of Aranza*–Cooper; Poor Soldier (27) Alexander the Great: *Alexander*–Cooper; Maid of Lodi

Mr (1) Town and Country; Bluebeard (3) Wives as They Were and Maids as They Are; Mother Goose (6) Beggar's Opera; Jew and the Doctor (8) Columbus; Shipwrecked (10) Soldier's Daughter; Shipwrecked (14) Which Is the Man?; Fortress (16) Siege of Belgrade; Honest Thieves (18) Time's a Tell-Tale; Adopted Child; Jack in Distress (20) Cheap Living; Cymon and Sylvia; Musical Festivity (22) Ella Rosenberg*; Waterman; Mr. H! (24) Wanderer; Absent Man; Ella Rosenberg (27) Cabinet*; Wood Demon*

Ap (3) Sighs; Harlequin Mariner (7) Curfew; Midas (11) Indian Princess*; Invisible Girl*; Raising the Wind

1809-1810

Mgr.: Alexander Placide; *acting mgr.:* J. William Green; *orch. leader:* Remoussin. *Stock:* Bray, J., Caulfield, Clarke. Clough, Foster, Fox, Jones, W., Ringwood, Rutherford, Spear, Sully, M., Sr., Utt; *Mrs.* Bray, J., Clarke, Green, J. W., Lipman, Placide, A.. Turnbull, J., Utt; *Misses* Placide, E., Placide, J., Sully, E., Sully, S.; *Masters* Green, Placide, H., Sully, M., Jr.

SE: T. A. Cooper: F 12-Mr 7; Master John Howard Payne: Mr 26-Ap 30.

(No Fall Season)

F (6) School for Scandal; Honest Thieves (7) Abaellino; No Song, No Supper (9) Pizarro; Spoil'd Child (10) Adrian and Orrilla; Love Laughs at Locksmiths (12) Hamlet: *Hamlet*–Cooper; House to Be Sold (14) Honeymoon: *Duke of Aranza*–Cooper; Plot and Counterplot (16) Othello: *Othello*–Cooper; Village Lawyer (19) Gamester: *Beverly*–Cooper; Children in the Wood (21) Adelgitha: *Michael Ducas*–Cooper; Hunters and the Milk Maid; Purse (23) Revenge: *Zanga*–Cooper; Honest Thieves (26) Robbers: *Charles de Moor*–Cooper; Milliners; Devil to Pay (27) Wheel of Fortune; *Pendruddock*–Cooper; Don Juan (28) Macbeth: *Macbeth*–Cooper; Wedding Day

Mr (1) Richard III: *Richard*–Cooper; Review (2) Othello: *Othello*–Cooper; Lock and Key (3) Pizarro: *Rolla*–Cooper; Prize, Ten Thousand Pounds (5) Pizarro: *Rolla*–Cooper; Raising the Wind (6) Rule a Wife and Have a Wife: *Leon*–Cooper; Midas (7) Alexander the Great: *Alexander*–Cooper; Catherine and Petruchio (10) Wood Demon; Two Strings to Your Bow (12) Man and Wife*; Quaker; Jack in Distress (14) Begone Dull Care*; Forty Thieves (16) Indian Princess; Animal Magnetism (20) King Lear; Harlequin Hurry-Scurry; Jew and the Doctor (21) John Bull; Death of Captain Cook; dances by Catawba Indians (23) Man and Wife; House to Be Sold (26) Douglas: *Young Norval*–Payne; Forty Thieves (28) Mountaineers: *Octavian*–Payne; Animal Magnetism (30) Hamlet: *Hamlet*–Payne; Spoil'd Child

Ap (2) Lovers' Vows: *Frederick*–Payne; Tekeli (4) Romeo and Juliet: *Romeo*–Payne; Jack in Distress; Farmer (6) Tancred and Sigismunda: *Tancred*–Payne; Adopted Child (7) Lovers' Vows: *Frederick*–Payne; Woodcutters; Weathercock (9) Pizarro: *Rolla*–Payne; High Life below Stairs (11) Barbarossa; *Selim*–Payne; Foundling of the Forest (13) Mahomet: *Zaphna*–Payne; Highland Reel (14) Tancred and Sigismunda: *Tancred*–Payne; Lock and Key (16) Jane Shore: *Lord Hastings*–Payne; Wood Demon (23) Clergyman's Daughter: *Theodore*–Payne; Vulcan's Gift (25) Mahomet: *Zaphna*–Payne; Bluebeard (27) Mountaineers: *Octavian*–Payne; Foundling of the Forest; Caledonian Lasses (30) Orphan: *Chamont*–Payne; Miss in Her Teens

My (3) Gordian Knot*; Hunter of the Alps (5) Point of Honor; Ella Rosenberg (9) Grieving's a Folly; Catch Him Who Can* (11) Gordian Knot; No Song, No Supper (12) Curfew; Rosina (16) She Stoops to Conquer; Family Picture; Care and Mirth

1810-1811

Mgr.: Alexander Placide; *acting mgr.;* William Twaits; *orch leader:*
Leaumont. *Stock:* Barton, Berry, Caulfield, Clarke, Collins, Foster,
Jones, W., McDonald, Morse, Sully, M., Sr., Utt, Young; *Mrs.* Clarke,
Poe, D., Placide, A., Utt, Young; *Misses* Clarke, C., Placide, E., Placide,
J., Thomas; *Masters* Lege, C., Placide, H.
SE: John H. Dwyer: Ja 19-F 16, 25-Mr 9; Mrs. Beaumont: Mr 13-
Ap 22; Beaumont: Mr 29-Ap 22.

(No Fall Season)
Ja (7) Soldier's Daughter; Ella Rosenberg (9) Adopted Child;
Pizarro (11) Heir at Law; Love Laughs at Locksmiths (12) Pizarro;
Adopted Child (14) She Stoops to Conquer; Prize, Ten Thousand
Pounds (16) John Bull; Weathercock (19) Laugh when You Can:
Gossamer–Dwyer; Fortune's Frolic (21) West Indian: *Belcour*–Dwyer;
Wives Metamorphosed (25) Beaux's Stratagem: *Archer*–Dwyer; Purse
(28) Suspicious Husband: *Ranger*–Dwyer; All the World's a Stage (30)
Dramatist: *Vapid*–Dwyer; Spoil'd Child
Romeo and Juliet: *Mercutio*–Dwyer; Fortune's Frolic
F (1) School for Scandal: *Charles Surface*–Dwyer; Of Age Tomor-
row (4) Laugh when You Can: *Gossamer*–Dwyer; Telemachus (8)
Way to Get Married: *Tangent*–Dwyer; Rosina (9) Cure for the Heart-
ache: *Young Rapid*–Dwyer; Padlock (13) Deserted Daughter: *Cherril*–
Dwyer; Liar: *Young Wilding*–Dwyer (15) Rivals: *Captain Absolute*–
Dwyer; Lying Valet (16) Mountaineers: *Octavian*–Dwyer; Jew and
the Doctor (18) Road to Ruin; Animal Magnetism (20) Doubtful
Son*; Of Age Tomorrow (23) Belle's Stratagem; Children in the
Wood (25) Everyone Has His Fault: *Sir Robert Ramble*–Dwyer;
Animal Magnetism (26) Speed the Plough: *Henry*–Dwyer; Irishman in
London (27) Mountaineers: *Octavian*–Dwyer; Ways and Means (28)
Mr (1) Way to Get Married: *Tangent*–Dwyer; Of Age Tomorrow (2)
School for Scandal: *Charles Surface*–Dwyer; Jew and the Doctor (4)
Wild Oats: *Rover*–Dwyer; Liar (6) Heir at Law: *Dick Dowlas*–Dwyer;
Review (8) West Indian: *Belcour*–Dwyer; Three Weeks after Mar-
riage: *Sir Charles Rachet*–Dwyer (9) Suspicious Husband: *Ranger*–
Dwyer; Three Weeks after Marriage: *Sir Charles Rachet*–Dwyer (11)
Poor Gentleman; Yes or No* (13) Grecian Daughter: *Euphrasia*–Mrs.
Beaumont; Sultan: *Roxalana*–Mrs. Beaumont (15) Isabella: *Isabella*–
Mrs. Beaumont; Farmer (19) Venice Preserved: *Belvidera*–Mrs. Beau-
mont; Citizen: *Maria*–Mrs. Beaumont (20) Foundling of the Forest:
Unknown Female–Mrs. Beaumont; My Grandmother (23) Othello;
Tekeli (25) Jane Shore: *Jane Shore*–Mrs. Beaumont; Agreeable Sur-
prise (27) Foundling of the Forest:*Unknown Female*–Mrs. Beaumont;
No Song, No Supper (29) Pizarro: *Rolla*–Beaumont, *Elvira*–Mrs. Beau-
mont; Agreeable Surprise
Ap (1) Winter's Tale*: *Hermoine*–Mrs. Beaumont; Catherine and
Petruchio: *Catherine*–Mrs. Beaumont, *Petruchio*–Beaumont (3) Stranger: *Stranger*–Beaumont, *Mrs. Haller*–Mrs. Beaumont; Telemachus:
Telemachus–Beaumont (5) Belle's Stratagem: *Letitia Hardy*–Mrs. Beaumont, *Doricourt*–Beaumont; Barnaby Brittle (6) Abaellino; Children in
the Wood (8) Macbeth: *Macbeth*–Beaumont, *Lady Macbeth*–Mrs. Beaumont; Hunter of the Alps (15) Midnight Hour; Hit or Miss*; Whim
upon Whim (17) Winter's Tale: *Hermoine*–Mrs. Beaumont; Two
Strings to Your Bow (19) Macbeth: *Macbeth*–Beaumont, *Lady Macbeth*–

Mrs. Beaumont; Don Juan: *Don Juan*–Beaumont (22) Merchant of
Venice: *Shylock*–Beaumont, *Portia*–Mrs. Beaumont; Ambrosia and
Matilda (24) Henry IV; Lying Valet (26) Cinderella; Town and Coun-
try; Woodcutters (29) Wonder; Highland Reel; Hurry-Scurry
    My (2) Man and Wife; Blue Devils; Bluebeard (7) Poor Lodger*;
Of Age Tomorrow; Harlequin's Restoration (9) Richard III; Love
Laughs at Locksmiths (14) Grandfather's Will; Black Beard, the
Pirate (18) Thomas and Sally; musical concert (20) Birthday; Black
Beard, the Pirate; Review

1 8 1 1 - 1 8 1 2

    Mgr.: Alexander Placide; *acting mgr.:* William Twaits; *scenists:* J.
West, Holmes; *orch. leader:* Leaumont. *Stock:* Anderson, J., Barton,
Berry, Burke, T., Caulfield, Clarke, Durang, J., Garelli, Green, J. W.,
Hanna, Knox, Mayberry, McDonald, Robertson, H., Utt, Young; *Mrs.*
Clarke, Green, J. W., Placide, A., Utt, Young; *Misses* Clarke, C., Placide,
E., Placide, J., Thomas; *Masters* Lege, C., Placide, H.
    (No Fall Season)
    Ja (31) Adelgitha; Jew and the Doctor
    F (3) Lovers' Vows; Animal Magnetism (5) Child of Nature;
Children in the Wood (7) Birthday; Raising the Wind; Children in the
Wood (10) Othello (12) Point of Honor; Fortune's Frolic (14) Rivals;
My Grandmother (15) Lovers' Vows; Animal Magnetism (19) Alex-
ander the Great; Irishman in London (20) Heir at Law; Rosina (22)
Gustavus Vasa; Agreeable Surprise; Birthday of the Immortal Wash-
ington (24) Abaellino; Farmer (25) Everyone Has His Fault; High
Life below Stairs (26) Road to Ruin; Modern Antiques (27) Foundling
of the Forest; Midnight Hour (28) Lady of the Lake*; Catherine and
Petruchio (29) School for Scandal; Budget of Blunders*
    Mr (2) Lady of the Lake; Review; Raising the Wind (4) Rivers;
Prisoner at Large (6) Modern Honor*; Of Age Tomorrow (7) Rivers;
Budget of Blunders (9) Modern Honor; Poor Soldier (12) Modern
Honor; Lying Valet (13) Lady of the Lake; Mountaineers (16) Our-
selves*; Spoil'd Child (18) Stranger; Rehearsal Disappointed; Purse
(20) Hamlet; Lock and Key (21) Pizarro; Lock and Key (30) Poor
Gentleman; Press Gang
    Ap (2) Honeymoon; Lock and Key (4) Honeymoon; Hunters and the
Milkmaid; Rehearsal Disappointed (6) Undescribable Something; Press
Gang (8) Othello; Preparations for Privateering; Lock and Key (10)
Blind Boy*; Hunters and the Milkmaid; Padlock (11) She Stoops to
Conquer; Trial by Jury (13) Way to Get Married; Blind Boy (16)
Macbeth; No Song, No Supper (17) Abaellino; Modern Antiques (20)
Exile*; Quaker; Paul and Alexis [Wandering Boys] (22) Macbeth;
Paul and Alexis [Wandering Boys] (24) Town and Country; Exile
(28) Doubtful Son; Shakespeare's Jubilee (30) Columbus; Exile
    My (1) Pizarro; Adopted Child (4) Glory of Columbia; Foundling
of the Forest (6) Birthday; Bear Hunters; Of Age Tomorrow (8)
Alexander the Great; Tekeli (12) School for Scandal; Bee Hive (15)
Kiss*; Pavlo and Petrovna (20) Town and Country; Paul and Alexis
[Wandering Boys]
    (Company moves to Augusta)

1812-1813

Mgr.: Mrs. Alexander Placide. *Stock:* Anderson, J., Burke, T., Caulfield, Clarke, Hanna, Turnbull, J., Utt; *Mrs.* Burke, T., Clarke, Utt; *Misses* Placide, E., Placide, J.; *Masters* Lege, C., Placide, H.

D (7) Clandestine Marriage; Hunters and the Milkmaid; Spoil'd Child (9, 11) Adrian and Orrilla; Mayor of Garratt (14) Doubtful Son; Family Picture; Mrs. Wiggins (21) Adrian and Orrilla; Family Picture; Mrs. Wiggins (23) Point of Honor; Widow Slow (28) Dramatist; Philosophers; Old Maid (30) Deserted Daughter; Mayor of Garratt

Ja (1) Wives as They Were and Maids as They Are; Children in the Wood (13) Midnight Hour; My Grandmother; Children in the Wood (18) Ways and Means; Of Age Tomorrow; No Song, No Supper

1813-1814; 1814-1815

(No Performances)

1815-1816

Mgr.: Joseph G. Holman; *scenist:* J. West; *orch. leader:* Charles Gilfert. *Stock:* Cross, Drummond, W. C., Durang, J., Hardinge, Hedderley, Hilson, T., Holmes, Horton, Hume, Lindsley, Mayberry, McDonald, Rivers, Robinson, Tyler, J., Utt, Waring, L., Young, E.; *Mrs.* Barrett, G. L., Gilfert, C., Horton, Waring, L., Young, E.; *Miss* Haines.

SE: T. A. Cooper: Mr 20-Ap 8; Aaron J. Phillips: Ap 19-24.

N (1) Road to Ruin; My Grandmother (3) Poor Gentleman; Love Laughs at Locksmiths (4) School of Reform; 'Tis All a Farce* (6) Heir at Law; Sleep Walker* (8) She Stoops to Conquer; Sprigs of Laurel (10) John Bull; 'Tis All a Farce (11) Poor Gentleman; Sleep Walker (13) Mountaineers; Darkness Visible (15) Rivals; Sprigs of Laurel (17) Who Wants a Guinea?; Love Laughs at Locksmiths (18) Speed the Plough; Darkness Visible (20) Speed the Plough; Sleep Walker (22) Mountaineers; 'Tis All a Farce (24) Merchant of Venice; Lock and Key (25) Road to Ruin; My Grandmother (27) Richard III; Spoil'd Child (29) School of Reform; Agreeable Surprise

D (1) Fraternal Discord; Lock and Key (2) She Stoops to Conquer; Agreeable Surprise (4) Soldier's Daughter; Poor Soldier (6) Education*; Sprigs of Laurel (8) Rule a Wife and Have a Wife; Review (9) Education; Fortune's Frolic (11) Henry IV; Day after the Wedding (13) Castle Spectre; Highland Reel (15) George Barnwell; Prisoner at Large (16) Heir at Law; Agreeable Surprise (18) Iron Chest; 'Tis All a Farce (20) Miller and His Men*; Day after the Wedding; Blue Devils (22) Point of Honor; Miller and His Men (23) Mountaineers; Love Laughs at Locksmiths (26) Rule a Wife and Have a Wife; Miller and His Men (27) Abaellino; Miller and His Men (29) Castle Spectre; Fortune's Frolic (30) George Barnwell; Lock and Key

Ja (1) Sons of Erin; Poor Soldier (3) Abaellino; Prisoner at Large (5) Curfew; Review (6) Sons of Erin; Miller and His Men (8) Provoked Husband; Sprigs of Laurel (9) Venice Preserved; Highland Reel (10) Honeymoon; Miller and His Men (12) Jane Shore; Love Laughs at Locksmiths (15) Wonder; My Grandmother (16) Fair Penitent; Raising the Wind (17) Abaellino; Irishman in London (19) Gamester; Irishman in London (22) Cymbeline; Raising the Wind (24) School for Scandal; Weathercock (26) As You Like It; Village Lawyer

(27) Wonder; Weathercock (29) Deaf and Dumb; Catherine and Petruchio (31) Much Ado about Nothing; Highland Reel

`F` (2) Foundling of the Forest; Turn Out (3) Jane Shore; Love Laughs at Locksmiths (5) Macbeth; 'Tis All a Farce (7) Wives as They Were and Maids as They Are; Lock and Key (9) Earl of Essex; Sleep Walker (10) Provoked Husband; Romp (12) Othello; Turn Out (14) Votary of Wealth*; Miller and His Men (16) Alexander the Great; Agreeable Surprise (17) Soldier's Daughter; Village Lawyer (19) Fair Penitent; Prize, Ten Thousand Pounds (21) Honeymoon; Romp (22) Glory of Columbia; Poor Soldier (23) Stranger; Sprigs of Laurel (26) Alexander the Great; 'Tis All a Farce (27) Much Ado about Nothing; Review (28) Jane Shore; Sleep Walker; Sailor's Hornpipe (29) School for Scandal; Purse

Mr (1) Wonder; Prize, Ten Thousand Pounds (2) Votary of Wealth; Miller and His Men (4) Rivals; Romp (5) Speed the Plough; Love Laughs at Locksmiths (6) Deaf and Dumb; Turn Out (8) Poor Gentleman; Review (11) Pizarro; 'Tis All a Farce (13) Know Your Own Mind; Devil to Pay (15) She Stoops to Conquer; Turn Out (16) Maid and the Magpie*; Prize, Ten Thousand Pounds (18) Maid and the Magpie; Devil to Pay (20) Hamlet: *Hamlet*–Cooper; Day after the Wedding (22) Curfew: *Fitzharding*–Cooper; Highland Reel (23) Richard III: *Richard*–Cooper; Spoil'd Child (25) Othello: *Othello*–Cooper; Review (27) Coriolanus: *Coriolanus*–Cooper; Irishman in London (29) Mountaineers: *Octavian*–Cooper; Catherine and Petruchio: *Petruchio*–Cooper (30) Iron Chest: *Sir Edward Mortimer*–Cooper; Purse

Ap (1) Honeymoon: *Duke of Aranza*–Cooper; Sleep Walker (3) Macbeth: *Macbeth*–Cooper; Devil to Pay (5) School for Scandal: *Charles Surface*–Cooper; Lying Valet (6) Pizarro: *Rolla*–Cooper; Lock and Key (8) Romeo and Juliet: *Romeo*–Cooper; Spoil'd Child (15) Maid and the Magpie; Sleep Walker; Harlequin's Vagaries (17) Busy Body; Adopted Child (19) Douglas: *Young Norval*–Phillips; St. Patrick's Day (20) Point of Honor: *Durimel*–Phillips; Maid and the Magpie (22) Adrian and Orrilla: *Adrian*–Phillips; My Grandmother (24) Adelgitha: *Adelgitha*–Phillips; Love a la Mode: *Sir Archy*–Phillips (26) Maid and the Magpie; Of Age Tomorrow; Harlequin's Vagaries (27) Maid and the Magpie; Rule a Wife and Have a Wife (29) Deserted Daughter; Paul and Virginia

My (1) Everyone Has His Fault; Tale of Mystery (3) Belle's Stratagem; Rosina (4) Speed the Plough; Paul and Virginia (6) Peasant Boy; Tekeli (8) Ship-Launch; Don Juan; Will (10) Lovers' Vows; Bridal Ring* (11) Peasant Boy; Sylvester Daggerwood; Tale of Mystery (13) Child of Nature; Ella Rosenberg

1816-1817

Mgr.: Joseph G. Holman; *scenist:* J. West; *orch. leader;* Charles Gilfert. *Stock:* Adamson, Andrews, Boyle, Brown, F., Caldwell, J. H., Cross, Durang, J., Fennell, J., Jr., Holloway, Horton, Legg, Mayberry, M'Cullock, McDonald, Nichols, W., Palmer, Saunders, Spiller, Tyler, J., Young, E.; *Mrs.* Barrett, G. L., Gilfert, C., Holman, J. G., Horton, Smith, Waring, L., Young, E.; *Misses* Haines, Lattimer, Lettine, Moore, Smith; *Masters* Lege, C., Utt.

N (4) Will; Review (6) West Indian; Of Age Tomorrow (8) Three and Deuce; Poor Soldier (11) Belle's Stratagem; Agreeable Surprise

(13) Rivals; Raising the Wind (15) Road to Ruin; Spoil'd Child (16) Sons of Erin; Day after the Wedding (18) Gamester; Three and Deuce (20) Love in a Village; Review (22) Stranger; Romp (23) Speed the Plough; Poor Soldier (25) Romeo and Juliet; Agreeable Surprise (27) Farmer's Wife*; Raising the Wind (29) Cymbeline; Of Age Tomorrow (30) Laugh when You Can; Spoil'd Child

D (2) Pizarro; Fortune's Frolic (4) Farmer's Wife; Liar (6) Provoked Husband; Budget of Blunders (7) Belle's Stratagem; Lock and Key (9) Jane Shore; Irishman in London (11) Cabinet; Budget of Blunders (13) Honeymoon; Prisoner at Large (14) Laugh when You Can; Agreeable Surprise (16) Wonder; Three and Deuce (18) Cabinet; Liar (20) Othello; Day after the Wedding (21) Forest of Bondy; Three and Deuce (23) Macbeth; Romp (26) Love in a Village; How to Die for Love (27) George Barnwell; Prisoner at Large (28) Forest of Bondy; Raising the Wind (30) Venice Preserved; Killing No Murder

Ja (1) Foundling of the Forest; Jew and the Doctor (3) Mountaineers; Irishman in London (4) Forest of Bondy; Sleep Walker (6) Douglas; Killing No Murder (9) Wives as They Were and Maids as They Are; Bombastes Furioso (10) Curfew; Fortune's Frolic; Pizarro (11) Forest of Bondy; Bombastes Furioso; Day after the Wedding (13) Castle Spectre; Maid and the Magpie (15) Wives as They Were and Maids as They Are; Tale of Mystery (17) Lovers' Vows; Killing No Murder (18) Miller and His Men; Bombastes Furioso (20) Romeo and Juliet; How to Die for Love (22) Farmer's Wife; Sleep Walker (24) Earl of Essex; Love, Law and Physic (25) Aethiop*; Fortune's Frolic (27) Forest of Bondy; Love, Law and Physic (29) Much Ado about Nothing; No Song, No Supper (31) Wives as They Were and Maids as They Are; No Song, No Supper

F (1) Aethiop; Bombastes Furioso (3) Heir at Law; Love, Law and Physic (5) School for Scandal; Eight to One; Rosina (7) Poor Gentleman; Of Age Tomorrow (10) Aethiop; Village Lawyer (12) Maid of the Mill; Catherine and Petruchio (14) School for Scandal; Rosina (15) Aethiop; How to Die for Love (17) Bertram*; Liar (19) Bertram; Matrimony (21) Bertram; No Song, No Supper (22) Glory of Columbia; Review (24) Aethiop; Bombastes Furioso (25) Forest of Bondy; Three and Deuce (26) Love in a Village; Love, Law and Physic (27) Macbeth; Weathercock (28) Provoked Husband; Killing No Murder

Mr (1) Farmer's Wife; Forest of Bondy; Sleep Walker (3) Rule a Wife and Have a Wife; Forest of Bondy (4) Cabinet; Day after the Wedding; Bombastes Furioso (5) Henry VIII; Matrimony (7) Henry VIII; Agreeable Surprise (8) Poor Gentleman; Village Lawyer (10) Mountaineers; Fortune's Frolic (12) John of Paris*; Miller and His Men (21) Hamlet; Three and Deuce (22) Heir at Law; Poor Soldier (24) Provoked Husband; Sylvester Daggerwood; Spoil'd Child (25) Abaellino; Lock and Key (26) John of Paris; Miller and His Men (27) Peasant Boy; Killing No Murder (29) John of Paris; Sylvester Daggerwood; Jew and the Doctor (31) John of Paris; Tekeli

Ap (7) King Lear; Harlequin Skeleton; Pas de Deux (9) Town and Country; Paul and Virginia (11) Who Wants a Guinea?; Highland Reel (12) Point of Honor; Sylvester Daggerwood; Turn Out (14) Man and Wife; Blind Boy (16) Hero of the North; Death of Captain

Cook (18) Haunted Tower; Killing No Murder (19) She Stoops to Conquer; Highland Reel (21) Alexander the Great; Padlock (23) Fortress; Love Laughs at Locksmiths (25) School of Reform; Midnight Hour (26) Soldier's Daughter; Devil to Pay (28) Barbarossa; Turn Out (30) Child of Nature; Boarding House
My (2) King Lear; For Freedom! Ho!

1817-1818

Mgr.: Charles Gilfert; *acting mgr.:* Charles Young; *scenists:* J. West, Spanoletti; *box-keeper:* Edward Young; *orch. leader:* Charles Gilfert. *Stock:* Carpenter, Clarke, Cregier, Dalton, Faulkner, T., Fennell, J., Jr., Hilson, T., Hopkins, Hyatt, G., Major, Meholla, Mude, Nicholas, W., Page, Quin, Schinotti, Stewart, Spiller, Trevor, Tyler, J., Utt; *Mrs.* Barrett, G. L., Clarke, Claude, J., Faulkner, T., Gilfert, C., Holman, J. G., Spiller, Waring, L., Young, E.; *Misses* Clarke, C., Lettine; *Masters* Clarke, E., Foucard.

SE: John H. Dwyer: Ja 15, F 4, 9, 16, Mr 11; Williams: F 11-14; T. A. Cooper: Mr 25-Ap 20; Benjamin Charles Incledon: Ap 13-24.

D (12) Speed the Plough; No Song, No Supper (13) Will; Agreeable Surprise (15) Way to Get Married (17) Cure for the Heartache; Broken Sword (19) Heir at Law; Frightened to Death (20) Mountaineers; Sylvester Daggerwood; Bombastes Furioso (22) Laugh when You Can; Broken Sword (24) Romeo and Juliet; Of Age Tomorrow (26) Poor Gentleman; Don Juan (27) Abaellino; Love Laughs at Locksmiths (29) Douglas; Poor Soldier (31) She Stoops to Conquer; Maid and the Magpie
Ja (1) George Barnwell; Don Juan (3) Lovers' Vows; Review (5) School of Reform; Sleep Walker (7) John Bull; Lock and Key (8) Forest of Bondy; Sylvester Daggerwood; Battle of New Orleans (9) Heir at Law; Sprigs of Laurel (10) Poor Gentleman; Love Laughs at Locksmiths (12) School for Scandal; 'Tis All a Farce (14) Apostate*; Prize, Ten Thousand Pounds (15) Laugh when You Can: *Gossamer*–Dwyer; Don Juan (16) Merchant of Venice; Highland Reel (17) Foundling of the Forest; Sprigs of Laurel (19) As You Like It; Adopted Child (21) Apostate; Sleep Walker (23) Henry IV; 'Tis All a Farce (24) School for Scandal; Purse (26) Know Your Own Mind; Blue Devils; Shipwreck (28) Belle's Stratagem; Rosina (30) Jane Shore; Punch's Festival
F (2) Apostate; Liar (3) Town and Country; Punch's Festival (4) Romeo and Juliet: *Mercutio*–Dwyer; Punch's Festival (5) Jane Shore; Punch's Festival (6) Hamlet; Punch's Festival (7) Apostate; Punch's Festival (9) Much Ado about Nothing: *Benedict*–Dwyer; Spoil'd Child (11) Pizarro: *Rolla*–Williams; Poor Soldier (13) Othello: *Othello*–Williams; Review (14) Mountaineers: *Octavian*–Williams; Paul and Virginia (16) Wonder: *Don Felix*–Dwyer; Prisoner at Large (18) Corsair*; Lock and Key (20) Corsair; Highland Reel (21) Corsair; Liar (23) Peasant Boy; Inn-keeper's Daughter* (24) Point of Honor; Inn-keeper's Daughter (25) George Barnwell; Inn-keeper's Daughter (26) Wild Oats; 'Tis All a Farce (27) Fraternal Discord; Killing No Murder (28) Wives as They Were and Maids as They Are; Hamlet Travestie*
Mr (2) Richard III; Devil to Pay (4) Columbus; Bombastes Furioso (6) John Bull; Inn-keeper's Daughter (7) School of Reform; Shipwreck

(9) Fortune's Frolic; Inn-keeper's Daughter (11) The West-Indian: *Belcour*–Dwyer; Fortune's Frolic (13) Farmer's Wife; Jew and the Doctor (14) Man and Wife; Rosina (16) Adelmorn; Tekeli (23) Accusation*; Brother and Sister* (25) Venice Preserved: *Pierre*–Cooper; Review (27) Macbeth: *Macbeth*–Cooper; Spoil'd Child (28) Honeymoon: *Duke of Aranza*–Cooper (30) Gamester: *Beverly*–Cooper; Brother and Sister

Ap (1) Hamlet: *Hamlet*–Cooper; Purse (3) Bertram: *Bertram*–Cooper; Romp (4) Rule a Wife and Have a Wife: *Leon*–Cooper; Inn-keeper's Daughter (6) Wheel of Fortune: *Pendruddock*–Cooper; Catherine and Petruchio (8) Apostate: *Malec*–Cooper; Rosina (10) Othello: *Othello*–Cooper; Bombastes Furioso (11) Aethiop: *Aethiop*–Cooper; Fortune's Frolic (13) Quaker: *Steady*–Incledon; Sylvester Daggerwood; Waterman: *Tom Tug*–Incledon (14) Romeo and Juliet: *Romeo*–Cooper; Raising the Wind (15) Alexander the Great: *Alexander*–Cooper; Of Age Tomorrow (17) Love in a Village: *Hawthorn*–Incledon; Irishman in London (18) Village Lawyer: *Scout*–Incledon; Rosina; Lock and Key (20) Julius Caesar*: *Mark Antony*–Cooper; Purse (22) Maid of the Mill: *Farmer Giles*–Incledon; Matrimony (24) Lord of the Manor: *Rashley*–Incledon; Animal Magnetism (25) School for Scandal; Inn-keeper's Daughter (27) Everyone Has His Fault; Broken Sword (28) Wandering Minstrel* (29) Tempest; Out of Place*

My (1) Such Things Are; Critic (2) Married Yesterday*; Mayor of Garratt; Two Strings to Your Bow (4) Coriolanus; Wedding Day (6) Siege of Belgrade; Modern Antiques (8) Zorinski; Divertisement; Hunter of the Alps (9) Adelgitha; Out of Place (11) New Way to Pay Old Debts; Honest Thieves (13) Battle of Hexham; Children in the Wood (15) Siege of Belgrade; John of Paris (16) Ella Rosenberg; Wedding Day; Turn Out (18) Surrender of Calais; Highland Reel (19) Animal Magnetism; Agreeable Surprise; Valentine and Orson (20) Rivals; Past Ten O'Clock (21) She Stoops to Conquer; Spoil'd Child (23) Timour the Tartar*; Prisoner at Large (26) L'Ambigue Comique

1818-1819

Mgr.: Charles Gilfert; *acting mgr.:* Charles Young; *scenists:* J. West, Schinotti; *orch. leader:* Charles Gilfert; *box-keeper:* Edward Young. *Stock:* Brooks, Brown, F., Clarke, Dalton, Drummond, W. C., Faulkner, T., Fennell, J., Jr., Finn, H. J., Hilson, T., Horton, Hyatt, G., Mude, Nichols, W., Quin, Seward; *Mrs.* Barrett, G. L., Clarke, Drummond, W. C., Faulkner, T., Gilfert, C., Waring, L., West, J., Young, E.; *Miss* Clarke, C.

SE: Aaron J. Phillips: N 16-27; F 2-22; T. A. Cooper: F 1-5, 24-Mr 1, Ap 13-28; Cleary: F 6-26, Mr 3, Ap 24-30.

O (29) Merchant of Venice; Irishman in London (30) Richard III; Fortune's Frolic (31) Falls of Clyde*; Past Ten O'Clock

N (2) Hamlet; Falls of Clyde (4) School for Scandal; Children in the Wood (6) Wild Oats; Sprigs of Laurel (7) Devil's Bridge; Sleep Walker (9) Othello; 'Tis All a Farce (10) School of Reform; Falls of Clyde (11) Henry IV; Broken Sword (12) Apostate; Love a la Mode (13) Busy Body; Critic (14) Apostate; Love a la Mode (16) Devil's Bridge: *Count Belino*–Phillips; Prisoner at Large (18) Maid of the Mill: *Lord Aimworth*–Phillips; Critic (20) Love in a Village: *Young Meadows*–Phillips; Animal Magnetism (21) Timour the Tartar; Love a

la Mode (23) Cabinet: *Count Orlando*–Phillips; Children in the Wood
(25) Devil's Bridge: *Count Belino*–Phillips; Sleep Walker (27) Foun-
tainbleau Races: *Henry*–Phillips; Brother and Sister
   (Company moves to Savannah)
   F (1) Venice Preserved: *Pierre*–Cooper; Love Laughs at Locksmiths
(2) Devil's Bridge: *Count Belino*–Phillips; Irishman in London (3)
Macbeth: *Macbeth*–Cooper; Of Age Tomorrow (5) Hamlet: *Hamlet*–
Cooper; Purse (6) Othello: *Othello*–Cleary; Spoil'd Child (8) Richard
III: *Richard*–Cleary; My Grandmother (10) Forty Thieves; Laugh when
You Can (12) Stranger: *Stranger*–Cleary; Sprigs of Laurel (13)
Spoil'd Child; Forty Thieves (15) Cabinet: *Orlando*–Phillips; Animal
Magnetism (17) John of Paris: *John*–Phillips; Poor Soldier (19)
Honeymoon: *Duke of Aranza*–Cleary; Falls of Clyde (20) Lock and
Key; Forty Thieves (22) Duenna: *Don Carlos*–Phillips; Love Laughs at
Locksmiths (24) Bertram: *Bertram*–Cooper; Sprigs of Laurel (26)
Othello: *Othello*–Cooper, *Iago*–Cleary; Agreeable Surprise (27) Rule
a Wife and Have a Wife: *Leon*–Cooper; Forty Thieves
   Mr (1) Green Man*: *The Green Man*–Cooper; Liar: *Young Wilding*–
Cooper (3) Adelgitha: *Michael Ducas*–Cleary; Inn-keeper's Daughter
   (Company moves to Savannah)
   Ap (12) Cure for the Heartache; Cinderella (13) Hamlet: *Hamlet*–
Cooper; Spoil'd Child (14) School for Scandal: *Charles Surface*–Cooper;
Sleeping Draught* (15) Bertram: *Bertram*–Cooper; Sleep Walker (16)
Pizarro: *Rolla*–Cooper; No Song, No Supper (17) Cinderella; Prisoner
at Large (19) Alexander the Great: *Alexander*–Cooper; Forty Thieves
(20) Robbers: *Charles de Moor*–Cooper; Agreeable Surprise (21) Much
Ado about Nothing: *Benedict*–Cooper; Falls of Clyde (22) Romeo and
Juliet: *Romeo*–Cooper; Sleeping Draught (23) Foundling of the Forest;
Tale of Mystery (24) Iron Chest: *Sir Edward Mortimer*–Cleary;
Fortune's Frolic (26) Gamester: *Beverly*–Cooper; Catherine and
Petruchio: *Petruchio*–Cooper (27) Alberti: *Alberti*–Cleary; Love
Laughs at Locksmiths (28) Julius Caesar: *Mark Antony*–Cooper,
Brutus–Cleary; Sleeping Draught (30) Alberti: *Alberti*–Cleary; Sprigs
of Laurel
   My (1) Poor Gentleman; Turn Out (3) Rob Roy MacGregor; Critic
(4) Clandestine Marriage; Killing No Murder (5) Education; Cinderel-
la (6) Rob Roy MacGregor; Irishman in London (7) Everyone Has His
Fault; Shipwreck (10) Adrian and Orrilla; Young Quaker (12) Castle
Spectre; Sea Serpent*

1 8 1 9 - 1 8 2 0

Mgr.: Charles Gilfert; *acting mgr.:* Thomas Hilson; *scenists:* J. West,
Schinotti; *orch. leader:* Charles Gilfert; *box-keeper:* Edward Young.
Stock: Allen, Brooks, Brown, F., Clarke, Dalton, Faulkner, T., Fennell,
J. Jr., Finn, H. G., Green, Hanna, Hayes, Howard, J., Kenyon, Nichols,
W., Placide, H., Pritchard, J., Quin, Ringwood, Robertson, W., Steele,
Thomas, Warrell, Wheatley, F., Wilson; *Mrs.* Barrett, G. L., Clarke,
Drummond, W. C., Faulkner, T., Gilfert, C., Hayes, Thomas, Waring,
L., West, J., Wheatley, F., Wheatley, S., Young, E.; *Misses* Clarke, C.,
Placide, E.; *Master* Wheatley, W.
   SE: T. A. Cooper: F 2, 11-14, Mr 17-27, Ap 17-My 1; Henry Wallack:
Mr 1-11; West Horse Troupe: F 3-10, Ap 3-15.
   D (21) Cure for the Heartache; Poor Soldier (22) Wonder; Prize,
Ten Thousand Pounds (24) Belle's Stratagem; Of Age Tomorrow (27)

George Barnwell; Falls of Clyde (29) Soldier's Daughter; Turn Out (31) Brutus*; Irishman in London

Ja (1) Will; Sixty-third Letter (5) Brutus; Where Shall I Dine? (7) Honeymoon; Weathercock (10) She Would Be a Soldier*; Married Yesterday; Purse (12) Sons of Erin; Spoil'd Child; Shelty's Frolic (14) She Would Be a Soldier; Blue Devils; Sixty-third Letter (15) Jealous Wife; Shelty's Frolic; Agreeable Surprise (17) Macbeth; Where Shall I Dine?; Personation* (19) Wanted—A Wife*; Prisoner at Large (21) Everyone Has His Fault; Matrimony (22) Wanted—A Wife; Prize, Ten Thousand Pounds (24) Clandestine Marriage; High Life below Stairs (26) Jew of Lubeck*; Married Yesterday; Turn Out (31) John Bull; Poor Soldier

F (1) Othello; Rosina (2) Hamlet: *Hamlet*–Cooper; Sprigs of Laurel (3) Animal Magnetism; Timour the Tartar (4) Midnight Hour; Timour the Tartar (5) Honest Thieves; Timour the Tartar (7) Flora's Birthday; My Grandmother; Timour the Tartar (9) High Life below Stairs; Bluebeard; Timour the Tartar (10) Sleeping Draught; Bluebeard; Timour the Tartar (11) Julius Caesar: *Mark Antony*–Cooper; Of Age Tomorrow (12) Honeymoon: *Duke of Aranza*–Cooper; Agreeable Surprise (14) Brutus: *Brutus*–Cooper; Prisoner at Large (16) Aethiop; Modern Antiques (18) Evadne*; Love Laughs at Locksmiths (19) School for Scandal; Devil to Pay (21) Apostate; Harlequin's Frolic (23) Wives as They Were and Maids as They Are; Harlequin's Frolic (25) Curfew; Drunken Provincial; 'Tis All a Farce (26) Heir at Law; Don Juan (28) Merry Wives of Windsor; Don Juan

Mr (1) Pizarro: *Rolla*–Wallack; Honest Thieves (3) Macbeth: *Macbeth*–Wallack; Fortune's Frolic (4) Mountaineers: *Octavian*–Wallack; Don Juan (6) Romeo and Juliet: *Romeo*–Wallack; Prize, Ten Thousand Pounds (7) Wonder: *Don Felix*–Wallack; Sleep Walker (8) Coriolanus: *Coriolanus*–Wallack; Lock and Key (10) Merchant of Venice: *Shylock*–Wallack; Three and Deuce (11) Pizarro: *Rolla*–Wallack; Harlequin's Frolic (15) Votary of Wealth; Forest of Bondy (17) Bertram: *Bertram*–Cooper; High Life below Stairs (18) Venice Preserved: *Jaffier*–Cooper; Harlequin's Frolic (22) Macbeth: *Macbeth*–Cooper; Romp (24) Rule a Wife and Have a Wife: *Leon*–Cooper; Broken Sword (25) Alfonso of Castile: *Alfonso*–Cooper; Adopted Child (27) Robbers: *Charles de Moor*–Cooper; Hunter of the Alps (29) Blue Devils; Barber of Seville*; Broken Sword

Ap (3) Midnight Hour; Timour the Tartar (4) My Grandmother; Timour the Tartar (5) Animal Magnetism; Timour the Tartar (7) Matrimony; Secret Mine; West Horse Troupe (8) Ways and Means; Secret Mine; West Horse Troupe (10) Fortune's Frolic; Tiger Horde; West Horse Troupe (12) Three Weeks after Marriage; Forty Thieves; West Horse Troupe (14) Lodoiska; La Perouse; West Horse Troupe (15) La Perouse; Tiger Horde; West Horse Troupe (17) Gamester: *Beverly*–Cooper; No Song, No Supper (19) Road to Ruin; Origin of Harlequin; Shelty's Frolic (21) Alfonso of Castile: *Orsino*–Cooper; Lying Valet (22) Wheel of Fortune: *Pendruddock*–Cooper; Teleki (24) Provoked Husband: *Lord Townly*–Cooper; Catherine and Petruchio: *Petruchio*–Cooper (26) Richard III: *Richard*–Cooper; Catherine and Petruchio (28) Revenge: *Zanga*–Cooper; Origin of Harlequin (29) Jane Shore: *Lord Hastings*–Cooper; Irishman in London

My (1) Revenge: *Zanga*–Cooper; Paul and Virginia (3) Lady of the Lake; Ways and Means (5) Lady of the Lake; Midnight Hour

(6) Town and Country; Spoil'd Child (8) Rivals; Purse; Actress of All
Work (10) School for Scandal; Sprigs of Laurel (12) She Would and
She Would Not; False and True; Dermot and Kathleen (13) Wives as
They Were and Maids as They Are; Turnpike Gate (15) Wild Oats;
Barber of Seville (18) Steward*; Actress of All Work; Adopted Child

1 8 2 0 - 1 8 2 1

Mgr.: J. H. Caldwell (N 22-D 26). *Stock:* Benton, Burke, T., Entwistle,
Fielding, Gray, J., Higgins, Hutton, J., Jefferson, T., Judah, Keene, A.,
M'Cafferty, Petrie, R. P., Russell, R., Scholes, Taylor, C. W.; *Mrs.*
Burke, T., Entwistle, Hutton, J., Legg, Russell, R., Williams; *Miss*
Placide, E.

N (22) Soldier's Daughter; Turnpike Gate (23) West Indian; Liar
(24) Stranger; Three and Deuce (25) Devil's Bridge; Spoil'd Child
(27) Pizarro; Rendezvous (29) Devil's Bridge; Poor Soldier

D (1) Much Ado about Nothing; Forest of Bondy (2) Guy Mannering*; Liar (4) Aethiop; Rosina (5) Guy Mannering; Don Juan (6)
Henry Quatre*; Of Age Tomorrow (8) Don Giovanni*; Suspicious Husband (9) Marmion*; Paul and Virginia (11) Aethiop; Weathercock
(13) Young Quaker; Padlock (14) Dramatist; Feast of Apollo; Review
(15) Vampire*; Sandy and Jemmy; Three and Deuce (16) Forest of
Bondy; No Song, No Supper (18) Country Girl; Lady of the Lake
(20) Love in a Village; Three Weeks after Marriage (22) As You
Like It; Hunter of the Alps (23) Wonder; Romp; Scottish Ghost (26)
Virginius*; Forty Thieves

(Company moves to New Orleans)

Mgr.: Charles Gilfert (Mr 16-My 30); *acting mgr.:* Thomas Hilson;
scenist: Grain; *orch. leader:* Charles Gilfert. *Stock:* Dalton, Faulkner,
T., Finn, H. J., Green, Hockney, Horton, Hyatt, G., Kenyon, Marshall,
Nichols, W., Pemberton, Placide, H., Robertson, W., Wheatley, F.; *Mrs.*
Anderson, Barrett, G. L., Faulkner, T., Gilfert, C., Holman, J. G., Hor-
ton, Waring, L., Wheatley, F.; *Misses* Clarke, C., Lewin, Placide, E.;
Master Clarke, E.

SE: Master George F. Smith: Ap 6-14; T. A. Cooper: My 25-30.

Mr (16) Provoked Husband; Love Laughs at Locksmiths (17) Castle
Spectre; Ways and Means (19) Steward; Plot and Counterplot (21)
School for Scandal; Animal Magnetism (23) Virginius; Weathercock
(24) Secrets Worth Knowing; Falls of Clyde (26) Merchant of Venice;
Children in the Wood (28) Exile; Irishman in London (29) Iron Chest;
Hunter of the Alps (31) Adelgitha; Children in the Wood

Ap (2) Rob Roy MacGregor; Of Age Tomorrow (4) Exile; Budget of
Blunders (6) Richard III: *Richard–*Master Smith; Promissory Note
(7) Douglas: *Young Norval–*Master Smith; High Life below Stairs
(9) Farmer's Wife; Apprentice: *Dick–*Master Smith (11) Mountaineers:
*Octavian–*Master Smith; Rosina (13) Way to Get Married; Lady and
the Devil (14) Richard III: *Richard–*Master Smith; Fortune's Frolic
(16) King Lear; Prisoner at Large (18) Heart of Midlothian; Lady
and the Devil (23) Woodman's Hut; Sleeping Draught (25) Love in
a Village; Turn Out (27) Woodman's Hut; Two Strings to Your Bow
(28) Exile; Village Lawyer (30) Midnight Hour; Woodman's Hut

My (2) Hamlet; Sea Serpent (4) Heart of Midlothian; Critic (5)
Rochester; Blind Boy (7) Who Wants a Guinea?; Amateurs and Actors
(9) Battle of Bunker Hill; Day after the Wedding; Rendezvous (11)

Fatal Snowstorm; Romp (12) She Would Be a Soldier; Maid and the
Magpie (14) Merry Wives of Windsor; Warlock of the Glen* (16)
Wild Oats; La Perouse (18) Merry Wives of Windsor; Rendezvous (19)
Wives as They Were and Maids as They Are; Warlock of the Glen (21)
Ivanhoe; Sprigs of Laurel (25) Virginius: *Virginius*–Cooper; Agree-
able Surprise (26) Macbeth: *Macbeth*–Cooper; Blue Devils (28)
Bertram: *Bertram*–Cooper; Of Age Tomorrow (29) Virginius: *Virgin-
ius*–Cooper; Prisoner at Large (30) Revenge: *Zanga*–Cooper; Sleep
Walker

1 8 2 1 - 1 8 2 2

Mgr.: Charles Gilfert; *acting mgr.:* Thomas Hilson; *scenist:* Grain;
orch. leaders: Charles Gilfert, R. R. Bishop. *Stock:* Bernard, C., Bignall,
Brennen, Brosa, J., Brown, F., Dykes, Faulkner, T., Fouchard, Green,
Horton, Humber, Hyatt, G., Keene, A., Kenyon, Lyons, G., Marshall,
Pemberton, Placide, H., Robertson, W., Spiller, Stevenson, Young, E.;
Mrs. Brown, F., Faulkner, T., Gilfert, C., Horton, Spiller, Young, E.;
Misses Lewin, Placide, E.
SE: J. B. Booth: N 29-D 11, F 22-Mr 1.
N (7) Heir at Law; Bombastes Furioso (8) Devil's Bridge; Lovers'
Quarrels (9) School for Scandal; Review (10) Warlock of the Glen;
Turn Out (12) School for Scandal; Poor Soldier (14) Damon and
Pythias; Bombastes Furioso (17) Devil's Bridge; Roland for an Oliver
(19) Therese*; Budget of Blunders (21) Wallace*; Nature and Philo-
sophy* (23) Woodman's Hut; Three and Deuce (24) Therese; Two
Late for Dinner (26) Damon and Pythias; Love Laughs at Locksmiths
(28) Therese; Bombastes Furioso (29) Richard III: *Richard*–Booth;
Poor Soldier (30) Mountaineers: *Octavian*–Booth; Two Late for Dinner
D (1) John of Paris; Roland for an Oliver (3) King Lear: *King
Lear*–Booth; Nature and Philosophy (5) New Way to Pay Old Debts:
Sir Giles Overreach–Booth; Warlock of the Glen (7) Hamlet: *Hamlet*–
Booth; Rendezvous (10) New Way to Pay Old Debts: *Sir Giles Over-
reach*–Booth; Nature and Philosophy (11) Town and Country: *Reuben
Glenroy*–Booth; Mayor of Garratt: *Mayor*–Booth
(Company moves to Savannah)
F (13) Jealous Wife; No Song, No Supper (15) Exile; Bombastes
Furioso (16) Devil's Bridge; Roland for an Oliver (18) Jealous Wife;
Lady and the Devil (20) Two Late for Dinner; Guy Mannering (22)
Richard III: *Richard*–Booth; Budget of Blunders (23) Iron Chest:
Sir Edward Mortimer–Booth; Highland Reel (25) Poor Gentleman;
Eight to One; Rendezvous (27) Merchant of Venice: *Shylock*–Booth;
Poor Soldier (28) Distressed Mother: *Orestes*–Booth; Animal Mag-
netism
Mr (1) Othello: *Othello*–Booth; Irishman in London
(Company moves to Savannah)
Ap (8) Marion; Lady and the Devil; Harlequin Woodcutter (10)
Wallace; Review (13) Spectre Bridegroom*; Turn Out; Forty Thieves
(15) Virgin of the Sun; Budget of Blunders (17) Virgin of the Sun;
Fortune's Frolic (19) Fraternal Discord; Sprigs of Laurel (20) School
of Reform; Highland Reel (24) Virgin of the Sun; Critic (26) Merry
Wives of Windsor; Poor Soldier (27) School of Reform; Irishman in
London (29) Apostate; Fire and Water; Adopted Child
My (1) Guy Mannering; Broken Sword (3) Virgin of the Sun;
Nature and Philosophy (4) Foundling of the Forest; Falls of Clyde

(6) Riches; Is He Jealous?; Harlequin Woodcutter (8) Young Quaker; Hamlet Travestie (10) Pizarro; Is He Jealous?; Fire and Water (11) Romeo and Juliet; Sylvester Daggerwood (13) How to Grow Rich; Prize, Ten Thousand Pounds (15) Know Your Own Mind; Wandering Boys (17) Fraternal Discord; Wandering Boys

1822-1823

Mgr.: Charles Gilfert; *acting mgr.*: F. Brown; *scenist*: Brain; *orch. leader*: Charles Gilfert; *ballet master*: T. Williams. *Stock*: Brazier, Dyball, Faulkner, T., Hilson, T., Horton, Hughes, Kenyon, Marks, H., Moreland, H., Placide, H., Robertson, W., Somerville, Spiller; *Mrs.* Barrett, G. L., Brown, F., Faulkner, T., Gilfert, C., Hughes, Spiller; *Misses* Russell, Tilden; *Master* Carey.

(No Fall Season)
My (22) Adelgitha; Spectre Bridegroom (23) Fraternal Discord; Children in the Wood (24) Steward; Adopted Child (27) Gamester; Love Laughs at Locksmiths (28) Jew; Monsieur Tonson (30) Jane Shore; Sleep Walker (31) Law of Java; Don and Patty
Je (2) Jew; Past Ten O'Clock (3) Point of Honor; Ella Rosenberg (4) Merry Wives of Windsor; Don and Patty (6) Apostate; Review (7) Adrian and Orrilla; Cobbler's Daughter (9) King John; 'Tis All a Farce (11) Merry Wives of Windsor; Cobbler's Daughter (13) Wonder; Critic (14) John Buzzby*; Sprigs of Laurel (16) Rochester; Bombastes Furioso (18) Richard III; Children in the Wood (20) Romeo and Juliet; Spectre Bridegroom (21) Adrian and Orrilla; Cobbler's Daughter (23) Jealous Wife; Monsieur Tonson (25) Macbeth; Matrimony (27) Pizarro; Wandering Boys (28) Tale of Mystery; Harlequin Shipwreck (30) Gilderoy*; Manager in Distress; Actor of All Work
Jy (2) West Indian; Rugantino (4) Gilderoy; Festival of the 4th of July; Sailor's Hornpipe (7) Dramatist; Manager in Distress; Rugantino

1823-1824

Mgr.: Charles Gilfert; *acting mgr.*: F. Brown; *scenist*: Grain; *treas.*: Miller; *orch. leaders*: Charles Gilfert, Nicola, J. Eckhardt; *ballet master*: Trebuchet. *Stock*: Austin, Barrett, G. H., Durang, F., Faulkner, T., Hatton, Horton, Hughes, Hyatt, G., Keene, A., Kenyon, Lindsley, Lowry, Marks, H., Nichols, W., Robertson, W., Spiller, Stevenson, Tyke; *Mrs.* Barrett, G. H., Brown, F., Faulkner, T., Fulmer, Gilfert, C., Gray, Hughes, Reeves; *Misses* Russell, Tilden; *Master* Carey.
SE: Vincent De Camp: D 31-Ja 12, F 23-Mr 19; Henry Wallack: F 21-Ap 5; William Pelby: Ap 6-9.
N (26) Rivals; Raising the Wind (28) West Indian; Of Age Tomorrow; Love in a Village (29) Love in a Village; Lovers' Quarrels
D (1) Isabella; Irishman in London (3) Love in a Village; Tale of Mystery (5) Jealous Wife; Two Pages of Frederick the Great* (6) Brother and Sister; Rugantino (8) Spy*; Rosina (10) Fazio*; No Song, No Supper (12) Honeymoon; Two Pages of Frederick the Great (13) Spy; Raising the Wind (15) Henry VIII; Matrimony (17) Castle Spectre; Three and Deuce (19) Clari*; Spectre Bridegroom (20) Duel; Wandering Boys (22) Damon and Pythias; Nature and Philosophy; Broken Sword (26) Clari; Irish Tutor; Tom Thumb the Great (27) Richard III; Lovers' Quarrels (29) Henry VIII; Irish Tutor (31) Laugh when You Can: *Gossamer*–De Camp; Monsieur Tonson

Ja (1) George Barnwell: *George Barnwell*–De Camp; Tom Thumb
the Great (3) Road to Ruin: *Goldfinch*–De Camp; Sylvester Daggerwood (5) School for Scandal: *Sir Peter Teazle*–De Camp; High Life
below Stairs (7) Way to Get Married: *Tangent*–De Camp; Duel (8)
Washington*; Nature and Philosophy (9) Wild Oats: *Rover*–De Camp;
Sleeping Draught (10) Laugh when You Can: *Gossamer*–De Camp;
Critic: *Puff*–De Camp (12) Wine Does Wonders; Sylvester Daggerwood: *Sylvester*–De Camp; Don Giovanni: *Don*–De Camp (14) Washington; Duel (16) Guy Mannering; Midnight Hour (17) Devil's
Bridge; Wandering Boys (19) Tom Thumb the Great; Brother and
Sister; Love among the Roses* (21) Virginius; Ladies at Home; Joan
of Art (23) Isabella; Poor Soldier (24) John of Paris; Therese (26)
Much Ado about Nothing; Therese (28) Spy; Joan of Arc (30) Love
in a Village; Therese; Clari (31) Macbeth; Master Key

F (2) Know Your Own Mind; Forest of Rosenwald* (4, 6) Wonder;
Ladies at Home; Hunter of the Alps (9) Aethiop; Fortune's Frolic
(11) Poor Gentleman; Bombastes Furioso (13) Marmion; Review (14)
Aethiop; Irish Tutor (17, 18) Damon and Pythias; Joan of Arc (20)
Adrian and Orrilla; Brother and Sister (21) Pizarro: *Rolla*–Wallack;
Spectre Bridegroom (23) Suspicious Husband: *Ranger*–De Camp; Mon-
sieur Tonson: *Marbleau*–De Camp (24) Pizarro: *Rolla*–Wallack;
Lovers' Quarrels (25) Jealous Wife; Three and Deuce: rôle not given–
De Camp (26) Way to Get Married: *Tangent*–De Camp; Frightened to
Death (27) Richard III: *Richard*–Wallack; Irish Tutor (28) Fountain-
bleau Races; Bombastes Furioso

Mr (1) Tom and Jerry*; *Tom*–De Camp; Love Among the Roses (2)
Tom and Jerry: *Tom*–De Camp; Irishman in London (3) Tom and
Jerry: *Tom*–De Camp; Nature and Philosophy (4) Julius Caesar:
Cassius–Wallack; Fortune's Frolic (5) Tom and Jerry: *Tom*–De Camp;
Is He Jealous? (6) Tom and Jerry: *Tom*–De Camp; Matrimony (8)
Tom and Jerry: *Tom*–De Camp; Family Jars (10) Rob Roy MacGregor:
Rob Roy–Wallack, *Nicol Jarvie*–De Camp; Family Jars (12) Henry
IV: *Hotspur*–Wallack, *Falstaff*–De Camp; Ladies at Home (13) Two
Pages of Frederick the Great: *Frederick*–Wallack; Rendezvous: rôle
not given–De Camp (15) King John: *Faulconbridge*–Wallack; Adopted
Child: *Michael*–Wallack (17) Tom and Jerry: *Tom*–De Camp; Village
Lawyer (18) Tom and Jerry: *Tom*–De Camp; Poor Soldier (19) Guy
Mannering: *Dandie Dinmont*–Wallack; Match Making; Deaf as a Post:
rôle not given–De Camp (20) Coriolanus: *Coriolanus*–Wallack; Love
Laughs at Locksmiths (22) Venice Preserved; Liar (24) Zembuca*;
Review (26) Duel; Greece and Liberty* (27) Adrian and Orrilla;
Rendezvous (29) Zembuca; Hunter of the Alps (31) Pizarro: *Rolla*–
Wallack; Spoil'd Child

Ap (2) Bertram: *Bertram*–Wallack; Midnight Hour (3) Tom and
Jerry: *Tom*–Wallack; Bombastes Furioso (5) Douglas: *Young Norval*–
Wallack; Warlock of the Glen: *Andrew*–Wallack (6) Damon and
Pythias: *Damon*–Pelby; Budget of Blunders (7) Lady of the Lake;
Animal Magnetism (8) Virginius: *Virginius*–Pelby; Sleeping Draught
(9) Lady of the Lake: *Roderick Dhu*–Pelby; Foundling of the Forest
(12) Master of Ravenswood*; Poor Soldier (20) Review; Tom and
Jerry (21) Master of Ravenswood; Sprigs of Laurel (23) Adelgitha;
Lady and the Devil (24) Zembuca; Youthful Days of Mr. Hyatt; Two
Strings to Your Bow (26) Wallace; Monsieur Tonson (28) Love among

the Roses; Shakespeare's Jubilee; Catherine and Petruchio (30) Mountaineers; Turnpike Gate

My (1) Tom and Jerry; Liar (3) Town and Country; Weathercock (5) Belle's Stratagem; Ella Rosenberg (7) Rivals; Brother and Sister (8) New Way to Pay Old Debts; Boarding House (10) Manager in Distress; Way to Keep Him; Irish Tutor (12) Belle's Stratagem; Turn Out; Gile Tout Soul (14) Tekeli; Gile Tout Soul; Lying Valet (17) Bride of Abydos; Two Strings to Your Bow (19) Soldier's Daughter; Clari (21) To Marry or Not to Marry; Wedding Day (22) Tom and Jerry; Rendezvous (24) School of Reform; La Perouse (26) Bride of Abydos; Tom and Jerry

1824-1825

Mgr.: Charles Gilfert; *acting mgr.:* F. Brown; *scenists:* C. Bernard, Sera; *orch. leader:* Charles Gilfert. *Stock:* Andes, Barrett, G. H., Barry, J., Cooke, Faulkner, T., Fuller, Harper, Horton, Howard, J., Higgins, Hunter, Hyatt, G., Kenyon, Lamb, Lindsley, Mason, Singleton, Spiller, Stone, J. A., Taylor; *Mrs.* Barrett, G. H., Brown, F., De Sylvia, Gray, Gilfert, C., Harper, Horton, Neufville, Stone, J. A.; *Miss* Tilden.

SE: William A. Conway: D 1-Ja 3; J. B. Booth: Mr 18-30.

N (20) Town and Country; Rosina (22) Dramatist; Raising the Wind (23) Cure for the Heartache; Lovers' Quarrels (24) School for Scandal; Liar (26) Road to Ruin; Review (27) Tom and Jerry; Rendezvous (29) Much Ado about Nothing; Catherine and Petruchio

D (1) Hamlet: *Hamlet*-Conway; Irish Tutor (3) Venice Preserved: *Jaffier*-Conway; Liar (4) Macbeth: *Macbeth*-Conway; Day after the Wedding (6) Julius Caesar: *Brutus*-Conway; Nature and Philosophy (8) Othello: *Othello*-Conway; Poor Soldier (9) Rule a Wife and Have a Wife: *Leon*-Conway; No Song, No Supper (11) Tom and Jerry; Fortune's Frolic (13) Stranger: *Stranger*-Conway; Simpson and Company* (15) Tom and Jerry; Animal Magnetism (17) Coriolanus: *Coriolanus*-Conway; Simpson and Company (18) Cure for the Heartache; Raising the Wind (20) Gamester: *Beverly*-Conway; Day after the Wedding (22) Romeo and Juliet: *Romeo*-Conway; Three and Deuce (23) Coriolanus: *Coriolanus*-Conway; Simpson and Company (27) Apostate: *Hemeya*-Conway; Review: *Looney M'Twoolter*-Conway (29) Spy; Duel (31) Fair Penitent: *Horatio*-Conway; Actress of All Work; Raising the Wind

Ja (1) George Barnwell: *George Barnwell*-Conway; La Perouse (3) Fair Penitent: *Horatio*-Conway; Actor of All Work; Raising the Wind (5) Married and Single*; Day after the Wedding; No Song, No Supper (7) Lafayette*; Simpson and Company (10) Alladin* (14) Honeymoon; Vampire (15) Tom and Jerry; Irish Tutor (17) Alladin; Liar (21) Jealous Wife; Broken Sword (22) Alladin; Poor Soldier (24) Alladin; Three Weeks after Marriage (26) Aethiop; Duel (28) John Bull; Broken Sword (29) Wonder; Rosina (31) Bride of Abydos; Midnight Hour

F (2) Brutus; Sprigs of Laurel (4) Wallace; Irishman in London (5) Town and Country; Love among the Roses (7) Alladin; John of Paris (9) Richard III; Spectre Bridegroom (11) Zembuca; Love among the Roses (14) Steward; Sponge in Town (16) West Indian; Zembuca (18) Aethiop; Sponge in Town (21) Wonder; Alladin (23) Wood Demon; Wedding Day (24) Tom and Jerry; Love among the Roses

(25) Wood Demon; Simpson and Company (26) Alladin; Dramatist (28) Smiles and Tears; Wood Demon

Mr (1) Road to Ruin; Sponge in Town (2) Bride of Abydos; Liar (3) School for Scandal; Alladin (4) Wild Oats; Bombastes Furioso (7) Alasco*; Budget of Blunders (9) Smiles and Tears; Monsieur Tonson (11) Young Quaker; Tale of Mystery (12) Lafayette; Sponge in Town (14) Love Laughs at Locksmiths (16-17) Military Balls in honor of Lafayette (18) Richard III: *Richard*–Booth; Irishman in London (19) Iron Chest: *Sir Edward Mortimer*–Booth; Sponge in Town (21) New Way to Pay Old Debts: *Sir Giles Overreach*–Booth; Sleeping Draught (22) Alladin; Poor Soldier (23) Town and Country: *Reuben Glenroy*–Booth; Sponge in Town (25) King Lear: *King Lear*–Booth; Of Age Tomorrow (26) Othello: *Othello*–Booth; No Song, No Supper (28) King Lear: *King Lear*–Booth; Of Age Tomorrow (29) Merchant of Venice: *Shylock*–Booth; Lady and the Devil (30) Caius Gracchus*: *Caius*–Booth; Amateurs and Actors

Ap (4) Fauntleroy*; Love among the Roses; Love Laughs at Locksmiths (5) Foundling of the Forest; Spoil'd Child (6) Soldier's Daughter; Alladin (7) She Stoops to Conquer; Catherine and Petruchio (8) Ladies at Home; Married and Single; Love a la Mode (9) Rivals; Ella Rosenberg (11) Day after the Wedding; Fauntleroy; 'Tis All a Farce (12) Exile; Wandering Boys (13) Columbus; Eight to One; Tom Thumb the Great (14) Restoration*; Wedding Day; Lovers' Quarrels (15) Pizarro; Wood Demon (16) Mountaineers; Trick upon Trick*; Rugantiño (18) Matrimony; Way to Get Married; Three Weeks after Marriage (19) Restoration; Timour the Tartar (20) Alexander the Great; Ladies at Home (22) Provoked Husband; Miller and His Men

1825-1826

Mgr.: Joe Cowell; *scenists:* W. Isherwood, Wilkins. *Stock:* Blakely, T., Collingbourne, Hallam, J., Isherwood, H., Jamie, Jones, Kirby, Laidley, Lee, C., McDonald, Moreland, H., Parker, J., Rowe, G., Stickney, Stoker, Wilkinson; *Mrs.* Battersby, Cowell, J., Jones, Kirby, Rowe, G.; *Misses* Aspinall, Greer, Hanna; *Master* Collet.

SE: Edmund Kean: Mr 13-Ap 10.

(No Fall Season)

F (13) Floating Beacon*; Turnpike Gate (15) Floating Beacon; Turnpike Gate (20) Miller's Maid; Flora's Birthday; Two Strings to Your Bow (22) False Friend; Flora's Birthday; Turnpike Gate (25) Miller's Maid; La Perouse (27) False Friend; Sandy and Jenny; Two Strings to Your Bow

Mr (1) Oscar and Malvina; El Hyder (6) Storm; Cataract of the Ganges* (8) Brave Hussar; Cataract of the Ganges (10) Don Juan; Cataract of the Ganges (13) Richard III: *Richard*–Kean; Turnpike Gate (15) Othello: *Othello*–Kean; Two Strings to Your Bow (17) New Way to Pay Old Debts: *Sir Giles Overreach*–Kean; St. Patrick's Day; Day after the Wedding (20) King Lear: *King Lear*–Kean; Don Juan (22) Merchant of Venice: *Shylock*–Dean; Don Juan (27) New Way to Pay Old Debts: *Sir Giles Overreach*–Kean; Raising the Wind (28) Iron Chest: *Sir Edward Mortimer*–Kean; House that Jack Built (29) Macbeth: *Macbeth*–Kean; House that Jack Built (31) Hamlet: *Hamlet*–Kean; Turnpike Gate

Ap (3) Merchant of Venice: *Shylock*–Kean; House that Jack Built (5) Brutus: *Brutus*–Kean; Day after the Wedding (6) Iron Chest: *Sir Edward Mortimer*–Kean; Roland for an Oliver (7) Othello: *Othello*–Kean; Raising the Wind (10) Richard III: *Richard*–Kean; Irish Widow (12) Matrimony; Valentine and Orson (13) Presumption*; Idiot Witness (14) Forty Thieves; Three Witches; Little Red Riding Hood* (19) Forty Thieves; Little Red Riding Hood; Fatal Snowstorm (21) Gilderoy; Broken Sword (24) Bertram: *Bertram*–Kean; Agreeable Surprise

1826-1827

Mgr.: John Dyott; *acting mgr.:* F. Brown; *scenist:* Apparisso; *boxkeeper:* Daniel Burrie; *orch. leader:* Nicola. *Stock:* Adams, J. J., Allen, Essender, Estelle, Fielding, Frethey, Herbert, J., Horton, Kent, J., Lamb, Laws, Miller, Morris, Morton, Oatland, Parsons, C. B., Phillips, J. B., Pitt, Presto, Sarzedas, D. A., Williams, H. A.; *Mrs.* Brown, F., Hatch, Horton, Hughes, Read, Riddle, Sage; *Misses* Miller, Riddle, E., Riddle, S.

SE: Thomas S. Hamblin: Ja 24-F 5, 21-Mr 28; T. A. Cooper: F 7-Mr 7; Mrs. Charles Gilfert: Mr 26-My 7.

D (20) Laugh when You Can; Of Age Tomorrow (22) Cure for the Heartache; High Life below Stairs (23) She Stoops to Conquer; Raising the Wind (26) Town and Country; Rendezvous (27) Heir at Law; Review (29) Virginius (30) Wandering Boys; Weathercock

Ja (1) Wheel of Fortune; Spoil'd Child (3) Pizarro; Promissory Note (5) Will; Lady and the Devil (6) Tale of Mystery; No Song, No Supper (8) William Tell*; Promissory Note (10) William Tell; Of Age Tomorrow (12) Foundling of the Forest; Wandering Boys (13) Laugh when You Can; Intrigue (15) William Tell; Poor Soldier (17) Paul Pry*; Promissory Note (19) Paul Pry; Lovers' Quarrels (20) Soldier's Daughter; Spoil'd Child (22) Paul Pry; Wedding Day (24) Hamlet: *Hamlet*–Hamblin; Nature and Philosophy (26) Virginius: *Virginius*–Hamblin; Poor Soldier (27) Soldier's Daughter; Rendezvous (29) William Tell: *William Tell*–Hamblin; Three and Deuce (31) Macbeth: *Macbeth*–Hamblin; Nature and Philosophy

F (2) Damon and Pythias: *Damon*–Hamblin; Romp (3) Iron Chest: *Sir Edward Mortimer*–Hamblin; Lovers' Quarrels (5) Pizarro: *Rolla*–Hamblin; Catherine and Petruchio: *Petruchio*–Hamblin (7) Virginius: *Virginius*–Cooper; Day after the Wedding (9) Damon and Pythias: *Damon*–Cooper; Of Age Tomorrow (10) Bertram: *Bertram*–Cooper; Romp (12) Othello: *Othello*–Cooper; Promissory Note (14) Rule a Wife and Have a Wife: *Leon*–Cooper; Romp (16) Macbeth: *Macbeth*–Cooper; Liar (17) Honeymoon: *Duke of Aranza*–Cooper; Wandering Boys (19) Damon and Pythias: *Damon*–Cooper; Catherine and Petruchio: *Petruchio*–Cooper (21) Brutus: *Brutus*–Hamblin; Romp (22) Point of Honor; Spoil'd Child (23) Othello: *Othello*–Hamblin, *Iago*–Cooper; Raising the Wind (24) Venice Preserved: *Jaffier*–Cooper, *Pierre*–Hamblin; High Life below Stairs (26) Romeo and Juliet: *Romeo*–Hamblin, *Mercutio*–Cooper (27) Paul Pry; No Song, No Supper (28) Julius Caesar: *Mark Antony*–Cooper, *Cassius*–Hamblin; Intrigue

Mr (1) Town and Country; Wandering Boys (2) Douglas: *Glenalvon*–Cooper, *Young Norval*–Hamblin; Tale of Mystery (3) Othello: *Othello*–Hamblin, *Iago*–Cooper; Blue Devils (5) King John: *King John*–Cooper, *Faulconbridge*–Hamblin; Is He Jealous? (7) Venice Preserved: *Jaffier*–Hamblin, *Pierre*–Cooper; Spoil'd Child (9) Stranger: *Stranger*–

Hamblin; Is He Jealous?; Blue Devils (10) Mountaineers: *Octavian–*
Hamblin; Sylvester Daggerwood; Day after the Wedding (12) King
Lear: *Edgar*–Hamblin; Matrimony (14) Wonder: *Don Felix*–Hamblin;
Frightened to Death (16) Lovers' Vows: *Frederick*–Hamblin; Turn
Out (17) Rule a Wife and Have a Wife: *Leon*–Hamblin; Frightened to
Death (19) William Tell: *William Tell*–Hamblin; Who's the Dupe?
(21) Honeymoon: *Duke of Aranza*–Hamblin; Robinson Crusoe (23)
Hamlet: *Hamlet*–Hamblin; Helpless Animals! Men without Women!
(24) Wedding Day; Robinson Crusoe (26) Wonder: *Don Felix*–Hamblin,
Violante–Mrs. Gilfert; Midnight Hour (28) Gamester: *Beverly*–
Hamblin, *Mrs. Beverly*–Mrs. Gilfert; Is He Jealous? (30) School for
Scandal: *Lady Teazle*–Mrs. Gilfert; Poor Soldier (31) Robinson Crusoe;
Who's the Dupe?
Ap (3) Much Ado about Nothing: *Beatrice*–Mrs. Gilfert; Review
(4) Jealous Wife; Tale of Mystery (6) Merchant of Venice: *Portia*–
Mrs. Gilfert; Turn Out (7) Foundling of the Forest; Weathercock (9)
Jealous Wife: *Elvira*–Mrs. Gilfert; Spectre Bridegroom (16) Hypocrite:
Charlotte–Mrs. Gilfert; Therese (18) Sweethearts and Wives; Author
and Actor; Swedish Patriotism (20) Tom and Jerry; Two Pages of
Frederick the Great (21) Much Ado about Nothing: *Beatrice*–Mrs.
Gilfert; Sweethearts and Wives (23) Apostate: *Florinda*–Mrs. Gilfert;
High Life below Stairs (25) Alexander the Great; Prisoner at Large
(26) Tom and Jerry: *Corinthian Kate*–Mrs. Gilfert; Liar (28) Blind
Boy; Killing No Murder (30) Much Ado about Nothing: *Beatrice*–
Mrs. Gilfert; Nature and Philosophy
My (2) Paul Pry; Tom and Jerry (4) Sweethearts and Wives; Two
Pages of Frederick the Great (5) Castle Spectre: *Angela*–Mrs. Gilfert;
Blue Devils (7) Provoked Husband: *Lady Townly*–Mrs. Gilfert; 'Twas
I* (9) Richard III; Fish out of Water (11) Sweethearts and Wives;
'Twas I; Fish out of Water (16) Dramatist; Lady and the Devil (18)
To Marry or Not to Marry; Matrimony (23) Will; Three and Deuce

1827-1828

Mgr.: John B. Irving; *acting mgr.:* Robert J. Scott. *Stock:* Ansell,
Barton, Estelle, Herbert, J., Hosack, Keene, A., Kenyon,[1] Laws, Moses,
Parsons, C. B., Read, Roberts, J., Simpson, Stone, J. A., West, William-
son; *Mrs.* Brown, F., Hughes, La Combe, Monier, V., Read, Simpson,
Toney.
SE: Thomas S. Hamblin: D 5-Ja 4, 30-F 6; Vincent De Camp: Ja 14-
F 8; John Barnes: F 13-Mr 18; Mrs. Eliza Povey Knight: F 29-Mr 28;
John Mills Brown, Watkins Burroughs, and Mrs. Robertson: Ap 9-26;
Villalave Family: F 5-Mr 1.
N (19) Sweethearts and Wives; Family Jars (21) Heir at Law; One
Hundred Pound Note (23) Bertram; One Hundred Pound Note (24)
Sweethearts and Wives; One Hundred Pound Note (26) Paul Pry;
Lottery Ticket (28) One Hundred Pound Note; Before Breakfast; Day
after the Fair (30) Mountaineers; Rendezvous
D (1) She Stoops to Conquer; Lottery Ticket (3) Devil's Bridge;
Day after the Fair (5) Virginius: *Virginius*–Hamblin; Lottery Ticket
(7) Coriolanus: *Coriolanus*–Hamblin; Bombastes Furioso (8) Stranger:
Stranger–Hamblin; Sleeping Draught (10) Rob Roy MacGregor: *Rob*

[1]After Scott's death, Kenyon was appointed acting manager (see *Courier,* March 24, April
7, 1828.)

Roy–Hamblin; 'Tis All a Farce (12) Revenge: *Zanga*–Hamblin; Turn Out (14) Stranger: *Stranger*–Hamblin; Sleep Walker (17) Fatal Dowry*: *Romont*–Hamblin; Is He Jealous?; Day after the Fair (19) Town and Country: *Reuben Glenroy*–Hamblin; Before Breakfast (21) Pizarro: *Rolla*–Hamblin; Falls of Clyde (22) Paul Pry; Rendezvous (24) Lottery Ticket; Gamester: *Beverly*–Hamblin (26) Damon and Pythias: *Damon*–Hamblin; Lovers' Quarrels (31) Aethiop: *Aethiop*–Hamblin; Lovers' Quarrels

Ja (2) Brutus: *Brutus*–Hamblin; Family Jars (4) Virginius: *Virginius*–Hamblin; Hunter of the Alps (7) Devil's Bridge; Village Lawyer (8) She Would be a Soldier; Day after the Fair; Battle of New Orleans (11) Heir at Law; Turnpike Gate (14) Laugh when You Can: *Gossamer*–De Camp; Monsieur Tonson: *Marbleau*–De Camp (16) Hypocrite: *Dr. Cantwell*–De Camp; Hops and Steps: *Bowkitt*–De Camp; Promissory Note (18) Dramatist: *Vapid*–De Camp; Lottery Ticket (22) Peter Wilkins*; Simpson and Company: *Simpson*–De Camp (23) Paul Pry: *Paul Pry*–De Camp; Peter Wilkins: *Phelim O'Scud*–De Camp (25) Lovers' Quarrels; Peter Wilkins: *Phelim O'Scud*–De Camp (26) Peter Wilkins: *Phelim O'Scud*–De Camp; Monsieur Tonson: *Marbleau*–De Camp (28) Critic: *Puff*–De Camp; Peter Wilkins: *Phelim O'Scud*–De Camp (30) Honeymoon: *Duke of Aranza*–Hamblin, *Rolando*–De Camp; Sylvester Daggerwood; Blue Devils: *Megrim*–De Camp

F (1) William Tell: *William Tell*–Hamblin, *Michael*–De Camp; High Life below Stairs: *Lord Duke*–De Camp (2) Romeo and Juliet: *Romeo*–Hamblin, *Mercutio*–De Camp; Simpson and Company: *Simpson*–De Camp (4) Tom and Jerry: *Tom*–De Camp; 102: *Phillip Garbois*–De Camp (5) Villalave Family (6) Hamlet: *Hamlet*–Hamblin; Review (7) Villalave Family (8) Flying Dutchman; Family Jars (9) Villalave Family (11) Richard III; One Hundred Pound Note; Magpie and the Maid (12) Villalave Family (13) Sweethearts and Wives: *Billy Lackaday*–Barnes; Mogul Tale: *Johnny Atkins*–Barnes (14) Villalave Family (15) Soldier's Daughter: *Governor Heartall*–Barnes; Sprigs of Laurel: *Nipperkin*–Barnes (16) Villalave Family (18) Comedy of Errors: *Dromio*–Barnes; Turnpike Gate: *Crack*–Barnes (19) Villalave Family (20) Comedy of Errors: *Dromio*–Barnes; Turnpike Gate: *Crack*–Barnes (22) Laroque, the Regicide*: *Laroque*–Barnes; Comedy of Errors: *Dromio*–Barnes (23) Maid and the Magpie; Mogul Tale: *Johnny Atkins*–Barnes (25) Illustrious Stranger: *Bowell*–Barnes; School for Scandal: *Sir Peter Teazle*–Barnes (26) Villalave Family (27) Hypocrite: *Mauworm*–Barnes; Day after the Wedding (28) Comedy of Errors: *Dromio*–Barnes; Villalave Family (29) Love in a Village: *Rosetta*–Mrs. Knight, *Justice Woodstock*–Barnes; Day after the Wedding.

Mr (1) Villalave Family (4) Brother and Sister: *Don Christophal*–Barnes, *Donna Isadora*–Mrs. Knight; Lady and the Devil; Rendezvous (6) Guy Mannering: *Dominie*–Barnes, *Julia*–Mrs. Knight (8) Love in a Village: *Justice Woodstock*–Barnes, *Rosetta*–Mrs. Knight; Illustrious Stranger: *Bowell*–Barnes (10) Clari: *Clari*–Mrs. Knight; Family Jars: *Delph*–Barnes (12) Lord of the Manor: *Annette*–Mrs. Knight, *Moll Flagon*–Barnes; Turn Out: *Marian*–Mrs. Knight, *Gregory*–Barnes (14) Devil's Bridge: *Rosalvina*–Mrs. Knight, *Pietro*–Barnes; Brother and Sister: *Donna Isadora*–Mrs. Knight, *Don Christophal*–Barnes (17) Rosina: *Rosina*–Mrs. Knight, *William*–Barnes; Charles II: *Mary*–Mrs. Knight (18) Rivals: *Sir Anthony Absolute*–Barnes, *Lydia Languish*–

Mrs. Knight; No Song, No Supper: *Endless*–Barnes, *Margaretta*–Mrs. Knight (19) Turn Out: *Marian*–Mrs. Knight; Poor Soldier (21) Foundling of the Forest: *Unknown Female*–Mrs. Knight; Paul and Virginia (22) Guy Mannering: *Julia*–Mrs. Knight; Irishman in London (24) Clari: *Clari*–Mrs. Knight; Raising the Wind (26) Rob Roy MacGregor: *Diana*–Mrs. Knight; Lady and the Devil (28) Haunted Tower: *Adela*–Mrs. Knight; John of Paris

Ap (7) Forest of Bondy; Tekeli (9) Stranger: *Stranger*–Burroughs, *Peter*–Brown, *Mrs. Haller*–Mrs. Robertson; Fortune's Frolic: *Robin*–Brown, *Dolly*–Mrs. Robertson (11) Bride of Abydos: *Selim*–Burroughs, *Zulieka*–Mrs. Robertson; Spectre Bridegroom: *Dickory*–Brown (12) Iron Chest: *Sir Edward Mortimer*–Burroughs, *Samson*–Brown, *Helen*–Mrs. Robertson; We Fly by Night: *Gaby Grim*–Brown (14) Matrimony: *Delaval*–Burroughs, *O'Clogherty*–Brown, *Clara*–Mrs. Robertson; Reprobate*: *Napthala*–Burroughs, *Celesta*–Mrs. Robertson, *Benedick*–Brown; Spoil'd Child (16) Metamorphoses*: *Aurelia, Captain Hector, Dorothy Dryloves*–Mrs. Robertson; Miller's Maid: *Giles*–Burroughs, *Matty*–Brown, *Phoebe*–Mrs. Robertson; Two Gregories: *Gregory*–Burroughs, *Fanchette*–Mrs. Robertson (18) Speed the Plough; Ruffian Boy* (22) Metamorphoses: *Aurelia, Captain Hector, Dorothy Dryloves*–Mrs. Robertson; Reprobate: *Napthala*–Burroughs, *Celesta*–Mrs. Robertson, *Benedick*–Brown; Race for a Dinner (23) School of Reform: *Robert Tyke*–Brown, *Mrs. Fernent*–Mrs. Robertson; Review: *Caleb Quotem*–Burroughs, *John Lump*–Brown (25) Day after the Wedding: *Lady Freelove*–Mrs. Robertson; El Hyder: *Harry Clifton*–Mrs. Robertson; Turnpike Gate: *Crack*–Burroughs, *Joe Steadfast*–Brown, *Peggy*–Mrs. Robertson (26) Reprobate: *Napthala*–Burroughs, *Celesta*–Mrs. Robertson, *Benedick*–Brown; Metamorphoses: *Aurelia, Captain Hector, Dorothy Dryloves*–Mrs. Robertson

1828-1829

Mgr.: J. J. Adams; *scenist:* West. *Stock:* Brown, J. M., De Camp, V., Durang, F., Evans, Fielding, Green, C. L., Johnson, Katen, Lear, Maguire, Moore, J., Moreland, H., Rice, D., Stevens, Waldgrave; *Mrs.* Barnes, J., Brown, J. M., Durang, F., Hill, Hutin; *Misses* Coster, Kelly, L., Stevens.

SE: George Holland: D 5-10; T. A. Cooper: D 12-19; Clara Fisher: Mr 11-Ap 8.

N (20) Pizarro; Fortune's Frolic (21) Honeymoon; Raising the Wind (24) Alexander the Great; Irishman in London (26) Mountaineers; High Life below Stairs (27) Romeo and Juliet; Rendezvous (28) Bertram; Fortune's Frolic

D (1) School for Scandal; Monsieur Tonson (3) Hamlet; Three Weeks after Marriage (5) Belle's Stratagem; Day after the Fair: rôle not given–Holland (6) Whims of a Comedian: seven rôles–Holland; How to Die for Love; Deaf as a Post (8) Isabella: *Carlos*–Holland; Secret; Somnambulist (9) Whims of a Comedian: seven rôles–Holland; Animal Magnetism; Day after the Fair (10) School of Reform: *Tyke*–Holland; Mayor of Garratt: *Jerry Sneak*–Holland; Hamlet Travestie: *Hamlet*–Holland (12) Macbeth: *Macbeth*–Cooper; Family Jars (13) Honeymoon: *Duke of Aranza*–Cooper; Frightened to Death (15) Bertram: *Bertram*–Cooper; Monsieur Tonson (16) Three and Deuce; Deaf as a Post; Deserter, the Robber, and Frederick the Great (17)

Damon and Pythias: *Damon*–Cooper; Where Shall I Dine? (18) Midnight Hour; How to Die for Love; Raising the Wind (19) Gamester: *Beverly*–Cooper; Catherine and Petruchio: *Petruchio*–Cooper (20) Broken Sword; Lottery Ticket
(Company moves to Savannah)
Ja 17-*F* 15. Villalave Family
F (16) Belle's Stratagem; Irishman in London (17) Venice Preserved; Raising the Wind (18) Town and Country; Lady and the Devil (19) Belle's Stratagem; X. Y. Z. (21) She Stoops to Conquer; Prize, Ten Thousand Pounds (23) Jealous Wife; X. Y. Z. (24) She Stoops to Conquer; Prize, Ten Thousand Pounds (25) Pizarro; High Life below Stairs (26) Wonder; Rosina (27) Honeymoon; Irishman in London (28) Wives as They Were and Maids as They Are; Of Age Tomorrow
Mr (2) Romeo and Juliet; Prize, Ten Thousand Pounds (4) Soldier's Daughter; One Hundred Pound Note (5) Alexander the Great; Spectre Bridegroom (6) Rivals; Ladies at Home (9) Gambler's Fate; Wandering Boys (11) Belle's Stratagem: *Letitia Hardy*–Clara Fisher; Actress of All Work: six rôles–Clara Fisher (13) Will: *Albina Mandeville*–Clara Fisher; Old and Young: five rôles–Clara Fisher (16) Man and Wife: *Helen Worrett*–Clara Fisher; Spoil'd Child: *Little Pickle*–Clara Fisher (18) Country Girl: *Peggy*–Clara Fisher; One Hundred Pound Note: *Maria*–Clara Fisher (20) She Would and She Would Not: *Hypolita*–Clara Fisher; Dead Shot: *Louisa*–Clara Fisher (23) School for Scandal: *Lady Teazle*–Clara Fisher; Incincibles: *Victoria*–Clara Fisher (24) Merchant of Venice; Irishman in London (25) Paul Pry: *Phoebe*–Clara Fisher; Old and Young: five rôles–Clara Fisher (27) Invincibles: *Victoria*–Clara Fisher; Yard Arm and Yard Yarm; Dead Shot: *Louisa*–Clara Fisher (30) Bold Stroke for a Husband: *Donna Olivia*–Clara Fisher; Actress of All Work: seven rôles–Clara Fisher
Ap (1) Wind Does Wonders: *Bessare*–Clara Fisher; Romp: *Priscilla Tomboy*–Clara Fisher (3) Much Ado about Nothing: *Beatrice*–Clara Fisher; Actress of All Work: seven rôles–Clara Fisher (4) Highland Reel: *Moggy M'Gilpin*–Clara Fisher; Is He Jealous?: *Harriet*–Clara Fisher; Old and Young: four rôles–Clara Fisher (6) Therese: *Therese*–Clara Fisher; Romp: *Priscilla Tomboy*–Clara Fisher (8) William Tell: *Albert*–Clara Fisher; Spoil'd Child: *Little Pickle*–Clara Fisher (10) Richard III; Family Jars (11) Tom Thumb the Great; Young Widow; Sleeping Draught (20) Foundling of the Forest; Easter Frolics (22) Tom and Jerry; Day after the Wedding (24) Virginius; Tom Thumb the Great (25) William Tell; Irish Tutor (27) Paul Jones; Valentine and Orson (29) Adeline; Rumfustian; Bee Hive
My (1) Foundling of the Forest; Family Jars (2) Richard III; Rendezvous (8) Manager in Distress; Lady of the Lake; Turn Out

1 8 2 9 - 1 8 3 0

Mgrs.: J. J. Adams (N 9-D 22), Thomas Faulkner, John B. Irving, Charles L. Green (D 23-Ap 19); *orch. leader:* George William Gronlund; *treas.:* Willard. *Stock:* Barry, J., Blake, W. R., Brown, J. M., Collins, Hamblin, T. S., Jones, S. I., Lyons, G., Maddox, Plumer, C., Rice, D., Sarzedas, D. A., Scott, J., Southwell, H., Sowerby, F., Thorne, C. R., Tuthill, H., Wells, Woodhull, J.; *Mrs.* Barry, J., Bernard, Blake, W. R.,

Brown, J. M., Collins, Green, C. L., Hamblin, T. S., Plumer, C., Scott, J., Woodhull, J.; *Misses* Coster, Wells.

SE: Mme. Feron: N 25-D 14; T. A. Cooper: Ja 29-Mr 4; Mr. and Mrs. John Sloman: F 22-Mr 8; Clara Fisher: Mr 10-26; Herr Andre Cline and Company: N 9-23.

N (9) Fortune's Frolic; Soldier's Daughter; Cline Company (10) Wonder: Is He Jealous? (11) Virginius; Honest Thieves; Cline Company (13) Will; Day after the Wedding; Cline Company (14) Damon and Pythias; Young Widow; Cline Company (20) School for Scandal; Bath Road; Cline Company (21) Robbers; Family Jars; Cline Company (23) Rienzi; Wedding Day; Cline Company (25) Barber of Seville: *Rosina*–Mme. Feron; Lady and the Devil (27) Cabinet: *Floretta*–Mme. Feron; Is He Jealous? (28) Father and Daughter; Young Widow (30) Marriage of Figaro: *Susannah*–Mme. Feron; Inn-keeper's Daughter; Actress of All Work

D (2) Rob Roy MacGregor: *Diana*–Mme. Feron; Marriage of Figaro: *Susannah*–Mme. Feron (4) Siege of Belgrade: *Lilla*–Mme. Feron; Father and Daughter (5) Belle's Stratagem: *Letitia Hardy*–Mme. Feron; Lady and the Devil (7) Merchant of Venice; Prize, Ten Thousand Pounds: *Caroline*–Mme. Feron (9) Barber of Seville: *Rosina*– Mme. Feron; Ambrose and Gwinnett (11) Quartetti: *Mad. de Lucival*–Mme. Feron; One Hundred Pound Note; No Song, No Supper: *Margaretta*–Mme. Feron (14) Exile: *Catherine*–Mme. Feron; Napoleon Bonaparte*; of Age Tomorrow (16) Quartetti; Clari; Scape Grace (18) Broken Sword; Animal Magnetism (21) Ambrose Gwinnett; Mutineer (23) Charles II; Valentine and Orson (24) Ambrose Gwinnett; Mutineer (26) Broken Sword; Mutineer (28) Death Fetch; Don Juan (30) Robbers; Irish Tutor

Ja (1) George Barnwell; Jamie of Aberdeen; Animal Magnetism (2) Death Fetch; Mutineer (4) Ambrose Gwinnett; Jamie of Aberdeen; Richard III (one act) (6) Last of the Mohicans; Weathercock (8) Charles II; Love in a Bustle; Broken Sword (11) Father and Daughter; Race for a Dinner; Inn-keeper of Abbeville (13) Man and Wife; Inn-keeper of Abbeville (15) Omala, the Red Indian; Village Lawyer (18) Conquest of Taranto; Love in a Bustle (20) Venice Preserved; Winning a Husband; Giovanni in London (22) Ambrose and Gwinnett; Omala, the Red Indian (25) Who Wants a Guinea?; Rendezvous (27) Conquest of Taranto; Irishman in London (29) Damon and Pythias: *Damon*–Cooper; Is He Jealous?

F (1) Gamester: *Beverly*–Cooper; Three and Deuce (3) Virginius: *Virginius*–Cooper; Gretna Green* (5) Othello: *Othello*–Cooper; Irish Tutor (8) Bertram: *Bertram*–Cooper; 'Twas I (10) Wives as They Were and Maids as They Are; Of Age Tomorrow (12) Julius Caesar: *Antony*–Cooper; Gretna Green; Mutineer (15) Rule a Wife and Have a Wife: *Leon*–Cooper; Touch and Take* (17) Stranger: *Stranger*–Cooper; Liar: *Young Wilding*–Cooper (19) Revenge: *Zanga*–Cooper; One Hundred Pound Note (20) Othello: *Iago*–Cooper; Mutineer (22) Isabella: *Isabella*–Mrs. Sloman; Fish out of Water: *Sam Savory*–Sloman (23) Julius Caesar: *Mark Antony*–Cooper; Day after the Wedding (24) Venice Preserved: *Belvidera*–Mrs. Sloman; Master's Rival: *Paul Shack*–Sloman (25) Romeo and Juliet: *Mercutio*–Cooper; Of Age Tomorrow (26) Isabella: *Isabella*–Mrs. Sloman; Intrigue: *Tom*–Sloman (27) Damon and Pythias; Liar: *Young Wilding*–Cooper

Mr (1) Jane Shore: *Jane Shore*–Mrs. Sloman; Master's Rival: *Paul Shack*–Sloman (2) Macbeth: *Macbeth*–Cooper; Is He Jealous? (3) School for Scandal: *Lady Teazle*–Mrs. Sloman; Family Jars: *Delph*–Sloman (4) Richard III: *Richard*–Cooper; Catherine and Petruchio: *Petruchio*–Cooper (5) Evadne: *Evadne*–Mrs. Sloman; Animal Magnetism: *La Fleur*–Sloman (8) Jealous Wife: *Sir Harry*–Sloman, *Mrs. Oakly*–Mrs. Sloman; Married Bachelor: *Sharp*–Sloman (10) Belle's Stratagem: *Letitia Hardy*–Clara Fisher; Actress of All Work: six rôles–Clara Fisher (12) Will: *Albina Mandeville*–Clara Fisher; Old and Young: four rôles–Clara Fisher (15) Man and Wife: *Helen Worrett*–Clara Fisher; Spoil'd Child: *Little Pickle*–Clara Fisher (17) Romeo and Juliet: *Juliet*–Clara Fisher; Mutineer (19) Lovers' Vows: *Amelia*–Clara Fisher; Gretna Green: *Betty Finnikin*–Clara Fisher (22) Douglas: *Young Norval*–Miss Fisher; Simpson and Company: *Mrs. Simpson*–Clara Fisher (24) Clari: *Clari*–Clara Fisher; Dead Shot: *Louisa*–Clara Fisher (26) Wedding Day: *Lady Contest*–Clara Fisher; Ten Mowbrays: ten rôles–Clara Fisher (29) Epigrammatist*; Secret (31) Young Lovers; Dead Shot; Winning a Husband

Ap (2) Rip Van Winkle; Dumb Girl of Genoa (5) Devil's Bridge; Dumb Girl of Genoa (12) Presumptive Evidence; Green-Eyed Monster (14) Death Fetch; Dumb Girl of Genoa (16) Rip Van Winkle; Two Friends (19) Point of Honor; Botheration

1830-1831

Mgr.: Thomas Faulkner; *acting mgr., treas., box-keeper:* Henry J. Riley; *scenist:* Sera. *Stock:* Bristow, Brown, F., Clarke, N. B., Davis, W., Eberle, H., Hill, F. S., Jackson, Riddle, Stammers, Stanley, G. B., Waldron, Waters; *Mrs.* Fulmer, Hughes, Justis, Riddle, Turner, W. A.; *Misses* Dunham, Riddle, E., Riddle, C.

SE: Miss Rock: N 29-D 20, F 23, Mr 11-23; Mrs. Mary Duff: D 21, F 22-Mr 25; Edwin Forrest: F 21-Mr 7; T. A. Cooper: Mr 1-18.

N (18) Speed the Plough; Raising the Wind (19) Laugh when You Can; Irishman in London (22) She Stoops to Conquer; Animal Magnetism (24) Poor Gentleman; Three Weeks after Marriage (25) Speed the Plough; Fortune's Frolic (26) Honeymoon; Raising the Wind (29) Belle's Stratagem: *Letitia Hardy*–Miss Rock; One Hundred Pound Note

D (1) Soldier's Daughter: *Widow Cheerly*–Miss Rock; Citizen: *Maria*–Miss Rock (3) Romeo and Juliet: *Juliet*–Miss Rock; Lovers' Quarrels (6) Wives as They Were and Maids as They Are: *Miss Dorrillon*–Miss Rock; Therese: *Therese*–Miss Rock (8) Bride of Lammermoor: *Lucy Ashton*–Miss Rock; Irish Tutor (10) Bride of Lammermoor: *Lucy Ashton*–Miss Rock; Citizen: *Maria*–Miss Rock (13) Know Your Own Mind: *Lady Bill*–Miss Rock; Winning a Husband: *Mrs. Deborah Griskin*–Miss Rock (15) Luke the Laborer*; Wedding Day: *Lady Contest*–Miss Rock; Matrimony: *Lady Clara*–Miss Rock (17) Is He Jealous?: *Harriet*–Miss Rock; Perfection*: *Kate O'Brien*–Miss Rock; Luke the Laborer (20) To Marry or Not to Marry: *Hester*–Miss Rock; Perfection: *Kate O'Brien*–Miss Rock (21) Isabella: *Isabella*–Mrs. Duff; Warlock of the Glen

F (21) Damon and Pythias: *Damon*–Forrest; Three Weeks after Marriage (22) Isabella: *Isabella*–Mrs. Duff; Rendezvous (23) Hamlet: *Hamlet*–Forrest, *Ophelia*–Miss Rock; Bath Road (24) Jane Shore: *Jane Shore*–Mrs. Duff; Winning a Husband (25) Virginius: *Virginius*–For-

rest; Irishman in London (26) Pizarro: *Rolla*–Forrest, *Elvira*–Mrs.
Duff; Raising the Wind (28) Brutus: *Brutus*–Forrest; Therese:
Garwin–Forrest
   Mr (1) Damon and Pythias: *Damon*–Cooper, *Calanthe*–Mrs.
Duff; Rendezvous (2) Metamora: *Metamora*–Forrest; Rendezvous (5) Meta-
mora: *Metamora*–Forrest; Fortune's Frolic (7) Othello: *Othello*–For-
rest; Black Eyed Susan* (10) Gamestor. *Beverly*–Cooper, *Mrs. Beverly*–
Mrs. Duff; Irish Tutor (11) Honeymoon: *Duke of Aranza*–Cooper; Day
after the Wedding: *Lady Freelove*–Miss Rock (14) Wives as They
Were and Maids as They Are: *Sir William Dorrillon*–Cooper, *Miss Dor-
rillon*–Miss Rock; Citizen: *Maria*–Miss Rock (16) Bertram: *Bertram*–
Cooper, *Imogene*–Miss Duff; Black Eyed Susan (18) Henry IV:
Falstaff–Cooper; Rendezvous (21) Stranger: *Mrs. Haller*–Mrs. Duff;
Bohemian Mother: *Mathilda*–Mrs. Duff (23) School for Scandal: *Lady
Teazle*–Miss Rock; Perfection: *Kate O'Brien*–Miss Rock (25) Distressed
Mother: *Hermione*–Mrs. Duff; Lady and the Devil (28) Charles XII;
Blind Boy
   Ap (4) West Indian; Critic

1 8 3 1 - 1 8 3 2

Mgr.: Vincent De Camp; *scenist:* West; *treas.:* J. C. Lozier; *box-
keeper:* Edward Young. *Stock:* Barton, Doyne, Fenno, W. A., Field, J.
M., Gordon, Hart, Holland, G., Hughes, Langton, Millar, Nickerson,
Pinder, Waldron, Young, C.; *Mrs.* Brown, F., Hughes, Pinder, Preston,
T.; *Miss* Barry.
   SE: James Hackett: Ja 31-F 8, 16-20; Charles Kean: F 10-18, Mr 5-
12; Clara Fisher: F 21-22, Mr 2, 15-21; T. A. Cooper: F 27-Mr 2.
   (No Fall Season)
   Ja (31) Jonathan in England: *Solomon Swap*–Hackett; Uncle Ben;
Monsieur Tonson
   F (1) Times: *Industrious Doolittle*–Hackett; Three Weeks after Mar-
riage; Therese (2) Rip Van Winkle: *Rip Van Winkle*–Hackett; Broken
Sword; Rendezvous (3) Jonathan in England: *Solomon Swap*–Hackett;
Ella Rosenberg; Mischief Making (4) Rip Van Winkle: *Rip Van
Winkle*–Hackett; Militia Training: *Major Joe Bunker*–Hackett; Mon-
sieur Tonson: *Marbleau*–Hackett (6) Kentuckian: *Nimrod Wild-
fire*–Hackett; Sylvester Daggerwood: *Sylvester*–Hackett; Militia
Training: *Major Joe Bunker*–Hackett; Is He Jealous? (8) Man and
Wife; Sylvester Daggerwood: *Sylvester*–Hackett; Broken Sword (10)
New Way to Pay Old Debts: *Sir Giles Overreach*–Kean; Mischief Mak-
ing (11) Merchant of Venice: *Shylock*–Kean; Deaf as a Post (13)
Richard III: *Richard*–Kean; Lottery Ticket (15) Brutus: *Brutus*–Kean;
Day after the Wedding (16) Paul Pry: *Paul Pry*–Hackett; Militia
Training: *Major Joe Bunker*–Hackett; How to Die for Love (17)
Stranger: *Stranger*–Kean; Deaf as a Post (18) Othello: *Othello*–Kean,
Iago–Hackett; Three Weeks after Marriage (20) Jonathan in England:
Solomon Swap–Hackett; Kentuckian: *Nimrod Wildfire*–Hackett (21)
Belle's Stratagem: *Letitia Hardy*–Clara Fisher; Youth, Love and Folly
(22) Will: *Albina Mandeville*–Clara Fisher; Perfection (27) Henry
IV: *Falstaff*–Cooper; Blind Boy; School for Scandal: *Sir Peter Teazle*–
Cooper; Day after the Fair (29) Sweethearts and Wives; Romeo and
Juliet: *Romeo*–Cooper; School for Scandal; Secret
   Mr (1) Hamlet: *Hamlet*–Cooper; Whims of a Comedian; Two Gregor-

ies (2) Much Ado about Nothing: *Benedict*–Cooper, *Beatrice*–Clara Fisher; Husband at Sight: *Catherine*–Clara Fisher (5) Richard III: *Richard*–Kean; Family Jars (7) Iron Chest: *Sir Edward Mortimer*–Kean; No, No; Animal Magnetism (9) Hamlet: *Hamlet*–Kean; 102 (12) Town and Country: *Reuben Glenroy*–Kean; Hamlet Travestie (13) Macbeth; First of April (14) Pizarro; Sweethearts and Wives (15) School for Scandal: *Lady Teazle*–Clara Fisher; First of April (16) Wonder: *Violante*–Clara Fisher; Dead Shot: *Louisa*–Clara Fisher (19) As You Like It: *Rosalind*–Clara Fisher; Gretna Green: *Betty*–Clara Fisher (20) Soldier's Daughter; Irish Tutor (21) Miller's Maid: *Phoebe*–Clara Fisher; Two Friends: *Rose*–Clara Fisher; Old and Young: four rôles–Clara Fisher (24) How to Die for Love; Inn-keeper's Daughter; Blue Devils (26) Sergeant's Wife; Seeing Is Believing (27) Charles II; Hamlet Travestie (28) Castle Spectre; Miller and His Men (29) Maid and the Magpie; Married Bachelor; Amateurs and Actors (30) Miller's Maid; Seeing Is Believing; Two Thompsons

1832-1833

Mgr.: Vincent De Camp. *Stock:* Barton, Beckwith, Brown, Brown, F., Field, J. M., Flynn, T., Gay, Hart, Hilson, T., Hyatt, G.; *Mrs.* Brown, F., Flynn, T., Gay, Hilson, T., Preston, T.; *Misses* Meadowcraft, Smith.

SE: Josephine Clifton: N 26-D 17, F 15; James Wallack: F 4-25; Master Joseph Burke: F 26-Mr 15.

N (26) Venice Preserved: *Belvidera*–Josephine Clifton; Race for a Dinner (28) Romeo and Juliet: *Juliet*–Josephine Clifton; Spectre Bridegroom (30) Fazio: *Bianca*–Josephine Clifton; Two Thompsons

D (1) Sleeping Draught; Personation; Dumb Girl of Genoa (3) Smoked Miser; Fazio: *Bianca*–Josephine Clifton; Pay Me for My Eye (5) Is It a Lie?*; Therese: *Therese*–Josephine Clifton; Three Weeks after Marriage: *Lady Rachett*–Josephine Clifton (7) Pizarro: *Elvira*–Josephine Clifton; Monsieur Tonson (8) Fazio: *Bianca*–Josephine Clifton; Brigand (10) Heir at Law; Turnpike Gate (12) Fazio: *Bianca*–Josephine Clifton; Sprigs of Laurel; Brigand (14) Macbeth: *Lady Macbeth*–Josephine Clifton; Illustrious Stranger (15) Poor Soldier; Merchant of Venice; Tale of Mystery (17) Hunchback: *Julia*–Josephine Clifton; Is He Jealous? (19) Cure for the Heartache; Hunter of the Alps (21) Two Strings to Your Bow; One Hundred Pound Note; Tom and Jerry (22) Therese; Turnpike Gate; Brigand (26) Antoine the Savage; Three Wishes (27) Gambler's Fate; Lady and the Devil (31) Timour the Tartar; Lady and the Devil

Ja (1) Lady and the Devil; Timour the Tartar (4) Catherine and Petruchio; Timour the Tartar (5) Of Age Tomorrow; Timour the Tartar (7) Victorine; Venetian Models; Nature and Philosophy (11) Child of Nature; Citizen; Nature and Philosophy (14) Victorine; Cataract of the Ganges

F (4) Rent Day: *Martin Heywood*–Wallack; My Aunt: *Dick Dashall*–Wallack (11) Rent Day: *Martin Heywood*–Wallack; Wolf and the Lamb (13) Wonder: *Don Felix*–Wallack; Children in the Wood: *Walter*–Wallack (15) Rob Roy MacGregor: *Rob Roy*–Wallack, *Helen*–Josephine Clifton; Adopted Child: *Michael*–Wallack (18) Town and Country: *Reuben Glenroy*–Wallack; Mogul Tale (21) Brigand: *Massaroni*–Wallack; Rent Day: *Martin Heywood*–Wallack (22) Brigand: *Massaroni*–Wallack; Children in the Wood: *Walter*–Wallack (23) Mountaineers: *Octavian*–Wallack; My Aunt: *Dick Dashall*–Wallack (25) School for Scandal: *Charles Surface*–Wallack; Brigand: *Massaroni*–Wallack (26) Douglas: *Young Norval*–Master Burke; Irish Tutor: *Terry*–Master Burke (27) Heir at Law: *Dr. Pangloss*–Master Burke; Whirligig Hall (28) Merchant of Venice: *Shylock*–Master Burke; Irishman in London: *Murtoch Delaney*–Master Burke

Mr (1) John Bull: *Dennis Bulgruddy*–Master Burke; Weathercock: *Tristram Fickle*–Master Burke (2) Romeo and Juliet: *Romeo*–Master Burke; Review: *Looney M'Twoolter*–Master Burke (4) Richard III: *Richard*–Master Burke; Sprigs of Laurel (6) Man and Wife: *Cornelius O'Dedimus*–Master Burke; Whirligig Hall (7) John Bull: *Dennis Bulgruddy*–Master Burke; Weathercock: *Tristram Fickle*–Master Burke (8) Paul Pry: *Paul Pry*–Master Burke; Review: *Looney M'Twoolter*–Master Burke (9) Hypocrite: *Mauworm*–Master Burke; Honest Thieves: *Teague*–Master Burke (11) Poor Gentleman: *Ollapod*–Master Burke; March of Intellect: six rôles–Master Burke (12) Weathercock: *Tristram Fickle*–Master Burke; High Life below Stairs: *Lord Duke*–Master Burke; Irish Tutor: *Terry*–Master Burke (13) Speed the Plough: *Sir Abel Handy*–Master Burke; Poor Soldier: *Darby*–Master Burke (15) Of Age Tomorrow: *Frederick*–Master Burke; Barney Brallaghay: *Barney*–Master Burke; March of Intellect: six rôles–Master Burke (18) School for Scandal; Sleep Walker (20) Paul Pry; Therese (21) Rent Day; Catherine and Petruchio (25) Clari; Is He Jealous?; Ambrose Gwinnett (26) Robbers; Beggar on Horseback (27) As You Like It; Sprigs of Laurel (28) Bertram; Two Thompsons (29) Cure for the Heartache; Matrimony; Review (30) Personation; Robbers

Ap (1) School of Reform; Nature and Philosophy; Sprigs of Laurel *My* (10) Marion; Napoleon Bonaparte

Queen Street Theatre

Mgr.: Hart; *treas.*: Theodore I. Smith. *Stock*: Beckwith, Field, J. M., Flynn, T., Forbes, W. C., Gay, Harrington, W., Hilson, T., Preston, T.; *Mrs.* Brown, F., Flynn, T., Gay, Hilson, T., Preston, T.; *Miss* Smith.

Ap (2) Pizarro; Pay Me for My Eye (3) Ambrose Gwinnett; Sprigs of Laurel (4) Paul Pry; Sleep Walker (8) Fraternal Discord; Is He Jealous?; Devil to Pay (27) Pizarro

My (4) Mother Goose (7) Napoleon Bonaparte; Mother Goose (17) George Barnwell; Tom and Jerry (20) Wandering Boys

Ju (12) Bohemian Girl; Hide-and-Go-Seek (15) Weathercock; How to Die for Love

1833-1834

Queen Street Theatre

Mgrs.: Hart and W. Hardy (D 9-Mr 5, Ap 18-30), Palmer and W. Harrington's Circus (Mr 10-Ap 10); *treas.*: Garmon. *Stock*: Bailey, Cadwallader, Carter, J., Claveau, Coult, Derious, Dickerson, Downs, Dykes, Field, J. M., Garson, T. E., Langton, Lyons, G., Preston, T., Richards, D.; *Mrs.* Dykes, Lyons, G., Palmer, Preston, T., Richards, D.; *Miss* Carter.

SE: T. D., ("Jim Crow") Rice: D 9-20; Zip Coon: D 21-Ja 1; Ravel Family (Gabriel, Sr., Gabriel, Jr., Jerome, Dominique, Gean, Emilie, Antoine, Francois, Louis Marzetti and Jean Pebernard): Ja 7-27, F 20-Mr 3, Ap 18-25; G. H. ("Yankee") Hill: Mr 21.

D (9) Stranger; Nature and Philosophy (11) Venice Preserved; Oh'
Hush: *Gambo Cuff*–Rice (12) Adeline; Miss in Her Teens (13) Hypo-
crite; Oh! Hush: *Gambo Cuff*–Rice (14) Paul Pry; One Hundred Pound
Note (17) Paul Jones; Oh! Hush: *Gambo Cuff*–Rice (18) Evadne; High
Life below Stairs (19) Wandering Boys; No Song, No Supper (20)
Waggaries at Wapping; Oh! Hush: *Gambo Cuff*–Rice; Is He Jealous?
(21) Jane Shore; Turn Out; Zip Coon (23) Charlotte Temple; 'Twas
I; Zip Coon (24) Therese; Two Thompsons; Zip Coon (27) Charlotte
Temple; Spectre Bridegroom; Zip Coon (28) Day after the Wedding;
Tom and Jerry; Jack in Distress; Zip Coon (31) Lady of the Lake;
Robinson Crusoe and His Good Man Friday; Zip Coon
   Ja (1) George Barnwell; Bluebeard; Zip Coon (3) Bohemian Girl;
Fortune's Frolic (4) George Barnwell; Massaniello; Dumb Girl of
Genoa (6) George Barnwell; Massaniello (7-8) Ravel Family (11)
Miller's Maid; Ravel Family (15) Invisible Harlequin; Turn Out; Ravel
Family (17) Monsieur Molinet; Conscript and the Soldier; Luke the
Laborer; Ravel Family (18) Godenski; Hypocrite; Ravel Family (22)
Monsieur Molinet; Death of Abel; Miller's Maid; Ravel Family (24)
Warlock of the Glen; Ravel Family (25) Chimney Sweepers; La Petite
Matelot; George Barnwell; Ravel Family (27) Jocko; Young Widow;
Ravel Family
   F (20) Sweethearts and Wives; Ravel Family (22) Hail Columbia;
Sweethearts and Wives; Ravel Family (24-26) Massaniello; Ravel
Family (27) Warlock of the Glen; Day after the Wedding; Death of
Abel; Ravel Family (28) Jocko; Lady and the Devil; Ravel Family
   Mr (1) Chimney Sweepers; Ravel Family (3) Jocko; Lady and the
Devil; Ravel Family (5) Douglas; Tom and Jerry (6) Soldier's
Daughter; Cupboard Love (10) Don Juan; circus (11) Spectre Bride-
groom; circus (14-15, 18) Forest of Bondy; circus (19) Harlequin
Statues; circus (20) Shipwrecked Sailor; Spectre Bridegroom; circus
(21) Forest Rose: *Jonathan Ploughboy*–Hill; circus (22) Tekeli; circus
(25-28) Mazeppa; circus
   Ap (3, 7-9) Timour the Tartar; circus (10) Oh! Hush; circus (18)
Soldier and the Peasant; Ravel Family (21) Jocko; Chimney Sweepers;
Ravel Family (23) Harlequin Statues; Ravel Family (25) Vulcan and
Cyclops; Idiot Witness; Ravel Family (26) Day after the Wedding;
Secret (28) Robber's Wife; Turn Out (30) Therese; Bluebeard

1834-1835

Mgrs.: Hart and W. Hardy (O 13-D 8, Mr 4-Ap 20); G. Sweet and
Hough's Circus, Palmer, *mgr.* (Ja 14-F 29). *Stock:* Bailey, Barnes, J.,
Benson, Camden, Dickson, A., Field, J. M., Finn, H. J., Forbes, W. C.,
Hood, Kelsey, Logan, T. D., Lyons, G., Richings, Sloman, J.; *Mrs.*
Bailey, Barnes, J., Carter, Hart, Lyons, G., Sharp; *Misses* Adamson,
Barnes, C., Clarke, E.
   SE: G. H. ("Yankee") Hill: N 14-24; Tyrone Power: D 2-8; T. A.
Cooper: Mr 4-30; Priscilla Cooper: Mr 16-30; James Hackett: Mr 31-
Ap 10.
   O (13) Damon and Pythias; Irish Tutor (14) Perfection; Crossing
the Line (15) New Way to Pay Old Debts; Irish Tutor (16) Soldier's
Daughter; Teddy, the Tiler (21) John Bull; Crossing the Line (22)
Town and Country; Aeronaut (23) Othello; One Hundred Pound Note
(25) Brian Boroihme; Crossing the Line (28) Stranger; Poor Soldier
(30) Iron Chest; Teddy, The Tiler

N (3) Tom Cringle*; Two Friends (4) Tom Cringle; Simpson and Company (5) Tom Cringle; Perfection (6) Tom Cringle; Raising the Wind (7) Tom Cringle; Irishman in London (8) Tom Cringle; Irish Tutor (10) Abaellino; Teddy, the Tiler (11) Black Eyed Susan; Two Friends (12) Pizarro; balloon ascension (14) Jonathan in England: *Solomon Swap*-Hill; Black Eyed Susan (15) Green Mountain Boy: *Jebediah Homebred*-Hill; No Song, No Supper (17) Yankee Pedlar: *Zachariah*-Hill; Forest Rose: *Jonathan Ploughboy*-Hill (18) Jonathan in England: *Solomon Swap*-Hill; Green Mountain Boy: *Jebediah Homebred*-Hill (19) Simpson and Company: *Simpson*-Hill; Knight of the Golden Fleece: *Sysaco*-Hill (20) Yankee Pedlar: *Zachariah*-Hill; Irishman in London (21) Is He Jealous?: *Belmour*-Hill; Knight of the Golden Fleece: *Sysaco*-Hill; Ovid and Obid: *Obid*-Hill (24) Married and Single; Master's Rival (25) Legion of Honor; Paul Pry (27) Merchant of Venice; One Hundred Pound Note (28) Hypocrite; Falls of Clyde (29) Legion of Honor; Tom and Jerry

D (2) Perfection; Irish Ambassador: *Sir Patrick O'Plenipo*-Power; Irish Tutor: *Terry*-Power (3) Two Gregories; Born to Good Luck: *Paudeen O'Rafferty*-Power; Rendezvous (5) Is He Jealous?; Nervous Man and the Man of Nerve: *M'Shane*-Power; Secret (6) Wild Oats: *Rover*-Power; Teddy, the Tiler (8) Wild Oats: *Rover*-Power; My Aunt

Ja 14-*F* 29. G. Sweet and Hough's Circus

Mr (4) Othello: *Iago*-Cooper; Lottery Ticket (5) Soldier's Daughter; Family Jars (6) Othello: *Iago*-Cooper; Lottery Ticket (7) Romeo and Juliet: *Romeo*-Cooper; Sprigs of Laurel (9) Damon and Pythias: *Damon*-Cooper; Dead Shot (10) School for Scandal; Turnpike Gate (11) Venice Preserved: *Pierre*-Cooper; Wool Dealer (12) Honeymoon; Mogul Tale (13) Hunchback; Hypocrite (14) Damon and Pythias: *Damon*-Cooper; Lottery Ticket (16) Virginius: *Virginius*-Cooper, *Virginia*-Priscilla Cooper; Dead Shot (17) St. Patrick's Day; Jocko (18) Much Ado about Nothing: *Benedict*-Cooper, *Beatrice*-Priscilla Cooper; Secret (19) Alexander the Great; Lottery Ticket (20) Gamester: *Beverly*-Cooper; Secret (21) Much Ado about Nothing: *Benedict*-Cooper, *Beatrice*-Priscilla Cooper; Rendezvous (23) Hunchback: *Walter*-Cooper; Dead Shot (24) Romeo and Juliet: *Mercutio*-Cooper, *Juliet*-Priscilla Cooper (25) Othello: *Othello*-Cooper, *Desdemona*-Priscilla Cooper; Secret (26) In Yankee Land; Charles II (27) Hamlet: *Hamlet*-Cooper; Rendezvous (28) Rule a Wife and Have a Wife: *Leon*-Cooper; Perfection (30) Wives as They Were and Maids as They Are: *Sir William Dorrillon*-Cooper, *Miss Dorrillon*-Priscilla Cooper; Catherine and Petruchio: *Catherine*-Priscilla Cooper, *Petruchio*-Cooper (31) Nature and Philosophy; Kentuckian: *Nimrod Wildfire*-Hackett; Family Jars

Ap (1) Is He Jealous?; Fazio; Lady and the Devil (4) Rip Van Winkle: *Rip Van Winkle*-Hackett; Job Fox, the Yankee Pedlar: *Job Fox*-Hackett (6) Monsieur Mallett: *Monsieur Mallett*-Hackett; Militia Training: *Major Joe Bunker*-Hackett; Two Gregories (7) Isabella; Lady and the Devil (8) Jonathan Doubikins: *Jonathan*-Hackett; Sylvester Daggerwood: *Sylvester Daggerwood*-Hackett; Perfection; Kentuckian: *Nimrod Wildfire*-Hackett (9) Fazio; Of Age Tomorrow (10) Clari; Day after the Wedding; Monsieur Mallett: *Monsieur Mallett*-Hackett (11) Merchant of Venice; Tom Cringle (13) Lottery Ticket; Rake's Progress (14) Golden Farmer; Spoil'd Child (15) Popping the

Question; Warlock of the Glen; Jealous Lover; Robinson Crusoe and His Good Man Friday (16) George Barnwell; Therese (20) Forest of Rosenwald; Young Widow

1835-1836

Mgrs.: Hart and W. Hardy (N 17-Mr 24). *Stock:* Bailey, Barnes, J., Judah, E., Mason, C., Young, C.; *Mrs.* Barnes, J., Carter, Hart; *Miss* Barnes, C.

SE: Il Diavolo Antonio and Family: N 23-D 9.

N (17) Othello; Nature and Philosophy (18) Richard III; Married Bachelor (19) Merchant of Venice; Monsieur Tonson (20) Pizarro; Jew and the Doctor (21) Richard III; Prescription for Happiness (23) Charles II; Nature and Philosophy; Antonio Family (24) Therese; Antonio Family (25) Stranger; Antonio Family (26) Adeline; Antonio Family (30) Warlock of the Glen; Married Bachelor; Antonio Family

D (1) Richard III; Napoleon Bonaparte; Antonio Family (2) Douglas; Antonio Family (3) Simpson and Company; Is He Jealous?; Antonio Family (4) Adeline; Antonio Family (5) Miller and His Men; Antonio Family; Dutch Brothers (7) Therese; Beggar on Horseback; Antonio Family (8) Barbarossa; Will Watch, the Bold Smuggler; Antonio Family; Sylvester Daggerwood (9) Bluebeard; Antonio Family (10) Pizarro; Bluebeard

F (9) Soldier's Daughter; Family Jars (10) Stranger; Rival Soldiers (11) Romeo and Juliet; Devil to Pay (12) School for Scandal; Sprigs of Laurel (13) Jane Shore; Turnpike Gate (15) Steward; Unfinished Gentleman (16) Hunchback; Unfinished Gentleman (17) Will; Golden Farmer (18) Douglas; Sweethearts and Wives (19) Honeymoon; Mogul Tale (20) Hypocrite; Therese (22) Wife*; Deuce Is in Her (23) Wife; Family Jars (24) Last Days of Pompey; Perfection (25) Last Days of Pompey; Nature and Philosophy (26) Last Days of Pompey; Deuce Is in Her (27) Last Days of Pompey; Two Thompsons (29) Wallace; Last Days of Pompey

Mr (1) Jane Shore; Forty Thieves (2) Hunchback; Forty Thieves (3) Romeo and Juliet; Rival Soldiers (4) Wallace; Mogul Tale (5) Evadne; Devil to Pay (7) Hypocrite; Maid and the Magpie (8) Evadne; Family Jars (9) Rob Roy MacGregor; Wedding Day (10) Wallace; Maid and the Magpie (11) Isabella; Three Weeks after Marriage (12) Wife; Family Jars (14) Cherry and Fair Star; Douglas (15) Cherry and Fair Star; Sweethearts and Wives (16) Cherry and Fair Star; Spectre Bridegroom (17) Cherry and Fair Star; Two Thompsons (18) Cherry and Fair Star; Unfinished Gentleman (21) Last Days of Pompey; Jewess (22) Cherry and Fair Star; Unfinished Gentlefan (23) Jewess; Spectre Bridegroom (24) Virgin of the Sun; Comedy of Errors

Seyle's "New" Theatre

Mgr.: T. Preston (Mr 2-28); *orch. leader:* Schmidt. *Stock:* Anderson, D., Cooke, Ellis, W., Gilbert, J. G., Lanning, W. M., Watt; *Mrs.* Preston, T., Watt; *Miss* Farren.

Mr (2) Hunchback; Young Widow (9) Charles II; Nature and Philosophy (10) Wife; Two Gregories (11) Wife; Irishman in London (14) Othello (16) Miller's Maid; No Song, No Supper (17) Bertram; Matrimony (18) Stranger; Rendezvous (21) Apostate; Perfection (22) Love a la Mode; Irishman in London; School for Scandal (scenes) (23) Spoil'd Child; Crossing the Line; Perfection (28) Bertram; Hunter of the Alps

Queen Street Theatre

Mgr.: W. M. Lanning (Mr 29-Ap 12); *orch. leader:* Schmidt. *Stock:* Anderson, D. A., Bailey, Barnes, J., Cooke, Ellis, Gilbert, J. G., Judah, E., Mason, C., Preston, T., Watt, Young, C.; *Mrs.* Barnes, J., Carter, Preston, T., Watt; *Misses* Barnes, C., Farren.

SE: Mertevais and Hinson: Ap 7-11.

Mr (29) Rob Roy MacGregor; Bombastes Furioso (30) Pizarro; Review (31) Wife; Perfection

Ap (1) George Barnwell; Spoil'd Child (5) Alonzo the Brave; Hunter of the Alps (6) George Barnwell; Alonzo the Brave (7) Catherine and Petruchio; Irishman in London; Mertevais and Hinson (9) Raising the Wind; Young Widow; Mertevais and Hinson (11) Warlock of the Glen; Rendezvous; Mertevais and Hinson (12) Iron Chest; Therese

1836-1837

Queen Street Theatre

(No Fall Season)

Ravel Family (Gabriel, Sr., Gabriel, Jr., Jerome, Gean, Dominique, Emilie, Antoine, Francois, Louis Marzetti, and Jean Perbernard, with Butler, *mgr.*) combined with Palmer's Pavilion Circus (*mgr.*: Johnson, *equestrian mgr.*: Gullen) rent theatre (Mr 10-My 15) for performances of horsemanship and gymnastics. Mr 10, 13-14 Vol-au-Vent was presented.

1837-1838

New Charleston Theatre

Mgr.: William Abbot; *orch. leader:* H. Marks; *scenist:* Chizzola. *Stock:* Andrews, L. S., Barnes, J., Durivage, O. E., Edwin, Flynn, T., Harrison, Herbert, J., Irving, R., Jamieson, G., Latham, W. H., Sedley, H., Thoman, J. W., Timm, Weston, J. M.; *Mrs.* Barnes, J., Herbert, J., Knight, A., Sharp, Timm; *Misses* Barnes, C., Melton, Monier, V.

SE: Ellen Tree: D 18-30; T. A. Cooper and Priscilla Cooper: Ja 4-15; Josephine Clifton: Ja 11; John M. Vandenhoff: Ja 24-F 9; Charles K. Mason: F 12-23, Mr 7-30, Ap 23-28; James Hackett: Mr 8-16; J. B. Booth: Mr 13-29; Coney and Blanchard's Dogs (Hector and Bruin): Ap 1-5.

D (15) Honeymoon; Waterman (18) Hunchback: *Julia*–Ellen Tree; Inn-keeper's Bride (19) Hunchback: *Julia*–Ellen Tree; Swiss Cottage* (20) Belle's Stratagem: *Letitia Hardy*–Ellen Tree; Swiss Cottage (21) Wife: *Mariana*–Ellen Tree; Waterman (22) Wonder: *Violante*–Ellen Tree; Perfection (23) Hunchback: *Julia*–Ellen Tree (26) Ion: *Ion*–Ellen Tree; Rendezvous (27) Honeymoon: *Juliana*–Ellen Tree; Day after the Wedding: *Lady Elizabeth*–Ellen Tree (28) Ion: *Ion*–Ellen Tree; Barrack Room: *Clarisse*–Ellen Tree (29) Hamlet; Loan of a Lover (30) Swiss Cottage: *Lisette*–Ellen Tree; Gentleman in Difficulties; Rendezvous

Ja (1) Guy Mannering; Loan of a Lover (3) Guy Mannering; My Fellow Clerk (4) Much Ado about Nothing: *Benedict*–Cooper, *Beatrice*–

Priscilla Cooper; Gentleman in Difficulties (5) Hunchback: *Master Walter*–Cooper, *Julia*–Priscilla Cooper; Happiest Day of My Life (6) Honeymoon: *Duke of Aranza*–Cooper, *Juliana*–Priscilla Cooper; Swiss Cottage (9) Gamester: *Beverly*–Cooper, *Mrs. Beverly*–Priscilla Cooper; Happiest Day of My Life (10) Venice Preserved: *Jaffier*–Cooper, *Belvidera*–Priscilla Cooper; Happiest Day of My Life (11) Fazio: *Bianca*–Josephine Clifton; Perfection: *Kate O'Brien*–Josephine Clifton (12) School for Scandal: *Charles Surface*–Cooper, *Lady Teazle*–Priscilla Cooper; Blue Devils (13) Captive; Two Thompsons (15) Much Ado about Nothing: *Benedict*–Cooper, *Beatrice*–Priscilla Cooper; Gentleman in Difficulties (17) Octavia Bragaldi; Sprigs of Laurel (18) Jane Shore; Turnpike Gate (19) Rivals; Youthful Queen (20) Octavia Bragaldi; Day after the Wedding; Two Thompsons (22) Poor Gentleman; Youthful Queen (23) School for Scandal; Lucille (24) Cato: *Cato*–Vandenhoff; Loan of a Lover (25) Othello: *Othello*–Vandenhoff; My Fellow Clerk (26) Virginius: *Virginius*–Vandenhoff; Two Gregories (27) Cato: *Cato*–Vandenhoff; Virginny Mummy (29) Coriolanus: *Coriolanus*–Vandenhoff; Black and White (30) Virginius: *Virginius*–Vandenhoff; Virginny Mummy (31) King Lear: *King Lear*–Vandenhoff; Jim Crow in London

F (1) Damon and Pythias: *Damon*–Vandenhoff; Black and White (2) Brutus: *Brutus*–Vandenhoff; Peacock and the Crow (3) Fazio: *Fazio*–Vandenhoff; Ransom (5) Hamlet: *Hamlet*–Vandenhoff; Roman Actor; Jim Crow in London (6) Damon and Pythias: *Damon*–Vandenhoff; Two Gregories (7) Hamlet: *Hamlet*–Vandenhoff; Roman Actor (8) Julius Caesar: *Brutus*–Vandenhoff; Day after the Wedding (9) Macbeth: *Macbeth*–Vandenhoff; Hunter of the Alps (12) New Way to Pay Old Debts: *Sir Giles Overreach*–Mason; Two Gregories (13) Pizarro: *Rolla*–Mason; Turn Out (14) Devil's Bridge; High Life below Stairs (15) Stranger: *Stranger*–Mason; Swiss Cottage (16) She Stoops to Conquer; Charles XII (17) Pizarro: *Rolla*–Mason; Rendezvous (19) Devil's Bridge; Happiest Day of My Life (20) Charles XII; Waterman; My Fellow Clerk (21) Stranger; Swiss Cottage (22) Cinderella; Rendezvous (23) Richard III: *Richard*–Mason; My Fellow Clerk (24) Cinderella; Hunter of the Alps (25) Race Course; Hunter of the Alps (27) Cinderella; Dumb Belle (28) Cinderella; Soldier's Courtship

Mr (1) Poor Gentleman; Critic (2) Cinderella; Dumb Belle (3) Paul Pry; Charles XII (5) Cinderella; Young Huzzar (6) Hamlet; Is He Jealous? (7) Richard III: *Richard*–Mason; Dumb Belle (8) Innkeeper's Bride; Monsieur Tonson: *Marbleau–Hackett*; Kentuckian: *Nimrod Wildfire*–Hackett (9) Jonathan in England: *Jonathan*–Hackett; Monsieur Mallett: *Monsieur Mallett*–Hackett; Is He Jealous? (10) Rip Van Winkle: *Rip Van Winkle*–Hackett; Militia Training: *Major Joe Bunker*–Hackett; Dumb Belle (12) Henry IV: *Falstaff*–Hackett, *Hotspur*–Mason; Is He Jealous? (13) New Way to Pay Old Debts: *Sir Giles Overreach*–Booth (14) Jonathan in England: *Jonathan*–Hackett; Monsieur Mallett: *Monsieur Mallett*–Hackett; Kentuckian: *Nimrod Wildfire*–Hackett (15) Paul Pry: *Paul Pry*–Hackett; Monsieur Tonson: *Marbleau*–Hackett (16) Henry IV: *Falstaff*–Hackett, *Hotspur*–Mason; Family Jars (17) Cinderella; Family Jars (19) New Way to Pay Old Debts: *Sir Giles Overreach*–Booth; Dumb Belle (20) Richard III: *Richard*–Booth; Family Jars (21) Othello: *Iago*–Booth, *Othello*–Mason; Young Widow (22) King Lear: *King Lear*–Booth; Secret (23) Iron Chest: *Sir Edward Mortimer*–Booth; Sudden Thoughts;

Review: *John Lump*–Booth (24) Merchant of Venice: *Shylock*–Booth; Sudden Thoughts (26) Cinderella; Young Widow (27) King Lear: *King Lear*–Booth; Sudden Thoughts (28) Richard III: *Richard*–Booth; Kill or Cure (29) Julius Caesar: *Cassius*–Booth; Review: *John Lump*–Booth (30) Rob Roy MacGregor: *Rob Roy*–Mason; Dead Shot

Ap (1) Cherokee Chief; Venetian Statues; Orang-ou-tang (2) Orang-ou-tang; Coney and Blanchard's Dogs (3) Forest of Bondy; Jack Robinson and His Monkeys (4) Cherokee Chief; Jack Robinson and His Monkeys (5) Knights of the Cross; Don Juan (6) Inn-keeper's Bride; Daughter to Marry; Young Hussar (7) Rob Roy MacGregor; Fortune's Frolic (9) Marriage of Figaro; Daughter to Marry (10) Marriage of Figaro; Lady and the Devil (11) Fatal Dowry; Chameleon (12) Napoleon; High Life below Stairs; Idiot Witness (16) King's Fool; Critic (17) Clari; Napoleon; Bombastes Furioso (18) Iron Chest; Spring and Autumn (19) Honeymoon; Barrack Room (20) King's Fool; Barrack Room (21) Fatal Dowry; Idiot Witness (23) Wife: *Julian St. Pierre*–Mason; Two Friends (24) Much Ado about Nothing; Hunter of the Alps (25) Cinderella; Beulah Spa; Family Jars (26) Point of Honor; Tale of Mystery: *Romaldi*–Mason (27) Dream at Sea; Animal Magnetism (28) Macbeth: *Macbeth*–Mason; Animal Magnetism

1838-1839

Mgr.: William Abbott; *acting mgr.:* H. J. Conway; *orch. leader:* H. Marks; *scenist:* Hillyard. *Stock:* A'Beckett, T., Barber, Benson, Burton, Clifford, Drummond, W. C., Eberle, H., Finn, H. J., Henkins, H., Latham, W. H., McBride, McClure, Marino, Reed, Rodney, Sprague, H. N., Stewart, Timm, Weston, J. M.; *Mrs.* Eberle, H., Knight, A., McClure, Timm; *Misses* Horn, McBride, M. C.

SE: Bedouin Arabs Company: D 26-Ja 8, My 7; Alexander Wilson: Ja 9-18; Fanny Davenport (supported by Mr. and Mrs. Edward L. Davenport): Ja 28-F 2; Madame Otto's Opera Troupe (Madame Otto, Miss Jane Shirreff, Messrs. Thomas Bishop, William F. Brough, Giacon, Zerlina): F 11-23, Mr 18-Ap 6, My 2-10; Love (magician): F 28-Mr 6; Josephine Clifton: Ap 15-17; Ravel Family (Gabriel, Jerome, Dominique, Emelie, Gean, Antoine): Ap 22-My 7; Mrs. E. L. Conway: My 30.

D (18) She Stoops to Conquer; Loan of a Lover (20) Lady of Lyons*; Mr. and Mrs. Peter White (21) Lady of Lyons; Middy Ashore (22) Last Man*; Middy Ashore; Pleasant Neighbors* (24) Faith and Falsehood*; Bengal Tiger* (26) Pleasant Neighbors; Two Gregories; Mr. and Mrs. Peter White; Bedouin Arabs Company (27) 'Twas I; My Young Wife and My Old Umbrella; Two Gregories; Bedouin Arabs Company (28) My Young Wife and My Old Umbrella; Lottery Ticket; Bedouin Arabs Company (31) Uncle John*; Pacha's Pets*; Lady of Lyons; Bedouin Arabs Company

Ja (1) Lady of Lyons; Bedouin Arabs Company (3) Hunchback; Bedouin Arabs Company (4) Lady of Lyons; Bedouin Arabs Company (5) Jane Shore; Mr. and Mrs. Peter White; Bedouin Arabs Company (7) Kate Kearney*; Our Mary Anne*; Bedouin Arabs Company (8) Kate Kearney; Our Mary Anne; Dead Shot; Bedouin Arabs Company (9) Richard III: *Richard*–Wilson; Widow's Victim (10) Brutus: *Brutus*–Wilson; Unfinished Gentleman (11) Pizarro: *Rolla*–Wilson; Our Mary Anne (12) Merchant of Venice: *Shylock*–Wilson; My Young Wife and My Old Umbrella (14) King Lear: *King Lear*–Wilson; My

Neighbor's Wife (15) Town and Country: *Reuben Glenroy*–Wilson; My Neighbor's Wife (16) Richard III: *Richard*–Wilson; My Neighbor's Wife (17) Brutus: *Brutus*–Wilson; My Master's Rival (18) Virginius: *Virginius*–Wilson; Mountaineers: *Octavian*–Wilson (19) Jane Shore; Kate Kearney (21) Lady of Lyons; My Neighbor's Wife (22) Stranger; My Master's Rival (23) Pleasant Neighbors; Kate Kearney; Duchess de la Vaubaliere (24) Duchess de la Vaubaliere; Uncle John; Dumb Belle (25) Lady of Lyons; Critic (26) Stranger; Hunting a Turtle (28) Dumb Boy of Manchester: *Tom*–Fanny Davenport; Spoil'd Child: *Little Pickle*–Fanny Davenport (29) Dumb Boy of Manchester: *Tom*–Fanny Davenport; Manager's Daughter (30) School for Scandal: *Sir Peter Teazle*–Fanny Davenport; Old and Young (31) Richard III: *Richard*–Fanny Davenport; Hunting a Turtle

F (1) Merchant of Venice: *Shylock*–Fanny Davenport; farce (2) Richard III: *Richard*–Fanny Davenport; Critic (4) Lady of Lyons; Hunting a Turtle (5) Hamlet; My Neighbor's Wife (6) Gamester; 'Twas I (7) Stranger; Our Mary Anne (8) Love Chase; Middy Ashore (11-12) Amilie; To Be or Not to Be (13) Amilie; My Wife's Husband (15) Fra Diavolo; Our Mary Anne (16) Fra Diavolo; Mr. and Mrs. Peter White (18) Lady of Lyons; Widow's Victim (19) Fra Diavolo; Fighting by Proxy (20) Deaf as a Post; Love Chase (21) Guy Mannering; John Jones (22) Fra Diavolo; Unfortunate Man (23) Amilie; Fighting by Proxy (25) Love Chase; No Song, No Supper (26) Rob Roy MacGregor; No, No (27) Barrack Room; Sudden Thoughts (28) Romeo and Juliet; Mr. Love

Mr (1) Lady of Lyons; Mr. Love (4) She Stoops to Conquer; Mr. Love (5) Comedy of Errors; Ladder of Love; Mr. Love (6) She Stoops to Conquer; Mr. Love (7) Apostate; Adopted Child (8) Rent Day; farce (9) Comedy of Errors; Fighting by Proxy; Mr. and Mrs. Peter White (11) Damon and Pythias; Ladder of Love (12) Victorine; Adopted Child (13) Victorine; Stranger (14) Velasco; Bengal Tiger; My Handsome Husband (15) William Tell; Deaf as a Post (16) Apostate; Deaf as a Post (18) Fra Diavolo; Our Mary Anne (19) Amilie; Spectre Bridegroom (20) Cinderella; Middy Ashore (21) Cinderella; Is He Jealous? (22) Love in a Village; Dead Shot (23) Fra Diavolo; No Song, No Supper (25) Cinderella; Dead Shot (26) La Somnambula; Spectre Bridegroom (27) La Somnambula; Sudden Thoughts

Ap (1) La Somnambula; My Unlucky Day (2) Rob Roy MacGregor; No Song, No Supper (3) Love in a Village; Sudden Thoughts; Fra Diavolo (Act III) (4) La Somnambula; Spectre Bridegroom (5) Fra Diavolo; My Neighbor's Wife (6) Golden Farmer; Pleasant Neighbors; Cherry Bounce (8) Tempest; Catching an Heiress (9) Velasco; Cherry Bounce (10) Lucille; As You Like It (11) Tempest; Loan of a Lover (13) Mountaineers; Crossing the Line (15) Fazio: *Bianca*–Josephine Clifton; My Handsome Husband (16) Hunchback: *Julia*–Josephine Clifton; Crossing the Line (17) Lady of Lyons: *Pauline*–Josephine Clifton; My Handsome Husband (18-19) Jewess; Two Gregories (20) Jewess; Cherry Bounce (22) Jewess; Mr. and Mrs. Peter White; Ravel Family (23) My Handsome Husband; Ravel Family (24) Mr. and Mrs. Peter White; Ravel Family (25) Jewess; My Neighbor's Wife; Ravel Family (26) Three-faced Frenchman; Ravel Family (27) Spectre Bridegroom; Ravel Family (29) Venetian Carnival; Ravel Family (30) Louie et el Pascha; Milliners; Ravel Family

My (1) Three-faced Frenchman; Ravel Family (2) La Somnambula; Dumb Belle (3) Jewess; Godenski; Ravel Family (4) L'Uomo Rosso; Touch and Take; Ravel Family (6) L'Uomo Rosso; Three-faced Frenchman; Michel et Christine*; Ravel Family (7) Red Man; Bedouin Arabs Company; Ravel Family (8) Der Freischutz; Deaf as a Post (9) Der Freischutz; Ladder of Love (10) La Somnambula; Lady and the Devil (11) Luke the Laborer; Youthful Queen (13) Jewess; Ladder of Love (14) Lady of Lyons; Lovers' Quarrels (15) Much Ado about Nothing; Agnes de Vere (16) Sweethearts and Wives; Agreeable Surprise (17) Charles XII; Bee Hive (18) Paul Pry; Monsieur Jacques (20) Macbeth; Quaker (21) Jewess; Monsieur Jacques (22) Maid of Croissey; Cinderella; Legion of Honor (23) Honeymoon; Perfection (24) Tam O'Shanter; Tom and Jerry; Removing the Deposits (25) Golden Farmer; Fortune's Frolic; Raising the Wind (27) Foundling of the Forest; Therese (28) West Indian; One Hundred Pound Note; Divertisement (30) Houfer, the Tell of the Tyrol; Tam O'Shanter; You Can't Marry Your Grandmother: rôle not given–Mrs. Conway

1839-1840

Mgr.: William Abbott; *acting mgr.:* Thomas Ward; *scenist:* S. B. Stockwell; *orch. leader:* H. Marks, assisted by A. Gambati, Guadella; *machinists:* W. B. Donaldson, Manville; *treas.:* C. M. Melton. *Stock:* Beck, Clifford, Colvin, Drummond, W. C., Fuller, J. B., Gannon, Hautonville, Henkins, H., Latham, W. H., Reed, R., Sprague, H. N., Timm, Weston, J. M.; *Mrs.* Brooks, Gannon, Hautonville, Hughes, Shaw, Timm; *Misses* Gannon, M., McBride, M. C., Shaw, C., Shaw, J., Warren.

SE: Ravel Family (Antoine, Dominique, Francois, Gabriel, Gean, Jerome, Louis Marzetti, Jean Pebernard, and others): N 19-27; William E. Burton: N 28-D 9; Madame Otto Opera Troupe (Madame Otto, Mrs. Thomas A'Beckett, Miss Jane Shirreff, Messrs. William F. Brough, Henry Sherman, Boullan, Thomas A'Beckett, John Wilson, John): D 13-27, Ja 20-F 3; Master and Miss Wells: D 30-Ja 17; Charles Thomas Parsloe: Ja 4-25; Charlotte Barnes (supported by Mr. and Mrs. J. Barnes): F 4-10; Charles Kean: F 11-22; Mrs. Fanny Fitzwilliam: F 24-Mr 9, Ap 8-13; Seguin Opera Company (Mr. and Mrs. Arthur E. S. Seguin, James Henry Horncastle): Mr 11-28; Mr. and Mrs. John Sloman: Mr 30-Ap 6.

N (19) Wonder; Married Rake (21) Simpson and Company; Ravel Family (22) Mischief Making; Race for a Dinner; Ravel Family (25) Married Rake; Jocko; L'Uomo Rosso; Ravel Family (26) Ladder of Love; Ravel Family (27) Spoil'd Child; Ravel Family (28) Sweethearts and Wives: *Billy Lackaday*–Burton; John Jones: *Guy Goodluck*–Burton (29) Breach of Promise: *Sudden*–Burton; Mummy: *Toby Tramp*–Burton; Spoil'd Child (30) Ladder of Love; Giovanni in London: *Seperello*–Burton; Man about Town*: *Skirts*–Burton

D (2) His First Champagne: *Dick Watt*–Burton; Mummy: *Toby Tramp*–Burton; Giovanni in London: *Seperello*–Burton (3) Begone Dull Care: *Old Revel*–Burton; Critic (4) His First Champagne: *Dick Watt*–Burton; John Jones: *Guy Goodluck*–Burton; State Secrets: *Gregory*–Burton (5) School for Scandal: *Sir Peter Teazle*–Burton; State Secrets: *Gregory*–Burton (7) Der Wachter: *Der Wachter*–Burton; Turning the Tables: *Jack Humphries*–Burton; Forty Winks: *Toby Munns*–Burton (9) Old English Gentleman: *Squire Broadlands*–Burton; But However:

Cabel Chizzler–Burton; John Jones: *Guy Goodluck*–Burton (10) Lady of Lyons; Loan of a Lover (11) Lady of Lyons; Charles XII (12) Hamlet; Agreeable Surprise (13-14) La Somnambula; Spoil'd Child (16) La Somnambula; My Handsome Husband (17) Fra Diavolo; Rendezvous (18) La Diavolo; Dumb Belle (19) Cinderella; Lottery Ticket (20) La Somnambula; Cramond Brig* (21) Rob Roy Mac-Gregor; Married Rake (23) Cinderella; Dumb Belle (24) Fra Diavolo; Cramond Brig (26) Native Land*; Lottery Ticket (27) Native Land; Amilie (selections) (28) Jane Shore; Wandering Boys (30) Unfinished Gentleman; Mischief Making; La Sylphide (31) Charles XII; Agreeable Surprise

Ja (1) Wandering Boys; La Sylphide (3) Jewess; La Sylphide (4) Jewess; Robinson Crusoe and His Good Man Friday: *Friday*–Parsloe (6) Lottery Ticket; La Bayadere (7) Robinson Crusoe and His Good Man Friday: *Friday*–Parsloe; La Bayadere (8) Spoil'd Child; La Bayadere (9-11) Cabin Boy: *Pug*–Parsloe; La Bayadere (13) Irish Tutor: *Terry*–Master Wells; La Bayadere (14) Simpson and Company; Loan of a Lover; Flore et Zephyr (15) La Bayadere: *Polichinel*–Parsloe; Pickwick Club (16) Pickwick Club; Flore et Zephyr (17) Flore et Zephyr; La Bayadere; Weathercock (18) Pickwick Club; Don Juan: *Scaramouch*–Parsloe (20) La Somnambula; You Can't Marry Your Grandmother (21) Amilie; Illustrious Stranger (22) Amilie; Cabin Boy: *Pug*–Parsloe (23) Cinderella; No Song, No Supper (24) Massaniello; Middy Ashore (25) George Barnwell; Jamie of Aberdeen: *Sawney*–Parsloe (27) Massaniello; Illustrious Stranger (28) Massaniello; musical concert (29) Massaniello; Husband at Sight (30) La Somnambula; Husband at Sight (31) Barber of Seville; My Handsome Husband

F (1) Barber of Seville; Massaniello (Act II) (3) Castle of Andalusia; Mountain Sylph; Barber of Seville (Act I) (4) School for Scandal: *Lady Teazle*–Charlotte Barnes; Captive; Sprigs of Laurel (5) Rivals: *Lydia Languish*–Charlotte Barnes; Youthful Queen: *Christine*–Charlotte Barnes (6) Rivals: *Lydia Languish*–Charlotte Barnes; Fra Diavolo (7) Love Chase: *Constance*–Charlotte Barnes; La Fitte: *Theodore*–Charlotte Barnes (8) Octavia Bragaldi: *Octavia*–Charlotte Barnes; La Fitte: *Theodore*–Charlotte Barnes (10) Love: *Countess*–Charlotte Barnes; Scape Goat; Captive: *Captive*–Charlotte Barnes (11) Hamlet: *Hamlet*–Kean; Illustrious Stranger (12) Merchant of Venice: *Shylock*–Kean; Is He Jealous? (13) Richard III: *Richard*–Kean; Loan of a Lover (14) New Way to Pay Old Debts: *Sir Giles Overreach*–Kean; Frank Fox Phipps, Esq. (15) Macbeth: *Macbeth*–Kean; Frank Fox Phipps, Esq. (17) Iron Chest: *Sir Edward Mortimer*–Kean; Lady of Lyons: *Claude*–Kean (18) Richard III: *Richard*–Kean; Mischief Making (19) Macbeth: *Macbeth*–Kean; Weathercock (20) Town and Country: *Reuben Glenroy*–Kean; Critic (21) Stranger: *Stranger*–Kean; Married Rake (22) King Lear: *King Lear*–Kean; Frank Fox Phipps, Esq. (24) Country Girl: *Miss Peggy*–Fanny Fitzwilliam; Widow Wiggins: six rôles–Fanny Fitzwilliam (25) Will: *Albina Mandeville*–Fanny Fitzwilliam; Widow Wiggins: six rôles–Fanny Fitzwilliam (26) Englishmen in India: *Sally Scraggs*–Fanny Fitzwilliam; Mischief Making: *Madame Manette*–Fanny Fitzwilliam (27) Irish Widow: *Widow Brady*–Fanny Fitzwilliam; Widow Wiggins: six rôles–Fanny Fitzwilliam (28) Country Girl: *Miss Peggy*–Fanny Fitzwilliam; Middy Ashore: *Harry*–Fanny Fitzwilliam (29) Irish Widow: *Widow Brady*–Fanny Fitzwilliam; Peep into Seraglio: *Roxalana*–Fanny Fitzwilliam

Mr (2) Soldier's Daughter: *Widow Mackenzie*–Fanny Fitzwilliam; Widow Wiggins: six rôles–Fanny Fitzwilliam; Mischief Making: *Madame Manette*–Fanny Fitzwilliam (3) Will: *Albina Mandeville*–Fanny Fitzwilliam; Dead Shot: *Louisa Lovetrick*–Fanny Fitzwilliam (4) Englishmen in India: *Sally Scraggs*–Fanny Fitzwilliam; Foreign Airs and Native Graces: four rôles–Fanny Fitzwilliam (5) Man and Wife: *Helen Worrett*–Fanny Fitzwilliam; Foreign Airs and Native Graces: four rôles–Fanny Fitzwilliam (6) Soldier's Daughter: *Widow Mackenzie*–Fanny Fitzwilliam; Foreign Airs and Native Graces: four rôles–Fanny Fitzwilliam (7) Man and Wife: *Helen Worrett*–Fanny Fitzwilliam; Widow Wiggins: six rôles–Fanny Fitzwilliam (9) As You Like It: *Rosalind*–Fanny Fitzwilliam; Foreign Airs and Native Graces: four rôles–Fanny Fitzwilliam (10) Jane Shore; George Barnwell (11) La Gazza Ladra; You Can't Marry Your Grandmother (12) La Gazza Ladra; Chaos Is Come Again (13) La Diavolo; Chaos Is Come Again (14) Secret; Cinderella (16) La Gazza Ladra; Deaf as a Post (17) Marriage of Figaro; Married Rake (19) Der Freischutz; Secret (20) Fra Diavolo; Savage and the Maiden (21) Der Freischutz; Frank Fox Phipps, Esq. (23) Barber of Seville; Savage and the Maiden (24) Der Freischutz; Secret (25) Barber of Seville; Savage and the Maiden (26) Marriage of Figaro; Savage and the Maiden; Der Freischutz (one scene) (27) La Gazza Ladra; Savage and the Maiden; Une Bonne Bouche Musicale (28) Barber of Seville; Cinderella (Act I) (30) Love: *Countess*–Mrs. Sloman; Fish out of Water: *Sam Savory*–Sloman (31) Venice Preserved: *Belvidera*–Mrs. Sloman; Family Jars: *Delph*–Sloman

Ap (1) Hunchback: *Julia*–Mrs. Sloman; Wandering Minstrel: *Jem Baggs*–Sloman (2) Stranger: *Mrs. Haller*–Mrs. Sloman; Bath Road: *Tom*–Sloman (3) Isabella: *Isabella*–Mrs. Sloman; Victorine: *Victorine*–Mrs. Sloman, *Blaise*–Sloman (4) Isabella: *Isabella*–Mrs. Sloman; Wandering Minstrel: *Jem Baggs*–Sloman (6) Married Life: *Dove*–Sloman, *Mrs. Lynx*–Mrs. Sloman; Hercules, King of Clubs: *Tim*–Sloman (7) Richelieu; Secret (8) Soldier's Daughter: *Widow Mackenzie*–Fanny Fitzwilliam; Widow Wiggins: six rôles–Fanny Fitzwilliam (9) Heart of Midlothian: *Madge Wildfire*–Fanny Fitzwilliam; Mischief Making: *Madame Manette*–Fanny Fitzwilliam (10) As You Like It: *Rosalind*–Fanny Fitzwilliam; Foreign Airs and Native Graces: six rôles–Fanny Fitzwilliam (11) Irish Widow: *Widow Brady*–Fanny Fitzwilliam; Heart of Midlothian: *Madge Wildfire*–Fanny Fitzwilliam (13) Bold Stroke for a Husband: *Donna Olivia*–Fanny Fitzwilliam; Foreign Airs and Native Graces: six rôles–Fanny Fitzwilliam; Widow Wiggins: four rôles–Fanny Fitzwilliam (14) Richelieu; Spectre Bridegroom (15) Lady of the Lake; Black Eyed Susan (20) Washington; Illustrious Stranger (21) Woman's Wit; Maid of Croissey (22) Washington; Illustrious Stranger (23) William Tell; Actress of All Work (24-25) Washington; Maid of Croissey (27) Speed the Plough; Miller and His Men (28) Lady of Lyons; Washington (29) Everyone Has His Fault; Actress of All Work (30) Hypocrite; Beggar's Opera; Washington

My (1) Everyone Has His Fault; Actress of All Work (4) Isabella; Rural Felicity (6) Aladdin; Rural Felicity (7) Aladdin; Husband at Sight (8) Aladdin; Actress of All Work (9) Aladdin; Day after the Wedding (11) Provost of Bruges; P. P. (12) Aladdin; Rural Felicity (13) White Rose; Printer's Devil (14) Provost of Bruges; Printer's Devil (15) Hazard of the Die; Irish Lion; 1, 2, 3, 4, 5, by Advertisement (20) Roland for an Oliver; Washington; Manager in

Distress (21) Aladdin; Weathercock (22) Aladdin; Mischief Making
(23) William Tell; Roland for an Oliver (26-27) Aladdin; Critic

1840-1841

Mgr.: William Abbott; *acting mgr.:* J. B. Fuller; *scenist:* S. B. Stock-
well; *orch. leader:* H. Marks; *machinist:* W. B. Donaldson; *treas.:* J.
M. Weston. *Stock:* Bellamy, W., Field, J. R., Harrington, W., Lewellen,
McCutcheon, T., Merryfield, J., Pearson, H., Reed, R., Smith, Sprague,
H. N., Stafford; *Mrs.* Groves, E., Hughes, Rivers, Watson; *Misses*
Bunyie, Gannon, M., Hildreth, S., Melton.

SE: James S. Browne: N 9-20; Mrs. Shaw: N 24-D 5, 21-24; Henry
Placide: D 8-23, Ja 25-F 3; Fanny Ellsler (assisted by Mons. J. Sylvain,
Madame Arraline, and C. T. Parsloe): D 28-Ja 1; Edwin Forrest: Ja
11-23; La Compte Ballet Troupe (Madame La Compte, Mlle. Desjardins,
Mons. Kaiffer, La Compte): F 6, 24-Mr 8; Tyrone Power: F 8-19;
Martyn Opera Troupe (Messrs. Martyn, William F. Brough, Mrs.
Martyn, Miss Inverarity): F 20; Fitzgerald Tasistro: Ap 22-26;
Lewellen's Trained Horses: Ap 28-My 5, 8-15.

N (5) Wife; Irish Tutor (6) Hunchback; Man about Town (7) Jane
Shore; Spectre Bridegroom (9) Wild Oats: *Rover*-Browne; Robert
Macaire: *Robert*-Browne (10) Cure for the Heartache: *Ned Rapid*-
Browne; Maid of Croissey (11) Rivals: *Bob Acres*-Browne; Robert
Macaire: *Robert*-Browne (12) Speed the Plough: *Bob Handy*-Browne;
My Young Wife and My Old Umbrella: *Gregory Grizzle*-Browne (13)
Way to Get Married: *Tangent*-Browne; Robert Macaire: *Robert*-Browne
(14) Romeo and Juliet: *Mercutio*-Brown; Uncle Sam: *Sam Hobbs*-
Browne (16) Old English Gentleman: *Horace*-Browne; My Young Wife
and My Old Umbrella: *Gregory Grizzle*-Browne (17) She Stoops to
Conquer: *Young Marlowe*-Browne; Actress of All Work (18) School
of Reform: *Ferment*-Browne; Robert Macaire: *Robert*-Browne (19)
Wild Oats: *Rover*-Browne; Frightened to Death: *Phantom*-Browne
(20) Road to Ruin: *Goldfinch*-Browne; Review: *Caleb*-Browne (21)
Venice Preserved; Old and Young (23) Love; Barrack Room (24) Love
Chase: *Constance*-Mrs. Shaw; Barrack Room (25) Romeo and Juliet:
Juliet-Mrs. Shaw; Secret (26) Fazio: *Bianca*-Mrs. Shaw; Critic (28)
Lucille: *Lucille*-Mrs. Shaw; Barrack Room (30) Ion: *Ion*-Mrs. Shaw;
Loan of a Lover

D (1) Agnes de Vere: *Agnes*-Mrs. Shaw; Lucille: *Lucille*-Mrs. Shaw
(2) Il Maledetto: *Flora*-Mrs. Shaw; Irish Tutor (3) Ion: *Ion*-Mrs.
Shaw; Youthful Queen: *Christine*-Mrs. Shaw (4) Ernest Maltravers:
Alice-Mrs. Shaw; Lucille: *Lucille*-Mrs. Shaw (5) Love: *Countess*-Mrs.
Shaw; Waterman (8) Clandestine Marriage: *Lord Ogleby*-Placide;
Uncle John: *Uncle John*-Placide (9) School for Scandal: *Sir Peter
Teazle*-Placide; Mr. and Mrs. Pringle: *Mr. Pringle*-Placide (10) Poor
Gentleman: *Ollapod*-Placide; Popping the Question: *Primrose*-Placide
(11) Patrician and Parvenu: *Sir Timothy*-Placide; Waterman (12)
Charles II: *Capt. Copp*-Placide; Secret; Popping the Question: *Prim-
rose*-Placide (15) Secret Service: *Michael Perrin*-Placide; Charles II:
Capt. Copp-Placide (16) Simpson and Company: *Simpson*-Placide;
Popping the Question: *Primrose*-Placide; Irish Tutor: *Doctor O'Toole*-
Placide (17) Clandestine Marriage: *Lord Ogleby*-Placide; Mr. and Mrs.
Pringle: *Mr. Pringle*-Placide (18) Secret Service: *Michael Perrin*-
Placide; Bombastes Furioso: *General Bombastes*-Placide; Uncle John:

Uncle John–Placide (21) Lady of Lyons: *Pauline*–Mrs. Shaw; Youthful Queen: *Christine*–Mrs. Shaw (22) Douglas: *Young Norval*–Mrs. Shaw; Lucille: *Lucille*–Mrs. Shaw (23) As You Like It: *Rosalind*–Mrs. Shaw, *Touchstone*–Placide; Bombastes Furioso: *General Bombastes*–Placide (24) Romeo and Juliet: *Juliet*–Mrs. Shaw; Agnes De Vere: *Agnes*–Mrs. Shaw (28) La Sylphide: *La Sylphide*–Fanny Ellsler; Wolf and the Fox; Cachucha; Irish Tutor (29) Othello; Dead Shot (30) La Sylphide: *La Sylphide*–Fanny Ellsler; Lottery Ticket; Loan of a Lover; La Cracovienne

Ja (1) Nathalie: *Nathalie*–Fanny Ellsler; Our Mary Anne (4) Glencoe*; Spoil'd Child (5) Glencoe; Old and Young (6) William Tell; Midnight Hour (7) Honeymoon; Swiss Cottage; Water Party (8) Nicholas Nickleby*; Midnight Hour (9) Nicholas Nickleby; Water Party (11) Virginius: *Virginius*–Forrest; Swiss Cottage (12) Lady of Lyons: *Claude*–Forrest; No, No (13) Richelieu: *Richelieu*–Forrest; Spoil'd Child (14) Macbeth: *Macbeth*–Forrest; Our Mary Anne (15) Metamora: *Metamora*–Forrest; Shocking Events (16) Damon and Pythias: *Damon*–Forrest; Nicholas Nickleby (18) Gladiator: *Spartacus*–Forrest; Happiest Day of My Life (19) Richelieu: *Richelieu*–Forrest; Shocking Events (20) Metamora: *Metamora*–Forrest; No, No (21) Richard III: *Richard*–Forrest; Love in Humble Life (22) King Lear: *King Lear*–Forrest; Village Lawyer (23) Richelieu: *Richelieu*–Forrest; William Tell: *William Tell*–Forrest (25) Patrician and Parvenu: *Sir Timothy*–Placide; Secret Service: *Michael Perrin*–Placide (26) Bluebeard; Water Party (27) Uncle John: *Uncle John*–Placide; Tom Noddy's Secret*: *Tom*–Placide; Bluebeard (28) School for Scandal: *Sir Peter Teazle*–Placide; Bluebeard (29) Bluebeard; Mr. and Mrs. Pringle: *Mr. Pringle*–Placide; Bombastes Furioso: *General Bombastes*–Placide (30) Village Doctor: *Pierre Bonceur*–Placide; Uncle Sam: *Uncle Sam*–Placide; Scan Mag: *Mr. Singleton*–Placide

F (1) Stranger; Bluebeard (2) Forty Thieves; No, No; Shocking Events (3) Married Life: *Mr. Coddle*–Placide; Forty Thieves (5) John of Procida*; Roland for an Oliver (6) Marco Bomba; La Compte Ballet Troupe (8) Irish Ambassador: *Sir Patrick O'Plenipo*–Power; Irish Lion: *Tim Moore*–Power; Shocking Events (9) His Last Legs: *O'Callaghan*–Power; Irish Lion: *Tim Moore*–Power; Swiss Cottage (10) His Last Legs: *O'Callaghan*–Power; Irish Tutor: *Dr. O'Toole*–Power; Our Mary Anne (11) Born to Good Luck: *Paudeen O'Rafferty*–Power; Forty Thieves (12) Irish Ambassador: *Sir Patrick O'Plenipo*–Power; Happy Man: *Paddy Murphy*–Power; No, No (13) Nervous Man and the Man of Nerve: *McShane*–Power; Teddy, the Tiler: *Teddy*–Power; Pleasant Neighbors (15) Irish Attorney: *Pierce O'Hara*–Power; Omnibus: *Pat Rooney*–Power; Dead Shot (16) Born to Good Luck: *Paudeen O'Rafferty*–Power; Roland for an Oliver (17) John Bull: *Dennis Bulgruddy*–Power; Secret (18) Nervous Man and the Man of Nerve: *McShane*–Power; Omnibus: *Pat Rooney*–Power; Weathercock (19) Irish Attorney: *Pierce O'Hara*–Power; Paddy Carey: *Paddy*–Power; Lottery Ticket (20) Loan of a Lover; Soldier and the Peasant; Norma (22) Rent Day; White Horse of the Peppers (23) Lady of Lyons; White Horse of the Peppers (24) Lise and Colin; Love, Law and Physic; La Compte Ballet Troupe (25) Marco Bomba; White Horse of the Peppers; La Compte Ballet Troupe (26) La Somnambula; Bachelor's Buttons; La Compte Ballet Troupe (27) My Little Adopted; Robert le Diable; Bachelor's Buttons; La Compte Ballet Troupe

Mr. (1) La Bayadere; X. Y. Z.; La Compte Ballet Troupe (2) Doctor Dilworth; Robert le Diable; My Little Adopted; La Compte Ballet Troupe (3) La Bayadere; Doctor Dilworth; La Compte Ballet Troupe (4) La Bayadere; Two Queens; Marco Bomba; La Compte Ballet Troupe (5) La Somnambula; Shocking Events; La Compte Ballet Troupe (6) Man about Town; Two Queens; Lise and Colin; La Compte Ballet Troupe (8) La Sylphide; Love, Law and Physic; La Compte Ballet Troupe (9) Wonder; Victorine (10) Wallace; Perfection (11) Sea Captain; Swedish Patriotism (12) Wallace; Catching an Heiress (15) Sea Captain; Swedish Patriotism (16) Sea Captain; Catching an Heiress (17) Miser of Marseilles; St. Patrick's Day; Charles XII (18) Idiot Witness; Turned Head; Rum Old Commodore (22) Gustavus III (23) Gustavus III; Catching an Heiress (24) Gustavus III; Rum Old Commodore (25) Bride of Abydos; Manager in Distress; Ladies' Man (Company moves to Savannah)

Ap (22) Othello: *Othello*-Tasistro; Turned Head (23) Merchant of Venice: *Shylock*-Tasistro; Swiss Cottage (24) John of Procida: *John*-Tasistro; Our Mary Anne (26) Hamlet: *Hamlet*-Tasistro; Is He Jealous?: *Belcour*-Tasistro (28) Mazeppa; Lottery Ticket (29) Mazeppa; Ladies' Man (30) Mazeppa; Fortune's Frolic

My (1) Mazeppa; Bachelor's Buttons (3) Two Gregories; Couancheatah (4) Mazeppa; Lottery Ticket (5) St. George and the Dragon; Mummy; Mazeppa (scenes) (6) Sea Captain; Brigand (7) Miser of Marseilles; Bombastes Furioso (8) Mazeppa; State Secrets (10) How Do You Manage?; Two Greens (11) Miser of Marseilles; Bombastes Furioso; Timour the Tartar (15) Laugh when You Can; Quadrupeds

1841-1842

Mgr.: W. H. Latham; *acting mgr.:* Harry Tuthill; *scenist:* H. Isherwood; *orch. leader:* H. Marks; *treas.:* C. M. Melton. *Stock:* Barnes, J., Byrne, J., Codet, Dennison, Donaldson, W. B., Faulconbridge, Henry, W., Howard, C., Larkins, Massett, S. C. (alias Stephens), Phillips, A. J., Sathill, Sinclair, J.; *Mrs.* Barnes, J., Henry, W.; *Misses* Barnes, C., Henry, Melton.

SE: Seguin Opera Company (Mr. and Mrs. Arthur E. S. Seguin, Mr. and Mrs. Manvers, Misses Manvers, Coad): D 7-16, Mr 12-29; T. D. ("Jim Crow") Rice: D 30-Ja 1; Mrs. Fanny Fitzwilliam and John B. Buckstone: Ja 4-17, 31; Samuel W. Butler: F 1, 7-12; James Hackett: F 14-26.

N (15) Poor Gentleman; Loan of a Lover (16) Heir at Law; Dead Shot (17) Soldier's Daughter; Perfection (19) Turn Out; Lottery Ticket (20) Swiss Cottage; Dumb Belle (22) Paul Pry; Family Jars (23) Belle's Stratagem; Two Late for Dinner (24) Rob Roy MacGregor; Roland for an Oliver (25) Poor Gentleman; Roland for an Oliver (26) Heir at Law; Review (27) Wonder; musical concert (29) Rob Roy MacGregor; Of Age Tomorrow (30) Perfection; Irish Tutor; Dumb Girl of Genoa

D (1) Guy Mannering; Two Late for Dinner (2-3) Guy Mannering; Dumb Girl of Genoa (4) Paul Pry; Fortune's Frolic (6) Hunchback; Omnibus (7) La Somnambula; Lottery Ticket (8) Cinderella; Pleasant Neighbors (9) Fra Diavolo; Omnibus (10) La Somnambula; Pleasant Neighbors (11) Fra Diavolo; Omnibus (13) L'Elisire d'Amore*; Uncle Sam (14) Fra Diavolo (Act I); La Somnambula (Act

I); Cinderella (Act I); Shocking Events (15) La Gazza Ladra; L'Elisir d'Amore; Shocking Events (16) La Somnambula; Day after the Wedding (17) Fazio; Agreeable Surprise (18) Wife; Of Age Tomorrow (20) Lady of Lyons; Agreeable Surprise (21) Hunchback; Uncle Sam (23) Hunchback; Of Age Tomorrow (24) Douglas; Rob Roy MacGregor (25) Lady of Lyons (28) Lady of Lyons; No Song, No Supper (29) Englishman in India; Young Hussar (30) Uncle Sam: *Uncle Sam*–Rice; Sarcophagus: *Ginger Blue*–Rice; Gumbo Jim: *Gumbo Jim*–Rice (31) Lady of Lyons; Jim Crow in London: *Jim Crow*–Rice; Captive

Ja (1) Of Age Tomorrow; Foreign Prince: *Jim Crow*–Rice; Oh! Hush: *Gumbo Cuff*–Rice; Day after the Wedding (4) Out of Place: *Sally Sallikins*–Fanny Fitzwilliam; Snapping Turtles; Kiss in the Dark: *Selim Pettibone*–Buckstone (5) My Old Woman: *Countess Xenia*–Fanny Fitzwilliam, *Michael*–Buckstone; Foreign Airs and Native Graces: five rôles–Fanny Fitzwilliam, *Sam*–Buckstone; Omnibus (6) My Little Adopted: *Lauretta*–Fanny Fitzwilliam, *John Dibbs*–Buckstone; Out of Place: *Sally*–Fanny Fitzwilliam (7) My Old Woman: *Countess Zenia*–Fanny Fitzwilliam, *Michael*–Buckstone; Widow Wiggins: six rôles–Fanny Fitzwilliam; Make Your Wills: *Joseph Bragg*–Buckstone (8) Irish Widow: *Widow Brady*–Fanny Fitzwilliam; My Little Adopted: *Lauretta*–Fanny Fitzwilliam, *John Dibbs*–Buckstone; Kiss in the Dark: *Selim Pettibone*–Buckstone (10) Ladies' Club: *Mrs. Fitzsmyth*–Fanny Fitzwilliam, *Flammer*–Buckstone; Foreign Airs and Native Graces: five rôles–Fanny Fitzwilliam; Make Your Wills: *Joseph Bragg*–Buckstone (11) Soldier's Daughter: *Widow Mackenzie*–Fanny Fitzwilliam; Mischief Making: *Madame Manette*–Fanny Fitzwilliam, *Nicholas*–Buckstone (12) Banished Star: *Fanny Nonpariel*–Fanny Fitzwilliam; Ladies' Club: *Mrs. Fitzsmyth*–Fanny Fitzwilliam, *Flammer*–Buckstone; Uncle Sam (13) My Old Woman: *Countess Xenia*–Fanny Fitzwilliam; Widow Wiggins: six rôles–Fanny Fitzwilliam; Make Your Wills: *Joseph Bragg*–Buckstone (14) Banished Star: *Fanny Nonpariel*–Fanny Fitzwilliam; Snapping Turtles; Happy Man (15) Irish Widow: *Widow Brady*–Fanny Fitzwilliam; Foreign Airs and Native Graces: five rôles–Fanny Fitzwilliam; Kiss in the Dark: *Joseph Bragg*–Buckstone (17) Pet of the Petticoats: *Paul the Pet*–Fanny Fitzwilliam; Widow Wiggins: *Widow Brady*–Fanny Fitzwilliam; Make Your Wills: *Joseph Bragg*–Buckstone (19) London Assurance*; Shocking Events (20) London Assurance; Bar-keeper's Bride (21-22, 24-27) London Assurance (28) Field of Forty Footsteps*; Faint Heart Ne'er Won Fair Lady* (29) London Assurance (31) Foreign Airs and Native Graces: six rôles–Fanny Fitzwilliam; Widow Wiggins: *Widow Brady*–Fanny Fitzwilliam; Make Your Wills: *Joseph Bragg*–Buckstone

F (1) Hamlet: *Hamlet*–Butler; Loan of a Lover (2-3) London Assurance (4) Field of Forty Footsteps; Dead Shot (5) Lady of Lyons; Raising the Wind (7) Hamlet: *Hamlet*–Butler; My Fellow Clerk (8) Othello: *Othello*–Butler; Bath Road (9) Hamlet: *Hamlet*–Butler; Faint Heart Ne'er Won Fair Lady (10) Virginius: *Virginius*–Butler; Lottery Ticket (11-12) Avenger: *Walder*–Butler; Sleep Walker: *Somne*–Butler (14) Henry IV: *Falstaff*–Hackett; Uncle Sam (15) Kentuckian: *Nimrod Wildfire*–Hackett; Monsieur Mallett: *Monsieur Mallett*–Hackett; Faint Heart Ne'er Won Fair Lady (16) King Lear: *King Lear*–Hackett; Pleasant Neighbors (17) Henry IV: *Falstaff*–Hackett; Bath Road (18)

Kentuckian: *Nimrod Wildfire*–Hackett; Monsieur Mallett: *Monsieur Mallett*–Hackett (19) Jonathan in England: *Solomon Swap*–Hackett; Militia Training: *Major Joe Bunker*–Hackett; Fortune's Frolic (21) Merry Wives of Windsor: *Falstaff*–Hackett; Monsieur Mallett: *Monsieur Mallett*–Hackett (22) Lady of Lyons; Faint Heart Ne'er Won Fair Lady (23) Merry Wives of Windsor: *Falstaff*–Hackett; My Fellow Clerk (24) Romeo and Juliet; Monsieur Mallett: *Monsieur Mallett*–Hackett; Soldier's Daughter (25) Merry Wives of Windsor: *Falstaff*–Hackett; Irish Tutor (26) Jonathan in England: *Solomon Swap*–Hackett; Kentuckian: *Nimrod Wildfire*–Hackett; Monsieur Tonson: *Marbleau*–Hackett (28) Money; Bombastes Furioso; London Assurance
    Mr (1) Money; Happy Man (2) Wives as They Were and Maids as They Are; Money (4) Pizarro; Illustrious Stranger (7) Flying Dutchman; Black Eyed Susan (8) Belle's Stratagem; Black Eyed Susan (9) Flying Dutchman; Golden Farmer (12) La Somnambula; My Fellow Clerk (15) Fra Diavolo; Uncle Sam (16-17) L'Elisir d'Amore; Black Eyed Susan (18) La Somnambula; Irish Tutor (19) La Gazza Ladra; Omnibus (21-23) Norma (29) Norma (Act I); Fra Diavolo (Act III); Clari (30) Ambrose Gwinnett; Damon and Pythias; Masked Ball (31) Rory O'More; No, No; Flying Dutchman

1842-1843

Mgr.: W. C. Forbes; *scenist:* H. Isherwood; *orch. leaders:* Rink, Tscheruer. *Stock:* Bennie, Fleming, W. M., Fuller, J. B., Hall, J. H., Hill, G. H., Larkins, Maywood, R. C., Nagel, Phillips, H. B., Scott, J. R., Smith, Sullivan; *Mrs.* Bennie, Forbes, W. C., Hughes, Isherwood, H., Phillips, H. B.; *Miss* Ince, E.
    SE: James Hackett: Ja 11; Mons. Paul: Ja 9-21; Seguin Opera Company (Mr. and Mrs. Arthur E. S. Seguin, Messrs. Shrival, Thomas Archer, Miss Coad): Mr 3-18, Ap 10-27; John Sloman: F 24-27.
    D (19) Lady of Lyons; State Secrets (20) Pizarro; Perfection (21) Honeymoon; Dumb Belle (22) Bertram; Dead Shot (23) Hamlet; Secret (24) Sweethearts and Wives; Nick of the Woods (26) Kinsmen*; Nick of the Woods (28) Two Friends; Lady and the Devil (29) Maid of Croissey; Kinsmen (30) Stranger; Conscripts (31) Dream of Fate; Nick of the Woods; Conscripts
    Ja (2) Damon and Pythias; Dream of Fate (4) Maid of Croissey; Black Eyed Susan; Conscripts (5) Carpenter of Rouen*; State Secrets (6) Carpenter of Rouen; Pleasant Neighbors (7) Carpenter of Rouen; Lottery Ticket (9) Two Friends; Our Mary Anne; Mons. Paul (10) Raising the Wind; Prince and the Peasant; Pleasant Neighbors; Mons. Paul (11) Henry IV: *Falstaff*–Hackett; Mons. Paul (12) Spectre Bridegroom; Fawn's Leap; La Bayadere; Mons. Paul (13) Lady of Lyons; Mons. Paul (14) Barrack Room; Catherine and Petruchio; Mons. Paul (16) Love Chase; Golden Farmer; Mons. Paul (17) Our Mary Anne; Lottery Ticket; Mons. Paul (18) Carpenter of Rouen; Prince and the Peasant; Mons. Paul (19) Virginius; Actress of All Work; Mons. Paul (20) Soldier's Daughter; La Bayadere; Mons. Paul (21) Charles II; Hylas and Hebe; Mons. Paul (23) London Assurance; Bachelor's Buttons (24) London Assurance; My Sister Kate (25) Macbeth; Actress of All Work (26) Dream of Fate; Don Juan; Adam and Eve (27) William Tell; Don Juan (28) Sergeant's Wife; Last Man; State Secrets (30) Last Days of Pompey; Barrack Room (31) Last Days of Pompey; Raising the Wind

F (1) Last Days of Pompey; Dead Shot (2) De Montalt*; Quiet Day; Rendezvous (3) Last Days of Pompey; De Montalt (4) Two Friends; Blue Devils; Don Juan (6) What Will the World Say?; Quiet Day (7) Wife; Day after the Wedding (8) Joan of Arc; Home Squadron (9) What Will the World Say?; Spectre Bridegroom (10) Man with the Carpet Bag; Wreck Ashore; Lucky Stars (11) Wreck Ashore; Joan of Arc (13) Faustus*; Lucky Stars (14) Faustus; Our Mary Anne (15) Wives as They Were and Maids as They Are; Tom and Jerry (16) Barrack Room; State Secrets; Naval Engagements (17) School for Scandal; Richard III (18) Faustus; Animal Magnetism (20) Rent Day; My Uncle Foozle (21) Exile; Lucky Stars (22) What Will the World Say?; Siege of Charleston (23) Lady of Lyons; Perfection (24) My Uncle Foozle; Siege of Charleston (25) Therese; Boots at the Swan (27) Married Life; Wandering Minstrel; Boots at the Swan (28) Venice Preserved; Siege of Charleston

Mr (1) Faustus; My Uncle Foozle (2) Othello; Lucky Stars (3) La Somnambula; My Uncle Foozle (4) Barber of Seville; Raising the Wind (6) Barber of Seville; Our Mary Anne (7-8) Cinderella; Quiet Day (9) Fra Diavolo; Lucky Stars (10) Postillion of Lonjumeau; My Uncle Foozle (13) Massaniello; Young Widow (14) Postillion of Lonjumeau; Animal Magnetism (15) Marriage of Figaro; Olympic Revels (16) Cinderella; Massaniello (Act II) (17) Barber of Seville; Olympic Revels (18) La Somnambula; Lottery Ticket

Ap (10) La Gazza Ladra; My Uncle Foozle (11) Postillion of Lonjumeau; Animal Magnetism (12) Massaniello; Boots at the Swan (18) Master Clark; Mutiny at the Nore (19) La Gazza Ladra; Lady and the Devil (20) Der Freischutz; Barrack Room (21) La Somnambula; Olympic Revels (22) Rob Roy MacGregor; Two Greens (24) Blanche of Jersey; Olympic Revels (25) Der Freischutz; Boots at the Swan (26) La Gazza Ladra; My Uncle Foozle (27) Barber of Seville; Dead Shot (28) Jane Shore; Tekeli (29) Macbeth; Olympic Revels

My (1) Brutus; Bashful Man (2) Honeymoon; State Secrets (3) Stranger; Bombastes Furioso (4) Merchant of Venice; Our Mary Anne; Black Eyed Susan (5) Illustrious Stranger; Nicholas Flam, Attorney-at-Law; Aldgate Pump (6) Mountaineers; Illustrious Stranger (8) Love's Sacrifice; My Uncle Foozle (11) Culprit; Matrimony; Valet de Sham (12) Love's Sacrifice; Perfection (16) Wonder; Therese

1843-1844

Olympic Theatre

Mgr.: H. B. Phillips. *Stock:* Durivage, O. E., Graham, F., Meyers, Newton, Raphael, Sefton, J., Thompson, W. C., Welsh; *Mrs.* Cline, Phillips, H. B., Welsh; *Misses* Hall, Hood, La Rose.

N (1) Review; Little Back Parlor; Family Jars (2) Stage Struck Yankee; Dead Shot (3) Black Eyed Susan; Stage Struck Yankee (4) Crossing the Line; Dead Shot; Bombastes Furioso

(Company moves to Augusta)

Charleston Theatre

Mgr.: W. C. Forbes; *scenist:* Milner; *orch. leader:* Rink. *Stock:* Bellamy, W. H., Berger, Charles, J. S., Fuller, J. B., Hill, G. H., Johnston, T. B., Kemble, M'Cluskey, Pearson, H., Proctor, J., Raphael,

Ryder, W.; *Mrs.* Barrett, G., Brougham, J.,[1] Berger, O., Charles, J. S., Forbes, W. C., Kemble; *Misses* Charles, Grove, Lee, M. A., Phillips, M'Duall.

SE: John R. Scott: D 12-20; James Hackett: D 20-28; Charles William Macready: Ja 8-19; Falvy Williams and Mrs. J. Brougham: Ja 13, F 8-14; Edwin Forrest: F 15-17; J. B. Booth: F 19-24; James W. Wallack, Sr.: F 26-Mr 6, 12-16; Seguin Opera Company (Mr. and Mrs. Arthur E. S. Seguin and Thomas A'Beckett, Shrival): Mr 7-11; J. S. Silsbee: Ap 1-3.

N (2) Belle's Stratagem; Waterman (4) She Stoops to Conquer; Nature and Philosophy (6) Lady of Lyons; Valet de Sham (7) Sweethearts and Wives; Merchant and His Clerks (8) Wives as They Were and Maids as They Are; Merchant and His Clerks (9) Simpson and Company; La Bayadere (10) Merchant and His Clerks; La Bayadere (11) His Last Legs; La Bayadere (13) My Handsome Husband; La Bayadere; Rifle Brigade (14) Two Friends; La Sylphide; His Last Legs (15) Three Weeks after Marriage; La Sylphide; Pleasant Neighbors (16) Alma Mater; La Sylphide (18) Alma Mater; Dumb Girl of Genoa (20) One Hour; La Bayadere (21) Rifle Brigade; Dumb Girl of Genoa; Double Bedded Room; Cracovienne (22) Alma Mater; La Sylphide; La Polacco (23) My Handsome Husband; Broken Sword; Day in Paris (24) William Tell; La Bayadere (25) Lucille; Broken Sword (27) Jonathan in England; Wife for a Day; Irish Tutor (28) Green Mountain Boy; New Notions; Double Bedded Room (29) Seth Slope; Wife for a Day; Rifle Brigade (30) Knight of the Golden Fleece; Yankee Pedlar; Pretty Bar Maid

D (1) Cut and Come Again; His Last Legs (2) People's Lawyer; Forest Rose; Hunting a Turtle (4) Knight of the Golden Fleece; Honest Roguery; Wife for a Day (5) Green Mountain Boy; Incendiary; Yankee Pedlar (6) Loan of a Lover; Married Rake; La Bayadere (Act II) (7) Jonathan in England; La Sylphide; Dumb Belle (8) Damon and Pythias; Star Spangled Banner (9) Therese; Star Spangled Banner (11) Cut and Come Again; Forest Rose; Nick of the Woods (12) Macbeth: *Macbeth*–Scott; Hunting a Turtle (13) Virginius: *Virginius*–Scott; Wife for a Day (15) Richard III: *Richard*–Scott; His Last Legs (16) Othello: *Othello*–Scott; Day in Paris (18) Richelieu: *Richelieu*–Scott; Review (19) Love's Sacrifice: *Matthew Elmore*–Scott; Adopted Child (20) Henry IV: *Hotspur*–Scott, *Falstaff*–Hackett; Perfection (21) Rip Van Winkle: *Rip Van Winkle*–Hackett; His Last Legs; Pleasant Neighbors (22) Merry Wives of Windsor: *Falstaff*–Hackett; Irish Tutor (23) Man of the World: *Sir Pertinax McSycophant*–Hackett; Monsieur Mallett: *Monsieur Mallett*–Hackett; Militia Training: *Major Joe Bunker*–Hackett (27) Man of the World: *Sir Pertinax McSycophant*–Hackett; His Last Legs (28) Jonathan in England: *Solomon Swap*–Hackett; Kentuckian: *Nimrod Wildfire*–Hackett; Monsieur Tonson: *Marbleau*–Hackett (29) Charles II; My Master's Rival; Richard Number Three (30) Aline; Richard Number Three

Ja (1) Alma Mater; Cherry and Fair Star (3) His Last Legs; Cherry and Fair Star (4) Two Friends; Cherry and Fair Star (5) Perfection; Dumb Belle (6) Dead Shot; Day in Paris (8) Hamlet: *Hamlet*–Macready; My Wife's Second Floor (10) Macbeth: *Macbeth*–Macready;

---

[1] Mrs. Brougham came on special engagement with Williams, but remained with the company.

Valet de Sham (11) Richelieu: *Richelieu*–Macready; My Wife's Second
Floor (12) Werner: *Werner*–Macready; Hunting a Turtle (13) Love
Chase: *Fondlove*–Williams, *Constance*–Mrs. Brougham; Centogenarian:
Phillip–Williams (14) Werner: *Werner*–Macready (15) Othello:
Othello–Macready; His Last Legs (16) Lady of Lyons: *Claude*–Macready; Rendezvous (17) Virginius: *Virginius*–Macready; Lottery
Ticket (18) Werner: *Werner*–Macready; Rendezvous (19) Hamlet:
Hamlet–Macready; Secret
   (Company moves to Savannah)
   F (8) School for Scandal: *Sir Peter Teazle*–Williams, *Lady Teazle*–
Mrs. Brougham; My Wife's Second Floor (9) Youthful Queen: *Christine*–Mrs. Brougham; Grandfather Whitehead: *Grandfather Whitehead*–
Williams; Day after the Wedding (10) Hunchback: *Julia*–Mrs.
Brougham; Monsieur Tonson: *Marbleau*–Williams (12) Rivals:
Mrs. Malaprop–Mrs. Brougham, *Capt. Absolute*–Williams; Married Rake: *Mrs. Tricktrack*–Mrs. Brougham (13) Alma Mater; Grandfather Whitehead: *Grandfather Whitehead*–Williams (14) London Assurance: *Lady Gay*–Mrs. Brougham, *Sir Haricourt*–Williams; 102:
Phillip Garbois–Williams (15) Richelieu: *Richelieu*–Forrest; Rendezvous
(16) Metamora: *Metamora*–Forrest; His Last Legs (17) Othello:
Othello–Forrest; Day in Paris (19) New Way to Pay Old Debts: *Sir
Giles Overreach*–Booth; Swiss Cottage (20) Iron Chest: *Sir Edward
Mortimer*–Booth; State Secrets (21) Richard III: *Richard*–Booth; Boots
at the Swan (22) Apostate: *Pescara*–Booth; Wandering Minstrel (23)
King Lear: *King Lear*–Booth; My Wife's Second Floor (24) Hamlet:
Hamlet–Booth; Mayor of Garratt: *Jerry Sneak*–Booth (26) Pizarro:
Rolla–Wallack; Boots at the Swan (27) Wonder: *Don Felix*–Wallack;
Rent Day: *Martin Heywood*–Wallack (28) Merchant of Venice: *Shylock*–Wallack; Children in the Wood: *Walter*–Wallack (29) Pizarro:
Rolla–Wallack; My Aunt: *Dick Dashall*–Wallack
   Mr (2) Town and Country: *Reuben Glenroy*–Wallack; Irish Tutor
(4) Much Ado about Nothing: *Benedict*–Wallack; Brigand: *Allessandro*–
Wallack (5) Macbeth: *Macbeth*–Wallack; Boots at the Swan (6) Wild
Oats: *Rover*–Wallack; My Uncle Foozle (7) La Somnambula; His Last
Legs (8) Soldier's Daughter; Landlords, Beware (9) Postillion of
Lonjumeau; Dead Shot (11) L'Elisir d'Amore; Olympic Revels (12)
Wild Oats: *Rover*–Wallack; Married Rake (13) Richard III: *Richard*–
Wallack; How to Pay the Rent (14) Youthful Queen; Brigand: *Allessandro*–Wallack; My Aunt: *Dick Dashall*–Wallack (15) Much Ado about
Nothing: *Benedict*–Wallack; My Uncle Foozle (16) School for Scandal:
Charles Surface–Wallack; Catherine and Petruchio: *Petruchio*–Wallack
(18) Maurice, the Woodcutter; Broken Sword (19) Married Life; No,
No; Love Laughs at Locksmiths (20) Agnes de Vere; Simpson and
Company (21) Robert Emmett, the Irish Patriot; Charles XII (22)
Irish Ambassador; Graveyard Murder (23) Soldier's Daughter; Lovers'
Quarrels (25) Mazeppa; Dumb Girl of Genoa (26) Pizarro; Secret
(27) Simpson and Company; Mazeppa (28) Honeymoon; Spanish
Exile
   Ap (1) Spanish Exile; Forest Rose: *Jonathan Ploughboy*–Silsbee (2)
Yankee Land: *Lot Sop Sago*–Silsbee; State Secrets (3) Wool Pedlar:
Deuteronomy–Silsbee; Boston Tea Party: *Jake Fuller*–Silsbee; Bumps:
Able Heartshorn–Silsbee; Jonathan in England: *Solomon Swap*–Silsbee

1 8 4 4 - 1 8 4 5

Mgr.: W. C. Forbes; *acting mgr.:* H. J. Conway; *scenist:* J. C. Lamb; *machinists:* Galbrath, Valentine. *Stock:* Charles, J. S., Collins, Fleming, W. M., Fuller, J. B., Hardy, W., Jones, W. G., M'Cutcheon, T., Maywood, R. C., Mitchell, W., Phillips, H. B., Radcliffe, T.; *Mrs.* Charles, J. S., Chippendale, W., Dearing, Forbes, W. C., Isherwood, H., Mossop, G.; *Misses* Celeste, Gannon, M.

SE: Louis and Gustave Ellsler: N 20-30, Ja 13; Herr Andre Cline: Ja 9-13; J. S. Silsbee: N 25-30; Henry Placide: D 16-21; J. B. Booth: D 23-31; Josephine Clifton: Ja 27-28, F 5-8; Seguin Opera Company (Mr. and Mrs. Arthur E. S. Seguin, Miss Moss, Messrs. Andrews, Frazer): Ja 29-F 15; Robinson's Equestrian Company: F 24-Mr 1.

N (18) Love's Sacrifice; Roland for an Oliver (19) Stranger; King's Gardener (20) Lovers' Quarrels; Crusaders*: *Leonards*–Ellsler Brothers; Married Bachelor (21) Crusaders: *Leonards*–Ellsler Brothers; Day after the Wedding; King's Gardener (22) Dumb Belle; Hercules of Brittany; New Footman; Ellsler Brothers (23) Barrack Room; Maiden's Vow; Ellsler Brothers (25) Yankee Land: *Lot Sop Sago*–Silsbee; Valentine and Orson: *Valentine*–L. Ellsler, *Green Knight*–G. Ellsler (26) Our Mary Anne; Man about Town; Chapter of Accidents: *Pierre*–L. Ellsler, *Pantalo*–G. Ellsler (27) Sam Slick: *Sam*–Silsbee; Sudden Thoughts (28) Wool Dealer: *Deuteronomy*–Sillsbee; Forest Rose: *Jonathan Ploughboy*–Silsbee (29) Red Wood: *Josh Doolittle*–Sillsbee; Rendezvous; Ellsler Brothers (30) Yankee Land: *Lot Sop Sago*–Silsbee; Bumps; Jonathan in England (Act II): *Solomon Swap*–Silsbee; Red Wood (Act I): *Josh Doolittle*–Sillsbee; Man about Town; Ellsler Brothers

D (2) Man of the World; New Footman (3) Rights of Women; Day after the Wedding; Turning the Tables (4) Love's Sacrifice; His Last Legs (5) Millionaire; Secret; Maiden's Vow (6) Rights of Women; Perfection; Pleasant Neighbors (7) King's Gardener; Nick of the Woods; Irish Tutor (9) Bride of Lammermoor; My Wife's Come (10) Millionaire; Tam O'Shanter; Day in Paris (11) Rob Roy MacGregor; My Wife's Second Floor (12) Man of the World; Nick of the Woods (13) Werner; Cramond Brig; New Footman (14) Pizarro; My Wife's Come (16) Poor Gentleman: *Ollapod*–Placide; My Neighbor's Wife (17) Is He Jealous?; Grandfather Whitehead: *Grandfather Whitehead*–Placide; Sleeping Draught (18) Speed the Plough: *Sir Abel Handy*–Placide; Uncle Sam: *Sam Hobbs*–Placide (19) John Bull: *Job Thornberry*–Placide; Bombastes Furioso: *General Bombastes*–Placide (20) Dead Shot; Grandfather Whitehead: *Grandfather Whitehead*–Placide; Uncle John: *Uncle John*–Placide (21) Paul Pry: *Colonel Hardy*–Placide; Anatomist: *Monsieur Le Medicen*–Placide (23) Richard III: *Richard*–Booth; My Wife's Come (24) New Way to Pay Old Debts: *Sir Giles Overreach*–Booth; My Wife's Second Floor (25) Brutus: *Brutus*–Booth; Forty Thieves (26) King Lear: *King Lear*–Booth (27) Othello: *Iago*–Booth; Irish Tutor (28) Bertram: *Bertram*–Booth; Forty Thieves (30) Riches: *Luke*–Booth; Amateurs and Actors: *Geoffrey*–Booth (31) Richard III: *Richard*–Booth; King's Gardener

Ja (1) Fraternal Discord; Fortunio (3) Our Mary Anne; Fortunio (4) Post of Honor; Waterman (6) Yemassee*; Fortunio (7) Yemassee; His Last Legs (8) Companion in Arms; Fortunio; College Boy (9) Follies of a Night; Lesson for Husbands; Roland for an Oliver; Herr Cline (11) Sweethearts and Wives; Fortunio; Herr Cline (13)

Follies of a Night; Companion in Arms; Herr Cline and Ellsler Brothers (14) Bath Road; Robert Macaire; College Boy (15) My Wife's
Come; New Footman; Putnam* (16) Putnam; Post of Honor; State
Secrets (17) Putnam; Simpson and Company (18) Putnam; Asmodeus*
(20) Putnam; Mazeppa (21) Putnam; White Milliner (22) Merchant
of Venice; Mysteries of Paris (23) My Wife's Come; Mysteries of
Paris (24) Putnam; His Last Legs (25) Asmodeus; Mazeppa (27)
Hunchback: *Julia*–Josephine Clifton; Companion in Arms (28) Stranger: *Mrs. Haller*–Josephine Clifton; My Wife's Come (29) Bohemian
Girl; Post of Honor (30) Bohemian Girl; Young Widow (31) Bohemian Girl; Rendezvous

F (1) Bohemian Girl; Irish Tutor (3) La Somnambula; Ballet de
Sham (4) Cinderella; His Last Legs (5) Lady of Lyons: *Pauline*–
Josephine Clifton; Dumb Belle (6) Bohemian Girl; Intrigue (7)
Postillion of Lonjumeau; Is He Jealous? (8) Partrician's Daughter*:
Lady Mabel–Josephine Clifton; Perfection (10) Massaniello; Young
Widow (11) La Somnambula; Sudden Thoughts (12) Asmodeus; Towers
of London* (13) Fra Diavolo; My Aunt (14) Love Spell; Postillion
of Lonjumeau (15) Fra Diavolo; Married Bachelor (17) Norman
Leslie*; Ballet de Sham (18) Norman Leslie; Irish Tutor (19) Follies
of a Night; Fortunio (20) William Tell; Pleasant Neighbors; Actress
of All Work (21) Towers of London; Mysteries of Paris (22) Columbus; State Secrets (24) My Wife's Come; Robinson's Equestrian
Company (25) Rendezvous; Robinson's Equestrian Company (26) Lottery Ticket; Robinson's Equestrian Company (27) Timour the Tartar;
Robinson's Equestrian Company

Mr (1) Mazeppa; Robinson's Equestrian Company; Virginny Mummy (3) Alma Mater; Black Eyed Susan (4) William Tell; Ben, the
Boatswain (5) Hunter of Savoy; Rival Pages; Blue Jackets (6) Carpenter of Rouen; Blue Jackets (7) My Uncle Foozle; Nature and Philosophy; Tom Cringle (8) Floating Beacon; Ballet de Sham; Rival Pages
(10) Rory O'More; Victorine (11) Happiest Day of My Life; Ballet
de Sham (12) Foundling of the Forest; Widow's Victim (13) Virginius;
Widow's Victim (14) Foundling of the Forest; My Uncle Foozle (15)
Happiest Day of My Life; Widow's Victim; Nature and Philosophy (17)
Jonathan Bradford; Ali Pacha (26) Soldier's Daughter; White Horse
of the Peppers (28) Golden Farmer; Lady and the Devil

1845-1846

Mgr.: W. C. Forbes; *scenist:* J. C. Lamb; *orch. leader:* F. C. Cook.
Stock: Allen, A. J., Anderton, E. W., Arnold, G. J., Byrne, J., Ellis, W.,
Fuller, J. B., Gowan, Hall, J. H., Hunt, C., Matthewes, T., Meeker, W.
H., Milot, Oxley, J.; *Mrs.* Anderson, D. C., Byrne, J., Clairville, Duven-
elle, Forbes, W. C., James, Matthewes, C., Maywood, M., Wray; *Misses*
Celeste, Matthewes, H.

SE: Clara Ellis: N 4-17; Dan Marble: N 24-D 1; Anna Cora Mowatt
and W. H. Crisp: D 4-30, Ja 17-28; Julia Turnbull: Ja 1-16; James
Hackett: Ja 10; Henry Placide: D 24-30; Mr. and Mrs. Charles Kean:
F 2-20.

N (3) Money; Charles II (4) Hunchback: *Julia*–Clara Ellis; Young
America (5) Lady of Lyons: *Pauline*–Clara Ellis; Caudle's Lectures
(6) Love Chase: *Constance*–Clara Ellis; Therese (8) Stranger: *Mrs.
Haller*–Clara Ellis; Caudle's Lectures (10) Evadne: *Evadne*–Clara
Ellis; Our Mary Anne (11) Merchant of Venice; Perfection (12) Wife:

Marianna–Clara Ellis; Loan of a Lover (13) Fazio: *Bianca*–Clara Ellis; Swiss Cottage (14) Old Heads and Young Hearts: *Lady Alice Hawthorn*–Clara Ellis; Loan of a Lover (15) Pizarro: *Elvira*–Clara Ellis; Dumb Belle (17) Wrecker's Daughter: *Marian*–Clara Ellis; Love Chase: *Constance*–Clara Ellis (18) Richard III; Two Queens (19) Time Works Wonders; Roland for an Oliver (20) Hamlet; Swiss Cottage (21) Time Works Wonders; Two Queens (22) Henry IV; Angel of the Attic (24) Sam Patch in France: *Sam Patch*–Marble; Backwoodsman: *Sampson Hardhead*–Marble (25) Jonathan in England: *Solomon Swap*–Marble; Black Eyed Susan: *William*–Marble (26) Hue and Cry: *Lot*–Marble; Angel of the Attic; Luke the Laborer: *Phillip*–Marble (27) Forest Rose: *Jonathan Ploughboy*–Marble; Perfection; All the World's a Stage: *Dickory*–Marble (28) People's Lawyer: *Solomon Shingle*–Marble; Peaceful Pelton: *Deuteronomy*–Marble; Swiss Cottage (29) Sam Patch in France: *Sam Patch*–Marble; Loan of a Lover; Black Eyed Susan: *William*–Marble

D (1) Hue and Cry: *Lot*–Marble; Larboard Finn: *Bob Stay*–Marble; All the World's a Stage: *Dickory*–Marble (2) Sweethearts and Wives; Rent Day (3) Paul Pry; Raising the Wind (4) Lady of Lyons: *Pauline*–Anna Cora Mowatt, *Claude*–Crisp; 'Twas I (5) Honeymoon: *Juliana*–Anna Cora Mowatt, *Duke of Aranza*–Crisp; Used Up: *Sir Charles Coldstream*–Crisp (6) Wife: *Mariana*–Anna Cora Mowatt, *Julian St. Pierre*–Crisp; Used Up: *Sir Charles Coldstream*–Crisp (8) Stranger: *Mrs. Haller*–Anna Cora Mowatt, *Stranger*–Crisp; Ladder of Love (9) Lady of Lyons: *Pauline*–Anna Cora Mowatt, *Claude*–Crisp; Raising the Wind: *Jeremy Diddler*–Crisp (10) Romeo and Juliet: *Juliet*–Anna Cora Mowatt, *Romeo*–Crisp; 'Twas I (11) School for Scandal: *Lady Teazle*–Anna Cora Mowatt, *Charles Surface*–Crisp; Ladder of Love (12) Bride of Lammermoor; *Lucy Ashton*–Anna Cora Mowatt, *Edgar*–Crisp; Faint Heart Ne'er Won Fair Lady: *Duchess*–Anna Cora Mowatt, *Ruy Gomez*–Crisp (13) London Assurance: *Grace Harkaway*–Anna Cora Mowatt, *Dazzle*–Crisp; Raising the Wind: *Jeremy Diddler*–Crisp (15) Fashion *Gertrude*–Anna Cora Mowatt, *Count Jolimaitre*–Crisp; Robert Macaire: *Robert*–Crisp (16) Fashion: *Gertrude*–Anna Cora Mowatt, *Count Jolimaitre*–Crisp; Dumb Belle (17) Romeo and Juliet: *Juliet*–Anna Cora Mowatt, *Romeo*–Crisp; Used Up: *Sir Charles Coldstream*–Crisp (18) Fashion: *Gertrude*–Anna Cora Mowatt, *Count Jolimaitre*–Crisp; Swiss Cottage (19) Wives as They Were and Maids as They Are; Blue Dominoes (20) Fashion: *Gertrude*–Anna Cora Mowatt, *Count Jolimaitre*–Crisp; Blue Dominoes (22) Jane Shore: *Lord Hastings*–Crisp; Weathercock: *Tristram Fickle*–Crisp (23) Bride of Lammermoor: *Lucy Ashton*–Anna Cora Mowatt, *Edgar*–Crisp; Faint Heart Ne'er Won Fair Lady: *Duchess*–Anna Cora Mowatt, *Ruy Gomez*–Crisp (24) School for Scandal: *Lady Teazle*–Anna Cora Mowatt, *Charles Surface*–Crisp, *Sir Peter Teazle*–Placide; Double Bedded Room (25) Don Caesar de Bazan: *Maritana*–Anna Cora Mowatt, *Don Caesar*–Crisp; Grandfather Whitehead: *Grandfather Whitehead*–Placide (27) London Assurance: *Grace Harkaway*–Anna Cora Mowatt, *Dazzle*–Crisp, *Sir Harcourt*–Placide (29) Venice Preserved: *Belvidera*–Anna Cora Mowatt, *Pierre*–Crisp; Uncle John: *Uncle John*–Placide (30) West End: *Norah*–Anna Cora Mowatt, *Percy Ardent*–Crisp, *Sir William Daventry*–Placide; Uncle Sam: *Uncle Sam*–Placide (31) Damon and Pythias; Blue Dominoes

Ja (1) La Bayadere: *Zoloe*–Julia Turnbull; My Handsome Husband (2-3) Momentous Question; La Bayadere: *Zoloe*–Julia Turnbull (5`

Home Again; Secret; La Cracovienne; dances by Julia Turnbull (6)
Iron Chest; King and I; La Cracovienne; dances by Julia Turnbull
(7) Lucille; Charles II; dances by Julia Turnbull (8) William Tell;
No, No; dances by Julia Turnbull (9) Virginius; Rendezvous; dances
by Julia Turnbull (10) Henry IV: *Falstaff*–Hackett; Monsieur Mallett:
Monsieur Mallett–Hackett; dances by Julia Turnbull (12) Point of
Honor; Buy It Dear, 'Tis Made of Cashmere; dances by Julia Turnbull
(13) Home Again; Buy It Dear, 'Tis Made of Cashmere; dances by Julia
Turnbull; Two Queens (14) Catherine and Petruchio; Momentous Ques-
tion; dances by Julia Turnbull (15) Dumb Girl of Genoa: *Pyefinch*–
Julia Turnbull; King and I; Buy It Dear, 'Tis Made of Cashmere; dances
by Julia Turnbull (16) New Way to Pay Old Debts; Buy It Dear, 'Tis
Made of Cashmere; dances by Julia Turnbull (17) Romeo and Juliet:
Juliet–Anna Cora Mowatt, *Romeo*–Crisp; Raising the Wind: *Jeremy
Diddler*–Crisp (19) Hunchback: *Julia*–Anna Cora Mowatt, *Sir Thomas*–
Crisp; Used Up: *Sir Charles Coldstream*–Crisp (20) Honeymoon:
Juliana–Anna Cora Mowatt, *Duke of Aranza*–Crisp; Don Caesar de
Bazan: *Maritana*–Anna Cora Mowatt, *Don Caesar*–Crisp (21) Man and
Wife: *Helen*–Anna Cora Mowatt, *Charles Austencourt*–Crisp; Turn Out;
Richard III (22) Fashion: *Gertrude*–Anna Cora Mowatt, *Count
Jolimaitre*–Crisp; King and I (23) Richelieu; Review (24) Wife:
Mariana–Anna Cora Mowatt, *Julian St. Piere*–Crisp; Uncle Sam (26)
Love's Sacrifice: *Margaret Elmore*–Anna Cora Mowatt, *St. Lo*–Crisp;
Used Up: *Sir Charles Coldstream*–Crisp (27) Man and Wife: *Helen*–
Anna Cora Mowatt, *Charles Austencourt*–Crisp; Day after the Wedding:
Lady Freelove–Anna Cora Mowatt, *Colonel Freelove*–Crisp (28) Bride
of Lammermoor: *Lucy Ashton*–Anna Cora Mowatt, *Edgar*–Crisp; Faint
Heart Ne'er Won Fair Lady: *Ruy Gomez*–Crisp, *Duchess*–Anna Cora
Mowatt (29) Spy; Farmer's Story (30) Town and Country; Maidens,
Beware (31) Time Works Wonders; Angel of the Attic

F (2) Stranger: *Stranger*–Kean, *Mrs. Haller*–Mrs. Kean; Turn Out
(3) Much Ado about Nothing: *Benedict*–Kean, *Beatrice*–Mrs. Kean; No,
No (4) Ladder of Love; Macbeth: *Macbeth*–Kean, *Lady Macbeth*–Mrs.
Kean (5) Hunchback: *Sir Thomas*–Kean, *Julia*–Mrs. Kean; 'Twas I
(6) As You Like It: *Jacquez*–Kean, *Rosalind*–Mrs. Kean; Swiss Cottage
(7) Lady of Lyons: *Claude*–Kean, *Pauline*–Mrs. Kean; Dumb Belle (9)
Gamester: *Beverly*–Kean, *Mrs. Beverly*–Mrs. Kean; Follies of a Night:
Duke–Kean, *Duchess*–Mrs. Kean (10) Ion: *Ion*–Mrs. Kean, *Adrastos*–
Kean; Uncle Sam (11) Merchant of Venice: *Shylock*–Kean, *Portia*–Mrs.
Kean; Valet de Sham (12) Twelfth Night: *Duke Orsino*–Kean, *Viola*–
Mrs. Kean; My Handsome Husband (13) Much Ado about Nothing:
Benedict–Kean, *Beatrice*–Mrs. Kean; Two Queens (14) Romeo and
Juliet: *Romeo*–Kean, *Juliet*–Mrs. Kean; No, No (16) Hamlet: *Hamlet*–
Kean, *Ophelia*–Mrs. Kean; Our Mary Anne (17) Ion: *Ion*–Mrs. Kean,
Adrastos–Kean; Honeymoon: *Duke of Aranza*–Kean, *Juliana*–Mrs. Kean
(18) Wonder: *Don Felix*–Kean, *Violante*–Mrs. Kean; Somebody Else
(19) Macbeth: *Macbeth*–Kean, *Lady Macbeth*–Mrs. Kean; Turn Out
(20) Gamester: *Beverly*–Kean, *Mrs. Beverly*–Mrs. Kean; Follies of a
Night: *Duke*–Kean, *Duchess*–Mrs. Kean (21) Fashion; Somebody Else
(23) Rob Roy MacGregor; Corporal's Wedding (24) Wives as They
Were and Maids as They Are; Loan of a Lover (25) Cricket on the
Hearth; 'Twas I; You Can't Marry Your Grandmother (26) Barrack
Room; Cricket on the Hearth; Corporal's Wedding

1 8 4 6 - 1 8 4 7

Mgr.: W. C. Forbes; *acting mgr.:* J. B. Fuller; *orch. leader:* A. Gambati; *treas.:* Dennison. *Stock:* De Walden, T. B., Ellis, W., Meeker, W. H., Muillar, Oxley, J., Smith, G. H., Ward, T.; *Mrs.* Eastcott, Ellis, W., Forbes, W. C., Frary, Hardwick, McGowan, McLean, Wray; *Misses* Homer, Lee, M. A.

SE: Clara Ellis: N 18-D 7; J. W. Wallack: D 1-7; Anna Cora Mowatt and Edward L. Davenport: D 8-21; John Collins: D 22-Ja 2; John Sloman: Ja 4-13; Henry Placide: Ja 13-16; James R. Anderson: Ja 18-23; Edwin Forrest: Ja 25-F 6; Dan Marble: F 9-17; Seguin Opera Company (Mr. and Mrs. Arthur E. S. Seguin, Messrs. Frazer, G. Holman, Meyer, Miss Adelaide Phillips, and full chorus from Park Theatre, New York City): F 22-Mr 6.

N (5) Honeymoon; Raising the Wind (6) Hamlet (7) Iron Chest; Sweethearts and Wives (9) Is He Jealous?; Giselle; Rendezvous (10) Dead Shot; Giselle; Day in Paris (11) Our Mary Anne; Griselle; Lend Me Five Shillings (12) Perfection; Giselle; Uncle Sam (13) Barrack Room; Lend Me Five Shillings; La Fleur de Champ (14) Lady and the Devil; Turned Head; La Fleur de Champ (16) Happiest Day of My Life; Lend Me Five Shillings; Wept of Wish-ton-Wish* (17) Clari; La Fleur de Champ; Lottery Ticket (18) Soldier's Daughter: *Widow Cheerly*–Clara Ellis; Giselle (19) Stranger: *Mrs. Haller*–Clara Ellis; Dead Shot (20) Day after the Wedding; Wept of Wish-ton-Wish; Done Brown (21) Old Heads and Young Hearts: *Lady Alice*–Clara Ellis; Done Brown (23) Raising the Wind; Loan of a Lover; La Bayadere (24) Wrecker's Daughter: *Marian*–Clara Ellis; Make Your Wills (25) Money: *Clara*–Clara Ellis; Turned Head (26) Evadne: *Evadne*–Clara Ellis; Make Your Wills (27) Mary Stuart, Queen of Scotland*: *Mary*–Clara Ellis; Illustrious Stranger (28) King of the Commoners: *Madeline*–Clara Ellis; Uncle Sam

D (1) Pizarro: *Rolla*–Wallack, *Elvira*–Clara Ellis; Love, Law and Physic (2) Wife: *Mariana*–Clara Ellis, *Julian St. Pierre*–Wallack; My Aunt: *Dick Dashall*–Wallack (3) Wonder: *Don Felix*–Wallack, *Donna Violante*–Clara Ellis; Rent Day: *Martin Heywood*–Wallack (4) Hamlet: *Hamlet*–Wallack, *Queen*–Clara Ellis; Secret (5) King of the Commoners: *King James*–Wallack, *Madeline*–Clara Ellis; Swiss Swains (7) Richard III: *Richard*–Wallack, *Queen*–Clara Ellis; Ernestine: *Ernestine*–Clara Ellis, *Frederick*–Wallack (8) Romeo and Juliet: *Juliet*–Anna Cora Mowatt, *Romeo*–Davenport; Raising the Wind (9) Much Ado about Nothing: *Beatrice*–Anna Cora Mowatt, *Benedict*–Davenport; My Wife's Second Floor (10) Fazio: *Bianca*–Anna Cora Mowatt, *Fazio*–Davenport; Make Yours Wills (11) Love's Sacrifice: *Margaret Elmore*–Anna Cora Mowatt, *Matthew Elmore*–Davenport; Swiss Swains (12) Hunchback: *Julia*–Anna Cora Mowatt, *Sir Thomas*–Davenport; Black Eyed Susan: *William*–Davenport (14) Love: *Countess*–Anna Cora Mowatt, *Huron*–Davenport; Trumpeter's Daughter: *Madelon*–Anna Cora Mowatt, *Phillepot*–Davenport (15) Lady of Lyons: *Pauline*–Anna Cora Mowatt, *Claude*–Davenport; Black Eyed Susan: *William*–Davenport (16) Fashion: *Gertrude*–Anna Cora Mowatt, *Count Jolimaitre*–Davenport; Swiss Swains (17) Jane Shore: *Jane Shore*–Anna Cora Mowatt, *Dumont*–Davenport; My Wife's Second Floor (18) Stranger: *Stranger*–Davenport, *Mrs. Haller*–Anna Cora Mowatt; Honeymoon: *Juliana*–Anna Cora Mowatt, *Duke of Aranza*–Davenport (19) Bride of Lammermoor: *Lucy*

Ashton–Anna Cora Mowatt, *Edgar*–Davenport; Trumpeter's Daughter: *Madelon*–Anna Cora Mowatt, *Phillepot*–Davenport; Uncle Sam (21) Wives as They Were and Maids as They Are: *Miss Dorrillon*–Anna Cora Mowatt, *Bronzeley*–Davenport; Did You Ever Send Your Wife to Mount Pleasant?* (22) Love, Law and Physic; Irish Ambassador: *Sir Patrick O'Plenipo*–Collins; Teddy, the Tiler: *Teddy*–Collins (23) My Wife's Second Floor; Born to Good Luck: *Paudeen O'Rafferty*–Collins; How to Pay the Rent: *Morgan Rattler*–Collins (24) Nervous Man and the Man of Nerve: *McShane*–Collins; His Last Legs: *O'Callaghan*–Collins; Turned Head (25) Born to Good Luck: *Paudeen O'Rafferty*–Collins; Teddy, the Tiler: *Teddy*–Collins; Done Brown (26) Irish Attorney: *Pierce O'Hara*–Collins; How to Pay the Rent: *Morgan Rattler*–Collins (28) Soldier of Fortune: *Captain O'Rourke*–Collins; Irish Post: *Terrance O'Grady*–Collins; Illustrious Stranger (29) Born to Good Luck: *Paudeen O'Rafferty*–Collins; Irish Post: *Terrance O'Grady*–Collins; Young Ambassador (30) Irish Attorney: *Pierce O'Hara*–Collins; His Last Legs: *O'Callaghan*–Collins; Boots at the Swan (31) Soldier of Fortune: *Captain O'Rourke*–Collins; Teddy, the Tiler: *Teddy*–Collins; Pleasant Neighbors

Ja (1) Nervous Man and the Man of Nerve: *McShane*–Collins; Happy Man: *Paddy Murphy*–Collins; You Can't Marry Your Grandmother (2) Irish Ambassador: *Sir Patrick O'Plenipo*–Collins; How to Pay the Rent: *Morgan Rattler*–Collins; Happy Man: *Paddy Murphy*–Collins (4) Wizard of the Wave; Wandering Minstrel: *Jem Baggs*–Sloman (5) Wizard of the Wave; Lottery Ticket: *Wormwood*–Sloman (6) Wizard of the Wave; Wandering Minstrel: *Jem Baggs*–Sloman (7) Youthful Queen; Family Jars: *Delph*–Sloman; Animal Magnetism: *La Fleur*–Sloman (8) Imagination; Fish out of Water: *Sam Savory*–Sloman; Patriot's Wife (9) Soldier's Daughter: *Timothy Quaint*–Sloman; Patriot's Wife (11) My Master's Rival: *Paul Shack*–Sloman; Deaf as a Post: *Tristram Snappy*–Sloman; King of Clubs: *Tim*–Sloman (12) Wizard of the Wave; Young America (13) Rivals: *Sir Anthony Absolute*–Placide; Palo Alto (14) Double Bedded Room: *Dulcimer Pipes*–Placide; Napoleon's Old Guard: *Haversack*–Placide; Palo Alto (15) School for Scandal: *Sir Peter Teazle*–Placide; Prophecy (16) West End: *Sir William Daventry*–Placide; Napoleon's Old Guard: *Haversack*–Placide (18) Hamlet: *Hamlet*–Anderson; My Wife's Second Floor (19) Lady of Lyons: *Claude*–Anderson; Did You Ever Send Your Wife to Mount Pleasant? (20) Stranger: *Stranger*–Anderson; Boots at the Swan (21) Robbers: *Charles De Moor*–Anderson; Turned Head (22) Elder Brother: *Charles*–Anderson; Lady of Lyons: *Claude*–Anderson (23) Elder Brother: *Charles*–Anderson; Raising the Wind (25) Othello: *Othello*–Forrest; Boots at the Swan (26) King Lear: *King Lear*–Forrest; Did You Ever Send Your Wife to Mount Pleasant? (27) Damon and Pythias: *Damon*–Forrest; Uncle Sam (28) Hamlet: *Hamlet*–Forrest; Lottery Ticket (29) Macbeth: *Macbeth*–Forrest; Wolf and Lamb (30) Metamora: *Metamora*–Forrest; Make Your Wills

F (1) Metamora: *Metamora*–Forrest; Spectre Bridegroom (2) Metamora: *Metamora*–Forrest; Lottery Ticket (3) Gladiator: *Spartacus*–Forrest; Secret (4) Gladiator: *Spartacus*–Forrest; Dumb Belle (5) Macbeth: *Macbeth*–Forrest; Dumb Belle (6) Damon and Pythias: *Damon*–Forrest; Spectre Bridegroom (8) Skeleton Hand; Young Widow; Bob Short (9) Sam Patch in France: *Sam Patch*–Marble; Backwoods-

man: *Sampson Hardhead*–Marble; Animal Magnetism (10) Simpson
and Company; Forest Rose: *Jonathan Ploughboy*–Marble; Uncle Foozle's
Wedding Day (11) Hue and Cry: *Lot*–Marble; Black Eyed Susan:
William–Marble; Young Widow (12) Jonathan in England: *Solomon
Swap*–Marble; All the World's a Stage: *Dickory*–Marble; Married Rake
(13) Wool Dealer: *Deuteronomy*–Marble; Backwoodsman: *Sampson
Hardhead*–Marble; You Can't Marry Your Grandmother (15) Family
Ties: *Josh Sims*–Marble; Fortune's Frolic: *Robin Roughead*–Marble;
All the World's a Stage: *Dickory*–Marble (16) Spectre Bridegroom;
Wool Dealer: *Deuteronomy*–Marble; Black Eyed Susan: *William*–Marble
(17) Forest Rose: *Jonathan Ploughboy*–Marble; Fortune's Frolic: *Robin
Roughead*–Marble; Married Rake (22) La Somnambula; Wolf and the
Lamb (23) Postillion of Lonjumeau; Secret (24) Bohemian Girl;
Pleasant Neighbors (25) Norma; farce (26) Don Pasquale; farce
(27) Lovers' Quarrels; La Somnambula

Mr (1) Brewer of Preston; Blue Devils (2) Norma; farce (4) Fra
Diavolo; farce (5) Elixir of Love; Massaniello (Act II) (6) Norma;
Cinderella (Act I); Olympic Revels

1847-1848

Mgrs.: Lehman Family (Mons. Christien, Madame Anna, Mlles.
Adelaide, Caroline, Flora, Julie, Mathilda Lehman, supported by Messrs.
Charles Winther, Joseph Marzetti, Louis Ferrin, Eugene Carriere, Henry
Herz, Camillo Sivori, and Alcedid): N 4-17; Henry W. Preston (D 13-
Mr 28); *acting mgr.:* Thomas Ward; *orch. leader:* Henry Marks. *Stock:*
Bass, C., Crisp, W. H., Fredericks, W. S., Fuller, J. B., Peck, Robinson,
A., Shelley, W., Stuart, C.; *Mrs.* Crisp, W. H., McLean, Ward, T.; *Misses*
Amilee, Vallee, H.

SE: Charles Dibden Pitt: D 13-30; George Vandenhoff: Ja 4-7; John
Collins: Ja 6-11; Madame Bishop Opera Troupe (Mesdames Anna
Bishop, Assoluto di Cartello, M. Korinski, Messrs. William F. Brough,
Valtellina, A. Andrews, Bennetti, W. H. Reeves; R. N. C. Boscha,
Director): Ja 12-27; Madame Augusta Ballet Troupe (Madame Augusta,
Mons. Frederick, M. DeBar): F 14-24, Mr 22-28.

N (4-17) Lehman Family

D (13) Lady of Lyons: *Claude*–Pitt (20) Soldier's Daughter: *Gov-
ernor Heartall*–Pitt; King's Gardener (21) Stranger: *Stranger*–Pitt;
Catherine and Petruchio: *Petruchio*–Pitt (22) Richard III: *Richard*–
Pitt; farce (24) Richard III: *Richard*–Pitt; Pleasant Neighbors (25)
Hamlet: *Hamlet*–Pitt; Hunter of the Alps: *Felix*–Pitt (28) Hamlet:
Hamlet–Pitt; Swiss Cottage (29) Romeo and Juliet: *Romeo*–Pitt;
Honeymoon: *Duke of Aranza*–Pitt (30) Pizarro: *Rolla*–Pitt; Moun-
taineers: *Octavian*–Pitt (31) Lady of Lyons

Ja (1) Merchant of Venice (4) Belle's Stratagem: *Doricourt*–Van-
denhoff (5) Wonder: *Don Felix*–Vandenhoff; Secret (6) Born to Good
Luck: *Paudeen O'Rafferty*–Collins; Day after the Wedding (7) Liar:
Young Wilding–Vandenhoff; Dead Shot (8) Irish Ambassador: *Sir
Patrick O'Plenipo*–Collins; Born to Good Luck: *Paudeen O'Rafferty*–
Collins (10) Irish Post: *Terrance O'Grady*–Collins; Teddy, the Tiler:
Teddy–Collins; His Last Legs: *O'Callaghan*–Collins (11) How to Pay
the Rent: *Morgan Rattler*–Collins; Irish Ambassador: *Sir Patrick
O'Plenipo*–Collins; Dead Shot (12-14) La Somnambula; farce (15, 17-
18) Linda; Lady and the Devil (19) Soldier's Daughter; Raising the

Wind (20) Lucrezia Borgia; Raising the Wind (21) Love Spell; Anna
Bolena; Tancredi (22) Norma; La Somnambula (Act III) (24) Lucrezia
Borgia; Maid of Artoris (25) Maid of Artoris (26) Linda (27) La
Somnambula; Trancredi (31) Hunchback; Old Soldier

F (1) Man of the World; Simpson and Company (2-3) Wife; Box
and Cox (4) Henry IV; Faint Heart Ne'er Won Fair Lady (5) Man
of the World; Raising the Wind (7) School for Scandal; Don Caesar
de Bazan (8) Othello; Forty and Fifty (9) Sweethearts and Wives;
Box and Cox; Faint Heart Ne'er Won Fair Lady (11) Bride of Lam-
mermoor; Used Up (14-15) Faint Heart Ne'er Won Fair Lady; Nicholas
Flam, Attorney-at-Law; Giselle; Augusta Ballet Troupe (16) Double
Bedded Room; Giselle; Married Rake; Augusta Ballet Troupe (18)
Miller's Maid; Weathercock; Lend Me a Dollar; Augusta Ballet Troupe
(21) Artful Dodger; Nathalie; Augusta Ballet Troupe (22) Hamlet;
Rendezvous; Augusta Ballet Troupe (23) Therese; Artful Dodger;
Young Widow; Augusta Ballet Troupe (24) Nathalie; Perfection;
Rendezvous; Pas de Trois; Augusta Ballet Troupe

Mr (2-4) Farces and other entertainments (6) Iron Chest; farce
(7-15) Farces and other entertainments (16) Two Gregories; Merchant
of Venice (Act IV); Our Mary Anne (17) Petite Comedy; farces (20)
Honeymoon; My Uncle Foozle (22-23) Artful Dodger; Sleeping Beauty;
Augusta Ballet Troupe (24) Diana; Goddess of the Chase; Spirit of
the Fountain; Nathalie; Augusta Ballet Troupe (28) Brigand; My
Aunt; Robert Macaire; Augusta Ballet Troupe

1848-1849

Mgrs.: Alexander Robinson and G. N. Eldred (O 25-My 20); *acting
mgr.:* C. W. Hield; *wardrobist:* A. J. Allen. *Stock:* Cunningham, P. C.,
McDougall, R. W., Ollier, J., Sloman, J., Wood, C., Wood, J. S., Yates;
Mrs. Bernard, C., Hield, C. W., Wood, C.; *Misses* Parker, A., Pullman,
S. *Mgr.:* J. Heron (My 21-28).

SE: James E. Murdoch: O 25-N 1; Viennoise Children (directed by
Josephine Weiss): N 13-25, D 4-5, Mr 28-Ap 3; Seguin Opera Company
(Mr. and Mrs. Arthur E. S. Seguin, Messrs. G. Holman, W. H. Reeves,
Mesdames H. Phillips, S. Leach): D 7-16, Ja 1-6; Ravel Family (Antoine,
Dominique, Gabriel, Gean, Francois, Jerome Ravel, Louis Marzetti, Jean
Pebernard, and others): D 18-28; John Collins and Mr. and Mrs. Leati:
D 30; Charles William Macready: Ja 8-17; Mr. and Mrs. Charles
Dibden Pitt: Ja 29-F 2; Kilmeste Family: F 26-Mr 5; Tedesco Opera
Company (Madame Fortunata Tedesco, Mlle. Rosina Pico, Monsieur
Adelino Vietti, and others): Mr 14-15; Madame Bishop Opera Troupe
(Mesdames Anna Bishop, Assoluto di Cartello, M. Korinski, Messrs.
William F. Brough, A. Andrews, Valtellina, Bennetti, W. H. Reeves;
R. N. C. Boscha, director): Mr 16-24; Bedouin Arabs Company (M. S.
Phillips, mgr.): Ap 16-21; Herr Alexander: My 7-15; Heron Family
(Agnes and J. Heron, and others): My 21-28.

O (25) Honeymoon: *Duke of Aranza*–Murdoch (26) Lady of Lyons:
Claude–Murdoch; Vermont Wool Dealer (28) Romeo and Juliet: *Romeo*–
Murdoch; Faint Heart Ne'er Won Fair Lady (30) Lady of Lyons:
Claude–Murdoch; Forest Rose (31) Hamlet: *Hamlet*–Murdoch; Forest
Rose

N (1) Romeo and Juliet: *Romeo*–Murdoch; Honeymoon: *Duke of
Aranza*–Murdoch (2) Faint Heart Ne'er Won Fair Lady; Lady and the

Devil; Robert Macaire (3) Lady and the Devil; Luke the Laborer (13-25) Viennoise Children (27-28) Rob Roy MacGregor; Momentous Question (29) Venice Preserved; Irish Tutor (30) Barrack Room; Irish Tutor; Warlock of the Glen

D (1) Venice Preserved; Irish Tutor (2) Charles II; Warlock of the Glen (4) Viennoise Children; farce (5) Cramond Brig; Day after the Wedding; Viennoise Children (7) Bohemian Girl (8) La Somnambula (9) Norma (11) Bohemian Girl (12) L'Elisir d'Amore; Cramond Brig (13) Norma (14) Daughter of the Regiment (16) Fra Diavolo (18-19) Ravel Family (20-21) Douglas; Ravel Family (22-23) Love in Humble Life; Ravel Family (25) How Do You Manage?; Ravel Family (27-28) Who Do They Take Me For?; Ravel Family (30) Teddy, the Tiler: *Teddy*–Collins; musical concert by Collins and Mr. and Mrs. Leati

Ja (1) Fra Diavolo; My Aunt (3) Cinderella (4) Fra Diavolo; Massaniello (Act II) (5) La Somnambula; Olympic Revels (6) Der Freischutz; Olympic Revels (8) Macbeth: *Macbeth*–Macready (10) Richelieu: *Richelieu*–Macready (11) Stranger: *Stranger*–Macready; Youthful Queen (12) Hamlet: *Hamlet*–Macready; Youthful Queen (15) Merchant of Venice: *Shylock*–Macready; Cramond Brig (17) Werner: *Werner*–Macready; Mysterious Visitor (29) Hamlet: *Hamlet*–Pitt; Dead Shot: *Louisa Lovetrick*–Mrs. Pitt (30) Othello: *Othello*–Pitt; Hunting a Turtle: *Mrs. Turtle*–Mrs. Pitt (31) Iron Chest: *Sir Edward Mortimer*–Pitt; Dead Shot: *Louisa Lovetrick*–Mrs. Pitt

F (1) Pizarro: *Rolla*–Pitt; Hunting a Turtle: *Mrs. Turtle*–Mrs. Pitt (2) Richard III: *Richard*–Pitt; Husband at Sight: *Catherine*–Mrs. Pitt (25-Mr 5) Kilmeste Family

Mr (14-15) Tedesco Opera Company in concerts (16-24) Madame Bishop Opera Troupe in concerts (28-Ap 3) Vennoise Children

Ap (16-21) Bedouin Arabs Company

My (7-15) Herr Alexander (21) Old and Young; Waterman; Heron Family (22-23) Born to Good Luck; Day in Paris; Heron Family (24) Happy Man; Young Widow; Heron Family (25) Swiss Cottage; Deaf and Dumb; Heron Family (28) Richard III (Acts IV-V); Irish Tutor; Cobbler; Heron Family

1 8 4 9 - 1 8 5 0

Mgrs.: A. Macallister; *stage mgr.:* E. W. Anderton (D 10-Ja 14); F. C. Adams (Ja 24-My 4); *acting mgr.:* H. V. Lovell; *orch. leader:* Brauer. *Stock:* Bellamy, W. H., Chippendale, W., Crocker, J. W., Douglas W. B., Edwards, H., Gallot, J., Henkins, H., Kames, McDougall, R. W., Raymond, J. T., Thompson, W. C., Watson, C., Wesley; *Mrs.* Carpenter, Lovell, H. V., Montgomery, Penson; *Misses* Amilee, Carpenter.

SE: A. Macallister: D 10-Ja 14; William M. Fleming: F 8-11; Creole Minstrels: F 8-11; J. B. Booth: F 12-16; Master Edwin Booth: F 16; Fanny Davenport, Edward L. Davenport and Andrew Jackson Neafie: Mr 4-16; James Hudson: Mr 18-23; Havana Italian Opera Company (Signoras Fortunata Tedesco, Balbina Steffenone, Elisa Costini, Louisa Bellini; Signors Lorenzo Salvi, Dominico Colletti, Timoleon Baratini, Dominico Lorini, Ignazio Marini, Luigi Martinelli, Vicenzo Locatelli, Pietro Condi, Bottesini, Frederico Badiali, mgr.; Misses Angela Bossio, Carolina Vietti; Luigi Arditi, director): Mr 26-Ap 2; Charlotte Cushman (supported by Charles Walter Couldock): Ap 15-24.

D (10-Ja 14) A. Macallister, Prestidator

Ja (24) Stranger; Wilful Murder (25) Hunchback; Box and Cox (26) Lady of Lyons; Dead Shot (28) Rivals; Bamboozling (29) Othello; Phantom Breakfast (30) Honeymoon; Lottery Ticket (31) Lady of Lyons; Phantom Breakfast

F (1) Romeo and Juliet; Wilful Murder (2) She Stoops to Conquer; Tom Noddy's Secret (4) Richard III; Practical Man (5ᵀ) Money; Dead Shot (6) Wife; Young England (7) Rivals; Tom Noddy's Secret; Love's Sacrifice (8) Hamlet: *Hamlet*–Fleming; concert by Creole Minstrels (9) King Lear: *King Lear*–Fleming; concert by Creole Minstrels (11) Gamester: *Beverly*–Fleming; Honeymoon: *Duke of Aranza*–Fleming; concert by Creole Minstrels (12) New Way to Pay Old Debts: *Sir Giles Overreach*–Booth; Spectre Bridegroom (13) Richard III: *Richard*–Booth; Young America (14) Bertram: *Bertram*–Booth; Practical Man (15) Othello: *Iago*–Booth; Poor Pillicoddy (16) Iron Chest: *Sir Edward Mortimer*–Booth, *Wilford*–Master Edwin Booth; Mayor of Garratt: *Jerry Sneak*–Booth

Mr (4) Love: *Countess*–Fanny Davenport, *Huron*–Neafie; Lend Me Five Shillings (5) Hunchback: *Julia*–Fanny Davenport, *Sir Thomas*–Neafie; Faint Heart Ne'er Won Fair Lady (6) Love: *Countess*–Fanny Davenport, *Huron*–Neafie; Raising the Wind (7) Romeo and Juliet: *Juliet*–Fanny Davenport, *Romeo*–Neafie; Mother and Child Are Doing Well (8) Lady of Lyons: *Pauline*–Fanny Davenport, *Claude*–Neafie; Eton Boy (9) Maid of Mariendorpt*: *Metta*–Fanny Davenport, *General Kleiner*–Edward L. Davenport (11) Gamester: *Mrs. Beverly*–Fanny Davenport, *Beverly*–Neafie; Wilful Murder (12) Wife: *Mariana*–Fanny Davenport, *Julian St. Pierre*–Neafie; Spectre Bridegroom (13) Evadne: *Evadne*–Fanny Davenport, *Ludovica*–Neafie; Mother and Child Are Doing Well (14) Much Ado about Nothing: *Beatrice*–Fanny Davenport, *Benedict*–Neafie; Eton Boy (15) Maid of Mariendorpt: *Metta*–Fanny Davenport, *General Kleiner*–Neafie (16) Roman Father: *Horatio*–Fanny Davenport, *Horatius*–Neafie; Love Chase: *Constance*–Fanny Davenport, *Wildrake*–Neafie (18) Knight of Arva: *Connor*–Hudson; Dumb Belle; Irish Lion: *Tim Moore*–Hudson (19) Born to Good Luck: *Paudeen O'Rafferty*–Hudson; His Last Legs: *O'Callaghan*–Hudson (20) Knight of Arva: *Connor*–Hudson; Irish Secretary: *Paddy O'Rafferty*–Hudson; Day after the Wedding (21) How to Pay the Rent: *Morgan Rattler*–Hudson; Irish Lion: *Tim Moore*–Hudson; Lady and the Devil (22) Irish Secretary: *Paddy O'Rafferty*–Hudson; His Last Legs: *O'Callaghan*–Hudson; Raising the Wind (23) Soldier of Fortune: *Captain O'Rourke*–Hudson; Irish Recruit: *Dermot*–Hudson; Catherine and Petruchio: *Petruchio*–Hudson (26-27) Norma

Ap (1) Lucrezia Borgia (2) Ernani (15) Stranger: *Mrs. Haller*–Charlotte Cushman; College Boy (16) Macbeth: *Lady Macbeth*–Charlotte Cushman; Lottery Ticket (17) As You Like It: *Rosalind*–Charlotte Cushman; Dead Shot (18) Lady of Lyons: *Pauline*–Charlotte Cushman; Tom Noddy's Secret (19) Guy Mannering: *Meg Merrilies*–Charlotte Cushman; Perfection (20) Macbeth: *Lady Macbeth*–Charlotte Cushman; Honeymoon: *Juliana*–Charlotte Cushman (22) Guy Mannering: *Meg Merrilies*–Charlotte Cushman; Poor Pillicoddy (23) Ion: *Ion*–Charlotte Cushman; Young America (24) Henry VIII: *Catherine*–Charlotte Cushman; Simpson and Company: *Mrs. Simpson*–Charlotte Cushman (26) Love's Sacrifice; Hunting a Turtle (27) Poor Pillicoddy; Napoleon's Old Guard; Naval Engagements (29) Dombey and Son; Jacobite (30) Dombey and Son; Roland for an Oliver

My (1) Dombey and Son; Simpson and Company (2) Major Jones' Courtship*; Dombey and Son (3) Major Jones' Courtship; Woman— Her Love! Her Faith! Her Trials! (4) She Stoops to Conquer; Napoleon's Old Guard

1850-1851

Mgr.: H. S. Smith; *acting mgr.:* C. K. Mason. *Stock:* Brown, Clarke, F., Crocker, J. W., Cullen, Dearing, Ellsler, J., Jefferson, J. J., Josephs, Linden, R., Ollier, J., Ryan, R., Ryder, W., Walcot, C. M., Sr., Weaver, J. H.; *Mrs.* Chapman, Dearing, Jefferson, J. J., Myers; *Misses* Clarke, Dearing, E., Dearing, F., Lewis, E., Sinclair, A.

SE: Jenny Lind (supported by Messrs. Kyle, Braun, Julius Benedict, and Belletti): D 26-28; Haworth Grand Olio Company: Ja 7-11; Blangy Dance Troupe (Mlle. Blangy, Madame Blangy, Monsieurs Durand and Szollosky): Ja 27-F 8; Richard L. Graham: F 10-Mr 3; Miss Richardson: F 10-Mr 3, Ap 28-My 6, 12-14; Sir William Don: Ap 30-My 6; Italian Opera Company (Signors Sesto Benedetti, Lietti, Kreutzer, Pozzesi, Benvuevento, Rossi, Caresi, Guibilie, Parozzi, Coemans, Kensler, Signoras Truffi Benedetti, Garet, Mlles. Nathalie Fitzjames, Virginia Whiting): Mr 21-Ap 9; Andrew Jackson Neafie: My 7-12.

D (26-28) Jenny Lind

Ja (7-11) Haworth Grand Olio Company (20) Poor Gentleman; Forest Rose (21) Paul Pry; Sudden Thoughts (22) Honeymoon; My Precious Betsy (23) Stranger; Taming of the Shrew (24) Sweethearts and Wives; Napoleon (25) Wonder; Spectre Bridegroom (27) Forest Rose; L'Illusion d'une Peintre (28) Paul Pry; La Vivandiere (29) Sudden Thoughts; Giselle (30) Dead Shot; Giselle (31) Poor Pillicoddy; Nicodemus; La Vivandiere

F (1) Wonder; Azurine; Child of Air (3) Don Caesar de Bazan; Taming of the Shrew; Blangy Troupe (4) Virginius; Child of Air (5) Rivals; Sudden Thoughts; Blangy Troupe (6) William Tell; Ondine (7) Richard III; Napoleon; Blangy Troupe (8) Poor Gentleman; Ondine (10) Macbeth: *Macbeth*–Graham, *Lady Macbeth*–Miss Richardson; King and I (11) Othello: *Othello*–Graham, *Emilie*–Miss Richardson; Raising the Wind (12) Venice Preserved: *Pierre*–Graham, *Belvidera*–Miss Richardson; Poor Pillicoddy (13) Julius Caesar: *Brutus*–Graham, *Portia*–Miss Richardson; My Neighbor's Wife (14) Pizarro: *Rolla*– Graham, *Elvira*–Miss Richardson; Spitfire (15) Coriolanus: *Coriolanus*– Graham, *Volumnia*–Miss Richardson; King and I (17) Hamlet: *Hamlet*– Graham, *Gertrude*–Miss Richardson; Friend Waggles (18) Macbeth: *Macbeth*–Graham, *Lady Macbeth*–Miss Richardson; Spitfire (19) School for Scandal: *Charles Surface*–Graham, *Lady Teazle*–Miss Richardson; Boots at the Swan (20) Richard III: *Richard*–Graham, *Queen*–Miss Richardson; Spectre Bridegroom (21) Merchant of Venice: *Shylock*– Graham, *Jessica*–Miss Richardson; Taming of the Shrew (22) Bridal*: *Melantius*–Graham, *Evadne*–Miss Richardson; Guy Mannering: *Meg Merrilies*–Miss Richardson (24) Lady of Lyons; Major Jones' Courtship (25) She Stoops to Conquer; Raising the Wind (26) Gamester: *Mrs. Beverly*–Miss Richardson, *Beverly*–Graham; Wonder (27) Serious Family; Boots at the Swan (28) Werner: *Werner*–Graham, *Josephine*– Miss Richardson; Guy Mannering: *Meg Merrilies*–Miss Richardson

Mr (1) Spit Fire; Rivals (3) Bridal: *Melantius*–Graham, *Evadne*– Miss Richardson; Napoleon (4) Charles XII; Serious Family (21) Ernani (22) La Favorita (25) Ernani (27) Lucrezia Borgia (28) La Favorita (31) Il Guiramento

Ap (1) Lucrezia Borgia (4-5) Norma (7) Lucia di Lammermoor (9) Norma (14) Rivals; Who Speaks First? (15) Serious Family; Honeymoon (16) Iron Chest; Follies of a Night (17) Sweethearts and Wives; Used Up (19) Don Caesar de Bazan; Who Speaks First? (23) Serious Family; Jenny Lind in Charleston*; Widow's Victim (24) Love Chase; Delicate Ground; South Carolina's Contribution to the World's Fair (25) Follies of a Night; David Copperfield; Jenny Lind in Charleston (26) Lady of Lyons; Charles XII (28) Gamester: *Mrs. Beverly*–Miss Richardson; Lola Montez* (29) Othello: *Emilie*–Miss Richardson; Two Gregories (30) Used Up: *Sir Charles Coldstream*– Don; Rough Diamond: *Cousin Joe*–Don; Merchant of Venice (Act IV): *Jessica*–Miss Richardson

My (1) Jacobite: *John Duck*–Don; Taming of the Shrew: *Catherine*– Miss Richardson; Rough Diamond: *Cousin Joe*–Don (2) Fazio; Guy Mannering: *Meg Merrilies*–Miss Richardson (3) Lottery Ticket: *Wormwood*–Don; Douglas: *Lady Randolph*–Miss Richardson; Make Your Wills: *Joseph Bragg*–Don (5) Used Up: *Sir Charles Coldstream*–Don; Poor Pillicoddy: *John Peter*–Don; American Farmer (6) Jacobite: *John Duck*–Don; School for Scandal: *Lady Teazle*–Miss Richardson, *Charles Surface*–Don; Rough Diamond: *Cousin Joe*–Don (7) Richard III: *Richard*–Neafie; Two Gregories (8) Mohammed: *Mohammed*–Neafie; Lola Montez (9) Wife: *Julian St. Pierre*–Neafie; Two Gregories (10) Mohammed: *Mohammed*–Neafie; American Farmer (12) Oralloosa*: *Oralloosa*–Neafie; Don Caesar de Bazan: *Don Caesar*–Neafie, *Maritana*– Miss Richardson (13) Drunkard; Jenny Lind in Charleston (14) Richard III: *Queen*–Miss Richardson; Napoleon

1851-1852

Mgrs.: F. C. Adams (O 8-D 30); J. J. Jefferson and J. Ellsler (Ja 1- Mr 30); *acting mgr.:* M. E. Barry; *treas.:* J. Jenree. *Stock:* Allen, J. H., Crocker, J. W., Elton, Everett, Fletcher, Melville, D., Morton, C. H., Owens, T., Perry, H. A., Sandrue, Savage, S. S.; *Mrs.* Crocker, J. W., Ellsler, J., Jefferson, J. J., Melville, D., Wray; *Misses* Ludlow, K., Eveline.

SE: Parisian Ballet Troupe (Monsieurs Leon Espinosa, Vegas, Charles Hilariot, Gredlue, Eichrenback, Szollosy; Mlles. Antonio Hilariot, Jenny, Jeanette; director, Charles Thasy, mgr., L. Fiot): O 8-18; Montplasir Ballet Troupe (Monsieurs W. M. Montplasir, Cornet, Wiethoff, Johello, Martini, Hipolite Montplasir; Mesdame Adele Montplasir; Mlles. Bulan, Blondeau, Sissan, McGregor, Corby; director, Grossi, orch. leader, Gilles): O 20-N 8; Max Maretzek's Opera Company (Signors Max Maretzek, Lorini, Rosi, Benventano, Strini, Marini, Parozzi; Mlles. Angelina Bosio, Julia Gould, Rose de Vries): N 10-29; Mozart's Don Giovanni Opera Company (Signors Sesto Benedetti, Lorini, Benventano, Sanquirico, Rossi, Parozzi; Signors Vietti, Carolina Vietti, Teresa Truffi; Mlles. Julia Gould, Virginia Whiting): D 1-13; New Orleans Burlesque Opera Company (mgr.: Samuel S. Sandford): D 15-27; Julia Bennett: Ja 26-31; Julia Dean: F 2-14, 23-Mr 6; Charles Burke: Mr 8- 20; Junius Brutus Booth, Sr.: Mr 22-30.

O (8) Parisian Ballet Troupe (9) Love in Humble Life; Jolly Miller; Parisian Ballet Troupe (10) La Diable a Quarte; Barber's Trouble; Parisian Ballet Troupe (11) Yankee Doodle; Barber's Trouble; Parisian Ballet Troupe (13) Parisian Ballet Troupe (15) Jolly Miller; Parisian Ballet Troupe (16) Goddess of the Dance; Fou; Monsieur Deschalumeau (17) Perfection; La Truondaix (18) Monsieur Deschalumeau; Day in Paris; Fou (20) L'Ombre; Perfection; Montplasir Ballet Troupe (21) Judgment of Paris; Day in Paris; Montplasir Ballet Troupe (22) School for Tigers; Loan of a Lover; Caliph of Bagdad (23) Redowska; Loan of a Lover; Ketley; Montplasir Ballet Troupe (24) Secret; Montplasir Ballet Troupe (25) Day after the Wedding; Montplasir Ballet Troupe (27-28) Day in Paris; Catarina (29) Perfection; Catarina

N (1) Box and Cox; Montplasir Ballet Troupe (4) Bad Night; Montplasir Ballet Troupe (5-6) La Diable a Quatre; Montplasir Ballet Troupe (7-8) L'Ombre; Montplasir Ballet Troupe (10) Lucia di Lammermoor (12) Il Puritani (14) Don Pasquale (15) Il Puritani (17) La Somnambula (19) Norma (21) La Favorita (22) Norma (24) Ernani (26) Norma (28) Ernani (29) La Favorita

D (1) Lucrezia Borgia (3) Barber of Seville (5) Barber of Seville; Lucia di Lammermoor (one scene) (6) Lucrezia Borgia (8) Don Giovanni (9) Norma (10) Roberto Devereux (11) Don Giovanni (12) Il Guiramento (13) Don Giovanni (15-20) Child of the Prairie (22-25) Cinderella; Shin-de-Heela (27) La Somnambula

Ja (1) Rivals; Sudden Thoughts (3) Poor Gentleman; Michael Earle (6) Pride of the Market; Beauty and the Beast (7) Isabelle; Beauty and the Beast (8) Soldier's Daughter; Beauty and the Beast (9) Hunchback; Slasher and Crasher (10) Dream at Sea; Poor Pillicoddy (12) Stranger; Somebody Else (13) Othello; Spectre Bridegroom (14) Hunchback; My Neighbor's Wife (15) Honeymoon; Peeping in at Six P. M.* (17) Paul Pry; Michael Earle (19) Money; Dead Shot (20) Don Caesar de Bazan; Dream at Sea (21) Rivals; Glance at New York (22) Cricket on the Hearth; Glance at New York (23) Don Caesar de Bazan; Glance at New York (24) Idiot Witness; Glance at New York (26) She Stoops to Conquer: *Miss Hardcastle*–Julia Bennett; Loan of a Lover: *Gertrude*–Julia Bennett (27) Ladies' Battle: *Countess de Autrival*–Julia Bennett; Roland for an Oliver (28) Lady of Lyons: *Pauline*–Julia Bennett; Sudden Thoughts (29) London Assurance: *Lady Gay Spanker*–Julia Bennett; Dead Shot (30) Ladies' Battle: *Countess de Autrival*–Julia Bennett; All that Glitters is Not Gold (31) Love Chase: *Constance*–Julia Bennett; Grist at the Mill: *Francine*–Julia Bennett

F (2) Hunchback: *Julia*–Julia Dean; Slasher and Crasher (3) Romeo and Juliet: *Juliet*–Julia Dean; Rendezvous (4) Lady of Lyons: *Pauline*–Julia Dean; Somebody Else (5) Stranger: *Mrs. Haller*–Julia Dean; Spectre Bridegroom (6) Love: *Countess*–Julia Dean; My Neighbor's Wife (7) Lucretia Borgia: *Lucretia Borgia*–Julia Dean; Michael Earle (9) Lady of Lyons: *Pauline*–Julia Dean; Rough Diamond: *Margery*–Julia Dean (10) Love Chase: *Constance*–Julia Dean; Dead Shot (11) Wife: *Mariana*–Julia Dean; Who Speaks First? (12) Evadne: *Evadne*–Julia Dean; Poor Pillicoddy (13) Hunchback: *Julia*–Julia Dean; Rough Diamond (14) Love's Sacrifice: *Margaret Elmore*–Julia Dean; Faint Heart Ne'er Won Fair Lady: *Duchess*–Julia Dean (23) Gamester: *Mrs.*

Beverly–Julia Dean; Swiss Swains (24) Lady of Lyons: *Pauline*–Julia Dean; Mother and Child Are Doing Well (25) Romeo and Juliet: *Juliet*–Julia Dean; Hunting a Turtle (26) Wife: *Mariana*–Julia Dean; Mother and Child Are Doing Well (27) School for Scandal: *Lady Teazle*–Julia Dean; Mother and Child Are Doing Well (28) Hunchback: *Julia*–Julia Dean; Swiss Swains

Mr (1) Fazio: *Bianca*–Julia Dean; Love Chase: *Constance*–Julia Dean (2) Wrecker's Daughter: *Marian*–Julia Dean; Slasher and Crasher (3) Lucretia Borgia: *Lucretia Borgia*–Julia Dean; My Precious Betsy (4) London Assurance: *Lady Gay Spanker*–Julia Dean; Mr. and Mrs. Peter White (5)· Pizarro: *Elvira*–Julia Dean; My Precious Betsy (6) Wrecker's Daughter: *Marian*–Julia Dean; Honeymoon: *Juliana*–Julia Dean (8) People's Lawyer: *Solomon Shingle*–Burke; Illustrious Stranger: *Benjamin Bowell*–Burke (9) Toodles*: *Timothy*–Burke; Ole Bull: *Ebenezer Calf*–Burke (10) Rip Van Winkle: *Rip Van Winkle*–Burke; Ole Bull: *Ebenezer Calf*–Burke (11) Sweethearts and Wives: *Billy Lackaday*–Burke; Lady of the Lions: *Clod Meddlenot*–Burke (12) Jacobite: *John Duck*–Burke; People's Lawyer: *Solomon Shingle*–Burke (13) Breach of Promise: *Sudden*–Burke; Lady of the Lions: *Clod Meddlenot*–Burke (15) Grandfather Whitehead: *Grandfather Whitehead*–Burke; Wool Dealer: *Deuteronomy*–Burke (16) Poor Pillicoddy: *John Peter*–Burke; Kiss in the Dark: *Pettibone*–Burke; Toodles: *Timothy*–Burke (17) Comedy of Errors: *Dromio*–Burke; Wool Dealer: *Deuteronomy*–Burke (18) Comedy of Errors: *Dromio*–Burke; Glance at New York: *Mose*–Burke (19) Hamlet; Kiss in the Dark: *Pettibone*–Burke (20) Golden Farmer: *Jemmy Twitcher*–Burke; Glance at New York: *Mose*–Burke (22) Richard III: *Richard*–Booth; Swiss Swains (23) Othello: *Iago*–Booth; Hunting a Turtle (24) New Way to Pay Old Debts: *Sir Giles Overreach*–Booth; My Precious Betsy (25) Hamlet: *Hamlet*–Booth; My Neighbor's Wife (26) Iron Chest: *Sir Edward Mortimer*–Booth; Review (27) King Lear: *King Lear*–Booth; Mother and Child Are Doing Well (29) Richard III: *Richard*–Booth; Perfection (30) New Way to Pay Old Debts: *Sir Giles Overreach*–Booth; Sudden Thoughts

1852-1853

Mgr.: John Sloman; *acting mgr.*: G. H. Barrett; *orch. leader:* Chatel. *Stock:* Allen, J. H., Bokee, Clifford, J. W., Davenport, A. H., Dennison, Dickenson, G. K., Douglas, W. B., Hield, C. W., Keene, A., Morton, C. H., O'Neil, Oxley, J., Shepherd, R. A., Sloan, J., Stuart, C., Warden, E. A.; *Mrs.* Allen, J. H., Barrett, G. H., Chekini, Hield, C. W., Sloan, J., Sloman, J., Stafford, Williams; *Misses* Bokee, Cruise, A., Faulkrod, E. V., Graham, M. A., Reede, Roberts, Somers, Walters.

SE: Julia Dean: N 22-D 4, F 14-26; Lola Montez: D 6-10; George Vandenhoff and Mrs. C. Sinclair: D 20-30; Bateman Family (Mr. and Mrs. H. L., Kate, and Ellen): Ja 12-29; Andrew Jackson Neafie: Ja 31-F 12; Ole Bull Company (Maurice Strakosch, Madame Amalie Strakosch, and Signora Adelina Patti): F 8; Rousett Sisters Dance Troupe: Ap 4-16; Steffanone's Opera Company (Madame Balbina Steffanone and others): My 10-12.

N (11) School for Scandal; Lola Montez (12) Grist at the Mill; Eton Boy; Lola Montez (13) Somebody Else; His Last Legs; How to Settle Accounts with Your Laundress (15) London Assurance; How to Settle Accounts with Your Laundress (17) School for Scandal; Eton

Boy (18) Honeymoon; How to Settle Accounts with Your Laundress
(19) Child of the Regiment; Omnibus; Lola Montez (20) London
Assurance; Mesmerism .(22) Hunchback: *Julia*–Julia Dean; His Last
Legs (23) Love: *Countess*–Julia Dean; Eton Boy (24) Evadne:
Evadne–Julia Dean; Child of the Regiment (25) Lady of Lyons:
Pauline–Julia Dean; Mesmerism (26) Evadne: *Evadne*–Julia Dean;
Somebody Else (27) Stranger: *Mrs. Haller*–Julia Dean; Love Chase
(29) Ingomar: *Parthenia*–Julia Dean; Dumb Belle (30) Ingomar:
Parthenia–Julia Dean; Child of the Regiment.

D (1) Ingomar: *Parthenia*–Julia Dean; Omnibus (2) Romeo and
Juliet: *Juliet*–Julia Dean; Somebody Else (3) Hunchback: *Julia*–Julia
Dean; Morning Call: *Mrs. Chillington*–Julia Dean (4) Wife: *Mariana*–
Julia Dean; Morning Call: *Mrs. Chillington*–Julia Dean (6) Maritana:
Maritana–Lola Montez; Rough Diamond (8) Maritana: *Maritana*–Lola
Montez; Little Jockey (9) Lola Montez in Bavaria: *Lola Montez*–
Lola Montez; Little Jockey (10) Lola Montez in Bavaria: *Lola
Montez*–Lola Montez; Child of the Regiment (11) Robert Macaire; Per-
fection (13) Somnambulist; Married and Settled; Mesmerism (15)
Flowers of the Forest; Irish Lion (16) London Assurance; Irish Lion
(17) Hamlet; Catherine and Petruchio (18) Othello; Secret (20) School
for Scandal: *Charles Surface*–Vandenhoff, *Lady Teazle*–Mrs. Sinclair;
Man without a Head (21) Lady of Lyons: *Claude*–Vandenhoff,
Pauline–Mrs. Sinclair; Secret (22) Stranger: *Stranger*–Vandenhoff, *Mrs.
Haller*–Mrs. Sinclair; Wedding Day (23) Love's Sacrifice: *Matthew
Elmore*–Vandenhoff, *Margaret Elmore*–Mrs. Sinclair; Rough Diamond
(24) Ingomar: *Ingomar*–Vandenhoff, *Parthenia*–Mrs. Sinclair; Little
Jockey (25) Where There's a Will There's a Way: *Donna Francisco*–
Mrs. Sinclair, *Don Manuel*–Vandenhoff; Catherine and Petruchio:
Petruchio–Vandenhoff, *Catherine*–Mrs. Sinclair; Robert Macaire (28)
Othello: *Iago*–Vandenhoff, *Desdemona*–Mrs. Sinclair; farce (29) Much
Ado about Nothing: *Benedict*–Vandenhoff, *Beatrice*–Mrs. Sinclair; Little
Jockey (30) Stranger: *Stranger*–Vandenhoff, *Mrs. Haller*–Mrs. Sinclair;
School for Scandal: *Charles Surface*–Vandenhoff, *Lady Teazle*–Mrs.
Sinclair (31) Pizarro; Young America

Ja (1) All that Glitters Is Not Gold; New Lovers; Irish Tutor (4)
Little Devil; All that Glitters Is Not Gold; Child of the Regiment (5)
Macbeth; Young America; Rob Roy MacGregor (6) Rob Roy Mac-
Gregor; Alarming Sacrifice (7) Romeo and Juliet; Robert Macaire
(8) Douglas; Little Devil; Alarming Sacrifice (10) Rough Diamond;
Rob Roy MacGregor (11) Richard III; Wanted, One Thousand Milliners
(12) Young Couple; Swiss Cottage; Wanted, One Thousand Milliners
(13) Young Couple; Spoil'd Child; Rendezvous (14) Merchant of
Venice; Perfection; Young Couple; How to Settle Accounts with Your
Laundress (15) Her Royal Highness; Young Couple; Somnambulist
(17) Richard III; Paul Pry; Young Couple; Young America (18) Old
and Young; Novel Expedient; Merchant of Venice (20) Macbeth; Young
Couple; Novel Expedient (21) Paul Pry; Young Couple; Used Up
(22) Richard III; Swiss Cottage; Little Devil (24) Old School and the
New; Young Scamp; Bombastes Furioso; Novel Expedient (26) Old
School and the New; Young Couple; Bombastes Furioso; Old Guard
(27) Merchant of Venice; Her Royal Highness; Young Scamp; Somebody Else (28) Richard III; Old and Young; Novel Expedient; Rough
Diamond (29) Sweethearts and Wives; Young Couple; Spoil'd Child;
Rendezvous (31-F 2) Corsican Brothers*: *Fabien* and *Louis*–Neafie

F (3) Corsican Brothers: *Fabien* and *Louis*–Neafie; Young Jockey
(4) Corsican Brothers: *Fabien* and *Louis*–Neafie; Irish Lion (5)
Corsican Brothers: *Fabien* and *Louis*–Neafie; Match in the Dark (7)
Richelieu: *Richelieu*–Neafie; Matrimony: *De Laval*–Neafie (8) Eton
Boy; Nature and Philosophy; concert by Ole Bull Company (9) Damon
and Pythias: *Damon*–Neafie; Rival Pages (10) Mohammed: *Moham-
med*–Neafie; Sam Patchieno (11) Virginius: *Virginius*–Neafie; Mesmer-
ism; Sam Patchieno (12) Macbeth: *Macbeth*–Neafie; Sam Patchieno
(14) Hunchback: *Julia*–Julia Dean; Match in the Dark (15) Gamester:
Mrs. Beverly–Julia Dean; Rival Pages (16) Love's Sacrifice: *Margaret
Elmore*–Julia Dean; Nature and Philosophy (17) Pizarro: *Elvira*–Julia
Dean; All that Glitters Is Not Gold (18) Lady of Lyons: *Pauline*–Julia
Dean; Novel Expedient (19) Madeline: *Madeline*–Julia Dean; All that
Glitters Is Not Gold (21) Fazio: *Bianca*–Julia Dean; Morning Call:
Mrs. Chillington–Julia Dean (22) Madeline: *Madeline*–Julia Dean;
Honeymoon (23) Much Ado about Nothing: *Beatrice*–Julia Dean; Some-
body Else; Go-to-Bed Tom (24) Lucretia Borgia: *Lucretia Borgia*–
Julia Dean; Nature and Philosophy (25) Lucretia Borgia: *Lucretia
Borgia*–Julia Dean; Child of the Regiment (26) Ingomar: *Parthenia*–
Julia Dean; Love Chase: *Constance*–Julia Dean (28) Critic; Two
Friends
Mr (1) All that Glitters Is Not Gold; Black Eyed Susan; Good for
Nothing (2) Richard III; How to Settle Accounts with Your Land-
lady (15-27) Donetti's Troupe of Acting Monkeys
Ap (4-16) Roussett Sisters Dance Troupe
My (10-12) Concerts by Steffanone's Opera Company

1853-1854

Mgr.: John Sloan; *orch. leader:* Chatel; *scenist:* Granville Perkins;
wardrobist: Reed; *machinist:* Jackson; *prompter:* W. A. Anderton.
Stock: Ashmer, J. G., Bradshaw, J. J., Cunningham, R. D., Edwards, H.,
Evain, W. H., Hind, T. J., Hill, C. B., Marchant, G. F., Marshall, Oxley,
J., Spencer, Uhl, Warwick, J. H., Watts; *Mrs.* Ashmer, J. G., Bradshaw,
J. J., Cunningham, R. D., Jones, M., Sloan, J.; *Misses* Harris, Henri,
Keough, E., Linden.
SE: S. C. Campbell's Minstrels: S 26-O 2; Kunkel's Nightingale
Burlesque Opera Troupe (*mgr.*: John T. Ford): O 17-28, My 1-9; Mlle.
Leontine Pouguad French Ballet Troupe: N 21-D 3; John Sefton: D 5-
10; Julia Dean: D 12-27; F. S. Chanfrau: Ja 2-14; Mrs. George P. Farren:
Ja 16-21; Ole Bull Company (Maurice Strakosch, Madame Amalie
Strakosch, and Signora Adelina Patti): Ja 23-24; Mr. and Mrs. Barney
Williams: Ja 30-F 11; Anna Cora Mowatt: F 20-Mr 6; Aeolian Minstrels
Company: Mr 7-10; Ravel Family (supported by Mlle. Yrca Mathias,
danseuse, and the Martinetti Brothers): Mr 20-Ap 8, Ap 24-26; Soto
Dance Troupe (supported by George W. Smith): Ap 10-15; Madame
Siminski Musical Company: Ap 20.
S (26-O 2) Campbell's Minstrels
O (17-22) Kunkel's Nightingale Burlesque Opera Troupe (24-26)
Uncle Tom's Cabin (Kunkel's Troupe) (27-28) Kunkel's Nightingale
Burlesque Opera Troupe (31) John Bull; Dead Shot
N (1) Love's Sacrifice; Mesmerism (2) Stranger; Child of the
Regiment (3) Wife; Omnibus (4) Lady of Lyons; Child of the Regi-
ment (5) Stranger; Child of the Regiment (7) Romeo and Juliet;

Perfection (8) Merchant of Venice; Nature and Philosophy (9) Lady of Lyons; Rough Diamond (10) Othello; Kate Carraway (11) Richelieu; Married Rake (12) Pizarro; Kate Carraway (14) Macbeth; Fortune's Frolic (15) John Bull; Perfection (16) Macbeth; How to Settle Accounts with Your Washerwoman (17) Damon and Pythias; Swiss Cottage (18) School for Scandal; Trying It On (19) Richard III; Married Rake (21) Cramond Brig; Paquerette (23) Naval Engagements; Monsieur Deschalumeau (24) Roland for an Oliver; La Bayadere (25) Momentous Question; Trisac, the Duelist (26) Bamboozling; Graciosa (28) Grist to the Mill; Night in Venice (29) Naval Engagements; La Bayadere (30) Therese; Massaneillo Tarentelle

D (1) Richard III; Pouguad Troupe (2) La Tisbe; Massaniello Tarentelle; Pouguad Troupe (3) La Tisbe; La Maja de Sevillea; Robert Macaire (5) Golden Farmer: *Jemmy Twitcher–*Sefton; Swiss Cottage; Siamese Twins* (6) Golden Farmer: *Jemmy Twitcher–*Sefton; He's Not A-Miss: *Prince–*Sefton; Bamboozling (7) Beulah Spa: *Hector* and *Magnus–*Sefton; La Tisbe; First Night: *Dufard–*Sefton (8) Merchant of Venice; First Night: *Dufard–*Sefton (9) French Spy; First Night: *Dufard–*Sefton; Sketches in India: *Count Glorieux–*Sefton (10) Mobb, the Outlaw: *Jemmy Twitcher–*Sefton; Spirit Rappings and Table Movings: *The Medium–*Sefton (12) Fazio: *Bianca–*Julia Dean; Jenny Lind at Last (13) Hunchback: *Julia–*Julia Dean; Trying It On (14) Rough Diamond; Gamester: *Mrs. Beverly–*Julia Dean (15) Lady of Lyons: *Pauline–*Julia Dean; How to Settle Accounts with Your Washerwoman (16) Love: *Countess–*Julia Dean; Jenny Lind at Last (17) Ingomar: *Parthenia–*Julia Dean; Morning Call: *Mrs. Chillington–*Julia Dean (19) Macbeth: *Lady Macbeth–*Julia Dean; Dead Shot (20) Adrienne, the Actress: *Adrienne–*Julia Dean; Roland for an Oliver (21) Ingomar: *Parthenia–*Julia Dean; Kate Carraway (22) Adrienne, the Actress: *Adrienne–*Julia Dean; Nature and Philosophy (23) Duke's Wager: *Gabrielle–*Julia Dean; Mesmerism (24) Rough Diamond; Wrecker's Daughter: *Marian–*Julia Dean (26) Evadne: *Evadne–*Julia Dean; Good for Nothing (27) Jane Shore: *Jane Shore–*Julia Dean; Love Chase: *Constance–*Julia Dean (28) Joan of Arc; Lola Montez; Spirit Rappings and Table Movings (29) Hamlet; Jenny Lind at Last (30) Virginius; Roland for an Oliver (31) Good for Nothing; French Spy

Ja (1) French Spy; farce (2) Poor Gentleman: *Ollapod–*Chanfrau; Toodles: *Timothy–*Chanfrau (4-5) Toodles: *Timothy–*Chanfrau; Jack Sheppard: *Blueskin–*Chanfrau (6) Husband at Sight; Stage Struck Barber: three rôles–Chanfrau; Black Eyed Susan: *William–*Chanfrau (7) Broken Sword; Stage Struck Barber: three rôles–Chanfrau; Toodles: *Timothy–*Chanfrau (9) Model of a Wife: *Bonnefoe–*Chanfrau; Mose: *Mose–*Chanfrau; Pleasant Neighbors (10) Black Eyed Susan: *William–*Chanfrau; Pleasant Neighbors; Mose: *Mose–*Chanfrau (11) Poor Gentleman: *Ollapod–*Chanfrau; Mose: *Mose–*Chanfrau (12) Stage Struck Barber: three rôles–Chanfrau; Dombey and Son: *Captain Cuttle–*Chanfrau (14) First Night: *Dufard–*Chanfrau; Toodles: *Timothy–*Chanfrau; Mose in California: *Mose–*Chanfrau (16) Gamester: *Mrs. Beverly–*Mrs. Farren; Cramond Brig (17) Jane Shore: *Jane Shore–*Mrs. Farren; Naval Engagements (18) Lucretia Borgia: *Lucretia Borgia–*Mrs. Farren; Lola Montez (19) Stranger: *Mrs. Haller–*Mrs. Farren; Mary Tudor (20) Evadne: *Evadne–*Mrs. Farren; St. Mary's Eve (21) Wrecker's Daughter: *Marian–*Mrs. Farren; Lucretia

Borgia: *Lucretia Borgia*–Mrs. Farren (23-24) Ole Bull Company
(25) She Stoops to Conquer; Milly (26) Charleston Fireman*;
All that Glitters Is Not Gold (27) She Stoops to Conquer;
Omnibus (28) Hamlet; Milly (30) Born to Good Luck: *Paudeen
O'Rafferty*–Williams; In and Out of Place: *Letty*–Mrs.
Williams; Lime-
rick Boy: *Paddy*–Williams (31) Barney, the Baron: *Barney*–Williams;
Happy Man: *Paddy Murphy*–Williams; In and Out of Place: *Letty*–
Mrs. Williams
    F (1) Irish Assurance and Yankee Modesty: *Pat*–Williams, *Nancy*–
Mrs. Williams; Limerick Boy: *Paddy*–Williams (2) Shandy Maguire:
Shandy–Williams; Our Gal: *Caroline*–Mrs. Williams; Barney, the
Baron: *Barney*–Williams (3) Shandy Maguire: *Shandy*–Williams; Law
for Ladies: five rôles–Mrs. Williams; Happy Man: *Paddy Murphy*–
Williams (6) Ireland as It Is: *Ragged Pat*–Williams, *Judy*–Mrs. Wil-
liams; Law for Ladies: five rôles–Mrs. Williams (7) Our Gal: *Caroline*–
Mrs. Williams; Ireland as It Is: *Ragged Pat*–Williams, *Judy*–Mrs.
Williams (8) Uncle Pat's Cabin: *Nickey Malone*–Williams, *Widow
Casey*–Mrs. Williams; In and Out of Place: *Letty*–Mrs. Williams (9)
Uncle Pat's Cabin: *Nickey Malone*–Williams, *Widow Casey*–Mrs. Wil-
liams; Custom of the Country: *Melissa*–Mrs. Williams; Irish Tutor:
Terry–Williams (10) Ireland and America: *Jemmy*–Williams, *Peggy*–
Mrs. Williams; Irish Thrush and the Swedish Nightingale: *Dennis*–
Williams, *Jenny Lind*–Mrs. Williams (11) Connecticut Courtship:
Jemima–Mrs. Williams; Teddy, the Tiler: *Teddy*–Williams; Brian
O'Lynn: *Brian*–Williams, *Shelah*–Mrs. Williams; Irish Thrush and the
Swedish Nightingale: *Dennis*–Williams, *Jenny Lind*–Mrs. Williams
(13) King Lear; Somebody Else (14) Nick of the Woods; Charles
XII (15) Rob Roy MacGregor; Child of the Regiment (16) Pizarro;
Raising the Wind (17) Richelieu; Trying It On (18) Broken Sword;
Raising the Wind (20) Much Ado about Nothing: *Beatrice*–Anna Cora
Mowatt; Dead Shot (21) Ingomar: *Parthenia*–Anna Cora Mowatt;
How to Settle Accounts with Your Washerwoman (22) As You Like It:
Rosalind–Anna Cora Mowatt; Married Rake (23) Lady of Lyons:
Pauline–Anna Cora Mowatt; Irish Lion (24) As You Like It: *Rosalind*–
Anna Cora Mowatt; Somebody Else (25) Armand: *Blanche*–Anna Cora
Mowatt; Milly (27) Ion: *Ion*–Anna Cora Mowatt; His Last Legs (28)
Armand: *Blanche*–Anna Cora Mowatt; Young America
    Mr (1) Corinna*: *Corinna*–Anna Cora Mowatt; Sketches in India
(2) Romeo and Juliet: *Juliet*–Anna Cora Mowatt; Jenny Lind (3)
Stranger: *Mrs. Haller*–Anna Cora Mowatt; Faint Heart Ne'er Won Fair
Lady: *Duchess*–Anna Cora Mowatt (4) King Rene's Daughter*:
Iolanthe–Anna Cora Mowatt; Honeymoon: *Juliana*–Anna Cora Mowatt
(6) Hunchback: *Julia*–Anna Cora Mowatt; His Last Legs (7) Momen-
tous Question; Aeolian Minstrels (8) Broken Sword; Aeolian Minstrels
(9) Henry VIII; Soldier, the Sailor, the Tinker, and the Tailor; Aeolian
Minstrels (10) Joan of Arc; Aeolian Minstrels (13) Jewess; Catherine
and Petruchio (14) Agnes de Vere; His Last Legs (15) Faint Heart
Ne'er Won Fair Lady; National Guard (16) Forest of Bondy; Drunk-
ard's Dream (17) Drunkard's Dream; St. Patrick's Day (18) Road to
Ruin; Day after the Wedding (20) Two Gregories; Ravel Family (21)
Mesmerism; Ravel Family (22) Young America; Ravel Family
(23) How to Settle Accounts with Your Washerwoman; Ravel
Family (24) Omnibus; Ravel Family (27) Raising the Wind;
Ravel Family (29, 31) Green Monster; Ravel Family

Ap (1) Three-faced Frenchman; Judgment of Paris; Ravel Family (4) Robert Macaire; Ravel Family (5-7) Mazulum; Ravel Family (8) Three-faced Frenchman; Young America; Ravel Family (10) Mr. and Mrs. Peter White; Soto Dance Troupe (12) Miller's Maid; Soto Dance Troupe (13) Slasher and Crasher; Soto Dance Troupe (14) Kiss in the Dark; His Last Legs; Soto Dance Troupe (15) Soto Dance Troupe; farce (17) Maid and the Magpie; Slasher and Crasher (20) Siminski Musical Company (24-26) Ravel Family
My (1-9) Kunkel's Burlesque Opera Troupe

1854-1855

Mgr.: John Sloan; *acting mgr.:* John Sloman (O 30-Mr 31); *scenist:* W. A. Ashe. *Stock:* Aiken, G. L., Langdon, G. C., Littell, J., Nagle, J. E., Rea, F., Weston, J. M., Williams, E. B.; *Mrs.* Archbold, Cappell, Duffield, Littell, J., Rea, F., Sloan, J., Thorpe; *Misses* Barre, D., Cappell, C., Saxton, K. *Mgr.:* W. H. Crisp (Ap 10-23). *Stock:* Chippendale, W., Fuller, J. B., Morton, A. T.; *Mrs.* Crisp, W. H.; *Misses* Adeline, Crisp, J., Dickens, J., Saxon, K.

SE: Annette Ince: O 30-N 11; Mrs. W. J. Noah: N 13-D 2; Julia Dean: D 4-16; Mrs. Charles Howard (supported by Mr. Howard): D 18-Ja 6; Mons. Bihin: Ja 4-6; Henry Farren and Louisa Howard: Ja 9-13; Niblo's English Opera Troupe (Messrs. Irving, St. Albyn; Mlle. Nau): Ja 16-20; Coney and Webb's Trained Dogs: Ja 22-27; Mr. and Mrs. Fred Conway: F 6-17; Eliza Logan: F 19-Mr 3, Ap 10-23.

O (30) Hunchback: *Julia*–Annette Ince; High Pressure! Express! (31) Love's Sacrifice: *Margaret*–Annette Ince; Bamboozling

N (1) Lady of Lyons: *Pauline*–Annette Ince; Trying It On (2) Love: *Countess*–Annette Ince; My Little Adopted (3) Romeo and Juliet: *Juliet*–Annette Ince; Phenomenon in a Smock Frock (4) Ingomar: *Parthenia*–Annette Ince; Morning Call (6) Camille: *Camille*–Annette Ince; Your Life's in Danger (7) Camille: *Camille*–Annette Ince; Phenomenon in a Smock Frock (8) Fazio: *Bianca*–Annette Ince; As Like as Two Peas (9) Stranger: *Mrs. Haller*–Annette Ince; Your Life's in Danger (10) Evadne: *Evadne*–Annette Ince; Honeymoon: *Juliana*–Annette Ince (11) Ion: *Ion*–Annette Ince; My Little Adopted (13) Fazio: *Bianca*–Mrs. Noah; Moustache Mania (14) Hunchback: *Julia*–Mrs. Noah; As Like as Two Peas (15) Lucretia Borgia: *Lucretia Borgia*–Mrs. Noah; Bamboozling (16) Macbeth: *Lady Macbeth*–Mrs. Noah; Your Life's in Danger (17) Lady of Lyons: *Pauline*–Mrs. Noah; Bamboozling (20) Lucretia Borgia: *Lucretia Borgia*–Mrs. Noah; Soldier's Daughter: *Widow Cheerly*–Mrs. Noah (21) School for Scandal: *Lady Teazle*–Mrs. Noah; Your Life's in Danger (22) Much Ado about Nothing: *Beatrice*–Mrs. Noah; My Little Adopted (23) Macbeth: *Lady Macbeth*–Mrs. Noah; Phenomenon in a Smock Frock (25) Lucretia Borgia: *Lucretia Borgia*–Mrs. Noah; Moustache Mania (27) Evadne: *Evadne*–Mrs. Noah; Fire Eater (28) Duchess Eleanor*: *Duchess*–Mrs. Noah; To Paris and Back for Five Pounds (29) Duchess Eleanor: *Duchess*–Mrs. Noah; Trying It On (30) Stranger: *Mrs. Haller*–Mrs. Noah; His Last Legs

D (1) Venice Preserved: *Belvidera*–Mrs. Noah; Fire Eater (2) Rob Roy MacGregor: *Helen*–Mrs. Noah; Love Chase: *Constance*–Mrs. Noah; Souvenir de Charleston (4) Evadne: *Evadne*–Julia Dean; As Like as Two Peas (5) Gamester: *Mrs. Beverly*–Julia Dean; To Oblige Benson

(6) Ingomar: *Parthenia*–Julia Dean; Moustache Mania (7) Love: *Countess*–Julia Dean; To Paris and Back for Five Pounds (8) Romeo and Juliet: *Juliet*–Julia Dean; To Paris and Back for Five Pounds (9) Fazio: *Bianca*–Julia Dean; Honeymoon: *Juliana*–Julia Dean (11) Jealous Wife: *Mrs. Oakly*–Julia Dean; How to Settle Accounts with Your Washerwoman (12) Hunchback: *Julia*–Julia Dean; Phenomenon in a Smock Frock (13) Lady of Lyons: *Pauline*–Julia Dean; Rough Diamond (14) Jealous Wife: *Mrs. Oakly*–Julia Dean; His Last Legs (15) Lady of Lyons: *Pauline*–Julia Dean; Rough Diamond (16) Stranger: *Mrs. Haller*–Julia Dean; Morning Call: *Mrs. Chillington*–Julia Dean (18) Belle's Stratagem: *Letitia Hardy*–Mrs. Howard; Jenny Lind: *Jenny Lind*–Mrs. Howard (19) Grist to the Mill: *Francine*–Mrs. Howard; D—— in Paris Is D—— (20) As Like as Two Peas; Time Tries All: *Laura*–Mrs. Howard; Unprotected Female: *Polly Crisp*–Mrs. Howard (21) School for Scandal: *Lady Teazle*–Mrs. Howard; Rough Diamond: *Margery*–Mrs. Howard (22) Moustache Mania; All that Glitters Is Not Gold: *Martha*–Mrs. Howard; Loan of a Lover: *Gertrude*–Mrs. Howard (23) Follies of a Night: *Duchess*–Mrs. Howard; Young Scamp: *Joseph*–Mrs. Howard; Jenny Lind: *Jenny Lind*–Mrs. Howard (24) Somnambulist: *Ernestine*–Mrs. Howard; Perfection: *Kate O'Brien*–Mrs. Howard; To Paris and Back for Five Pounds (27) Belle's Stratagem: *Letitia Hardy*–Mrs. Howard; Kate Kearney: *Kate Kearney*–Mrs. Howard (28) La Bayadere: *Ninka*–Mrs. Howard; Love Chase: *Constance*–Mrs. Howard (29) Pride of the Market: *Marton*–Mrs. Howard; La Bayadere: *Ninka*–Mrs. Howard (30) Kate Kearney: *Kate Kearney*–Mrs. Howard; La Bayadere: *Ninka*–Mrs. Howard

Ja (1) Hamlet: *Ophelia*–Mrs. Howard; Unprotected Female (3) London Assurance: *Lady Gay Spanker*–Mrs. Howard; Perfection: *Kate O'Brien*–Mrs. Howard (4) Welch Girl: *Julia*–Mrs. Howard; Mons. Bihin (5) Pride of the Market: *Marton*–Mrs. Howard; Mons. Bihin (6) Somnambulist: *Ernestine*–Mrs. Howard; Mons. Bihin (8) Hamlet; To Oblige Benson (9) Anthony and Cleopatra: *Anthony*–Farren, *Cleopatra*–Louisa Howard; Play, Plot and Passion: *Mons. Desmarets*–Farren, Mad. de Fontanges–Louisa Howard (10) Esmerelda: *Esmerelda*–Louisa Howard, *Quasimodo*–Farren; Delicate Ground: *Pauline*–Louisa Howard, *Sangfroid*–Farren (11) Antony and Cleopatra: *Antony*–Farren, *Cleopatra*–Louisa Howard; One Hundred Years Old; Green Bushes*: *Wild Murtogh*–Farren, *Miami*–Louisa Howard (12) Liberty, Equality, and Fraternity; Play, Plot and Passion: *Mons Desmarets*–Farren, Mad. de Fontanges–Louisa Howard (13) Two Loves in a Life: *Father Radcliffe*–Farren, *Ruth Ravenscar*–Louisa Howard; Green Bushes: *Wild Murtogh*–Farren, *Miami*–Louisa Howard (15) Forest of Bondy; Orang-ou-tang (16) La Somnambula; To Oblige Benson (17) La Somnambula; Phenomenon in a Smock Frock (18) Lucia di Lammermoor (Acts I-II); Bohemian Girl (Act III); How to Settle Accounts with Your Washerwoman (19) Lucia di Lammermoor; Bohemian Girl (Act III); Your Life's in Danger (20) His Last Legs; musical concert (22) Forest of Bondy; Orang-ou-tang (23) Two Buzzards; Trust to Luck; Dog Witness (24) Two Buzzards; Dog Witness (25-26) Butcher's Dog of Ghent; Don Juan (27) Cattle Stealer; Jocko; Red Indian (29) Hamlet; Dead Shot (30) Othello; Actress of All Work (31) William Tell; My Aunt

F (1) Black Eyed Susan; Dead Shot; My Aunt (2) Damon and Pythias; Man about Town (3) Poor Pillicoddy; Man about Town; Disowned and His Poor Dog Tray (5) Ingomar; Two Buzzards (6) Lady of Lyons: *Pauline*–Mrs. Conway, *Claude*–Conway; Perfection (7) Macbeth: *Macbeth*–Conway, *Lady Macbeth*–Mrs. Conway; To Oblige Benson (8) Merchant of Venice: *Shylock*–Conway, *Portia*–Mrs. Conway; Irish Lion (9) Romeo and Juliet: *Romeo*–Conway, *Juliet*–Mrs. Conway; Moustache Mania (10) Money: *Clara*–Mrs. Conway, *Evelyn*–Conway; Mesmerism (12) Stranger: *Stranger*–Conway, *Mrs. Haller*–Mrs. Conway; Sunshine through Clouds (14) All that Glitters Is Not Gold: *Martha*–Mrs. Conway, *Stephen*–Conway; Ireland as It Is (Act I); Therese (15) Much Ado about Nothing: *Benedict*–Conway, *Beatrice*–Mrs. Conway; Mesmerism (16) Money: *Clara*–Mrs. Conway, *Evelyn*–Conway; Irish Lion (17) Ann Blake*: *Thorald*–Conway, *Ann Blake*–Mrs. Conway; Love Chase (19) Evadne: *Evadne*–Eliza Logan; Wind Mill (20) Hunchback: *Julia*–Eliza Logan; Wind Mill (21) Lady of Lyons: *Pauline*–Eliza Logan; Sunshine through Clouds (22) Romeo and Juliet: *Juliet*–Eliza Logan; Your Life's in Danger (23) Love's Sacrifice: *Margaret*–Eliza Logan; As Like as Two Peas (24) Lucretia Borgia: *Lucretia Borgia*–Eliza Logan; Honeymoon: *Juliana*–Eliza Logan (26) Love: *Countess*–Eliza Logan; Perfection (27) Ion: *Ion*–Eliza Logan; Charles II (28) Ingomar: *Parthenia*–Eliza Logan; Wind Mill

Mr (1) Adrienne, the Actress: *Adrienne*–Eliza Logan; Your Life's in Danger (2) Fazio: *Bianca*–Eliza Logan; How to Settle Accounts with Your Washerwoman (3) Adrienne, the Actress: *Adrienne*–Eliza Logan; Matrimonial Squabbles; Jealous Wife: *Mrs. Oakly*–Eliza Logan (5) Serious Family; My Precious Betsy (6) George Barnwell; Sketches in India (7) Money; Swiss Cottage (8) Asmodeus; Serious Family (9) Richelieu; Young America (10) Therese; Serious Family (12) Time Works Wonders; Somebody Else (13) Richelieu; Swiss Cottage (14) Time Works Wonders; Young America (15) Don Caesar de Bazan; Somebody Else (16) Don Caesar de Bazan; Sketches in India (17) Robbers; Man without a Head (19) Robbers; My Precious Betsy (20) Time Works Wonders; Your Life's in Danger (21) Robbers; Young America (22) Ben Bolt; Morning Call; P. P. (23) Serious Family; Faint Heart Ne'er Won Fair Lady (24) Ben Bolt; Morning Call; P. P. (26) Michael Bonham* (27) Michael Bonham; address by William Gilmore Simms (28) Michael Bonham (29) Money; Young Scamp (30) Werner; As Like as Two Peas

Ap (10) Pizarro: *Elvira*–Eliza Logan; Simpson and Company (11) Stranger: *Mrs. Haller*–Eliza Logan; Wreck Ashore (12) Honeymoon: *Juliana*–Eliza Logan; Lady of the Lake (13) Jane Shore: *Jane Shore*–Eliza Logan; Robert Macaire; Two Murderers (14) Lucretia Borgia: *Lucretia Borgia*–Eliza Logan; Black Eyed Susan (16) Hunchback: *Julia*–Eliza Logan; Pretty Piece of Business (17) Fazio: *Bianca*–Eliza Logan; Wreck Ashore; Lady of the Lake (18) Gamester: *Mrs. Beverly*–Eliza Logan; My Precious Betsy; Lady of the Lake (19) Taming of the Shrew: *Catherine*–Eliza Logan; Lady of the Lake (20) Soldier's Daughter: *Widow Cheerly*–Eliza Logan; Lucille (21) Adelgitha: *Adelgitha*–Eliza Logan; Match in the Dark (23) Bride of Lammermoor: *Lucy Ashton*–Eliza Logan; Adelgitha: *Adelgitha*–Eliza Logan; Lady of the Lake: *Ellen*–Eliza Logan

1855-1856

Mgr.: John Sloan; *acting mgr.:* J. B. Fuller; *scenist:* Granville Perkins; *wardrobist:* Cassels; *machinist:* Furze; *orch. leader:* E. Fenelon. *Stock:* Aiken, F., Bland, W. H., Dawson, G., Douglas, W. B., Floyd, W. R., Grattan, H. P., Haviland, Lanagan, Lomas, Loveday, Meyer, F., Miller, D. J., Raymond, J. T., Reeves, W. H., Reynolds, Smith, G. W.; *Mrs.* Austen, Bailey, Grattan, H. P., Reeves, W. H., Sloan, J.; *Misses* Barre, D., Fisher, K., Grattan, A., Grattan, V., Hall, E., Ingersoll, Lewis, E., Maxwell, Morant, F., Terry, T., Wilton, E.

SE: Mlle. Rachel (supported by Mlles. Sarah, Dinah, and Lia): D 10-17; S. C. Campbell's Minstrels: F 19-25; Julia Dean (Hayne): F 27-Mr 12; Agnes Robertson: Mr 13-29; Dion Boucicault: Mr 17-29; F. S. Chanfrau (supported by Miss Albertine): Ap 7-21.

O (15) Waterman; Still Water Runs Deep; Peg Woffington* (16) Hamlet (17) Lady of Lyons; Swiss Swains (18) Ingomar (19) Love's Sacrifice; Swiss Cottage (20) Still Water Runs Deep; Swiss Cottage (22) Macbeth; Poor Pillicoddy (23) Peg Woffington; Kiss in the Dark (24) Still Water Runs Deep; Mesmerism (25) Old Heads and Young Hearts (26) Still Water Runs Deep; Illustrious Stranger (27) Married Life; Illustrious Stranger (29) Guy Mannering; Love in Livery (30) Married Life (31) Hunchback; State Secrets

N (1) Victorine; Married Life (2) State Secrets; Married Life (3) Single Life; Love in Livery (5) Victorine; Loan of a Lover (6) Single Life; Kiss in the Dark (7) Married Life; Still Water Runs Deep (8) As You Like It; Waterman (9) Victorine; Swiss Swains (10) Single Life; Married Life (12) School for Scandal; Drawing Room Divertisement (13) As You Like It; Drawing Room Divertisement (14) Guy Mannering; Loan of a Lover (15) Married Life; Single Life (16) School for Scandal (17) Rivals; Spectre Bridegroom (19) Dream at Sea; Grimshaw, Bagshaw, and Bradshaw (20) Rivals; Grimshaw, Bagshaw, and Bradshaw (21) Merchant of Venice; Bob Nettles (22) Dream at Sea; Bob Nettles (23) Rivals; Bob Nettles (24) Merchant of Venice; Bob Nettles (26-27) Twelfth Night (28) Single Life; Still Water Runs Deep (29) Bob Nettles; Wandering Boys (30) As You Like It; Bob Nettles

D (1) Game of Love; Spectre Bridegroom (3) Game of Love; As Like as Two Peas (4) Game of Love; To Oblige Benson (5) Game of Love; Poor Pillicoddy (6) Honeymoon; My Uncle Foozle (7) Love Chase; Drawing Room Divertisement (8) Merry Wives of Windsor; Bob Nettles (10) Le Depit Amoureux; La Chapeau d'un Horloger (12) Adrienne, the Actress: *Adrienne*–Mlle. Rachel (13) Le Tartuffe (17) Adrienne, the Actress: *Adrienne*–Mlle. Rachel (22) Merry Wives of Windsor; Bob Nettles (24) Stranger; My Uncle Foozle (25) Rob Roy MacGregor; State Secrets (27) Richard III; Mother Bailey* (28) Rob Roy MacGregor; My Uncle Foozle (29) London Assurance; Object of Interest (31) Jane Shore; Still Water Runs Deep

Ja (1) Iron Chest; Loan of a Lover (2) Bride of Lammermoor; All that Glitters Is Not Gold (3) Old Heads and Young Hearts; Blue Devils (4) Married Life; All that Glitters Is Not Gold (5) Jack Cade*; Windmill (7) Jack Cade; Windmill (8) Willow Copse; William Tell; 102 (9) Bride of Lammermoor; 102; (10) Bottle*; 102 (11) Bottle; My Uncle Foozle (12) Bottle; Honeymoon (14) Bottle; Single Life (15) Bottle; Grimshaw, Bagshaw, and Bradshaw (16) Willow

Copse; Object of Interest (17) Hamlet; Irish Tutor (18) Lucretia
Borgia; Lola Montez (19) Lucretia Borgia; Simpson and Company
(21) Money; Mystery (22) Iron Chest; Object of Interest (23) Morn-
ing Call; Rake's Progress (24) Lucretia Borgia; Mr. and Mrs. Peter
White (25) Follies of a Night; Eudia*; La Bayadere (Act I) (26)
Wives as They Were and Maids as They Are; Lola Montez (28) Wives
as They Were and Maids as They Are; Eudia (29) Little Treasure;
Naval Engagements; Lend Me Five Shillings (30) Money; Mr. and
Mrs. Peter White (31) Paul Pry; Good for Nothing; P. P.

F (1) Paul Pry; Lend Me Five Shillings (2) Serious Family; Rich-
ard III (4) Wonder; Eton Boy (5) Married Life; Mystery (6) Little
Treasure; Serious Family (7) Wonder; P. P. (8) Jane Shore; La
Bayadere (9) Man of Many Friends; Tom and Jerry (11) Flowers of
the Forest; Mischief Making (12) Man of Many Friends; Tom and
Jerry (13) Flowers of the Forest; Mischief Making (14) Corsican
Brothers; Lend Me Five Shillings (15) Corsican Brothers; Rough
Diamond (16) Isabelle; Asmodeus (18) School of Reform; Lola
Montez; Vivandiere of Chapultepec (19-25) Campbell's Minstrels (26)
Isabelle; Wandering Minstrel (27) Romeo and Juliet: *Juliet*–Julia
Dean; Sudden Thoughts (28) Hunchback: *Julia*–Julia Dean; Rough
Diamond (29) Ingomar: *Parthenia*–Julia Dean; Number One Round
the Corner

Mr (1) Gamester: *Mrs. Beverly*–Julia Dean; Swiss Swains (3)
Griseldis: *Griseldis*–Julia Dean; Morning Call: *Mrs. Chillington*–Julia
Dean (4) Evadne: *Evadne*–Julia Dean; Sudden Thoughts (5) Lady of
Lyons: *Pauline*–Julia Dean; Bob Nettles (6) Mary of Mantua: *Mary*–
Julia Dean; Wind Mill (7) Griseldis: *Griseldis*–Julia Dean; Mesmerism
(8) Adrienne, the Actress: *Adrienne*–Julia Dean; Eton Boy (10) Fazio:
Bianca–Julia Dean; Love Chase: *Constance*–Julia Dean (11) Mary of
Mantua: *Mary*–Julia Dean; As Like as Two Peas (12) Love: *Countess*–
Julia Dean; Mesmerism (13) Milly: *Milly*–Agnes Robertson; Young
Actress: six rôles–Agnes Robertson; P. P. (14) Monsieur Jacques;
Andy Blake: *Andy*–Agnes Robertson; Young Actress: six rôles–Agnes
Robertson (15) Monsieur Jacques; Milly: *Milly*–Agnes Robertson;
Young Actress: six rôles–Agnes Robertson (17) Young Actress: six
rôles–Agnes Robertson; Violet: *Violet*–Agnes Robertson, *Grimaldi*–
Boucicault (18) Violet: *Violet*–Agnes Robertson, *Grimaldi*–Boucicault;
Andy Blake: *Andy Blake*–Agnes Robertson (19) Chameleon: four rôles–
Agnes Robertson; Used Up: *Sir Charles Coldstream*–Boucicault; Bob
Nettles: *Bob Nettles*–Agnes Robertson, *Mons. Tourbillon*–Boucicault
(20) Cat Changed into a Woman: *Minette*–Agnes Robertson, *Karl*–
Boucicault; Violet: *Violet*–Agnes Robertson, *Grimaldi*–Boucicault (21)
Used Up: *Sir Charles Coldstream*–Boucicault; Cat Changed into a
Woman: *Minette*–Agnes Robertson, *Karl*–Boucicault; Rachel's Coming:
six rôles–Agnes Robertson (24) How to Settle Accounts with Your
Washerwoman; Devil's in It: *Cario*–Agnes Robertson; Chameleon: four
rôles–Agnes Robertson (25) Old Guard: *Haversack*–Boucicault; Milly:
Milly–Agnes Robertson; Young Actress: six rôles–Agnes Robertson
(26) Sudden Thoughts; Bob Nettles: *Bob Nettles*–Agnes Robertson,
Mons. Tourbillon–Boucicault; Young Actress: six rôles–Agnes Robertson (27) Used Up: *Sir Charles Coldstream*–Boucicault; Andy Blake:
Andy Blake–Agnes Robertson; Rachel's Coming: six rôles–Agnes Robertson (28) London Assurance: *Dazzle*–Boucicault, *Grace*–Agnes Robertson;

Love and Money: *Lord Fipley*–Boucicault, Lady Rose–Agnes Robertson (29) London Assurance: *Dazzle*–Boucicault, *Grace*–Agnes Robertson; Young Actress: six rôles–Agnes Robertson (31) Leap Year*; Somebody Else

Ap (1) Leap Year; Mesmerism (2) Leap Year; Sweethearts and Wives (3) Leap Year; Sweethearts and Wives; Love and Murder (4) Leap Year; Love and Murder (5) Take that Girl Away; That Blessed Baby (7) Model of a Wife: *Bonnefoe*–Chanfrau; French Spy: *Ben*–Chanfrau; Stage Struck Barber: *Jeremiah*–Chanfrau (8) People's Lawyer: *Solomon Shingle*–Chanfrau; Paddy Mile's Boy: *Paddy*–Chanfrau; Toodles: *Timothy*–Chanfrau (9) Black Eyed Susan: *William*–Chanfrau; First Night: *Dufard*–Chanfrau; Toodles: *Timothy*–Chanfrau (10) People's Lawyer: *Solomon Shingle*–Chanfrau; Mose in California: *Mose*–Chanfrau (11) Ireland as It Is: *Ragged Pat*–Chanfrau; Mose in California: *Mose*–Chanfrau; Stage Struck Barber: *Jeremiah*–Chanfrau (12) Glance: *Mose*–Chanfrau; Ireland as It Is: *Ragged Pat*–Chanfrau; Toodles: *Timothy*–Chanfrau (14) Ocean Child: *Harry Helm*–Chanfrau; Glance: *Mose*–Chanfrau (15) Model of a Wife: *Bonnefoe*–Chanfrau; Stage Struck Barber: *Jeremiah*–Chanfrau; Ocean Child: *Harry Helm*–Chanfrau (16) Linda, the Cigar Girl: *Mose*–Chanfrau; First Night: *Dufard*–Chanfrau (17) Linda, the Cigar Girl: *Mose*–Chanfrau; Stage Struck Barber: *Jeremiah*–Chanfrau (18) Linda, the Cigar Girl: *Mose*–Chanfrau; Ireland as It Is: *Ragged Pat*–Chanfrau (19) O'Flannigan and the Fairies: *O'Flannigan*–Chanfrau; Toodles: *Timothy*–Chanfrau; Mose in California: *Mose*–Chanfrau (21) Poor Gentleman: *Ollapod*–Chanfrau; Bob Nettles: *Mons. Tourbillon*–Chanfrau

1856-1857

Mgr.: John Sloan; *acting mgr.*: W. L. Ayling; *orch. leader:* de Carlo Vitto; *machinist:* C. Herbert; *treas.:* T. A. Burns; *prompter:* C. B. Harrison. *Stock:* Arnold, M. A., Crocker, F. S., Dowling, Drew, F., Fisher, G., Grace, J. R., Greatorex, Green, T. C., Marchant, G. W., Parks, Raymond, J. T., Silsbee, Williams, E. B. (Adam Brock); *Mrs.* Ayling, W. L., Harrison, C. B., Marchant, G. F., Silsbee, Sloan, J.; *Misses* Blake, F., Crocker, E. V., Cushnie, G., Gray, N., Holdridge, Hosmer, A.

SE: John Wallack Lester (J. Lester Wallack): N 17-29; James W. Wallack: D 1-13; Agnes Robertson and Dion Boucicault: D 15-27; Andrew J. Neafie: Ja 12-17; Annette Ince: Ja 19-F 14; Max Maretzek's Opera Company (Max Maretzek, Bertucca Maretzek, F. Brignoli, A. Amodio, Dominico Colletti, L. Quinto, L. Muller; Signoras Bertucca Maretzek, L. Avogardo): F 16-17; Fanny Davenport: F 18-28, Mr 16-Ap 4; John Drew: Mr 2-14; Fannie Morant: Ap 14-21; Madame D'Angri Opera Company (Madame and Mlle. D'Angri; Messrs. Theodore Thomas, Louis Schreiber, Abella): My 11.

N (3) School for Scandal; farce (5) Honeymoon; Box and Cox (6) Still Water Runs Deep; Slasher and Crasher (7) Married Life; Kiss in the Dark (8) Old Chateau*; Lottery Ticket (10) Othello; First Night (11) Old Chateau; Slasher and Crasher (12) Lady of Lyons; Lottery Ticket (13) Ladies' Battle; First Night (14) Ladies' Battle; Married Life (15) Helping Hands; Bob Nettles (17) Morning Call: *Sir Edward Ardent*–Lester; Pauline: *Count Horace de Beauval*–Lester (18) Captain of the Watch: *Viscount de Ligny*–Lester; Pauline: *Count Horace de Beauval*–Lester (19) School for Scandal: *Charles Surface*–

Lester; Slasher and Crasher (20) Ernestine: *Frederick de Champeur-ville*–Lester; Captain of the Watch: *Viscount de Ligny*–Lester (22) Wild Oats: *Rover*–Lester; Box and Cox (24) Captain of the Watch: *Viscount de Ligny*–Lester; London Assurance: *Charles Courtly*–Lester (25) Wild Oats: *Rover*–Lester; Trying It On: *Walsingham Potts*–Lester (26) Bachelor of Arts*: *Harry Jasper*–Lester; Captain of the Watch: *Viscount de Ligny*–Lester (27) Ernestine: *Frederick de Champeurville*–Lester; Bachelor of Arts: *Harry Jasper*–Lester (28) Bachelor of Arts: *Harry Jasper*–Lester; Pauline: *Count Horace de Beauval*–Lester (29) She Stoops to Conquer: *Sir Charles Marlowe*–Lester; Rights and Wrongs of Women*: *Sir Brian de Beausex*–Lester

D (1) Hamlet: *Hamlet*–Wallack; Box and Cox (2) Much Ado about Nothing: *Benedict*–Wallack; Slasher and Crasher (3) Merchant of Venice: *Shylock*–Wallack; Lottery Ticket (4) Hamlet: *Hamlet*–Wallack; First Night (5) Stranger: *Stranger*–Wallack; Bob Nettles (6) Iron Chest: *Sir Edward Mortimer*–Wallack; My Aunt: *Dick Dashall*–Wallack (8) Don Caesar de Bazan: *Don Caesar*–Wallack; His Last Legs (9) Don Caesar de Bazan: *Don Caesar*–Wallack; Moustache Mania (10) Don Caesar de Bazan: *Don Caesar*–Wallack; My Aunt: *Dick Dashall*–Wallack (11) Wonder: *Don Felix*–Wallack; His Last Legs (12) Wife: *Julian St. Pierre*–Wallack; Rough Diamond (13) Scholar: *Erasmus Bookworm*–Wallack; Rent Day: *Martin Heywood*–Wallack (15) Violet: *Grimaldi*–Boucicault, *Violet*–Agnes Robertson; Young Actress: five rôles–Agnes Robertson (16) Love and Money: *Lord Fipley*–Boucicault, *Lady Rose*–Agnes Robertson; Young Actress: five rôles–Agnes Robertson (17) London Assurance: *Dazzle*–Boucicault, *Grace Harkaway*–Agnes Robertson; Young Actress: five rôles–Agnes Robertson (18) Violet: *Grimaldi*–Boucicault, *Violet*–Agnes Robertson; Chameleon: four rôles–Agnes Robertson (19) London Assurance: *Dazzle*–Boucicault, *Grace Harkaway*–Agnes Robertson; Chameleon: four rôles–Agnes Robertson (20) Phantom*: *Phantom*–Boucicault, *Lucy* and *Ada*–Agnes Robertson; Young Actress: five rôles–Agnes Robertson (22) Phantom: *Phantom*–Boucicault, *Lucy* and *Ada*–Agnes Robertson; Bluebelle: *Bluebelle*–Agnes Robertson (23) Andy Blake: *Andy Blake*–Agnes Robertson; Bluebelle: *Bluebelle*–Agnes Robertson (24) Victor and Hortense*: *Victor*–Boucicault, *Hortense*–Agnes Robertson; Andy Blake: *Andy Blake*–Agnes Robertson (25) Phantom: *Phantom*–Boucicault, *Lucy* and *Ada*–Agnes Robertson; Young Actress: five rôles–Agnes Robertson (26) Bob Nettles: *Bob*–Agnes Robertson, *Mons. Tourbillon*–Boucicault; Bluebelle: *Bluebelle*–Agnes Robertson (27) Victor and Hortense: *Victor*–Boucicault, *Hortense*–Agnes Robertson; Used Up: *Sir Charles Coldstream*–Boucicault; Chameleon: four rôles–Agnes Robertson (29) Bold Stroke for a Husband; Serious Husband (30) Macbeth; Moustache Mania (31) Othello; First Night

Ja (1) Marble Hearts*; Irish Lion (3) Heir at Law; My Precious Betsy (5) Marble Hearts; Spectre Bridegroom (6) Heir at Law; Irish Lion (7) Retribution*; Bombastes Furioso; Phenomenon in a Smock Frock (8) Retribution; Serious Family (9) Vicar of Wakefield*; Rough Diamond; My Fellow Clerk (10) Ambrose Gwinnett; Bombastes Furioso (12) Hamlet: *Hamlet*–Neafie; My Fellow Clerk (13) Macbeth: *Macbeth*–Neafie; Irish Lion (14) Corsican Brothers: *Fabien* and *Louis*–Neafie; Phenomenon in a Smock Frock (15) Corsican Brothers: *Fabien* and *Louis*–Neafie; My Fellow Clerk (16) Corsican Brothers: *Fabien*

and *Louis*–Neafie; Rough Diamond (17) Damon and Pythias: *Damon–*
Neafie; Don Caesar de Bazan: *Don Caesar*–Neafie (19) Romeo and
Juliet: *Juliet*–Annette Ince; Secret (20) Lady of Lyons: *Pauline*–
Annette Ince; Poor Pillicoddy (21) Hunchback: *Julia*–Annette Ince;
Crossing the Line (22) Love's Sacrifice: *Margaret Elmore*–Annette
Ince; Poor Pillicoddy (23) Armand: *Blanche*–Annette Ince; Honey-
moon: *Juliana*–Annette Ince (24) Wife: *Mariana*–Annette Ince; Cross-
ing the Line (26) Lucretia Borgia: *Lucretia Borgia*–Annette Ince;
Secret (27) Armand: *Blanche*–Annette Ince; Mesmerism (28) Evadne:
Evadne–Annette Ince; Poor Pillicoddy (29) Lucretia Borgia: *Lucretia
Borgia*–Annette Ince; Crossing the Line (30) Love: *Countess*–Annette
Ince; Morning Call: *Mrs. Chillington*–Annette Ince (31) Pizarro:
Elvira–Annette Ince; Mesmerism

F (2) Fashion; Faint Heart Ne'er Won Fair Lady: *Duchess*–Annette
Ince (3) Limerick Boy; Hunchback: *Julia*–Annette Ince (4) Fashion;
Most Unwarrantable Intrusion (5) Ingomar: *Parthenia*–Annette Ince;
Most Unwarrantable Intrusion (6) As You Like It: *Rosalind*–Annette
Ince; Ladies Beware (7) Rob Roy MacGregor; Review (9) Ion: *Ion*–
Annette Ince; Ladies Beware (10) As You Like It: *Rosalind*–Annette
Ince; Review (11) Mathilde*; Delicate Ground (12) Ingomar: *Par-
thenia*–Annette Ince; Limerick Boy (13) Virginius; Night with an
Artist (14) Fazio: *Bianca*–Annette Ince; Madeline: *Madeline*–Annette
Ince (16) Lucia di Lammermoor (17) Il Puritani (18) Adrienne, the
Actress: *Adrienne*–Fanny Davenport; Night with an Artist (19) Hunch-
back: *Julia*–Fanny Davenport; Mesmerism (20) Adrienne, the Actress:
Adrienne–Fanny Davenport; Ladies Beware (21, 23-25) Camille:
Camille–Fanny Davenport (26) Charlotte Corday: *Charlotte*–Fanny
Davenport; Dumb Belle (27) Lady of Lyons: *Pauline*–Fanny Daven-
port; London Assurance: *Lady Gay Spanker*–Fanny Davenport (28)
Charlotte Corday: *Charlotte*–Fanny Davenport; Dumb Belle

Mr (2) Irish Ambassador: *Sir Patrick O'Plenipo*–Drew; Temptation:
O'Brien–Drew (3) Irish Attorney: *Pierce O'Hara*–Drew; Temptation:
O'Brien–Drew (4) Irish Ambassador: *Sir Patrick O'Plenipo*–Drew;
Serious Family: *Capt. Murphy Maguire*–Drew (5) Knight of Arva:
Connor–Drew; His Last Legs: *O'Callaghan*–Drew (6) Knight of Arva:
Connor–Drew; Temptation: *O'Brien*–Drew (7) Rivals: *Sir Lucius
O'Trigger*–Drew; Black Eyed Susan: *William*–Drew (9) Comedy of
Errors: *Dromios*–Drew; Irish Attorney: *Pierce O'Hara*–Drew (10)
Comedy of Errors: *Dromios*–Drew; More Blunders than One: *Larry*–
Drew (11) Rivals: *Sir Lucius O'Trigger*–Drew; More Blunders than
One: *Larry*–Drew (12-13) Comedy of Errors: *Dromios*–Drew; White
Horse of the Peppers: *Gerald*–Drew (14) Nervous Man and the Man of
Nerve: *McShane*–Drew; Rory O'More: *Rory O'More*–Drew (16) Love:
Countess–Fanny Davenport; Two Bonny Castles (17) Camille: *Camille*–
Fanny Davenport (18) Love's Sacrifice: *Margaret Elmore*–Fanny Dav-
enport; Two Bonny Castles (19) Adrienne, the Actress: *Adrienne*–
Fanny Davenport; Two Bonny Castles (20) Valeria*: *Valeria* and
Lycisca–Fanny Davenport; Rough Diamond (21) Valeria: *Valeria* and
Lycisca–Fanny Davenport; Dumb Belle (23) Peg Woffington: *Peg*–
Fanny Davenport; Bob Nettles (24) Peg Woffington: *Peg*–Fanny
Davenport; Limerick Boy (25) Stranger: *Mrs. Haller*–Fanny Daven-
port; Box and Cox (26) Camille: *Camille*–Fanny Davenport (27)
Belle's Stratagem: *Letitia Hardy*–Fanny Davenport; Most Unwarrant-

able Intrusion (28) Medea*: *Medea*-Fanny Davenport; Belle's Strata-
gem: *Letitia Hardy*-Fanny Davenport (30) Medea: *Medea*-Fanny
Davenport; Somebody Else (31) Medea: *Medea*-Fanny Davenport; Bob
Nettles

Ap (1) Camille: *Camille*-Fanny Davenport; Peg Woffington: *Peg*-
Fanny Davenport (2) Camille: *Camille*-Fanny Davenport (3) Mona
Lisa*: *Therese*-Fanny Davenport; Honeymoon: *Juliana*-Fanny Daven-
port (4) Mona Lisa: *Therese*-Fanny Davenport; Most Unwarrantable
Intrusion (6-7) Days of Washington*; As Like as Two Peas (8) Days
of Washington; Somebody Else (9-10) Grandfather Whitehead; Medea
Burlesque (11) Pride of the Market; Camille Burlesque (13) All that
Glitters Is Not Gold; Camille Burlesque (14) Second Love*: *Eleanor*-
Fannie Morant; Somebody Else (15) Second Love: *Eleanor*-Fannie
Morant; Pride of the Market (16) Second Love: *Eleanor*-Fannie
Morant; Old Guard (17) Second Love: *Eleanor*-Fannie Morant; All
that Glitters Is Not Gold (18) Nocturnal Visitor: *Zephrina*-Fannie
Morant; Othello Travestie (20) Nocturnal Visitor: *Zephrina*-Fannie
Morant; Lola Montez; Othello Travestie (21) Play, Plot and Passion:
Madame De Fontagnes-Fannie Morant; How to Settle Accounts with
Your Washerwoman; Othello Travestie (24) Drunkard's Fate; Roguer-
ies of Thomas*; Maniac

My (11) Barber of Seville (scenes); Romeo and Juliet (Act III)

1857-1858

Mgr.: G. F. Marchant; *acting mgr.:* John Dyott; *scenist:* George
Evans; *machinist:* C. Herbert; *decorator:* Deverna; *upholsterer:* La-
rousseliere. *Stock:* Aiken, G. L., Beverly, Browne, J. F., Chippendale, F.,
Clinton, Durivage, O. E., Dwyer, Fiske, M. W., Harrison, C. B, Lewis,
H., Ralton, D. E., Rea, F., Smith, J. S., Smith, T. R.; *Mrs.* France,
Harrison, C. B., Jones, M., Marchant, G. F., Rea, F.; *Misses* Cappell,
C., Clifton, France, Haisman, S., Heyward, Moreland, A. G., Raymond,
A., Shaw, M.

SE: Avonia Jones: N 30-D 5, Ja 4-13; Fanny Davenport: D 7-19;
New Orleans English Opera Troupe (George Hodson, Fred Lyster, H.
Warton, Frank Trevor; Misses Rosalie Durand, Ada King, Georgia
Hodson; Antoine Rieff, director): Ja 18-F 6; Campbell's Minstrels: F
8-13; Edwin Booth: F 17-20; Mr. and Mrs. W. J. Florence: F 22-Mr 1,
8-13; Havana Italian Opera Company (Signors F. Brignoli, Tagliafico,
Stecchi Bottardi, A. Amodio, Assoni, D. Colletti, L. Muller, L. Quinto;
Signoras Marietta Gazzaniga, L. Avogardo; Miss Adelaide Phillips):
Mr 2-6; Keller Ballet Troupe: Mr 29-Ap 10; Charles Matthews (sup-
ported by Mrs. Matthews): Ap 12-19.

O (19) Jealous Wife; Loan of a Lover (21) Still Water Runs Deep;
Sketches in India (23) Town and Country; Box and Cox (24) Charles
XII; Sketches in India (26) King Lear; Loan of a Lover (27) Town
and Country; Family Jars (28) Lady of Lyons; Two Gregories (29)
Willow Copse; Jenny Lind (30) Willow Copse; Swiss Cottage (31)
Clari; Honeymoon

N (2) Hamlet; My Precious Betsy (3) Lucille; Mr. and Mrs. Dodson
(4) Lucille; Nothing to Nurse; Your Life's in Danger (5) Money;
Nothing to Nurse (6) Clari; Wonder (7) Richard III; Two Gregories
(10) Eustache; Brian O'Lynn (11) Mountain Maid; Willow Copse (12)
She Would and She Would Not; Your Life's in Danger (13) Eustache;

Still Water Runs Deep (14) Momentous Question; Mr. and Mrs. Dodson; Prince and the Watchman* (15) Azael*; farce (16) Azael; Swiss Cottage (18) Azael; Nothing to Nurse (19-20) Azael (21) Azael; Hunting a Turtle; Loan of a Lover (23) Home Again; Azael (24) Poor Gentleman; Hunter of the Alps (25) Money; Perfection (26) Courtier of Lyons*; Your Life's in Danger (27) Courtier of Lyons; Home Again (28) Courtier of Lyons; Iron Chest (30) Armand: *Blanche*–Avonia Jones; Swiss Cottage

D (1) Ingomar: *Parthenia*–Avonia Jones; Two Gregories (2) Second Love: *Eleanor*–Avonia Jones; Family Jars (3) Bride of Lammermoor: *Lucy Ashton*–Avonia Jones; Rose de Mal* (4) Romeo and Juliet: *Juliet*– Avonia Jones; Hunter of the Alps (5) Evadne: *Evadne*–Avonia Jones; French Spy (7) Wife: *Mariana*–Fanny Davenport; Who Speaks First? (8) Mona Lisa: *Therese*–Fanny Davenport; Perfection (9) Medea: *Medea*–Fanny Davenport; Mountain Maid (10) School for Scandal: *Lady Teazle*–Fanny Davenport; Kiss in the Dark (11) Gamester: *Mrs. Beverly*–Fanny Davenport; Nature versus Art: *Mrs. Oldfield*–Fanny Davenport (12) Macbeth: *Lady Macbeth*–Fanny Davenport; Conjugal Lesson (14) Camille: *Camille*–Fanny Davenport; Conjugal Lesson (15) Ingomar: *Parthenia*–Fanny Davenport; Conjugal Lesson (16) Hunchback: *Julia*–Fanny Davenport; Kiss in the Dark (17) Nature versus Art: *Mrs. Oldfield*–Fanny Davenport; Peg Woffington: *Peg*–Fanny Davenport (18) Virginia: *Virginia*–Fanny Davenport; Peg Woffington: *Peg*–Fanny Davenport (19) Camille: *Camille*–Fanny Davenport; Box and Cox (21) Othello; Review (25-26, 28) Aladdin (29) Aladdin; Poor Pillicoddy (30) Aladdin; Two Buzzards (31-Ja 1) Aladdin; Sunshine through Clouds

Ja (4) Evadne: *Evadne*–Avonia Jones; Two Buzzards (5) Love's Sacrifice: *Margaret Elmore*–Avonia Jones; Poor Pillicoddy (6) Fazio: *Bianca*–Avonia Jones; Loan of a Lover (7) Lady of Lyons: *Pauline*– Avonia Jones; My Precious Betsy (8) Child of the Regiment: *Marie*– Avonia Jones; King Rene's Daughter: *Iolanthe*–Avonia Jones (9) Child of the Regiment: *Marie*–Avonia Jones; Rob Roy MacGregor (11) London Assurance: *Grace Harkaway*–Avonia Jones; Two Buzzards (12) Bride of Lammermoor: *Lucy Ashton*–Avonia Jones; Child of the Regiment: *Marie*–Avonia Jones (13) Armand: *Blanche*–Avonia Jones; Little Treasure: *Gertrude*–Avonia Jones (14) Charles II; Loan of a Lover; Poor Pillicoddy (16) Charleston Theatre in an Uproar; Love in Livery; Nice Young Ladies; Lady's Maid; Paddy Mile's Boy (18) La Somnambula (19) Barber of Seville (20) Daughter of the Regiment (21) Bohemian Girl (22) La Somnambula (23) Fra Diavolo (25) Barber of Seville (26) Fra Diavolo (27) Il Trovatore (28) Fra Diavolo (29-30) Cinderella

F (1) Il Trovatore (2) Bohemian Girl (3) Barber of Seville; Midas (4) Cinderella (5) Daughter of the Regiment; Pocahontas (6) Beggar's Opera; Pocahontas (8-13) Campbell's Minstrels (17-18) Richelieu: *Richelieu*–Booth; Sketches in India (19) New Way to Pay Old Debts: *Sir Giles Overreach*–Booth; Catherine and Petruchio (20) Richard III: *Richard*–Booth; My Precious Betsy (22) Born to Good Luck: *Paudeen O'Rafferty*–Florence; Lesson for Husbands: six rôles–Mrs. Florence; Yankee Gal: *Peg Ann*–Mrs. Florence, *Barry O'Conner*– Florence (23) Ireland as It Is: *Ragged Pat*–Florence, *Judy*–Mrs. Florence; Mischievous Annie: five rôles–Mrs. Florence, *Tim*–Florence

(24) Temptation: *O'Brien*–Florence; Mischievous Annie: five rôles–
Mrs. Florence, *Tim*–Florence; Yankee Gal: *Peg Ann*–Mrs. Florence,
Barry O'Conner–Florence (25) Irish Lion: *Tim*–Florence; Lesson for
Husbands: six rôles–Mrs. Florence; Irish Baron: *Flannigan*–Florence,
Hulda–Mrs. Florence (26) Irish Lion: *Tim*–Florence; Working the
Oracle: eight rôles–Mrs. Florence; Mischievous Annie: five rôles–Mrs.
Florence, *Tim*–Florence (27) Temptation: *O'Brien*–Florence; Working
the Oracle: eight rôles–Mrs. Florence; Irish Baron: *Flannigan*–
Florence, *Hulda*–Mrs. Florence
  Mr (1) O'Flannigan and the Fairies: *O'Flannigan*–Florence; Young
Actress: five rôles–Mrs. Florence, *Mr. Camomile*–Florence; Good for
Nothing: *Nan*–Mrs. Florence, *Tim*–Florence (2) Lucrezia Borgia (3)
Barber of Seville (4) Il Trovatore (5) L'Elisir d'Amore (6) La
Traviata (8) Frederick the Great: *O'Neill*–Florence; Mischievous An-
nie: five rôles–Mrs. Florence, *Tim*–Florence; Good for Nothing: *Nan*–
Mrs. Florence, *Tim*–Florence (9) Irish Assurance and Yankee Modesty:
Pat–Florence, *Nancy*–Mrs. Florence; Thrice Married*: *Vivian*–Florence,
four rôles–Mrs. Florence; Box and Cox (10) Ireland as It Is: *Ragged
Pat*–Florence, *Judy*–Mrs. Florence; Young Actress: five rôles–Mrs.
Florence (11) Lesson for Husbands: six rôles–Mrs. Florence, *Tim*–
Florence; Irish Baron: *Flannigan*–Florence, *Hulda*–Mrs. Florence; Brian
O'Lynn: *Brian*–Florence (12) O'Flannigan and the Fairies: *O'Flan-
nigan*–Florence; Thrice Married: four rôles–Mrs. Florence; Working
the Oracle: eight rôles–Mrs. Florence (13) Irish Assurance and Yankee
Modesty: *Pat*–Florence, *Nancy*–Mrs. Florence; Thrice Married: four
rôles–Mrs. Florence; Sanguinary Bootjack; Florence and Smith at
Daggers' Points (15) Raffael, the Reprobate; Pioneer Patriot (22)
Simpson and Company; Swiss Swains (23) Maid of Croissey; Dobson
and Company (24) Simpson and Company; Two Buzzards; Paddy Mile's
Boy (25) Last Man; Swedish Nightingale (26) Milly; Loan of a Lover;
Beauty and the Beast; Jenny Lind (27) Charleston Fireman; Miseries
of Human Life; Smith and Fiske; Object of Interest (29-31) Keller
Ballet Troupe
  Ap (1-2) Last Days of Pompey; Keller Ballet Troupe (5) Uriel;
Keller Ballet Troupe (6-10) Azael; Keller Ballet Troupe (12) Married
for Money: *Mopus*–Matthews; Patter versus Clatter: *Capt. Patter*–
Matthews; Your Life's in Danger (13) Dowager: *Lord Alfred*–
Matthews; Eton Boy: two rôles–Matthews; Patter versus Clatter: *Capt.
Patter*–Matthews (14) Cool as a Cucumber: *Plumper*–Matthews; Comi-
cal Countess; He Would Be an Actor: *Motley*–Matthews (15) Married
for Money: *Mopus*–Matthews; He Would Be an Actor: *Motley*–Matthews
(16) London Assurance: *Dazzle*–Matthews; Cool as a Cucumber:
Plumper–Matthews (17) Dowager: *Lord Alfred*–Matthews; Used Up:
Sir Charles Coldstream–Matthews; Trying It On: *Walsingham Potts*–
Matthews (19) Take that Girl Away: *Charles*–Matthews; Two Can Play
at that Game: *Henry*–Matthews; Nicholas Nickleby: *Smike*–Matthews
(20) Ingomar; Swiss Cottage (21) Rob Roy MacGregor; Spectre Bride-
groom (22) Jewess; Three Jack Sheppards (23) Pizarro; Raising the
Wind (24) Serious Family; Lost Son (26) Serious Family; Lottery
Ticket (27) Guy Mannering; Major Jones' Courtship (28) Still Water
Runs Deep; My Young Wife and My Old Umbrella

1858-1859

Mgr.: G. F. Marchant; *orch. leader:* H. Eckhardt; *treas.:* J. Corrigan.
Stock: Barrett, J. H., Bernard, Browne, C. M., Coleman, E. B., Cooke,
H., Elmore, M., Fuller, J. B., Lemoyne, Lennox, W., Lewis, H., Metkiff,
Morton, C. H., Penistan, Richards, Rivers, Wallis, J. L.; *Mrs.* Eckhardt,
H., Elmore, M., Fuller, J. B., Gladstane, M., Lennox, W.; *Misses* Ashley,
Basson, Frost, A., Harcourt, Lawton, Miller, M., Norton, Raymond, A.

SE: C. M. Walcot, Jr.: N 16-20; W. E. Burton (supported by Mrs.
Hughes): N 29-D 11; James E. Murdoch: D 13-18; Maggie Mitchell:
D 21-Ja 8; Ravel Family (with Martinetti Brothers and M. Blondin):
Ja 10-22, F 15-24; Julia Dean (Hayne): Ja 24-F 5; New Orleans English
Opera Troupe (same cast as 1857-1858): F 28-Mr 8; Mr. and Mrs. W. J.
Florence: Mr 17-21; Edwin Booth: Mr 22-Ap 11.

N (15) School for Scandal; Alpine Maid (16) Not a Bad Judge: *La
Vater*–Walcot; Pretty Piece of Business: *Dr. Launcelot*–Walcot; King's
Gardener (17) Follies of a Night: *Pierre*–Walcot; Man without a Head:
Dr. Top–Walcot; Poor Pillicoddy (18) London Assurance: *Dazzle*–
Walcot; Kiss in the Dark (19) Knights of the Round Table*: *Tom
Titler*–Walcot; Pretty Piece of Business: *Dr. Launcelot*–Walcot (20)
Road to Ruin: *Goldfinch*–Walcot; 'Twas I (22-25, 27) Sea of Ice* (29)
Dombey and Son: *Capt. Cuttle*–Burton; Alpine Maid (30) Serious
Family: *Aminidab Sleek*–Burton; Wanted, One Thousand Milliners: *Joe
Bragg*–Burton

D (1) Breach of Promise: *Sudden*–Burton; Toodles: *Timothy*–Burton
(2) John Jones: *Guy Goodluck*–Burton; Wandering Minstrel: *Jem
Baggs*–Burton; Wanted, One Thousand Milliners: *Joe Bragg*–Burton
(3) Blue Devils: *Megrim*–Burton; Sweethearts and Wives: *Billy Lacka-
day*–Burton; Mummy: *Toby Tramp*–Burton (4) Serious Family:
Aminidab Sleek–Burton; Toodles: *Timothy*–Burton (6) Dombey and
Son: *Capt. Cuttle*–Burton; Wandering Minstrel: *Jem Braggs*–Burton
(7) David Copperfield: *Wilkins Micawber*–Burton; Blue Devils: *Meg-
rim*–Burton (8) David Copperfield: *Wilkins Micawber*–Burton; Wanted,
One Thousand Milliners: *Joe Bragg*–Burton (9) Paul Pry: *Paul Pry*–
Burton; Mummy: *Toby Tramp*–Burton (10) Dutch Governor: *Van
Dumer*–Burton; Breach of Promise: *Sudden*–Burton; John Jones: *Guy
Goodluck*–Burton (11) Sweethearts and Wives: *Billy Lackaday*–Burton;
Wanted, One Thousand Milliners: *Joe Bragg*–Burton (13-14) Lady of
Lyons: *Claude*–Murdoch; My Precious Betsy (15) Hamlet: *Hamlet*–
Murdoch; Kiss in the Dark (16) Money: *Evelyn*–Murdoch; Alpine Maid
(17) Time Works Wonders: *Young Mirable*–Murdoch; Catherine and
Petruchio: *Petruchio*–Murdoch (18) Macbeth: *Macbeth*–Murdoch; My
Precious Betsy (20) Sea of Ice; Lottery Ticket (21) Mysterious
Stranger: rôle not given–Maggie Mitchell; Milly: *Milly*–Maggie Mitchell
(22) Little Treasure: *Gertrude*–Maggie Mitchell; Kathy O'Sheal: *Kathy*–
Maggie Mitchell (23) French Spy: rôle not given–Maggie Mitchell;
Kathy O'Sheal: *Kathy*–Maggie Mitchell (24) Margot, the Poultry
Dealer: *Margot*–Maggie Mitchell; Youth of Frederick the Great: *Prince
Frederick*–Maggie Mitchell (25) Margot, the Poultry Dealer: *Margot*–
Maggie Mitchell; Milly: *Milly*–Maggie Mitchell; Richard (27) Pet of
the Petticoats: *Paul the Pet*–Maggie Mitchell; Kathy O'Sheal: *Kathy*–
Maggie Mitchell (28) Wept of Wish-ton-Wish; *Narramattah*–Maggie
Mitchell; Object of Interest: *Fanny*–Maggie Mitchell (29) Peg Woffing-

ton: *Peg*–Maggie Mitchell; Lady's Stratagem: five rôles–Maggie Mitchell (30) Husband at Sight: *Catherine*–Maggie Mitchell; Little Treasure: *Gertrude*–Maggie Mitchell; Four Sisters (31) Daughter of the Regiment: *Madeline*–Maggie Mitchell; Antony and Cleopatra: *Cleopatra*–Maggie Mitchell; Douglas: *Young Norval*–Maggie Mitchell

Ja (1) Wandering Boys: rôle not given–Maggie Mitchell; Richard: *Richard*–Maggie Mitchell; Kathy O'Sheal: *Kathy*–Maggie Mitchell (3) Green Bushes: *Miami*–Maggie Mitchell; Lady's Stratagem: five rôles–Maggie Mitchell (4) Mysterious Stranger: rôle not given–Maggie Mitchell; Antony and Cleopatra: *Cleopatra*–Maggie Mitchell (5) Wept of Wish-ton-Wish: *Narramattah*–Maggie Mitchell; Pet of the Petticoats: *Paul the Pet*–Maggie Mitchell (6) French Spy: rôle not given–Maggie Mitchell; Margot, the Poultry Dealer: *Margot*–Maggie Mitchell (7) Brigand Queen: *Olympia*–Maggie Mitchell; Asmodeus: *Carlo*–Maggie Mitchell; Four Sisters (8) Milly: *Milly*–Maggie Mitchell; Kathy O'Sheal: *Kathy*–Maggie Mitchell; Persecuted Dutchman (10) Robert Macaire; Vol au Vent; Ravel Family (11) Old and Young; Jocko; Ravel Family (12) Secret Marriage; Diana; Monsieur Deschalumeau; Ravel Family (13) Green Monster; Three Gladiators; Ravel Family (14) Isle of Nymphs; Three Gladiators; Ravel Family (15) Green Monster; Venetian Carnival; Ravel Family (17) Wanted, One Thousand Milliners; Magic Trumpet; Isle of Nymphs; Ravel Family (18) Soldier for Love; Monsieur Deschalumeau; Ravel Family (19) Harvest Home; Roman Gladiator; Vol au Vent; Ravel Family (20) Raoul; Three Gladiators; Diana; Ravel Family (21) Raoul; Hungarian Rendezvous; Ravel Family (22) Jocko; Raoul; Ravel Family (24) Hunchback: *Julia*–Julia Dean; farce (25) Ingomar: *Parthenia*–Julia Dean; Conjugal Lesson (26) Griseldis: *Griseldis*–Julia Dean; Conjugal Lesson (27) Wife: *Mariana*–Julia Dean; Sketches in India (28) Mary's Birthday: *Mary*–Julia Dean; Love Chase (29) Lady of Lyons: *Pauline*–Julia Dean; Sketches in India (31) Adrienne, the Actress: *Adrienne*–Julia Dean; Lady and a Gentleman in a Peculiarly Perplexing Predicament

F (1) Love: *Countess*–Julia Dean; Slasher and Crasher (2) Phillip of France*: *Marie*–Julia Dean; Slasher and Crasher (3) Duke's Wager: *Gabrielle*–Julia Dean; farce (4) Much Ado about Nothing: *Beatrice*–Julia Dean; Rough Diamond: *Marjorie*–Julia Dean (5) Camille: *Camille*–Julia Dean (7) Rivals; My Uncle Foozle (8) All that Glitters Is Not Gold; Alpine Maid (9) As You Like It; White Horse of the Peppers (10) Therese; Lend Me Five Shillings (11) Roland for an Oliver; King's Gardener; White Horse of the Peppers (12) Marble Hearts; My Uncle Foozle (15-21) Mazulme; Ravel Family (22-24) Esther; Ravel Family (28) La Somnambula

Mr (1) Crown Diamonds (2) Cinderella (3) Barber of Seville (4) Il Trovatore (5) Fra Diavolo (7) Don Pasquale (8) Bohemian Girl (9) Idiot Witness; Somebody Else; Artful Dodger (11) Ladies' Battle; Trying It On; 'Twas I (12) Highlander's Oath; Raising the Wind; Artful Dodger (14) Catherine and Petruchio; 'Twas I; Somebody Else (15) Lend Me Five Shillings; concert (16) Dead Shot; concert (17) Mischievous Annie: five rôles–Mrs. Florence; Born to Good Luck: *Paudeen O'Rafferty*–Florence (18) Knight of Arva: *Connor*–Florence; Lesson for Husbands: six rôles–Mrs. Florence (19) Temptation: *O'Brien*–Florence; Young Actress: five rôles–Mrs. Florence (21) Crossing the Frontier: *Marguerite*–Mrs. Florence; Advertising for a Wife: rôle not

given–Florence; Yankee Housekeeper: rôle not given–Mrs. Florence
(22) New Way to Pay Old Debts: *Sir Giles Overreach*–Booth; farce
(23) Hamlet: *Hamlet*–Booth; farce (24) Richelieu: *Richelieu*–Booth;
farce (25) Richard III: *Richard*–Booth; farce (26) Iron Chest: *Sir
Edward Mortimer*–Booth; Catherine and Petruchio: *Petruchio*–Booth
(28) Othello: *Othello*–Booth; farce (29) Apostate: *Pescara*–Booth; farce
(30) Richelieu: *Richelieu*–Booth (31) Hamlet: *Hamlet*–Booth; farce
   Ap (1) Macbeth: *Macbeth*–Booth; farce (2) Richard III: *Richard*–
Booth; farce (4) Macbeth: *Macbeth*–Booth; farce (5) King Lear: *King
Lear*–Booth; farce (6) Apostate: *Pescara*–Booth; farce (7) Iron Chest:
Sir Edward Mortimer–Booth; Black Eyed Susan (8) Othello: *Iago*–
Booth; farce (9) Richelieu: *Richelieu*–Booth; farce (11) Brutus:
Brutus–Booth; Who Speaks First?

1 8 5 9 - 1 8 6 0

   Mgr.: G. F. Marchant; *acting mgr.:* H. B. Phillips; *treas.:* J. Cor-
rigan; *orch. leader:* H. Eckhardt. *Stock:* Elmore, M., Fuller, J. B.,
Ralton, D. E., Raymond, J. T.; *Mrs.* Eckhardt, H., Elmore, M., Fuller, J.
B., Gladstane, M., Lingard, Phillips, H. B., Riggs; *Misses* Alinson, E.,
Estell, K., Gray, A., Marshall, L.
   SE: Polly Marshall: O 10-21; E. A. Sothern: O 24-29; John Collins:
O 31-N 10; Sandford Opera Company (Samuel S. Sandford, mgr.): N
·14-19; R. B. Buckley's Burlesque Opera Troupe (with Julia Gould):
N 21-25; Donetti and Woods' Trained Dogs: D 26-31; Marsh Juvenile
Comedians (B. G. Marsh, mgr.; Charlotte, Mary, Jenny, Annette, Annie,
George W., and Louis Marsh; Louisa Arnot, and others): Ja 2-14; Mr.
Love (magician): Ja 16-22; Ravel Family (and Miss Francis): Ja 25-
F 15; Italian Opera Company (G. Sbriglia, F. Gnone, N. Barilli;
Signoras Carolina Alaimo, Teresa Parodi, and chorus): F 20-Mr 3, 12-
14; French Comic Opera Company (with Mlle. Darcy): Mr 5-7; Edwin
Booth: Mr 20-Ap 4; Julia Dean (Hayne): Ap 2, 9-21; Mr. Jacobs
(magician): Ap 23-28.
   O (10) Countess for an Hour: *Catherine*–Polly Marshall; Unprotected
Female: *Polly*–Polly Marshall; Bobtail and Wagtail (11) Captain
Charlotte: *Charlotte*–Polly Marshall; Unprotected Female: *Polly*–Polly
Marshall; Spectre Bridegroom (12) Little Treasure: *Gertrude*–Polly
Marshall; Object of Interest: *Fanny*–Polly Marshall; Swiss Cottage
(13) Mischief Making: *Mad. Manette*–Polly Marshall; Morning Call;
Mr. and Mrs. Peter White: *Mrs. Peter White*–Polly Marshall (14) Little
Treasure: *Gertrude*–Polly Marshall; Object of Interest: *Fanny*–Polly
Marshall; Momentous Question (15) Little Dot: *Little Dot*–Polly
Marshall; Sergeant's Wife (17) Flowers of the Forest: *Starlight Bess*–
Polly Marshall; Bobtail and Wagtail (18) Two Queens: *Christine*–
Polly Marshall; Countess for an Hour: *Catherine*–Polly Marshall;
Thumping Legacy (19) Flowers of the Forest: *Starlight Bess*–Polly
Marshall; State Secrets (20) Captain Charlotte: *Charlotte*–Polly
Marshall; Madeline (21) Little Dot: *Little Dot*–Polly Marshall; Mous-
tache Mania: *Louisa*–Polly Marshall; Rough Diamond (22) St. Mary's
Eve; Our Wife; Perfection (24-28) Our American Cousin: *Lord Dun-
dreary*–Sothern (29) Our American Cousin: *Lord Dundreary*–Sothern;
Pauline (31) Irish Ambassador: *Sir Patrick O'Plenipo*–Collins; Teddy,
the Tiler: *Teddy*–Collins

N (1) Irish Attorney: *Pierce O'Hara*–Collins; How to Pay the Rent; Poor Pillicoddy (2) Nervous Man and the Man of Nerve: *McShane*–Collins; Magic Shirt: *Paddy*–Collins; Conjugal Lesson (3) Soldier of Fortune: *Capt. O'Rourke*–Collins; Teddy, the Tiler: *Teddy*–Collins; Widow's Victim (4) Irish Genius: three rôles–Collins; Born to Good Luck: *Paudeen O'Rafferty*–Collins (5) Rory O'More: *Rory O'More*–Collins; Momentous Question (7) His Last Legs: *O'Callaghan*–Collins; Born to Good Luck: *Paudeen O'Rafferty*–Collins; Young Widow (9) King O'Neill: *O'Neill*–Collins; Magic Shirt: *Paddy*–Collins; Wandering Minstrel (9) Irish Ambassador: *Sir Patrick O'Plenipo*–Collins: Irish Genius: three rôles–Collins; Swedish Nightingale (10) Rory O'More: *Rory O'More*–Collins; St. Mary's Eve (11) Victims*; Richard III on Horseback; Robert Macaire (12) Poor Gentleman; Our American Cousin (14-19) Sandford Opera Company in concerts (21-22) Bride of Lammermoor (23) Il Trovatore (24-25) La Somnambula

D (26-31) Donetti and Woods' Dogs

Ja (2) Brigand; Toodles (4) Maniac Lovers; Toodles (5) Naiad Queen (6) Naiad Queen; Nan, the Good for Nothing (7) Forty Thieves; Brian O'Lynn (9) Sea of Ice (10-11) Bottle Imp; Wandering Minstrel (12) Cinderella; Spectre Bridegroom (13) Serious Family; Toodles (14) Richard III; Trip to Coney Island (16-22) Love (magician) (25-F 15) Ravel Family

F (20) Ernani (21) La Traviata (22) Norma (23) La Favorita (24) Lucrezia Borgia (25) Don Giovanni (27) Il Trovatore (28) Il Polinto (29) Norma

Mr (1) Il Trovatore (2) La Favorita (3) Barber of Seville; Il Polinto (Act III) (5) La Chatte Metamorphosee; La Rose de St. Fleur (Act I) (6) La Corde Sensible; Les Deux Avengles; Jean le Sot (7) Jobin et Manette; Les Adventures d'une Canne (12) La Somnambula (13) Rigoletto (14) Lucrezia Borgia (19) Willow Copse; Sketches in India (20) New Way to Pay Old Debts: *Sir Giles Overreach*–Booth; farce (21) Othello: *Iago*–Booth; farce (22) Richelieu: *Richelieu*–Booth; farce (23) Much Ado about Nothing: *Benedict*–Booth; Slasher and Crasher (24) Richard III: *Richard*–Booth; farce (26) Marble Hearts: *Phidias*–Booth; farce (27) Hamlet: *Hamlet*–Booth (28) Richelieu: *Richelieu*–Booth; farce (29) Richard III: *Richard*–Booth (30) Iron Chest: *Sir Edward Mortimer*–Booth; Catherine and Petruchio: *Petruchio*–Booth (31) Macbeth: *Macbeth*–Booth

Ap (2) Romeo and Juliet: *Romeo*–Booth, *Juliet*–Julia Dean; Trying It On (3) Merchant of Venice: *Shylock*–Booth; Catherine and Petruchio (4) Brutus: *Brutus*–Booth; Don Caesar de Bazan: *Don Caesar de Bazan*–Booth (5) Gun Maker of Moscow; Stars and Stripes in Mexico (6) Gun Maker of Moscow; Black Eyed Susan (9) Evadne: *Evadne*–Julia Dean; Bobtail and Wagtail (10) Ingomar: *Parthenia*–Julia Dean; Spectre Bridegroom (11) Adrienne, the Actress: *Adrienne*–Julia Dean (12) Camille: *Camille*–Julia Dean (13) Fazio: *Bianca*–Julia Dean; Faint Heart Ne'er Won Fair Lady (14) Lady of Lyons: *Pauline*–Julia Dean; Rough Diamond (16) Hunchback: *Julia*–Julia Dean; Mr. and Mrs. Peter White (17) London Assurance: *Lady Gay Spanker*–Julia Dean (18) Wife: *Mariana*–Julia Dean; Limerick Boy (19) Ingomar: *Parthenia*–Julia Dean; Preparing for the Convention (20) Morning Call: *Mrs. Chillington*–Julia Dean; Madeline: *Madeline*–Julia Dean (21) Lucretia Borgia: *Lucretia Borgia*–Julia Dean; Five Dollars a Day (23-28) Jacobs (magician)

1860-1861

Mgr.: G. F. Marchant. No Stock.

SE: Mr. and Mrs. Henri Drayton: O 16-20; Adelina Patti and Company: N 5-7, 12-13; Cooper English Opera Troupe (H. C. Cooper, mgr., *Messrs.* Aynsley Cook, F. B. Boudinot, Brookhouse Bowler, Bruno, Holywell Collins, James Arnold, Hurley, Miller; *Mrs.* Gillespie, F. B. Boudinot; *Misses* Annie Milner, H. Payne, Kemp, Marie Barton, Manderville, Wickens): N 19-26; George Christy's Minstrels: D 17-20; Duprey and Green's New Orleans and Metropolitan Burlesque Opera Troupe: Ja 31-F 2.

O (16) Marry in Haste; Love's Labor Lost (17) Somnambula; Marry in Haste (18) Never Judge by Appearances (19) Love Is Blind: *Capt. Ravenworth*–Henri, *Julia*–Mrs. Henri (20) Nothing Venture, Nothing Have: *Gustave*–Henri, *Clarisse*–Mrs. Henri

N (5-7, 12-13) Adelina Patti and Company (19) La Somnambula (20) Norma (21) Daughter of the Regiment; Quaker (Acts I-II) (23) Il Trovatore (24) Bohemian Girl (26) La Traviata

D (17-22) George Christy's Minstrels

Ja (31-F 2) New Orleans and Metropolitan Burlesque Opera Company

1861-[1862]

Mgr.: G. F. Marchant. No Stock.

SE: Savannah Quartette Club (Carl Viewig, mgr.); O 15-16; The Thespian Family or The Queen Sisters: O 21-24; The Zouaves, French Soldiers of the Crimea: N 25-30.

O (15-16) Savannah Quartette Club (21, 24) Little Blanche; concert

N (25) Troubadour Soldier; Une Fille Terrible!; Soldier and Boarder (26) Tartar Peasant in Crimea; Les Deux Pecheurs; La Corde Sensible (27) Les Deux Avengles; The Past! The Present!! The Future!!! (28) Les Folies Dramatiques; Les Deux Pecheurs; drills by the Charleston Volunteers (29) Barber of Seville; La Chambre Deux Lits; drills by the Charleston Volunteers (30) Battalion of Forlorn Hope!; drills by the Charleston Volunteers

D (11) Theatre destroyed by fire

VIII: THE PLAY LIST

In the following list of plays the year of the nineteenth century in which the play was performed, the title variants, and doubtful authorships are given in parentheses.

Abaellino, or The Great Bandit; *Dunlap:* (02) F 8, 15, Mr 1; (04) Ja 31, F 13; (05) F 8; (06) My 14; (07) Mr 18, My 8, N 23; (08) D 14; (10) F 7; (11) Ap 6; (12) F 24, Ap 17; (15) D 27; (16) Ja 3, 17; (17) Mr 25, D 27; (34) N 10.

The Absent Man; *Bickerstaff:* (09) Mr 24.

Accusation, or The Family of D'Anglode; *Payne:* (18) Mr 23.

Actor of All Work; *Coleman:* (23) Ju 30; (25) Ja 3.

Actress of All Work; *Oxberry:* (20) My 8, 18; (24) D 31; (29) Mr 11, 30, Ap 3, N 30; (30) Mr 10; (40) Ap 23, 29, My 1, 8, N 17; (43) Ja 19, 25; (45) F 20; (55) Ja 30.

Adam and Eve: (43) Ja 26.

Adelgitha, or The Fruits of a Single Error; *Lewis:* (09) F 13; (10) F 21; (12) Ja 31; (16) Ap 24; (18) My 9; (19) Mr 3; (21) Mr 31; (23) My 22; (24) Ap 23; (55) Ap 21, 23.

Adeline, or The Victim of Seduction; *Payne:* (29) Ap 29; (33) D 12; (35) N 26, D 4.

Adelmorn, or The Outlaw; *Lewis:* (03) Mr 21, 25, Ap 18; (06) F 12; (08) My 6; (18) Mr 16.

The Adopted Child, or The Baron of Wilford Castle; *Birch:* (00) F 24, Mr 22; (01) Ja 23, Ap 24; (02) F 22; (03) F 7; (04) Ap 9, Ju 12, N 12; (05) F 8; (06) D 1; (07) N 23; (08) Ja 2; (09) Mr 18; (10) Ap 6; (11) Ja 9, 12; (12) My 1; (16) Ap 17; (18) Ja 19; (20) Mr 25, My 18; (22) Ap 29; (23) My 24; (24) Mr 15; (33) F 15; (39) Mr 7, 12; (43) D 19.

Adrian and Orrila, or A Mother's Vengeance; *Dimond:* (07) D 7, 12; (08) Ja 1, 16, Ap 8; (10) F 10; (12) D 9, 11, 21; (16) Ap 22; (19) My 10; (23) Ju 7, 21; (24) F 20, Mr 27.

Adrienne, the Actress; *Davenport:* (53) D 20, 22; (55) Mr 1, 3, D 12, 17; (56) Mr 8; (57) F 18, 20, Mr 19; (59) Ja 31; (60) Ap 11.

Advertising for a Wife: (59) Mr 21.

The Aeronaut: (34) O 22.

The Aethiop, or Child of the Desert; *Dimond:* (17) Ja 25, F 1, 10, 15, 24; (18) Ap 11; (20) F 16, D 4, 11; (24) F 9, 14; (25) Ja 26, F 18; (27) D 31.

Agnes De Vere, or The Broken Heart (or The Italian Wife): (39) My 15; (40) D 1, 24; (44) Mr 20; (54) Mr 14.

The Agreeable Surprise; *O'Keeffe:* (00) Ja 20; (01) Ap 27, N 23; (02) F 11, N 12; (03) N 9, D 21; (05) Ap 17; (06) Mr 14; (07) My 2, 13; (08) Mr 4; (11) Mr 25, 29; (12) F 22; (15) N 29, D 2, 16; (16) F 16, N 11, 25, D 14; (17) Mr 7, D 13; (18) My 19; (19) F 26, Ap 20; (20) Ja 15, F 12; (21) My 25; (26) Ap 24; (39) My 16, D 12, 31; (41) D 17, 20.

Aladdin, or The Wonderful Lamp; *(Morton)*: (25) Ja 10, 17, 22, 24, F 7, 21, 26, Mr 3, Ap 6; (40) My 6 7, 8, 9, 12, 21, 22, 26, 27; (57) D 25, 26, 28, 29, 30, 31; (58) Ja 1.

An Alarming Sacrifice; *Buckstone:* (53) Ja 6, 8.

Alasco: (25) Mr 7.

Alberti; *Harby:* (19) Ap 27, 30.

The Aldgate Pump: (43) My 5.

Alexander the Great, or The Rival Queens; *Lee:* (01) My 4; (02) Ja 22; (05) F 9; (06) My 10; (09) F 27; (10) Mr 7; (12) F 19, My 8; (16) F 16, 26; (17) Ap 21; (18) Ap 15; (19) Ap 19; (25) Ap 20; (27) Ap 25; (28) N 24; (29) Mr 5; (35) Mr 19.

Alfonso of Castile, or The True Patriot (or The Patriot Father); *Lewis:* (04) D 1, 3, 7; (05) Mr 8; (20) Mr 25, Ap 21.

Ali Pa(s)cha, or The Signet Ring; *Payne:* (45) Mr 17.

Aline, or The Rose of Killarney: (43) D 30.

All in the Wrong, or All in the Right at Last; *Murphy:* (03) F 21, Mr 5.

All that Glitters Is Not Gold, or The Factory Girl; *Morton:* (52) Ja 30; (53) Ja 1, 4, F 17, 19, Mr 1; (54) Ja 26, D 22; (55) F 14; (56) Ja 2, 4; (57) Ap 13, 17; (59) F 8.

All the World's a Stage; *Jackman:* (02) Mr 5, 23, D 22; (03) D 9; (06) Ja 3; (11) Ja 28; (45) N 27, D 1; (47) F 12.

Alma Mater, or Life at Oxford; *Boucicault:* (43) N 16, 18, 22; (44) Ja 1, F 13; (45) Mr 3.

Alonzo and Imogene; *Dibdin:* (02) Ap 5, My 14; (07) Ja 23.

Alonzo the Brave, or The Fair Imogene (or The Spectre Bride) ; *Milner:* (36) Ap 5, 6.

The Alpine Maid: (58) N 29, D 16; (59) F 8.

Amateurs and Actors; *Peake:* (21) My 7; (25) Mr 30; (32) Mr 29; (44) D 30.

Ambrose Gwinnett, or A Tale of the Seaside; *Jerrold:* (29) D 9, 21, 24; (30) Ja 4, 22; (33) Mr 25, Ap 3; (42) Mr 30; (57) Ja 10.

Ambrosia and Matilda: (11) Ap 22.

The American Brothers, or A Visit to Charleston; *(Hatton):* (07) Mr 14.

The American Farmer, or The Yankee in Jersey: (51) My 5, 10.

The American Heroine: (06) Ap 11.

American True Blue: (00) Ap 4.

Amilie, or The Love Test; *Haines* and *Rook:* (39) F 11, 12, 13, 23, Mr 19, D 27; (40) Ja 21, 22.

The Anatomist, or The Sham Doctor; *Ravenscroft:* (44) D 21.

Andy Blake, or The Irish Diamond; *Boucicault:* (56) Mr 14, 18, 27, D 23, 24.

Angel of the Attic; *Morton:* (45) N 22, 26; (46) Ja 31.

Animal Magnetism; *Inchbald:* (10) Mr 16, 28; (11) F 18, 25; (12) F 3, 15; (18) Ap 24, My 19, N 20; (19) F 15; (20) F 3, Ap 5; (21) Mr 21; (22) F 28; (24) Ap 7, D 15; (28) D 9; (29) D 18; (30) Ja 1, Mr 5, N 22; (32) Mr 7; (38) Ap 27, 28; (43) F 18, Mr 14, Ap 11; (47) Ja 7, F 9.

Anna Bolena; *Donizetti:* (48) Ja 21.

Ann(ie) Blake, or The Poor Dependent; *Marston:* (55) F 17.

Antoine the Savage, or The Rock of Charbonniere: (32) D 26.

Antony and Cleopatra; *Shakespeare:* (55) Ja 9, 11; (58) D 31; (59) Ja 4.

The Apostate; *Sheil:* (18) Ja 14, 21, F 2, 7, Ap 8, N 12, 14; (20) F 21; (22) Ap 29; (23) Ju 6; (24) D 27; (27) Ap 23; (36) Mr 21; (39) Mr 7, 16; (44) F 22; (59) Mr 29, Ap 6.

The Apprentice; *Murphy:* (21) Ap 9.

Arbitration, or Free and Easy; *Reynolds:* (08) Mr 14, 16, 21; (09) F 17.

Armand, or The Peer and the Peasant; *Mowatt:* (54) F 25, 28; (57) Ja 23, 27, N 30; (58) Ja 13.

The Artful Dodger; *Field:* (48) F 21, 23, Mr 22, 23; (59) Mr 9, 12.

As Like as Two Peas: (54) N 8, 14, D 4, 20; (55) F 23, Mr 30, D 3; (56) Mr 11; (57) Ap 6, 7.

As You Like It; *Shakespeare:* (01) Ap 8; (06) Ja 17; (16) Ja 26; (18) Ja 19; (20) D 22; (32) Mr 19; (33) Mr 27; (39) Ap 10; (40) Mr 9, Ap 10, D 23; (46) F 6; (50) Ap 17; (54) F 22, 24; (55) N 8, 13, 30; (57) F 6, 10; (59) F 9.

Asmodeus, or The Little Devil's Share: (45) Ja 18, 25, F 12; (55) Mr 8; (56) F 16; (59) Ja 7.

Author and Actor, or Fun and Frolic: (27) Ap 18.

The Avenger, or The Moor of Sicily: (42) F 11, 12.

Azael, or The Prodigal Son; *Ware:* (57) N 15, 16, 18, 19, 20, 21, 23; (58) Ap 6, 7, 8, 9, 10.

Azurine: (51) F 1.

Bachelor of Arts; *(Brougham):* (56) N 26, 27, 28.

Bachelor's Buttons; *Stirling:* (41) F 26, 27, My 1; (43) Ja 23.

The Backwoodsman; *(Reed):* (45) N 24; (47) F 9, 13.

A Bad Night: (51) N 4.

Ballet de Sham: (45) F 3, 17, Mr 8, 11.

Bamboozling; *Wilks:* (50) Ja 28; (53) N 26, D 6; (54) O 31, N 15, 17.

The Banished Star, or A Leaf from the Life of an Actress; *Buckstone:* (42) Ja 12, 14.

Barbarossa, or The Downfall of the Tyrant of Algiers; *Browne:* (06) Mr 26, Ap 11; (08) My 21; (10) Ap 11; (17) Ap 28; (35) D 8.

The Barber of Seville; *Rossini:* (20) Mr 29, My 15; (29) N 25, D 9; (40) Ja 31, F 1, 3, Mr 23, 25, 28; (43) Mr 4, 6, 17, Ap 27; (51) D 3, 5; (57) My 11; (58) Ja 19, 25, F 3, Mr 3; (59) Mr 3; (60) Mr 3; (61) N 29.

The Barber's Trouble: (51) O 10, 11.

The Barkeeper's Bride: (42) Ja 20.

Barnaby Brittle: (11) Ap 5.

Barney Brallaghay: (33) Mr 15.

Barney, the Baron: (54) Ja 31, F 2.

The Barrack Room; *Bayley:* (37) D 28; (38) Ap 19, 20; (39) F 27; (40) N 23, 24, 28; (43) Ja 14, 30, F 16, Ap 20; (44) N 23; (46) F 26, N 13; (48) N 30.

The Bashful Man; *(Moncrieff):* (43) My 1.

The Bath Road, or Married Yesterday: (29) N 20; (31) F 23; (40) Ap 2; (42) F 8, 17; (45) Ja 14.

Battalion of Forlorn Hope!: (61) N 30.

The Battle of Bunker Hill, or The Death of Gen. Warren; *Burke:* (01) Ap 22; (02) My 10; (04) D 28; (08) My 4; (21) My 9.

The Battle of Eutaw Springs and the Evacuation of Charleston; *Ioor:* (07) Ja 10, 14, F 23; (08) My 9.

The Battle of Hexham, or Days of Old; *Coleman:* (18) My 13.
The Battle of New Orleans, or The Glorious 8th of January; *Grice:* (18) Ja 8; (28) Ja 8.
The Bear Hunters; *Buckstone:* (12) My 6.
Beauty and the Beast: (52) Ja 6, 7, 8; (58) Mr 26.
The Beaux's Stratagem; *Farquhar:* (02) Ap 23; (11) Ja 25.
The Bedouin Arabs; *Ravel Family:* (38) D 26, 27, 28, 31; (39) Ja 1, 3, 4, 5, 7, 8, My 7.
The Bee Hive, or Industry Must Prosper: (12) My 12; (29) Ap 29; (39) My 17.
Before Breakfast: (27) N 28, D 19.
Beggar on Horseback: (33) Mr 26; (35) D 7.
Beggar's Opera; *Gay:* (09) Mr 6; (40) Ap 30; (58) F 6.
Begone Dull Care; *Reynolds:* (10) Mr 14; (39) D 3.
The Belle's Stratagem; *Cowley:* (00) Ja 4; (03) F 7; (07) Mr 9, D 14; (11) F 23, Ap 5; (16) My 3, N 11, D 7; (18) Ja 28; (19) D 24; (24) My 5, 12; (28) D 5; (29) F 16, 19, Mr 11, D 5; (30) Mr 10, N 29; (32) F 21; (37) D 20; (41) N 23; (42) Mr 8; (43) N 2; (48) Ja 4; (54) D 18, 27; (57) Mr 27, 28.
Ben Bolt; *Johnstone:* (55) Mr 22, 24.
Ben, the Boatswain, or Sailor's Sweethearts; *Wilks:* (45) Mr 4.
Bengal Tiger; *Dance:* (38) D 24; (39) Mr 14.
Bertram, or The Castle of St. Aldobrand; *Maturin:* (17) F 17, 19, 21; (18) Ap 3; (19) F 24, Ap 15; (20) Mr 17; (21) My 28; (24) Ap 2; (26) Ap 24; (27) F 10, N 23; (28) N 28, D 15; (30) F 8; (31) Mr 16; (33) Mr 28; (36) Mr 17, 28; (42) D 22; (44) D 28; (50) F 14.
Beulah Spa, or Two of the B'hoys; *Dance:* (38) Ap 25; (53) D 7.
The Bird Catcher: (04) Ap 16, 30; (07) Ju 1.
Birth, Death and Renovation of Harlequin, or The Enchanted Cavern; *Placide:* (05) My 9, 20; (06) F 7.
The Birthday, or The Twin Brothers (or Reconciliation); *Dibdin:* (01) Ja 24, F 14; (11) My 20; (12) F 7, My 6.
Black and White, or The Mistakes of a Morning: (38) Ja 29, F 1.
Black Beard, the Pirate; *(Sawyer):* (11) My 14, 20.
Black Eyed Susan, or All in the Downs (or The Fleet in Harbor); *Jerrold:* (31) Mr 7, 16; (34) N 11, 14; (40) Ap 15; (42) Mr 7, 8, 16, 17; (43) Ja 4, My 4, N 3; (45) Mr 3, N 25, 29; (46) D 12, 15; (47) F 11, 16; (53) Mr 1; (54) Ja 10; (55) F 1, Ap 14; (56) Ap 9; (57) Mr 7; (59) Ap 7; (60) Ap 6.
Blanche of Jersey; *Peake:* (43) Ap 24.
Blind Bargain, or Hear It Out; *Reynolds:* (05) D 6, 13; (06) F 18, D 1.
The Blind Boy, or Sarmatia's Heir; *Dunlap:* (12) Ap 10, 13; (17) Ap 14; (21) My 5; (27) Ap 28; (31) Mr 28; (32) F 27.
Blue Devils, or The Grumbling Englishman; *Coleman:* (02) Ap 19; (11) My 2; (15) D 20; (18) Ja 26; (20) Ja 14, Mr 29; (21) My 26; (27) Mr 3, 9, My 5; (28) Ja 30; (32) Mr 24; (38) Ja 12; (43) F 4; (47) Mr 1; (56) Ja 3; (58) D 3, 7.
Blue Domino: (45) D 19, 20, 31.
Blue Jackets; *Stirling:* (45) Mr 5, 6.
Bluebeard, or Female Curiosity; *Dunlap:* (01) Mr 20, 25, 27, Ap 22, N 27; (02) F 12, Ap 2; (03) Mr 18; (04) D 26, 28; (05) F 23; (06) Ja 15, F 18, My 13, 15; (07) F 27, 28, Mr 12; (08) Ja 27, Ap 8; (09) Mr 1; (10) Ap 25; (11) My 2; (20) F 9, 10; (24) Ja 1; (35) D 9, 10; (41) Ja 26, 28, 29, F 1.

Bluebelle; *Boucicault:* (56) D 22, 23, 26.

The Boarding House; *(Beazley):* (17) Ap 30; (24) My 8.

Bob Nettles, or To Parents and Guardians: (55) N 21, 22, 23, 24, 29, 30, D 8, 22; (56) Mr 5, 19, 26, Ap 21, N 15, D 5, 26; (57) Mr 23, 31.

Bob Short: (47) F 8.

Bobtail and Wagtail: (59) O 10, 17; (60) Ap 9.

The Bohemian Girl (or A Woman's Revenge): (33) Ju 12; (34) Ja 3.

The Bohemian Girl; *Balfe:* (45) Ja 29, 30, 31, F 1, 6; (47) F 24; (48) D 7, 11; (55) Ja 18, 19; (58) Ja 21, F 2; (59) Mr 8; (60) N 24.

The Bohemian Mother, or The Judgment Seat: (31) Mr 21.

A Bold Stroke for a Husband; *Cowley:* (04) Ap 2; (29) Mr 30; (40) Ap 13; (56) D 29.

The Bombardment of Tripoli by the American Fleet: (05) Mr 19.

Bombastes Furioso; *Barnes:* (17) Ja 9, 11, 18, F 1, 24, Mr 4, D 20; (18) Mr 4, Ap 10; (21) N 7, 14, 28; (22) F 15; (23) Ju 16; (24) F 11, 28, Ap 3; (25) Mr 4; (27) D 7; (36) Mr 29; (38) Ap 17; (40) D 18, 23; (41) Ja 29, My 7, 11; (42) F 28; (43) My 3, N 4; (44) D 19; (53) Ja 24, 26; (57) Ja 7, 10.

Boots at the Swan; *Selby:* (43) F 25, 27, Ap 12, 25; (44) F 21, 26, Mr 5; (46) D 30; (47) Ja 20, 25; (51) F 19, 27.

Born to Good Luck, or An Irishman's Fortune; *Power:* (34) D 3; (41) F 11, 16; (46) D 25, 29; (48) Ja 6, 8; (49) My 22, 23; (50) Mr 19; (54) Ja 30; (58) F 22; (59) Mr 17, N 4, 7.

The Boston Tea Party: (44) Ap 3.

Botheration, or A Ten Years' Blunder; *Oulton:* (30) Ap 19.

The Bottle, or The Drunkard's Fate; *Cruikshank:* (56) Ja 10, 11, 12, 14, 15.

The Bottle Imp; *Peake:* (60) Ja 10, 11.

Box and Cox; *Morton:* (48) F 2, 3, 9; (50) Ja 25; (51) N 1; (56) N 5, 22, D 1; (57) Mr 25, O 23, D 19; (58) Mr 9.

The Brave Hussar: (26) Mr 8.

The Brazen Mask, or Alberto and Rosabella: (08) F 1.

The Breach of Promise, or Second Thoughts; *Buckstone:* (39) N 29; (52) Mr 13; (58) D 1, 10.

The Brewer of Preston; *Adam:* (47) Mr 1.

Brian Boroihme, or The Maid of Erin; *Knowles:* (34) O 25.

Brian O'Lynn, or The Irish Mormon; *Johnson:* (54) F 11; (57) N 10; (58) Mr 11; (60) Ja 7.

The Bridal, or Maid's Tragedy; *Knowles:* (51) F 22, Mr 3.

The Bridal Ring, or A Victim of Revenge; *(Reynolds):* (16) My 10.

The Bride of Abydos; *Dimond:* (24) My 17, 26; (25) Ja 31, Mr 2; (28) Ap 11; (41) Mr 25.

The Bride of Lammermoor, or The Last Heir of Ravenswood; *Calcraft:* (30) D 8; (44) D 9; (45) D 12, 23; (46) Ja 28, D 19; (48) F 11; (55) Ap 23; (56) Ja 2, 9; (57) D 3; (58) Ja 12; (59) N 21, 22.

The Brigand, or The Banditti of the Quadagnola (or The Robbers of Italy); *Planché:* (32) D 8, 12, 22; (33) F 21, 22, 25; (41) My 6; (44) Mr 4, 14; (48) Mr 28; (60) Ja 2.

The Brigand Queen: (59) Ja 7.

The Broken Sword, or The Dumb Boy of the Mountains; *Dimond:* (17) D 17, 22; (18) Ap 27, N 11; (20) Mr 24, 29; (22) My 1; (23) D 22; (25) Ja 21, 28; (26) Ap 21; (28) D 20; (29) D 18, 26; (30) Ja 8; (32) F 2, 8; (43) N 23, 25; (44) Mr 18; (54) Ja 7, F 18, Mr 8.

Brother and Sister; *Dimond:* (18) Mr 23, 30, N 27; (23) D 6; (24) Ja 19, F 20, My 7; (28) Mr 4, 14.

Brutus, or The Fall of Tarquin (or Liberation of Rome); *Payne:* (19) D 31; (20) Ja 5, F 14; (25) F 2; (26) Ap 5; (27) F 21; (28) Ja 2; (31) F 28; (32) F 15; (38) F 2; (39) Ja 10, 17; (43) My 1; (44) D 25; (59) Ap 11; (60) Ap 4.

A Budget of Blunders; *Greffuhle:* (12) F 29, Mr 7; (16) D 6, 11; (21) Ap 4, N 19; (22) F 22, Ap 15; (24) Ap 6; (25) Mr 7.

Bumps: (44) Ap 3, N 30.

The Burning of the Frigate Philadelphia in the Harbor of Tripoli: (06) Mr 26.

The Busy Body; *Centlivre:* (04) Ap 16, Ju 12, D 5; (06) Mr 14; (16) Ap 17; (18) N 13.

But However, or Short of Change: (39) D 9.

The Butcher's Dog of Ghent: (55) Ja 25, 26.

Buy It Dear, 'Tis Made of Cashmere; *Horncastle:* (46) Ja 12, 13, 15, 16.

The Cabin Boy, or The Devil of Demeraro: (40) Ja 9, 10, 11, 22.

The Cabinet; *Dibdin;* (09) Mr 27; (16) D 11, 18; (17) Mr 4; (18) N 23; (19) F 15; (29) N 27.

Cachucha: (40) D 28.

Caius Gracchus; *Knowles:* (25) Mr 30.

Caledonian Lasses: (10) Ap 27.

The Caliph of Bagdad: (51) O 22.

Camille Burlesque: (57) Ap 11, 13.

Camille, or The Fate of a Coquette; *Wilkins:* (54) N 6, 7; (57) F 21, 23, 24, 25, Mr 17, 26, Ap 1, 2, D 14, 19; (59) F 5; (60) Ap 12.

The Camp, or Soldier's Festival: (06) D 15, 22; (08) Ja 18, 21, D 14.

Captain Charlotte: (59) O 11, 20.

Captain of the Watch; *Planché:* (56) N 18, 20, 24, 26.

The Captive; *(Conner):* (38) Ja 13; (40) F 4, 10; (41) D 31.

Care and Mirth: (02) My 12, 17; (03) N 14; (04) My 25; (05) Ap 8, 25; (06) D 5; (08) Ja 11, F 19; (10) My 16.

The Carmelite; *Cumberland:* (02) N 26, 29; (03) F 8.

The Carpenter of Rouen; *Jones:* (43) Ja 5, 6, 7, 18; (45) Mr 6.

The Castle Besieged: (01) Mr 16, Ap 6.

The Castle of Andalusia, or The Banditti; *O'Keeffe:* (02) F 1, 10, Ap 7; (06) Ja 27, F 28; (08) D 23, 28; (40) F 3.

The Castle of Sarento: (06) Mr 24.

The Castle Spectre, or The Secrets of Conway Castle; *Lewis:* (01) F 4, 6, 12, 16, 23, Mr 23, N 25; (02) Mr 26, N 13; (03) D 22; (05) Mr 9; (06) My 9, D 5, 27; (07) N 24, 28; (08) F 13; (15) D 13, 29; (17) Ja 13; (19) My 12; (21) Mr 17; (23) D 17; (27) My 5; (32) Mr 28.

The Cat Changed into a Woman: (56) Mr 20, 21.

The Cataract of the Ganges, or The Rajah's Daughter; *Moncrieff:* (26) Mr 6, 8, 10; (33) Ja 14.

Catarina, or The Bandit Queen: (51) O 27, 28, 29.

Catch Him Who Can; *Hook:* (10) My 9.

Catching an Heiress; *Selby:* (39) Ap 8; (41) Mr 12, 16, 23.

Catherine and Petruchio, or Taming the Shrew; *Garrick:* (01) Mr 4, 27; (02) D 13; (04) Ap 12; (05) Mr 9; (06) F 12, My 2; (07) Ap 28, D 19; (09) Ja 14, F 20; (10) Mr 7; (11) Ap 1; (12) F 28; (16)

Ja 29, Mr 29; (17) F 12; (18) Ap 6; (19) Ap 26; (20) Ap 24; (24) Ap 28, N 29; (25) Ap 7; (27) F 5, 19; (28) D 19; (30) Mr 4; (33) Ja 4, Mr 21; (35) Mr 30; (36) Ap 7; (43) Ja 14; (44) Mr 16; (46) Ja 14; (47) D 21; (50) Mr 23; (52) D 17, 25; (54) Mr 13; (58) F 19, D 17; (59) Mr 14, 26; (60) Mr 30, Ap 3.

Cato; *Addison:* (38) Ja 24, 27.

Cattle Stealer, or The Rover, the Dover, and His Dog: (55) Ja 27.

Caudle's Lectures: (45) N 5, 8.

The Centogenarian: (44) Ja 13.

The Chameleon: (38) Ap 11; (56) Mr 19, 24, D 18, 19, 27.

Chaos Is Come Again: (40) Mr 12, 13.

A Chapter of Accidents; *Lee:* (04) Ap 23; (06) Ja 31, N 12; (44) N 26.

Charles I: (07) Ap 3.

Charles II, or The Merry Monarch; *Payne:* (28) Mr 17; (29) D 23; (30) Ja 8; (32) Mr 27; (35) Mr 26, N 23; (36) Mr 9; (40) D 12, 15; (43) Ja 21, D 29; (45) N 3; (46) Ja 7; (48) D 2; (55) F 27; (58) Ja 14.

Charles XII; *Planché:* (31) Mr 28; (38) F 16, 20, Mr 3; (39) My 17, D 11, 31; (41) Mr 17; (44) Mr 21; (51) Mr 4, Ap 26; (54) F 14; (57) O 24.

Charleston Fireman, or The Meeting St. Heiress: (54) Ja 26; (58) Mr 27.

The Charleston Sailor, or A Preparation for a Cruise in the John Adams Frigate: (01) Mr 30; (02) Ap 12.

Charleston Theatre in an Uproar: (58) Ja 16.

Charlotte and Werter: (04) Ap 19.

Charlotte Corday, or The Assassination of Marat and Death of the Queen of France: (04) Ap 30.

Charlotte Corday, or The Reign of Terror; *Conner* or *Conway:* (57) F 26, 28.

Charlotte Temple: (33) D 23, 27.

Chaste Susanna: (05) My 1.

Cheap Living; *Reynolds:* (04) F 16, 20; (05) F 18; (09) Mr 20.

The Cherokee Chief, or Dogs of the Wreck: (38) Ap 1, 4.

Cherry and Fair Star, or The Children of Cypress: (36) Mr 14, 15, 16, 17, 18, 22; (44) Ja 1, 3, 4.

Cherry Bounce; *Raymond:* (39) Ap 6, 9, 20.

The Child of Nature: (00) Ja 20; (01) N 7, 21; (08) My 2, 28; (12) F 5; (16) My 13; (17) Ap 30; (33) Ja 11.

Child of the Air: (51) F 1, 4.

The Child of the Prairie: (51) D 15, 16, 17, 18, 19, 20.

The Child of the Regiment: (52) N 19, 24, 30, D 10; (53) Ja 4, F 25, N 2, 4, 5; (54) F 15; (58) Ja 8, 9, 12.

The Children in the Wood; *Morton:* (00) My 8; (03) Ap 14, N 17, D 3; (04) F 16, Ap 16, D 21; (05) F 7; (06) Mr 10, N 21; (07) F 9, My 18, D 12; (08) F 22; (10) F 19; (11) F 23, Ap 6; (12) F 5, 7; (13) Ja 1, 13; (18) My 13, N 4, 23; (21) Mr 26, 31; (23) My 23, Ju 18; (33) F 13, 22; (44) F 28.

The Chimney Sweepers, or The Broken Sword: (34) Ja 25, Mr 1, Ap 21.

Chit Chat; *Killigrew:* (00) F 27, 28.

Chrononhotonthologos; *Carey:* (07) Mr 18; (08) Ap 1.

Cinderella, or The Little Glass Slipper (or The Fairy and the Little Glass Slipper): (07) F 13, 14, 16, 17, 18, 25, Mr 6, Ap 15, My 15, D 26; (08) Ja 6, F 18; (09) Ja 2, F 18; (11) Ap 26; (19) Ap 12, 17, My 5; (38) F 22, 24, 27, 28, Mr 2, 5, 17, 26, Ap 25; (39) Mr 20, 21, 25, My 22, D 19, 23; (40) Ja 23, Mr 14, 28; (41) D 8, 14; (43) Mr 7, 8, 16; (45) F 4; (47) Mr 6; (49) Ja 3; (51) D 22, 23, 24, 25; (58) Ja 29, 30, F 4; (59) Mr 2; (60) Ja 12.

The Citizen; *Murphy:* (02) Mr 8; (11) Mr 19; (30) D 1; (31) Mr 14; (33) Ja 11.

The Clandestine Marriage; *Coleman* and *Garrick:* (06) Mr 5; (12) D 7; (19) My 4; (20) Ja 24; (40) D 8, 17.

Clari, or The Maid of Milan; *Payne:* (23) D 19, 26; (24) Ja 30, My 19; (28) Mr 10, 24; (29) D 16; (30) Mr 24; (33) Mr 25; (35) Ap 10; (38) Ap 17; (42) Mr 29; (46) N 17; (57) O 31, N 6.

Clemence and Waldemar, or The Painter through Love: (07) F 27, 28, Mr 6; (08) Ap 6.

The Clergyman's Daughter; *White:* (10) Ap 23.

The Clown's Triumph: (02) Mr 26.

The Cobbler: (49) My 28.

The Cobbler's Daughter, or All in the Wrong: (23) Ju 7, 11, 21.

The College Boy: (45) Ja 8, 14; (50) Ap 15.

Columbine's Choice, or Harlequin Statue: (08) Ap 18.

Columbus, or America Discovered (or A World Discovered); *Morton:* (00) F 10, 17; (07) Ap 6; (09) Mr 8; (12) Ap 30; (18) Mr 4; (25) Ap 13; (45) F 22.

A Comedy of Errors; *Shakespeare:* (28) F 18, 20, 22, 28; (36) Mr 24; (39) Mr 5, 9; (52) Mr 17, 18; (57) Mr 9, 10, 12, 13.

The Comet, or New Philosophy (or He Would Be an Astronomer); *(Milne):* (05) Ap 15.

The Comical Countess; *Brough:* (58) Ap 14.

A Companion in Arms: (45) Ja 8, 13, 27.

Comus; *Milton:* (05) Ap 22.

A Conjugal Lesson; *Danvers:* (57) D 12, 14, 15; (59) Ja 25, 26, N 2.

Connecticut Courtship: (54) F 11.

The Conquest of Taranto, or St. Clare's Eve; *Dimond:* (30) Ja 18, 27.

The Conscript and the Soldier: (34) Ja 17.

The Conscripts, or The Pledge of Truth: (42) D 30, 31; (43) Ja 4.

Cool as a Cucumber; *Jerrold:* (58) Ap 14, 16.

The Cooper, or Love in a Tub: (06) Mr 24, Ap 23.

Corinna, or The Improvisitrice: (54) Mr 1.

Coriolanus; *Shakespeare:* (07) Ap 22; (16) Mr 27; (18) My 4; (20) Mr 8; (24) Mr 20, D 17, 23; (27) D 7; (38) Ja 29; (51) F 15.

The Corporal's Wedding: (46) F 23, 26.

The Corsair; *Holland:* (18) F 18, 20, 21.

The Corsican Brothers; *Boucicault:* (53) Ja 31, F 1, 2, 3, 4, 5; (56) F 14, 15; (57) Ja 15, 16.

The Cosmetique Doctor, or The Man for the Ladies: (04) F 25, My 14.

Couancheatah: (41) My 3.

Count Benyowski, or The Conspiracy of Kamschatka; *Kenney:* (01) Ap 15; (02) F 5, 13; (07) My 25.

The Count of Narbonne: (00) F 27; (01) Ap 6.

A Countess for an Hour: (59) O 10, 18.

The Countess of Salisbury: (03) Mr 28.

The Country Girl, or Bachelor Outwitted; *Garrick:* (00) Ja 1, Ap 30;
(06) Mr 17, N 18, D 22; (20) D 18; (29) Mr 18; (40) F 24, 28.
The Courier of Lyons; *Reade:* (57) N 26, 27, 28.
Cracovienne: (43) N 21.
Cramond Brig, or The Gudeman of Ballangeich; *Murray:* (39) D 20,
24; (44) D 13; (48) D 5, 12; (49) Ja 15; (53) N 21; (54) Ja 16.
The Cricket on the Hearth; *Smith:* (46) F 25, 26; (52) Ja 22.
The Critic, or A Tragedy Rehearsed; *Sheridan:* (00) Mr 24; (01) F 2,
Mr 13; (02) D 10, 11; (03) Mr 4; (04) My 11; (05) Mr 1, 27;
(08) D 7; (18) My 1, N 13, 18; (19) My 3; (21) My 4; (22) Ap
24; (23) Ju 13; (24) Ja 10; (28) Ja 28; (31) Ap 4; (38) Mr 1, Ap
16; (39) Ja 25, F 2, D 3; (40) F 20, My 26, 27, N 26; (53) F 28.
Crossing the Frontier, or Marguerite's Colors: (59) Mr 21.
Crossing the Line, or Crowded Houses; *Almar:* (34) O 14, 21, 25; (36)
Mr 23; (39) Ap 13, 16; (43) N 4; (57) Ja 21, 24, 29.
The Crown Diamonds; *Auber:* (59) Mr 1.
The Crusaders; *Brown:* (44) N 20, 21.
The Culprit; *Bayley:* (43) My 11.
Cupboard Love: (34) Mr 6.
A Cure for Care: (08) My 17.
A Cure for the Heartache; *Morton:* (02) D 6; (03) Mr 2; (04) My 3;
(05) N 13; (07) My 30; (11) F 9; (17) D 17; (19) Ap 12, D 21;
(24) N 23, D 18; (26) D 22; (32) D 19; (33) Mr 29; (40) N 10.
The Curfew, or Vision of the Dead; *Tobin:* (08) Ja 8, 11, Ap 25; (09)
Ap 7; (10) My 12; (16) Ja 5, Mr 22; (17) Ja 10; (20) F 25.
The Custom of the Country; *Walcot:* (54) F 9.
Cut and Come Again: (43) D 1, 11.
Cymbeline; *Shakespeare:* (16) Ja 22, N 29.
Cymon and Sylvia, or Love and Magic; *Garrick:* (05) F 20, Mr 11;
(09) Mr 20.
Cymon, or Love Triumphant: (01) Ap 11.

D— in Paris is D—: (54) D 19.
Damon and Pythias, or The Test of Friendship; *Banim:* (21) N 14, 26;
(23) D 22; (24) F 17, 18, Ap 6; (27) F 2, 9, 19, D 26; (28) D 17;
(29) N 14; (30) Ja 29, F 27; (31) F 21, Mr 1; (34) O 13; (35)
Mr 9, 14; (38) F 1, 6; (39) Mr 11; (41) Ja 16; (42) Mr 30; (43)
Ja 2, D 8; (45) D 31; (47) Ja 27, F 6; (53) F 9, N 17; (55) F 2;
(57) Ja 17.
Darkness Visible: (15) N 13.
The Daughter of the Regiment, or The Gallant Twenty-First (or The
800 Fathers); *Fitzball:* (48) D 14; (58) Ja 20, F 5, D 31; (60)
N 21.
A Daughter to Marry: (38) Ap 6, 9.
David Copperfield; *(Brougham):* (51) Ap 25; (58) D 7, 8.
The Day after the Fair, or My Nervous Debility; *Somerset:* (27) N 28,
D 3, 17; (28) Ja 8, D 5, 9; (32) F 27.
The Day after the Wedding, or A Wife's First Lesson; *Kemble:* (15)
D 11, 20; (16) Mr 20, N 16, D 20; (17) Ja 11, Mr 4; (21) My 9;
(24) D 4, 20; (25) Ja 5, Ap 11; (26) Mr 17, Ap 5; (27) F 7, Mr
10; (28) F 27, 29, Ap 25; (29) Ap 22, N 13; (30) F 23; (31) Mr
11; (32) F 15; (33) D 28; (34) F 27, Ap 26; (35) Ap 10; (37)
D 27; (38) Ja 20, F 8; (40) My 9; (41) D 16; (42) Ja 1; (43) F

7; (44) F 9, N 21, D 3; (46) Ja 27, N 20; (48) Ja 6, D 5; (50) Mr 20; (51) O 25; (54) Mr 18.

A Day in Paris; *Selby:* (43) N 23, D 16; (44) Ja 6, F 17, D 10; (46) N 10; (49) My 22, 23; (51) O 18, 21, 27, 28.

Days of Old, or Riever's Ransom: (01) My 15.

The Days of Washington, or Love in 1776: (57) Ap 6, 7, 8.

De Montalt, or The Abbey of St. Clair; *Simmons:* (43) F 2.

The Dead Shot; *Buckstone:* (29) Mr 20, 27; (30) Mr 24, 31; (32) Mr 16; (35) Mr 9, 16, 23; (38) Mr 30; (39) Ja 8, Mr 22, 25; (40) Mr 3, D 29; (41) F 15, N 16; (42) F 4, D 22; (43) F 1, Ap 27, N 2, 4; (44) Ja 6, Mr 9, D 20; (46) N 10, 19; (48) Ja 7, 11; (49) Ja 29, 31; (50) Ja 26, F 5, Ap 17; (51) Ja 30; (52) Ja 19, 29, F 10; (53) O 31, D 19; (54) F 20; (55) Ja 29, F 1; (59) Mr 16.

Deaf and Dumb, or l'Abbé de l'Épée; *Dunlap:* (02) Ja 23, 25, 29; (16) Ja 29, Mr 6; (49) My 25.

Deaf as a Post: (24) Mr 19; (28) D 6, 16; (32) F 11, 17; (39) F 20, Mr 15, 16, My 8; (40) Mr 16; (47) Ja 11.

The Death Fetch, or The Student of Gohengen: (29) D 28; (30) Ja 2, Ap 14.

The Death of Abel: (34) Ja 22, F 27.

The Death of Captain Cook: (01) Ap 15; (02) My 5; (06) Mr 17, My 12; (07) Ja 26; (08) Mr 7; (10) Mr 21; (17) Ap 16.

Delays and Blunders, or The Vestil Buried Alive; *Reynolds:* (03) Ap 25.

Delicate Ground, or Paris in 1793; (51) Ap 24; (55) Ja 10; (57) F 11.

The Delinquent, or Seeing Company; *Reynolds:* (07) Ja 28.

Der Freischutz, or The Last Ball; *von Weber:* (39) My 8, 9; (40) Mr 19, 21, 24, 26; (43) Ap 20, 25; (49) Ja 6.

Der Wachter, or A Night's Adventure: (39) D 7.

Dermot and Kathleen: (06) Ap 11, 21; (20) My 12.

The Deserted Daughter, or The Faithful Scotchman; *Holcroft:* (00) Mr 10, 11, 12, 22; (06) Mr 21; (08) Ap 29; (11) F 13; (12) D 30; (16) Ap 29.

The Deserter; *Dibdin:* (01) Mr 11.

The Deserter of Naples: (08) My 2.

The Deserter, the Robber and Frederick the Great: (28) D 16.

The Deuce Is in Her, or The Widow's Stratagem: (36) F 22, 26.

The Devil among the Taylors: (05) My 2.

The Devil to Pay, or The Wives Metamorphosed; *Coffey:* (05) My 27; (10) F 26; (16) Mr 13, 18, Ap 3; (17) Ap 26; (18) Mr 2; (20) F 19; (33) Ap 8; (36) F 11, Mr 5.

The Devil's Bridge; *Arnold:* (18) N 7, 16, 25; (19) F 2; (20) N 25, 29; (21) N 8, 17; (22) F 16; (24) Ja 17; (27) D 3; (28) Ja 7, Mr 14; (30) Ap 5; (38) F 14, 19.

The Devil's in It; *Wilks:* (56) Mr 24.

Diana, Goddess of the Chase: (48) Mr 24.

Diana, or The Triumph of Love (or Love's Masquerade): (59) Ja 12, 20.

Did You Ever Send Your Wife to Mount Pleasant?: (46) D 21; (47) Ja 19, 26.

The Disowned and His Poor Dog Tray: (55) F 3.

The Distressed Mother; *Phillips:* (00) F 24; (22) F 28; (31) Mr 25.

A Divertisement: (18) My 8; (39) My 28.

Dobson and Company: (58) Mr 23.

Dog Witness: (55) Ja 23, 24.

Dombey and Son; *Brougham:* (50) Ap 29, 30, My 1, 2; (54) Ja 12; (58) N 29, D 6.

The Dominion of Fancy, or Harlequin Rambler: (07) Mr 30, Ju 1.

Don and Patty: (23) My 31, Ju 4.

Don Caesar de Bazan, or Love and Honor; *A'Beckett* and *Lemon:* (45) D 25; (46) Ja 20; (48) F 7; (51) F 3, Ap 19, My 12; (52) Ja 20, 23; (55) Mr 15, 16; (56) D 8, 9, 10; (57) Ja 17; (60) Ap 4.

Don Giovanni; *Mozart:* (51) D 8, 11, 13; (60) F 25.

Don Giovanni, or The Spectre on Horseback: (20) D 8; (24) Ja 12.

Don Juan, or The Libertine Destroyed; *(Delpini):* (01) F 13, Ap 8; (02) F 17; (03) Ap 14, N 19; (04) D 24; (05) D 23; (06) My 5, D 12; (07) F 21; (09) Ja 23; (10) F 27; (11) Ap 19; (16) My 8; (17) D 26; (18) Ja 1, 15; (20) F 26, 28, Mr 4, D 5; (26) Mr 10, 20, 22; (29) D 28; (34) Mr 10; (38) Ap 5; (40) Ja 18; (43) Ja 26, 27, F 4; (55) Ja 25, 26.

Don Pasquale; *Donizetti:* (47) F 26; (51) N 14; (59) Mr 7.

Donald M'Intosh's Travels, or The Register Office: (08) My 23.

Done Brown; *Coyne:* (46) N 20, 21, D 25.

The Double Bedded Room; *Morton:* (43) N 21, 28; (45) D 24; (47) Ja 14; (48) F 16.

The Doubtful Son; *Dimond:* (11) F 20; (12) Ap 28, D 14.

Douglas, or The Noble Shepherd; *Home:* (00) Ap 23; (02) F 24, N 17; (05) Ap 29, My 17; (06) Ap 23; (07) Ap 30; (08) Ap 13, D 10, 17; (10) Mr 26; (16) Ap 19; (17) Ja 6, D 29; (21) Ap 7; (24) Ap 5; (27) Mr 2; (30) Mr 22; (33) F 26; (34) Mr 5; (35) D 2; (36) F 18, Mr 14; (40) D 22; (41) D 24; (48) D 20, 21; (51) My 3; (53) Ja 8; (58) D 31.

The Dowager; *Matthews:* (58) Ap 13, 17.

Dr. Dilworth; *Oxenford:* (41) Mr 2, 3.

The Dramatist, or Stop Him Who Can; *Reynolds:* (02) N 5; (04) Ap 26; (07) F 13; (08) N 18; (11) Ja 30; (12) D 28; (20) D 14; (23) Jy 7; (24) N 22; (25) F 26; (27) My 16; (28) Ja 18.

Drawing Room Divertisement: (55) N 12, 13, D 7.

The Dream at Sea, or The Haunted Cave; *Buckstone:* (38) Ap 27; (52) Ja 10, 20; (55) N 19, 22.

The Dream of Fate, or The Rich Jew of Frankfort; *Barnett:* (42) D 31; (43) Ja 2, 26.

The Drunkard, or The Fallen Saved; *Smith:* (51) My 13.

The Drunkard's Dream: (54) Mr 16, 17.

The Drunkard's Fate: (57) Ap 24.

Drunken Provincial: (20) F 25.

The Duchess de la Vaubaliere; *Buckstone:* (39) Ja 23, 24.

Duchess Eleanor: (54) N 29.

The Duel, or My Two Nephews: (23) D 20; (24) Ja 7, 14, Mr 26, D 29; (25) Ja 26.

The Duenna, or The Double Elephant; *Sheridan:* (06) Ja 3, F 21; (08) N 28, D 7; (09) F 8; (19) F 22.

The Duke's Wager; *Butler:* (53) D 23; (59) F 3.

The Dumb Belle; *Bernard:* (38) F 27, Mr 2, 7, 10, 19; (39) Ja 24, My 2, D 18, 23; (41) N 20; (42) D 21; (43) D 7; (44) Ja 5, N 22; (45) F 5, N 15, D 16; (46) F 7; (47) F 4, 5; (50) Mr 18; (52) N 29; (57) F 26, 28, Mr 21.

The Dumb Boy of Manchester: (39) Ja 28, 29.
The Dumb Girl of Genoa, or The Bandit Merchant: (30) Ap 2, 5, 14; (32) D 1; (34) Ja 4; (41) N 30, D 2, 3; (43) N 18, 21; (44) Mr 25; (46) Ja 15.
The Dutch Brothers: (35) D 5.
The Dutch Governor, or 'Twould Puzzle a Conjuror: (58) D 10.

The Earl of Essex, or The Unhappy Favorite; *Brooke:* (01) Ja 30; (03) Ja 31; (16) F 9; (17) Ja 24.
Easter Frolics, or Harlequin Hurry-Scurry: (05) Ap 15; (29) Ap 20.
Education, or Friends and Enemies; *Morton:* (15) D 6, 9; (19) My 5.
Eight to One, or How to Nail a Manager: (17) F 5; (22) F 25; (25) Ap 13.
El Hyder, or Love and Bravery; *Barrymore:* (26) Mr 1; (28) Ap 25.
The Elder Brother, or Love Makes the Man; *Fletcher:* (05) Mr 4; (47) Ja 22, 23.
The Elixir of Love: *See* L'Elisir d'Amore.
Ella Rosenberg; *Kenney:* (09) Mr 22, 24; (10) My 5; (11) Ja 5; (16) My 13; (18) My 16; (23) Ju 3; (24) My 5; (25) Ap 9; (32) F 3.
The Embargo, or The Honest Countryman (or What News?); *Barker:* (08) Ap 27.
Englishmen in India; *Dimond:* (40) F 26, Mr 4; (41) D 29.
The Epigrammatist: (30) Mr 29.
Ernani; *Verdi:* (50) Ap 2; (51) Mr 21, 25, N 24, 28; (60) F 20.
Ernest Maltravers; *Medina:* (40) D 4.
Ernestine: (46) D 7; (56) N 20, 27.
Esmerelda, or The Hunchback of Notre Dame; *Fitzball:* (55) Ja 10.
Esther, or The Enchanted Rose: (59) F 22, 23, 24.
The Eton Boy: (50) Mr 8, 14; (52) N 12, 17, 23; (53) F 8; (56) F 4, Mr 8; (58) Ap 13.
Eudia, or The Fairies of the Lake: (56) Ja 25, 28.
Eustache, or The Condemned: (57) N 10, 13.
Evadne, or The Statue; *Sheil:* (20) F 18; (30) Mr 5; (33) D 18; (36) Mr 5, 8; (45) N 10; (46) N 26; (50) Mr 13; (52) F 12, N 24, 26; (53) D 26; (54) Ja 20, N 10, 27, D 4; (55) F 19; (56) Mr 4; (57) Ja 28, D 5; (58) Ja 4; (60) Ap 9.
Everyone Has His Fault; *Inchbald:* (01) F 18, My 18; (03) F 17; (04) My 31, D 10; (05) N 18; (08) Mr 30, My 19; (11) F 25; (12) F 25; (16) My 1; (18) Ap 27; (19) My 7; (20) Ja 21; (40) Ap 29, My 1.
The Examination of Doctor Lost: (02) My 5.
The Exile, or The Russian Daughter; *Reynolds:* (12) Ap 20, 24, 30; (21) Mr 28, Ap 4, 28; (22) F 15; (25) Ap 12; (29) D 14; (43) F 21.

Faint Heart Ne'er Won Fair Lady; *Planché:* (42) Ja 28, F 9, 15, 22; (45) D 12, 23; (46) Ja 28; (48) F 4, 9, 14, 15, O 28, N 2; (50) Mr 5; (52) F 14; (54) Mr 3, 15; (55) Mr 23; (57) F 2; (60) Ap 13.
The Fair Penitent; *Rowe:* (01) Mr 16; (04) Mr 3; (06) My 7; (16) Ja 16, F 19; (24) D 31; (25) Ja 3.
Faith and Falsehood, or The Fate of a Bushranger; *Rede:* (38) D 24.
The Falls of Clyde; *Soane:* (18) O 31, N 2, 10; (19) F 19, Ap 21, D 27; (21) Mr 24; (22) My 4; (27) D 21; (34) N 28.
False and True, or The Irishman's Medley: (09) Ja 12; (20) My 12.

False Friend, or The Assasin of the Rocks: (26) F 22, 27.
False Shame, or The American Orphan in Germany; *Dunlap:* (00) Mr 19, Ap 25, My 2.
Family Jars; *Lunn:* (24) Mr 8, 10; (27) N 19; (28) Ja 2, F 8, Mr 10, D 12; (29) Ap 10, My 1, N 21; (30) Mr 3; (32) Mr 5; (35) Mr 5, 31; (36) F 9, 23, Mr 8, 12; (38) Mr 16, 17, 20, Ap 25; (40) Mr 31; (41) N 22; (43) N 1; (57) O 27, D 2.
The Family Picture, or Sailor's Garland: (05) My 17; (06) F 17; (07) Ju 1; (10) My 16; (12) D 14, 21.
Family Ties, or The Will of Uncle Josh; *Field:* (47) F 15.
The Farmer; *O'Keeffe:* (00) F 10; (02) F 5, My 1; (03) N 11; (04) Ja 31, D 7; (05) N 18; (06) Ap 30; (07) My 30, N 18; (08) Ja 8; (09) Ja 16; (10) Ap 4; (11) Mr 15; (12) F 24.
The Farmhouse, or Female Duelist: (04) F 4, 17.
The Farmer's Story: (46) Ja 29.
The Farmer's Wife; *Dibdin:* (16) N 27, D 4; (17) Ja 22, Mr 1; (18) Mr 13; (21) Ap 9.
Fashion, or Life in New York; *Mowatt:* (45) D 15, 16, 18, 20; (46) Ja 22, F 21, D 16; (57) F 2, 4.
Fashionable Lover, or The Faithful Highlander: (08) Ap 27.
The Fatal Dowry; *Massinger:* (27) D 17; (38) Ap 11, 21.
The Fatal Snowstorm, or Lowina of Tobolskow: (21) My 11; (26) Ap 19.
Father and Daughter; *Ranger:* (29) N 28, D 4; (30) Ja 11.
The Fatherless Children: (04) Ap 9.
Fauntleroy, or The Fatal Forgery; *Stone:* (25) Ap 4, 11.
Faustus, the German Student: (43) F 13, 14, 18, Mr 1.
The Fawn's Leap: (43) Ja 12.
Fazio, or The Italian Wife; *Milman:* (23) D 10; (32) N 30, D 3, 8, 12; (35) Ap 1, 9; (38) Ja 11, F 3; (39) Ap 15; (40) N 26; (41) D 17; (45) N 13; (46) D 10; (51) My 2; (52) Mr 1; (53) F 21, D 12; (54) N 8, 13, D 9; (55) Mr 2, Ap 17; (56) Mr 10; (57) F 14; (58) Ja 6; (60) Ap 13.
The Feast of Apollo: (20) D 14.
The Festival, or The Fourth of July: (23) Jy 4.
A Fête: (05) Ap 19.
The Field of Forty Footsteps; *Farren:* (42) Ja 28, F 4.
Fighting by Proxy: (39) F 19, 23, Mr 9.
The Finger Post, or Five Miles Off: (06) D 10, 15, 22; (07) F 20.
Fire and Water; *Beazley:* (22) Ap 29, My 10.
The Fire Eater; *Selby:* (54) N 27, D 1.
The First Night, or The Debutante; *Parry:* (53) D 7, 8, 9; (54) Ja 14; (56) Ap 9, 16, N 10, 13, D 4, 31.
The First of April: (32) Mr 13, 15.
A Fish Out of Water, or The Cook Turned Secretary; *Lunn:* (27) My 9, 11; (30) F 22; (40) Mr 30; (47) Ja 8.
Five Dollars a Day, or Lodgings for the Convention: (60) Ap 21.
The Flitch of Bacon, or The Custom of Dunmow Priory; *Dudley:* (00) Mr 7, 8, Ap 2; (05) My 6.
The Floating Beacon, or The Norwegian Wreckers: (26) F 13, 15; (45) Mr 8.
Flora, or Hob in the Well: (06) Mr 5.
Flora's Birthday: (20) F 7; (26) F 20, 22.

Flore et Zephyr: (40) Ja 14, 16, 17.
Flowers of the Forest; *Buckstone:* (52) D 14; (56) F 11, 13; (59) O 17, 19.
The Flying Dutchman, or The Phantom Ship; *Dunlap:* (28) F 8; (42) Mr 7, 9, 31.
Follies of a Day, or The Marriage of Figaro; *Holcroft:* (01) Mr 30; (05) Ap 29.
Follies of a Night, or A Lesson for Husbands; *Planché:* (45) Ja 9, 13, F 19; (46) F 9, 20; (51) Ap 16, 25; (54) D 23; (56) Ja 25; (58) N 17.
Folly as It Flies, or Modern Dueling; *Reynolds:* (02) My 10; (07) F 9, 17.
For Freedom! Ho!; *Pocock:* (17) My 2.
The Force of Calumny: (05) My 23.
Foreign Airs and Native Graces; *Moncrieff:* (40) Mr 4, 5, 6, 9, Ap 10, 13; (42) Ja 5, 10, 15, 31.
The Foreign Prince: (42) Ja 1.
The Forest of Bondy, or Dog of Montargis: (16) D 21, 28; (17) Ja 4, 11, 27, F 25, Mr 1, 3; (18) Ja 8; (20) Mr 15, D 1, 16; (28) Ap 7; (34) Mr 14, 15, 18; (38) Ap 3; (54) Mr 16; (55) Ja 15, 22.
The Forest of Rosenwald, or The Bleeding Nun of Lindenberg (or The Travellers Benighted, or Raymond and Agnes); *Stokes:* (08) Ap 25, My 19; (24) F 2; (35) Ap 20.
The Forest Rose, or American Farmers; *Woodworth:* (34) Mr 21, N 17; (43) D 2, 11; (44) Ap 1, N 28; (45) N 27; (47) F 10, 17; (48) O 30, 31; (51) Ja 20, 27.
The Fortress: (09) Ja 14, 19, Mr 14; (17) Ap 23.
Fortune's Frolic, or The Merry Villagers (or The True Use of Riches, or The Ploughman Turned Lord); *Allingham:* (01) Mr 16; (02) F 1, 9, Mr 19, N 26; (03) N 28; (04) F 29; (08) D 5; (11) Ja 19, F 28; (12) F 12; (15) D 9, 29; (16) D 2; (17) Ja 25, Mr 10; (18) Mr 9, 11, Ap 11, O 30; (19) Ap 24; (20) Mr 3, Ap 10; (21) Ap 24; (22) Ap 17; (24) F 9, Mr 4, D 11; (28) Ap 9, N 20, 28; (29) N 9; (30) N 25; (31) Mr 5; (34) Ja 3; (38) Ap 7; (39) My 25, D 4; (42) F 19; (47) F 15, 17; (53) N 14.
Fortunio; *Planché:* (45) Ja 1, 3, 6, 8, 11, F 19.
Forty and Fifty: (48) F 8.
Forty Thieves: (07) D 18, 19; (08) F 3, 19; (09) Ja 25, F 16; (10) Mr 14, 26; (19) F 10, 13, 20, 27, Ap 19; (20) F 5, Ap 12, D 26; (22) Ap 13; (26) Ap 14, 19; (36) Mr 1, 2; (41) F 2, 3, 11; (44) D 25, 28; (60) Ja 7.
Forty Winks, or Blunders in a Bed Room; *Burton:* (39) D 7.
Foscari, or The Venetian Exile; *White:* (06) Ja 10, 13, F 24; (09) Ja 20.
The Fou, or The King's Jester: (51) O 16, 18.
The Foundling of the Forest; *Dimond:* (10) Ap 11, 27; (11) Mr 20, 27; (12) F 27, My 4; (16) F 2; (17) Ja 1; (18) Ja 17; (19) Ap 23; (22) My 4; (24) Ap 9; (25) Ap 5; (27) Ja 12, Ap 7; (28) Mr 21; (29) Ap 20, My 1; (39) My 27; (45) Mr 12, 14.
Fountainbleau Races, or Our Way in France: (08) My 25; (18) N 27; (24) F 28.
Fountainville Forest; *Boaden:* (00) Mr 31.
The Four Sisters: (58) D 30; (59) Ja 7.

Fra Diavolo, or The Inn of Terracina; *Auber:* (39) F 15, 16, 19, 22, Mr
    18, 23, Ap 3, 5, D 17, 18, 24; (40) F 6, Mr 13, 20; (41) D 9, 11, 14;
    (42) Mr 15, 29; (43) Mr 9; (45) F 13, 15; (47) Mr 4; (48) D 16;
    (49) Ja 1, 4; (58) Ja 23, 26, 28; (59) Mr 5.
Frank Fox Phipps, Esq.; *Selby:* (40) F 14, 15, 22, Mr 21.
Fraternal Discord; *Smith* or *Dunlap:* (04) D 17, 21, 27; (05) F 20, 27;
    (07) Ap 1; (08) Ap 21; (15) D 1; (18) F 27; (22) Ap 19, My 17;
    (23) My 23; (33) Ap 8; (45) Ja 1.
Frederick the Great: (58) Mr 8.
The French Spy, or The Fall of Algiers: (53) D 9, 31; (54) Ja 1;
    (56) Ap 7; (57) D 5; (58) D 23; (59) Ja 6.
Friend Waggles; *Morton:* (51) F 17.
Frightened to Death; *Oulton:* (17) D 19; (24) F 26; (27) Mr 14, 17;
    (28) D 13; (40) N 19.
The Fusilier, or The Clown Outwitted: (08) Ap 18.

The Gambler's Fate, or A Lapse of Twenty Years; *(Milner):* (29) Mr
    9; (32) D 27.
The Game of Love [Life]; *(Brougham):* (55) D 1, 3, 4, 5.
The Gamester; *Moore:* (06) My 2; (07) Ap 11; (09) F 16; (10) F
    19; (16) Ja 19, N 18; (18) Mr 30; (19) Ap 26; (20) Ap 17; (23)
    My 27; (24) D 20; (27) Mr 28, D 24; (28) D 19; (30) F 1; (31)
    Mr 10; (35) Mr 20; (38) Ja 9; (39) F 6; (46) F 9, 20; (50) F
    11, Mr 11; (51) F 26, Ap 28; (52) F 23; (53) F 15, D 14; (54)
    Ja 16, D 5; (55) Ap 18; (56) Mr 1; (57) D 11.
The Generous Cottager: (01) Ap 11; (02) Ap 28.
The Generous Farmer: (03) Mr 28.
Genevieve of Brabant, or Virtue of Triumphant: (00) My 2.
A Gentleman in Difficulties; *Bayley:* (37) D 30; (38) Ja 4, 15.
The Gentle Shepherd, or Patie and Roger: (01) Ap 22.
George Barnwell, or The London Merchant (or The London Apprentice);
    Lillo: (01) Ap 25; (04) Mr 7, D 26; (05) D 26; (06) Ja 20; (07)
    Ja 1, D 2; (08) D 24, 28; (15) D 15, 30; (16) D 27; (18) Ja 1, F
    25; (19) D 27; (24) Ja 1; (25) Ja 1; (30) Ja 1; (33) My 17;
    (34) Ja 1, 4, 6, 25; (35) Ap 16; (36) Ap 1, 6; (40) Ja 25, Mr 10;
    (55) Mr 6.
Gil Blas, or The Cave of the Robbers; *Moore:* (06) Ja 1, 6, F 21, My
    14, D 26.
Gilderoy, the Bonnie Boy, or The Reiver of Perth; *Barrymore:* (23) Ju
    30, Jy 4; (26) Ap 21.
Gile Tout Soul: (24) My 12, 14.
Giovanni in London, or The Libertine Reclaimed; *Moncrieff:* (30) Ja
    20; (39) N 30, D 2.
Giselle, or Les Wilis; *Gautier:* (46) N 9, 10, 11, 12, 18; (48) F 14, 15,
    16; (51) Ja 29, 30.
The Gladiator; *Bird:* (41) Ja 18; (47) F 3, 4.
A Glance at New York; *Baker:* (52) Ja 21, 22, 23, 24, Mr 18, 20.
A Glance, or New York as It Is: (56) Ap 12, 14.
Glencoe, or The Fate of the Donalds; *Talfourd:* (41) Ja 4, 5.
The Glory of Columbia; *Dunlap:* (05) Ap 8, 17; (07) D 22; (12) My 4;
    (16) F 22; (17) F 22.
Go-to-Bed-Tom; *Morton:* (53) F 23.
Goddess of the Dance: (51) O 16.

Godenski, or The Skates of Wilner: (34) Ja 18; (39) My 3.

The Golden Farmer, or The Last Crime; *Webster:* (35) Ap 14; (36) F 17; (39) Ap 6, My 25; (42) Mr 9; (43) Ja 16; (45) Mr 28; (52) Mr 20; (53) D 5, 6.

Good for Nothing; *Buckstone:* (53) Mr 1, D 26, 31; (56) Ja 31; (58) Mr 1, 8.

The Gordian Knot, or Causes and Effects; *Harby:* (10) My 3, 10.

Graciosa: (53) N 26.

Grandfather Whitehead; *Lemon:* (44) F 9, 13, D 17, 20; (45) D 25; (52) Mr 15; (57) Ap 9, 10.

Grandfather's Will: (05) D 18; (06) Ja 8, 11, D 31; (07) D 5; (11) My 14.

The Graveyard Murder: (44) Mr 22.

The Grecian Daughter; *Murphy:* (02) D 15, 16; (03) Mr 14; (05) N 22; (11) Mr 13.

Greece and Liberty: (24) Mr 26.

Green Bushes, or The Mississippi; *Buckstone:* (55) Ja 11, 13; (59) Ja 3.

The Green-Eyed Monster; *Pocock:* (30) Ap 12.

The Green Man; *Jones:* (19) Mr 1.

The Green Monster, or The Three Knights of Trineomalee; *Ravel Family:* (54) Mr 29, 31; (59) Ja 13, 15.

The Green Mountain Boy, or Love and Learning; *Jones:* (34) N 15, 18; (43) N 28, D 5.

Gretna Green, or Heigho for a Husband; *Beazley:* (30) F 3, 12, Mr 19; (32) Mr 19.

Grieving's a Folly; *Leigh:* (10) My 9.

Grimshaw, Bagshaw, and Bradshaw, or The Three Shaws; *Morton:* (55) N 19, 20; (56) Ja 15.

Griseldis, or The Patient Woman; *Field:* (56) Mr 3, 7; (59) Ja 26.

Grist to the Mill; *Planché:* (52) Ja 31, N 12; (53) N 28; (54) D 19.

Guilty or Not Guilty; *Dibdin:* (05) Mr 19.

Gumbo Jim: (41) D 30.

The Gun Maker of Moscow; *Brougham:* (60) Ap 5, 6.

Gustavus III, or The Masked Ball; *Auber:* (41) Mr 22, 23, 24; (42) Mr 30.

Gustavus Vasa, or The Deliverer of His Country; *Brooke:* (03) D 5; (12) F 22.

Guy Mannering, or The Gipsey's Prophecy; *Terry:* (20) D 2, 5; (22) F 20, My 1; (24) Ja 16, Mr 19; (28) Mr 6, 22; (38) Ja 1, 3; (39) F 21; (41) D 1, 2, 3; (50) Ap 19, 22; (51) F 22, 28, My 2; (55) O 29, N 14; (58) Ap 27.

Hail Columbia: (34) F 22.

Hamlet; *Shakespeare:* (01) Ap 27; (04) My 25; (05) Mr 21, N 28, D 20, 24; (06) Ap 14; (07) Ap 9; (08) Ap 4; (09) F 3; (10) F 12, Mr 30; (12) Mr 20; (16) Mr 20; (17) Mr 21; (18) F 6, Ap 1, N 2; (19) F 5, Ap 13; (20) F 2; (21) My 2, D 7; (24) D 1; (26) Mr 31; (27) Ja 24, Mr 23; (28) F 6, D 3; (31) F 23; (32) Mr 1, 9; (35) Mr 27; (37) D 29; (38) F 5, 7, Mr 6; (39) F 5, D 12; (40) F 11; (41) Ap 26; (42) F 1, 7, 9, D 23; (44) Ja 8, 19, F 24; (45) N 20; (46) F 16, N 6, D 4; (47) Ja 18, 28, D 25, 28; (48) F 22, O 31; (49) Ja 12, 29; (50) F 8; (51) F 17; (52) Mr 19, 25, D 17; (53)

D 29; (54) Ja 28; (55) Ja 1, 8, 29, O 16; (56) Ja 17, D 1, 4; (57) Ja 12, N 2; (58) D 15; (59) Mr 23, 31; (60) Mr 27.

Hamlet Travestie; *Poole:* (18) F 28; (22) My 8; (28) D 10; (32) Mr 12, 27.

Hampton Court Frolics, or The Lie of the Day: (04) Mr 26.

The Happiest Day of My Life; *Buckstone:* (38) Ja 5, 9, 10, F 19; (41) Ja 18; (45) Mr 11, 15; (46) N 16.

The Happy Family; *Smith:* (02) Ap 5.

The Happy Man, or Paddy in China; *Lover:* (41) F 12; (42) Ja 14, Mr 1; (47) Ja 1, 2; (49) My 24; (54) Ja 31, F 3.

Harlequin Dr. Faustus; *Woodward:* (07) Mr 23.

Harlequin Free Mason, or Friendship and Love: (06) Mr 31, My 22.

Harlequin Hurry-Scurry, or Christmas Gambols: (10) Mr 20.

Harlequin Mariner: (09) Ap 3.

Harlequin Shipwreck: (23) Ju 28.

Harlequin Skeleton, or The Crown Metamorphosed: (00) F 7; (06) Ja 13, 29, Ap 21; (17) Ap 7.

Harlequin Statues: (34) Mr 19, Ap 23.

Harlequin Woodcutter: (22) Ap 8, My 6.

Harlequin's Frolic, or Magic Gambols: (20) F 21, 23, Mr 11, 18.

Harlequin's Invasion: (01) F 25.

Harlequin's Restoration, or The Triumph of Love: (11) My 7.

Harlequin's Vagaries: (16) Ap 15, 26.

Harvest Home: (59) Ja 19.

The Haunted Tower; *Cobb:* (02) Mr 8; (09) Ja 12, F 1; (17) Ap 18; (28) Mr 28.

Hazard of the Die; *Jerrold:* (40) My 15.

He Would Be An Actor: (58) Ap 14, 15.

Hear Both Sides; *Holcroft:* (03) My 3.

The Heart of Midlothian, or The Lilly of St. Leonards (or The Highland Whistler): (21) Ap 18, My 4; (40) Ap 9, 11.

Hearts of Oak; *Allingham:* (05) My 6.

The Heir at Law; *Coleman:* (00) Ja 8, 11, 13, F 14, Mr 17; (02) Mr 23, D 18, 20; (09) Ja 9, 16; (11) Ja 11, Mr 6; (12) F 20; (15) D 16; (17) F 3, Mr 22, D 19; (18) Ja 9; (20) F 26; (21) N 7; (26) D 27; (27) N 21; (28) Ja 11; (32) D 10; (33) F 27; (41) N 16, 26; (57) Ja 3, 6.

Helping Hands, or The Blind Musician: (56) N 15.

Helpless Animals! Men without Women!: (27) Mr 23.

Henry IV; *Shakespeare:* (06) F 7, D 12; (07) My 20, D 28; (11) Ap 24; (15) D 11; (18) Ja 23, N 11; (24) Mr 12; (31) Mr 18; (32) F 27; (38) Mr 12, 16; (42) F 14, 17; (43) Ja 11, D 20; (45) N 22; (46) Ja 10; (48) F 4.

Henry VIII; *Shakespeare:* (02) Ap 12; (17) Mr 5, 7; (23) D 15, 29; (50) Ap 24; (54) Mr 9.

Henry Quatre, or France in the Olden Time; *Morton:* (20) D 6.

Her Royal Highness: (53) Ja 15, 27.

Hercules, King of Clubs: (40) Ap 6; (47) Ja 11.

Hercules of Brittany: (44) N 22.

The Hero of the North, or The Liberator of His Country; *Coleman:* (17) Ap 16.

He's Not A-Miss: (53) D 6.

Hide-and-Go-Seek, or All in the Dark: (33) Ju 12.

High Life below Stairs; *Garrick:* (01) Mr 20; (02) F 3; (04) D 15; (08) Mr 2, 11; (10) Ap 9; (12) F 25; (20) Ja 24, F 9, Mr 17; (21) Ap 7; (24) Ja 5; (26) D 22; (27) F 24, Ap 23; (28) F 1, N 26; (29) F 25; (33) Mr 12, D 18; (38) F 14, Ap 12.

High Pressure! Express!: (54) O 30.

The Highland Reel; *O'Keeffe:* (00) Ja 22, Mr 5; (01) My 1; (02) Ja 20, F 3, N 17; (03) F 17, D 12; (04) F 6, D 27; (06) Mr 3, Ap 18, D 6, 10; (07) Ja 23, D 2, 28; (08) My 23, D 16; (10) Ap 13; (11) Ap 29; (15) D 13; (16) Ja 9, 31, Mr 22; (17) Ap 11, 19; (18) Ja 16, F 20, My 18; (22) F 23, Ap 20; (29) Ap 4.

The Highlander's Oath: (59) Mr 12.

His First Champagne, or Wine Works Wonders: (39) D 2, 4.

His Last Legs; *Bernard:* (41) F 9, 10; (43) N 11, 14, D 1, 15, 21, 27; (44) Ja 3, 15, F 16, Mr 7, D 4; (45) Ja 7, 24, F 4; (46) D 24, 30; (48) Ja 10; (50) Mr 19, 22; (52) N 13, 22; (54) F 27, Mr 6, 14, Ap 14, N 30, D 14; (55) Ja 20; (56) D 8, 11; (57) Mr 5; (59) N 7.

Hit or Miss; *Pocock:* (11) Ap 15.

Home Again, or The Sisters; *(Fitzball):* (46) Ja 5, 13; (57) N 23, 27.

Home Squadron, or The Female Sailors: (43) F 8.

Homeward Bound, or The Sailor's Return: (00) Ap 14.

Honest Roguery: (43) D 4.

The Honest Thieves, or The Faithful Irishman; *Knight:* (02) Ap 7, 9; (07) Mr 18; (09) Mr 16; (10) F 6, 23; (18) My 11; (20) Mr 1; (29) N 11; (33) Mr 9.

The Honeymoon; *Tobin:* (05) D 28; (06) Ja 22, Ap 25, N 26; (07) F 25, Ap 24; (08) Ja 14, F 22, D 19; (09) F 25; (10) F 14; (12) Ap 2, 4; (16) Ja 10, F 21, Ap 1, D 13; (18) Mr 28; (19) F 19; (20) Ja 7, F 12; (23) D 12; (25) Ja 14; (27) F 17, Mr 21; (28) Ja 30, N 21, D 13; (29) F 27; (30) N 26; (31) Mr 11; (35) Mr 12; (36) F 19; (37) D 15, 27; (38) Ja 6, Ap 19; (39) My 23; (41) Ja 7; (42) D 21; (43) My 2; (44) Mr 28; (45) D 5; (46) Ja 20, F 17, N 5, D 18; (47) D 29; (48) Mr 20, O 25, N 1; (50) Ja 30, F 11, Ap 20; (51) Ja 22, Ap 15; (52) Ja 15, Mr 6, N 18; (53) F 22; (54) Mr 4, N 10, D 9; (55) F 24, Ap 12, D 6; (56) Ja 12, N 5; (57) Ja 23, Ap 3, O 31.

Hops and Steps: (28) Ja 16.

The Horse and the Widow; *Dibdin:* (01) Ja 28, F 11, Mr 2.

Houfer, the Tell of the Tyrol: (39) My 30.

The House that Jack Built: (26) Mr 28, 29, Ap 3.

A House to Be Sold; *Cobb:* (07) F 2, 6, Ap 22; (10) F 12, Mr 23.

How Do You Manage?: (41) My 10; (48) D 25.

How to Die for Love, or The Blank Cartridge: (16) D 26; (17) Ja 20, F 15; (28) D 6, 18; (32) F 16, Mr 24; (33) Ju 15.

How to Grow Rich; *Reynolds:* (22) My 13.

How to Pay the Rent; *Power:* (44) Mr 13; (46) D 26; (47) Ja 2; (48) Ja 11; (50) Mr 21; (59) N 1.

How to Settle Accounts with Your Landlady: (53) Mr 2.

How to Settle Accounts with Your Laundress; *Coyne:* (52) N 13, 15, 18; (53) Ja 14.

How to Settle Accounts with Your Washerwoman: (53) N 16, D 15; (54) F 21, Mr 23, D 11; (55) Ja 18, Mr 2; (56) Mr 24; (57) Ap 21.

Hue and Cry, or A Run at Hamstead: *(Reed):* (45) N 26, D 1; (47) F 11.

The Hunchback; *Knowles:* (32) D 17; (35) Mr 13, 23; (36) F 16, Mr 2; (37) D 18, 19, 23; (38) Ja 5; (39) Ja 3, Ap 16; (40) Ap 1, N 6; (41) D 6, 21, 23; (44) F 10; (45) Ja 27, N 4; (46) Ja 19, F 5, D 12; (48) Ja 31; (50) Ja 25, Mr 5; (52) Ja 9, 14, F 2, 13, 28, N 22, D 3; (53) F 14, D 13; (54) Mr 6, O 30, N 14, D 12; (55) F 20, Ap 16, O 31; (56) F 28; (57) Ja 21, F 3, 19, D 16; (59) Ja 24; (60) Ap 16.

Hungarian Rendezvous: (59) Ja 21.

Hunt the Slipper: (06) Ja 22.

The Hunter of Savoy: (45) Mr 5.

The Hunter of the Alps; *Dimond:* (07) Ja 8, 12, F 20, Mr 14, Ap 17; (08) F 26, D 19; (10) My 3; (11) Ap 8; (18) My 8; (20) Mr 27, D 22; (21) Mr 29; (24) F 4, 6, Mr 29; (28) Ja 4; (32) D 19; (36) Mr 28, Ap 5; (38) F 9, 24, 25, Ap 24; (47) D 25; (57) N 24, D 4.

The Hunters and the Milk Maid: (10) F 21; (12) Ap 4, 10, D 7.

Hunting a Turtle: (39) Ja 26, 31, F 4; (43) D 2, 12; (44) Ja 12; (49) Ja 30, F 1; (50) Ap 26; (52) F 25, Mr 23; (57) N 21.

Hurry Scurry, or The Devil Among the Mechanics: (11) Ap 29.

Husband at Sight; *Buckstone:* (32) Mr 2; (40) Ja 29, 30, My 7; (49) F 2; (54) Ja 6; (58) D 30.

The Hussard's Daughter: (05) Ap 6.

Hylas and Hebe: (43) Ja 21.

The Hypocrite; *Bickerstaff:* (27) Ap 16; (28) Ja 16, F 27; (33) Mr 9, D 13; (34) Ja 18, N 28; (35) Mr 13; (36) F 20, Mr 7; (40) Ap 30.

The Idiot Witness, or A Tale of Blood: (26) Ap 13; (34) Ap 25; (38) Ap 12, 21; (41) Mr 18; (52) Ja 24; (59) Mr 9.

Il Bondocane, or The Caliph Robber: (03) Ap 12.

Il Guiramento; *Rossi* and *Mercandante:* (51) Mr 31, D 12.

Il Maledetto: (40) D 2.

Il Polinto: (60) F 28, Mr 3.

Il Puritani; *Bellini:* (51) N 12, 15; (57) F 17.

Il Trovatore; *Verdi:* (58) Ja 27, F 1, Mr 4; (59) Mr 4, N 23; (60) F 27, Mr 1, N 23.

The Illustrious Stranger, or You Must Be Buried; *(Kenney):* (28) F 25, Mr 8; (32) D 14; (40) Ja 21, 27, F 11, Ap 20, 22; (42) Mr 4; (43) My 5, 6; (46) N 27, D 28; (52) Mr 8; (55) O 26, 27.

Imagination: (47) Ja 8.

In and Out of Place; *Johnson:* (54) Ja 30, 31, F 8.

In Yankee Land: (35) Mr 26.

The Incendiary: (43) D 5.

The Inconstant, or The Way to Win Him; *Farquhar:* (05) Ap 22.

Independence, or Which Do You Like Best, the Peer or the Farmer?; *Ioor:* (05) Mr 30; (06) F 26.

The Indian Princess, or La Belle Sauvage; *Barker:* (09) Ap 11; (10) Mr 16.

The Indian Princess, or The First Settlement of Virginia (or Pocahontas); *Custis:* (58) F 5, 6.

Ingomar, or The Son of the Wilderness (or The Barbarian and the Greek Maiden); *Lovell:* (52) N 29, 30, D 1, 24; (53) F 26, D 17, 21; (54) F 21, N 4, D 6; (55) F 5, 28, O 18; (56) F 29; (57) F 5, 12, D 1, 15; (58) Ap 20; (59) Ja 25; (60) Ap 10, 19.

Inkle and Yarico, or The American Heroine; *Coleman:* (01) Ap 25; (02) F 22, Mr 15, D 10, 11; (06) F 10; (07) My 8.

The Inn-keeper of Abbeville, or The Ostler and the Robber; *Burke:* (30) Ja 11, 13.

The Inn-keeper's Bride: (37) D 18; (38) Mr 8, Ap 6.

The Inn-keeper's Daughter: (18) F 23, 24, 25, Mr 6, 9, Ap 4, 25; (19) Mr 3; (29) N 30; (32) Mr 24.

Intrigue, or Married Yesterday; *Poole:* (27) Ja 13, F 28; (30) F 26; (45) F 6.

The Invincibles; *Morton:* (29) Mr 23, 27.

The Invisible Girl: (09) Ap 11.

The Invisible Harlequin, or The Enchanted Trumpet: (34) Ja 15.

Ion, or The Fate of Argos; *Talfourd:* (37) D 26, 28; (40) N 30, D 3; (46) F 10, 17; (50) Ap 23; (54) F 27, N 11; (55) F 27; (57) F 9.

Ireland and America, or Life in Both; *(Pilgrim):* (54) F 10.

Ireland as It Is: (54) F 6, 7; (55) F 14; (56) Ap 11, 12, 18; (58) F 23, Mr 10.

The Irish Ambassador, or A School for Diplomats; *Power:* (34) D 2; (41) F 8, 12; (44) Mr 22; (46) D 22; (47) Ja 2; (48) Ja 8, 11; (57) Mr 2, 4; (59) O 31, N 9.

Irish Assurance and Yankee Modesty; *(Pilgrim):* (54) F 1; (58) Mr 9, 13.

The Irish Attorney, or Galway Practice; *Power:* (41) F 15, 19; (46) D 26, 30; (57) Mr 3, 9; (59) N 1.

The Irish Baron: (58) F 25, 27, Mr 11.

The Irish Genius: (59) N 4, 9.

The Irish Lion; *Buckstone:* (40) My 15; (41) F 8, 9; (50) Mr 18, 21; (52) D 14, 16; (53) F 4; (54) F 23; (55) F 8, 16; (57) Ja 1, 6, 13; (58) F 25, 26.

Irish Post; *Planché:* (46) D 28, 29; (48) Ja 10.

Irish Recruit: (50) Mr 23.

Irish Secretary: (50) Mr 20, 22.

Irish Thrush and the Swedish Nightingale: (54) F 10, 11.

Irish Tutor, or New Lights; *Butler:* (23) D 26, 29; (24) F 14, 27, My 10, D 1; (25) Ja 15; (29) Ap 25, D 30; (30) F 5, D 8; (31) Mr 10; (32) Mr 20; (33) F 26, Mr 12; (34) O 13, 15, N 8, D 2; (40) Ja 13, N 5, D 2, 16, 28; (41) F 10, N 30; (42) F 25, Mr 18; (43) N 27, D 22; (44) Mr 2, D 7, 27; (45) F 1, 18; (48) N 29, 30, D 1; (49) My 28; (53) Ja 1; (54) F 9; (56) Ja 17.

The Irish Widow; *Garrick:* (01) Ja 24, N 27; (04) N 26; (07) D 26; (26) Ap 10; (40) F 29, Ap 11; (42) Ja 8, 15.

The Irishman in London; *Macready:* (01) Ap 29, My 6; (02) Mr 10, 24; (05) N 15, D 24; (08) N 11, 28; (09) F 13; (11) F 26; (12) F 19; (16) Ja 17, 19, Mr 27, D 9; (17) Ja 3; (18) Ap 17, O 29; (19) F 2, My 6, D 31; (20) Ap 29; (21) Mr 28; (22) Mr 1, Ap 27; (23) D 1; (24) Mr 2; (25) F 4, Mr 18; (28) Mr 22, N 24; (29) F 16, 27, Mr 24; (30) Ja 27, N 19; (31) F 25; (33) F 28; (34) N 7, 20; (36) Mr 11, 22, Ap 7.

The Iron Chest, or The Mysterious Murder; *Coleman:* (07) Mr 16; (15) D 18; (16) Mr 30; (19) Ap 24; (21) Mr 29; (22) F 23; (25) Mr 19; (26) Mr 28, Ap 6; (27) F 3; (28) Ap 12; (32) Mr 7; (34) O 30; (36) Ap 12; (38) Mr 23, Ap 18; (40) F 17; (44) F 20; (46) Ja 6, N 7; (48) Mr 6; (49) Ja 31; (50) F 16; (51) Ap 16;

(52) Mr 26; (56) Ja 1, 22, D 6; (57) N 28; (59) Mr 26, Ap 7; (60) Mr 30.

The Iron Mask, or The Island of St. Marguerite: (00) Mr 28.

Is He Jealous?; *Beazley:* (22) My 6, 10; (24) Mr 5; (27) Mr 5, 9, 28, D 17; (29) Ap 4, N 10, 27; (30) Ja 29, Mr 2, D 17; (32) F 6, D 17; (33) Mr 25, Ap 8, D 20; (34) N 21, D 5; (35) Ap 1, D 3; (38) Mr 6, 9, 12; (39) Mr 21; (40) F 12; (41) Ap 26; (44) D 17; (45) F 7; (46) N 9.

Is It a Lie?: (32) D 5.

Isabella, or The Fatal Marriage; *Southerne:* (03) F 18; (05) D 11; (11) Mr 15; (23) D 1; (24) Ja 23; (28) D 8; (30) F 22, 26, D 21; (31) F 22; (35) Ap 7; (36) Mr 11; (40) Ap 3, 4, My 4.

Isabelle, or Woman's Life (or The Maid, the Wife, and Widow): (52) Ja 7; (56) F 16, 26.

The Isle of Nymphs: (59) Ja 14, 17.

The Italian Monk; *Boaden:* (03) Mr 4, 9, 16.

Ivanhoe, or The Jew's Daughter: (21) My 21.

Jack Cade, or The Bondmen of Kent (or The Noble Kinsman);*Conrad:* (56) Ja 5, 7.

Jack in Distress, or American Tars on Shore: (09) Ja 27, Mr 18; (10) Mr 12, Ap 4; (33) D 28.

Jack Robinson and His Monkeys: (38) Ap 3, 4.

Jack Sheppard, or The Housebreaker: (54) Ja 4, 5.

The Jacobite; *Planché:* (50) Ap 29; (51) My 1, 6; (52) Mr 12.

Jamie of Aberdeen, or Love in a Mist: (30) Ja 1, 4; (40) Ja 25.

Jane Shore; *Rowe:* (03) N 19; (04) D 22; (07) Ja 21, D 23; (08) Ja 2; (10) Ap 16; (11) Mr 25; (16) Ja 12, F 3, 28, D 9; (18) Ja 30, F 5; (20) Ap 29; (23) My 30; (30) Mr 1; (31) F 24; (33) D 21; (36) F 13, Mr 1; (38) Ja 18; (39) Ja 5, 19, D 28; (40) Mr 10, N 7; (43) Ap 28; (45) D 22; (46) D 17; (53) D 27; (54) Ja 17; (55) Ap 13, D 31; (56) F 8.

The Jealous Lover: (35) Ap 15.

The Jealous Wife; *Coleman:* (01) Ap 13, My 6; (03) D 1, 19; (20) Ja 15; (22) F 13, 18; (23) Ju 23, D 5; (24) F 25; (25) Ja 21; (27) Ap 4, 9; (29) F 23; (30) Mr 8; (54) D 11, 14; (55) Mr 3; (57) O 19.

Jean le Sot: (60) Mr 6.

Jenny Lind: (54) Mr 2, D 18, 23; (57) O 29; (58) Mr 26.

Jenny Lind at Last: (53) D 12, 16, 29.

Jenny Lind in Charleston, or Fanatico per la Musica: (51) Ap 23, 25, My 13.

The Jew and the Doctor; *Dibdin:* (00) F 13, Mr 10, 11, 12; (01) F 4, 6, N 20, 25; (02) Ja 20, F 15, 16, D 3; (03) Mr 21; (06) Ja 10, D 31; (07) Ja 14; (08) Mr 23; (09) Mr 6; (10) Mr 20; (11) F 16, Mr 2; (12) Ja 31; (17) Ja 1, Mr 29; (18) Mr 13; (35) N 20.

The Jew of Lubeck: (20) Ja 26.

The Jew, or Benevolent Hebrew; *Cumberland:* (03) Ap 21; (04) F 4; (05) N 15, D 14; (07) Ju 3; (23) My 28, Ju 2.

The Jewess, or The Fate of Haman (or Massacre at York): (36) Mr 21, 23; (39) Ap 18, 19, 20, 22, 25, My 3, 13, 21; (40) Ja 3, 4; (54) Mr 13; (58) Ap 22.

Jim Crow in London: (38) Ja 31, F 5; (41) D 31.

Joan of Arc, or The Maid of Orleans: (24) Ja 21, 28, F 17, 18; (43) F 8, 11; (53) D 28; (54) Mr 10.
Job Fox, the Yankee Pedlar; *Bernard:* (35) Ap 4.
Jocko, or The Brazilian Ape: (34) Ja 27, F 28, Mr 3, Ap 21; (35) Mr 17; (39) N 25; (55) Ja 27; (59) Ja 22.
John Bull, or An Englishman's Fireside; *Coleman:* (03) N 23, 28, D 3; (04) F 8, 18, My 28, D 14; (05) D 4; (06) N 21; (07) Ja 12; (08) Ja 20, F 26, D 12; (10) Mr 21; (11) Ja 16; (15) N 10; (18) Ja 7, Mr 6; (20) Ja 31; (25) Ja 28; (33) Mr 1, 7; (34) O 21; (41) F 17; (44) D 19; (53) O 31, N 15.
John Buzzby, or A Day in Richmond; *Poole:* (23) Ju 14.
John et Manette (60) Mr 7.
John Jones, or The Most Unfortunate Man in the World: (39) F 21, N 28, D 4, 9; (58) D 2, 10.
John of Paris; *Pocock:* (17) Mr 12, 26, 29, 31; (18) My 15; (19) F 17; (21) D 1; (24) Ja 24; (25) F 7; (28) Mr 28.
John of Procida, or The Bridals of Messina; *Knowles:* (41) F 5, Ap 24.
The Jolly Miller: (51) O 9, 15.
Jonathan Bradford, or The Murder at the Road-Side Inn: (45) Mr 17.
Jonathan Doubikins, or A Trip to England: (35) Ap 8.
Jonathan in England; *Hackett:* (32) Ja 31, F 3, 20; (34) N 14, 18; (38) Mr 9, 14; (42) F 19, 26; (43) N 27, D 7, 28; (44) Ap 3, N 30; (45) N 25; (47) F 12.
The Judgment of Paris; *(Schomberg):* (51) O 21.
Julia, or The Italian Lover; *Jephson:* (04) Mr 13.
Julius Caesar; *Shakespeare:* (18) Ap 20; (19) Ap 28; (20) F 11; (24) Mr 4, D 6; (27) F 28; (30) F 12, 23; (38) F 8, Mr 29; (51) F 13.
Jupiter and Europa, or The Jealousy of Juno (or The Intrigues of Harlequin): (03) Mr 2, 7, 11, 23, 24, Ap 28, D 5; (04) F 13, D 10; (05) F 19; (06) Ja 8, 11; (08) Ap 6.

Kate Carraway, or The Miller of Whetstone: (53) N 10, 12, D 21.
Kate Kearney: (39) Ja 7, 8, 19, 23; (54) D 27, 30.
Kathy O'Sheal; *Pilgrim:* (58) D 22, 23, 27; (59) Ja 1, 8.
The Kentuckian, or A Trip to New York (or The Lion of the West); *Paulding:* (32) F 6, 20; (35) Mr 31, Ap 8; (38) Mr 8, 14; (42) F 15, 18, 26; (43) D 28.
Ketley, or The Mountain Rose: (51) O 23.
Kill or Cure: (38) Mr 28.
Killing No Murder; *Hook:* (16) D 30; (17) Ja 6, 17, F 28, Mr 27, Ap 18; (18) F 27; (19) My 4; (27) Ap 28.
The King and I; *Morton:* (46) Ja 6, 15, 22.
King Rene's Daughter: (54) Mr 4; (58) Ja 8.
King John; *Shakespeare:* (05) My 31; (23) Ju 9; (24) Mr 15; (27) Mr 5.
King Lear; *Shakespeare:* (07) My 13, 16; (10) Mr 20; (17) Ap 7, My 2; (21) Ap 16, D 3; (25) Mr 25, 28; (26) Mr 20; (27) Mr 12; (38) Ja 31, Mr 22, 27; (39) Ja 14; (40) F 22; (41) Ja 22; (42) F 16; (44) F 23, D 26; (47) Ja 26; (50) F 9; (52) Mr 27; (54) F 13; (57) O 26; (59) Ap 5.
The King of the Commoners; *White:* (46) N 28, D 5.
King O'Neill, or The Irish Brigade; *Gore:* (59) N 8.

The King's Fool: (38) Ap 16, 20.
The King's Gardener: (44) N 19, 21, D 7, 31; (47) D 20; (58) N 16.
The Kinsmen, or The Black Riders of the Congaree: (42) D 26, 29.
The Kiss; *Clark:* (12) My 15.
Kiss in the Dark: (42) Ja 4, 8, 15; (52) Mr 16, 19; (54) Ap 14; (55)
    O 23, N 6; (56) N 7; (57) D 10, 16; (58) N 18, D 15.
The Knight of Arva, or Conner the Rash; *Boucicault:* (50) Mr 18, 20;
    (57) Mr 5, 6; (59) Mr 18.
The Knight of the Golden Fleece, or The Yankee in Spain; *Stone:* (34)
    N 19, 21; (43) N 30, D 4.
The Knights of the Cross: (38) Ap 5.
The Knights of the Round Table; *Planché:* (58) N 19.
Know Your Own Mind; *Murphy:* (01) My 11; (16) Mr 13; (18) Ja
    26; (22) My 15; (24) F 2; (30) D 13.

L'Ambique Comique, ou La Prose Poesie et la Musique: (18) My 26.
L'Elisir d'Amore, or The Love Spell; *Donizetti:* (41) D 13, 15; (42)
    Mr 16, 17; (44) Mr 11; (45) F 14; (47) Mr 5; (48) Ja 21, D 12;
    (58) Mr 5.
L'Illusion d'une Peintre: (51) Ja 27.
L'Ombre, or The Maniac: (51) O 20, N 7, 8.
L'Uomo Rosso: (39) My 4, 6, N 25.
La Bayadere; *Auber:* (40) Ja 6, 7, 8, 9, 10, 11, 13, 15, 17; (41) Mr 1,
    3, 4; (43) Ja 12, 20, N 9, 10, 11, 13, 20, 24, D 6; (46) Ja 1, 2, 3, N
    23; (53) N 24, 29; (54) D 28, 29, 30; (56) Ja 25, F 8.
La Belle Dorothe: (05) Mr 19.
La Bonne Fille, or The Banditti: (04) My 3; (08) My 6.
La Chambre Deux Lits: (61) N 29.
La Capeau d'un Horloger: (55) D 10.
La Chatte Metamorphosee: (60) Mr 5.
La Corde Sensible: (60) Mr 6; (61) N 26.
La Cracovienne: (46) Ja 5, 6.
La Diable a Quatre: (51) O 10, N 5, 6.
La Favorita; *Donizetti:* (51) Mr 22, 28, N 21, 29; (60) F 23, Mr 2.
La Fitte, or The Pirate of the Gulf; *Conner:* (40) F 7, 8.
La Fleur de Champ: (46) N 13, 14, 17.
La Forêt Noire: (03) Mr 14; (07) My 27.
La Gazza Ladra, or The Maid of Paulaisseur; *Rossini:* (40) Mr 11,
    12, 16, 27; (41) D 15; (42) Mr 19; (43) Ap 10, 19, 26.
La Maja de Sevillea: (53) D 3.
La Petite Matelot: (34) Ja 25.
La Pe(y)rouse; *(Smith):* (03) My 10, D 1; (04) F 25; (05) F 9;
    (06) My 16; (07) D 5, 14; (08) Ap 4; (20) Ap 14, 15; (21) My
    16; (24) My 24; (25) Ja 1; (26) F 25.
La Polacco: (43) N 22.
La Rose de St. Fleur: (60) Mr 5.
La Somnambula; *Bellini:* (39) Mr 26, 27, Ap 1, 4, My 2, 10, D 13, 14,
    16, 20; (40) Ja 20, 30; (41) F 26, Mr 5, D 7, 10, 14, 16; (42) Mr
    12, 18; (43) Mr 3, 18, Ap 21; (44) Mr 7; (45) F 3, 11; (47) F 22,
    27; (48) Ja 12, 13, 14, 22, 27, D 8; (49) Ja 5; (51) N 17, D 27;
    (55) Ja 16, 17; (58) Ja 18, 22; (59) F 28, N 24, 25; (60) Mr 12,
    N 19.

La Sylphide: (39) D 30; (40) Ja 1, 3, D 28, 30; (41) Mr 8; (43) N 14, 15, 16, 22, D 7.

La Tisbe: (53) D 2, 3, 7.

La Traviata; *Verdi;* (58) Mr 6; (60) F 21, N 26.

La Truondaix: (51) O 17.

La Vivandiere: (51) Ja 28, 31.

The Ladder of Love; *Bayley:* (39) Mr 5, 11, My 9, 13, N 26, 30; (45) D 8, 11; (46) F 4.

Ladies at Home, or Gentlemen, We Can Do without You: (24) Ja 21, F 4, 6, Mr 12; (25) Ap 8, 20; (29) Mr 6.

Ladies' Battle, or Duel en Amour: (52) Ja 27, 30; (56) N 13, 14; (59) Mr 11.

Ladies Beware: (57) F 6, 9, 20.

The Ladies' Club; *Lemon:* (42) Ja 10, 12.

The Ladies' Man; *Burton:* (41) Mr 25, Ap 29.

The Ladies' Race, or The Four Jockeys: (04) F 18.

Lady and a Gentleman in a Peculiarly Perplexing Predicament: (59) Ja 31.

The Lady and the Devil; *Dimond:* (21) Ap 13, 18; (22) F 18, Ap 8; (24) Ap 23; (25) Mr 29; (27) Ja 5, My 16; (28) Mr 4, 26; (29) F 18, N 25, D 5; (31) Mr 25; (32) D 27, 31; (33) Ja 1; (34) F 28, Mr 3; (35) Ap 1, 7; (38) Ap 10; (39) My 10; (42) D 28; (43) Ap 19; (45) Mr 28; (46) N 14; (48) Ja 15, 17, 18, N 2, 3; (50) Mr 21.

The Lady of Lyons, or Love and Price; *Bulwer-Lytton:* (38) D 20, 21, 31; (39) Ja 1, 4, 21, 25, F 4, 18, Mr 1, Ap 17, My 14, D 10, 11; (40) F 17, Ap 28, D 21; (41) Ja 12, F 23, D 20, 25, 28, 31; (42) F 5, 22, D 19; (43) Ja 13, F 23, N 6; (44) Ja 16; (45) F 5, N 5, D 4, 9; (46) F 7, D 15; (47) Ja 19, D 13, 31; (48) O 26, 30; (50) Ja 26, 31, Mr 8, Ap 18; (51) F 24, Ap 26; (52) Ja 28, F 4, 9, 24, N 25, D 21; (53) F 18, N 4, 9, D 15; (54) F 23, N 1, 17, D 13, 15; (55) F 6, 21, O 17; (56) Mr 5, N 12; (57) Ja 20, F 27, O 28; (58) Ja 7, D 13, 14; (59) Ja 29; (60) Ap 14.

The Lady of the Lake, or The Knight of Snowden: (12) F 28, Mr 2, 13; (20) My 3, 5, D 18; (24) Ap 7, 9; (29) My 8; (33) D 31; (40) Ap 15; (55) Ap 12, 17, 18, 19, 23.

The Lady of the Lions; *Durivage:* (52) Mr 11, 13.

The Lady of the Rock; *Holcroft:* (07) Mr 16, Ap 1.

Lady's Maid: (58) Ja 16.

Lady's Stratagem: (58) D 29; (59) Ja 3.

Lafayette, or The Castle of Olmutz; *Woodworth:* (25) Ja 7, Mr 12.

The Lame Lover, or The Deuce Is in Him: (03) F 21.

Landlords, Beware: (44) Mr 8.

Larboard Fin: (45) D 1.

Laroque, the Regicide; *Stone:* (28) F 22.

The Last Days of Pompey; *Medina:* (36) F 24, 25, 26, 27, 29, Mr 21; (43) Ja 30, 31, F 1, 3; (58) Ap 1, 2.

The Last Man, or The Miser of Eltham Green; *Blake:* (38) D 22; (43) Ja 28; (58) Mr 25.

The Last of the Mohicans; *Glover:* (30) Ja 6.

Laugh when You Can, or The Laughing and Crying Philosopher; *Reynolds:* (00) F 3, 4, 7, My 8; (11) Ja 19, F 4; (16) N 30, D 14;

(17) D 22; (18) Ja 15; (19) F 10; (23) D 31; (24) Ja 10; (26) D 20; (27) Ja 13; (28) Ja 14; (30) N 19; (41) My 15.

Law for Ladies, or 'Tis So Reported: (54) F 3, 6.

The Law of Java, or The Upas Tree; *(Coleman):* (23) My 31.

Le Depit Amoureux: (55) D 10.

Le Tartuffe; *Molière:* (55) D 13.

Leap Year, or The Ladies' Privilege; *Buckstone:* (56) Mr 31, Ap 1, 2, 3, 4.

Legion of Honor, or The Veteran of 102: (34) N 25, 29; (39) My 22.

Lend Me a Dollar: (48) F 18.

Lend Me Five Shillings; *Morton:* (46) N 11, 13, 16; (56) Ja 29, F 1, 14; (59) F 10, Mr 15.

Les Adventures d'une Canne: (60) Mr 7.

Les Deux Avengles: (60) Mr 6; (61) N 27.

Les Deux Pecheurs: (61) N 26, 28.

Les Folies Dramatiques: (61) N 28.

Lesson for Husbands: (45) Ja 9; (58) F 22, 25, Mr 11; (59) Mr 18.

The Liar; *Foote:* (00) Ap 25; (01) Mr 6; (02) N 15, 29; (03) F 8, N 26; (04) Ju 7; (09) F 8; (11) F 13, Mr 4; (16) D 4, 18; (17) F 17; (18) F 2, 21; (19) Mr 1; (20) N 23, D 2; (24) Mr 22, My 1, N 24, D 3; (25) Ja 17, Mr 2; (27) F 16, Ap 26; (30) F 17, 27; (48) Ja 7.

Liberty, Equality, and Fraternity: (55) Ja 12.

Liberty in Louisiana; *Workman:* (04) Ap 4, 6, My 21.

The Lie of the Day; *O'Keeffe:* (05) Mr 4.

Life, or The World as It Goes; *Reynolds:* (02) My 3, 17; (03) F 12, 14, Mr 24.

The Limerick Boy; *Pilgrim:* (54) Ja 30, F 1; (57) F 3, 12, Mr 24; (60) Ap 18.

Linda, or The Pearl of Savoy: (48) Ja 15, 17, 18, 26.

Linda, the Cigar Girl, or Mose and His Conspirators: (56) Ap 16, 17, 18.

The Lion of the West: *See* The Kentuckian.

Lise and Colin, or The Wise Outwitted: (41) F 24, Mr 6.

The Little Back Parlor: (43) N 1.

Little Blanche, or The Vigilance Committee: (61) O 21, 24.

The Little Devil: (53) Ja 4, 8, 22.

Little Dot: (59) O 15, 21.

The Little Jockey: (52) D 8, 9, 24, 29.

Little Red Riding Hood: (26) Ap 14, 19.

Little Treasure: (56) Ja 29, F 6; (58) Ja 13, D 22, 30; (59) O 12, 14.

The Loan of a Lover; *Planché:* (37) D 29; (38) Ja 1, 24, D 18; (39) Ap 11, D 10; (40) Ja 14, F 13, N 30, D 30; (41) F 20, N 15; (42) F 1; (43) D 6; (45) N 12, 14, 29; (46) F 24, N 23; (51) O 22, 23; (52) Ja 26; (54) D 22; (55) N 5, 14; (56) Ja 1; (57) O 19, 26, N 21; (58) Ja 6, 14, Mr 26.

The Lock and Key; *Hoare:* (02) Mr 17, My 7, D 15, 16; (03) F 26; (05) N 25; (06) F 24; (07) My 20; (08) My 2, D 17; (10) Mr 2, Ap 14; (12) Mr 20, 21, Ap 2, 8; (15) N 24, D 1, 30; (16) F 7, Ap 6, D 7; (17) Mr 25; (18) Ja 7, F 18, Ap 18; (19) F 20; (20) Mr 8.

Lodoiska, or Rescue of the Princess of Poland; *Kemble:* (07) Mr 20, 23; (20) Ap 14.

Lola Montez in Bavaria: (52) D 9, 10.

Lola Montez, or Countess for an Hour; *(Coyne):* (51) Ap 28, My 8;

(52) N 11, 12, 19; (53) D 28; (54) Ja 18; (56) Ja 18, 26, F 18; (57) Ap 20.

London Assurance; *Boucicault:* (42) Ja 19, 20, 21, 22, 24, 25, 26, 27, 29, F 2, 3, 28; (43) Ja 23, 24; (44) F 14; (45) D 13, 27; (52) Ja 29, Mr 4, N 15, 20, D 16; (55) Ja 3, D 29; (56) Mr 28, 29, N 24, D 17, 19; (57) F 27; (58) Ja 11, Ap 16, N 18; (60) Ap 17.

The Lord of the Manor, or The Discarded Son; *(Burgoyne):* (18) Ap 24; (28) Mr 12.

The Lost Son: (58) Ap 24.

The Lottery Ticket, or The Lawyer's Clerk; *Beazley:* (27) N 26, D 1, 5, 24; (28) Ja 18; (32) F 13; (35) Mr 4, 6, 14, 19, Ap 13; (38) D 28; (39) D 19, 26; (40) Ja 6, D 30; (41) F 19, Ap 28, My 4, N 19, D 7; (42) F 10; (43) Ja 7, 17, Mr 18; (44) Ja 17; (45) F 26; (46) N 17; (47) Ja 5, 28, F 2; (50) Ja 30, Ap 16; (51) My 3; (56) N 8, 12, D 3; (58) Ap 26, D 20.

Louie et le Pascha: (39) Ap 30.

Love a la Mode, or The Rival Suitors; *Macklin:* (00) F 5, 6; (01) F 12; (04) Ap 26; (05) My 17; (08) Ja 14, 25, Mr 25; (16) Ap 24; (18) N 12, 14, 21; (25) Ap 8; (36) Mr 22.

Love among the Roses: (24) Ja 19, Mr 1, Ap 28; (25) F 5, 11, 24, Ap 4.

Love and Money; *Boucicault:* (56) Mr 28, D 16.

Love and Murder; *Brougham:* (56) Ap 3, 4.

The Love Chase, or The Widow Green; *Knowles:* (39) F 8, 20, 25; (40) F 7, N 24; (43) Ja 16; (44) Ja 13; (45) N 6, 17; (50) Mr 16; (51) Ap 24; (52) Ja 31, F 10, Mr 1, N 27; (53) F 26, D 27; (54) D 2, 28; (55) F 17, D 7; (56) Mr 10; (59) Ja 28.

Love in a Bustle: (30) Ja 8, 18.

Love in a Village; *Bickerstaff:* (01) N 21; (05) Mr 15; (06) F 14; (08) N 11, 23; (16) N 20, D 26; (17) F 26; (18) Ap 17, N 20; (20) D 20; (21) Ap 25; (23) N 28, 29, D 3; (24) Ja 30; (28) F 29, Mr 8; (39) Mr 22, Ap 3.

Love in Humble Life; *Payne:* (41) Ja 21; (48) D 22, 23; (51) O 9.

Love in Livery: (55) O 29, N 3; (58) Ja 16.

Love Is Blind: (60) O 19.

Love Laughs at Locksmiths, or The Guardian Outwitted; *Coleman:* (05) My 31, D 9, 14; (06) F 20, Ap 25, D 27; (07) F 4, D 16; (08) Ja 9, D 10, 21; (10) F 10; (11) Ja 11, My 9; (15) N 3, 17, D 23; (16) Ja 12, F 3, Mr 5; (17) Ap 23, D 27; (18) Ja 10; (19) F 1, 22, Ap 27; (20) F 18; (21) Mr 16, N 26; (23) My 27; (24) Mr 20; (25) Mr 14, Ap 4; (44) Mr 19.

Love, Law and Physic; *Kenney:* (17) Ja 24, 27, F 3, 26; (41) F 24, Mr 8; (46) D 1, 22.

Love, or The Countess and the Serf; *Knowles:* (40) F 10, Mr 30, N 23, D 5; (46) D 14; (50) Mr 4, 6; (52) F 6, N 23; (53) D 16; (54) N2, D 7; (55) F 26; (56) Mr 12; (57) Ja 30, Mr 16; (59) F 1.

Love Spell: *See* L'Elisir d'Amore.

Lovers' Quarrels, or Like Master Like Man: (21) N 8; (23) N 29, D 27; (24) F 24, N 23; (25) Ap 14; (27) Ja 19, F 3, D 26, 31; (28) Ja 25; (30) D 3; (39) My 14; (44) Mr 23, N 20; (47) F 27.

Lovers' Vows; *Dunlap* or *Payne:* (00) F 11, 12; (01) F 11, N 16, 18; (02) F 12, My 7, D 24; (04) D 20; (07) Ja 26, N 18; (08) F 8; (10) Ap 2, 7; (12) F 3, 15; (16) My 10; (17) Ja 17; (18) Ja 3; (27) Mr 16; (30) Mr 19.

Love's Labor Lost; *Shakespeare:* (60) O 16.
Love's Offering: (04) My 25.
Love's Orphan: (04) Ju 7.
Love's Sacrifice, or The Rival Merchants; *Lovell:* (43) My 8, 12, D 19;
  (44) N 18, D 4; (46) Ja 26, D 11; (50) F 7, Ap 26; (52) F 14, D
  23; (53) F 16, N 1; (54) O 31; (55) F 23, O 19; (57) Ja 22, Mr
  18; (58) Ja 5.
Lucia di Lammermoor; *Donizetti:* (51) Ap 7, N 10, D 5; (55) Ja 18,
  19; (57) F 16.
The Lucid Interval: (02) F 19.
Lucille, or A Story of the Heart: (38) Ja 23; (39) Ap 10; (40) N 28,
  D 1, 4, 22; (43) N 25; (46) Ja 7; (55) Ap 20; (57) N 3, 4.
Lucky Stars: (43) F 10, 13, 21, Mr 2, 9.
Lucret(z)ia Borgia; *Donizetti* or *Rees:* (48) Ja 20, 24; (50) Ap 1;
  (51) Mr 27, Ap 1, D 1, 6; (52) F 7, Mr 3; (53) F 24, 25; (54) Ja
  18, 21, N 15, 20, 25; (55) F 24, Ap 14; (56) Ja 18, 19, 24; (57) Ja
  26, 29; (58) Mr 2; (60) F 24, Mr 14, Ap 21.
Luke the Laborer, or The Lost Son Restored: (30) D 15, 17; (34) Ja
  17; (39) My 11; (45) N 26; (48) N 3.
The Lying Valet; *Garrick:* (01) Mr 9; (06) Mr 7, N 28; (11) F 15,
  Ap 24; (12) Mr 12; (16) Ap 5; (20) Ap 21; (24) My 14.

Macbeth; *Shakespeare:* (01) Mr 2; (02) F 9, D 8; (03) D 9; (04) D
  15; (06) Ja 24, Ap 16, My 13, 15; (07) Ja 6, Ap 28; (08) N 21;
  (09) F 10; (10) F 28; (11) Ap 8, 19; (12) Ap 16, 22; (16) F 5,
  Ap 3, D 23; (17) F 27; (18) Mr 27; (19) F 3; (20) Ja 17, Mr 3,
  22; (21) My 26; (23) Ju 25; (24) Ja 31, D 4; (26) Mr 29; (27)
  Ja 31, F 16; (28) D 12; (30) Mr 2; (32) Mr 13, D 14; (38) F 9,
  Ap 28; (39) My 20; (40) F 15, 19; (41) Ja 14; (43) Ja 25, Ap 29,
  D 12; (44) Ja 10, Mr 5; (46) F 4, 19; (47) Ja 29, F 5; (49) Ja 8;
  (50) Ap 16, 20; (51) F 10, 18; (53) Ja 5, 20, F 12, N 14, 16, D 19;
  (54) N 16, 23; (55) F 7, O 22; (56) D 30; (57) Ja 13, D 12; (58)
  D 18; (59) Ap 1, 4; (60) Mr 31.
Mad Bess: (06) Mr 3.
Madeline, or The Belle of Fabourg: (53) F 19, 22; (57) F 14; (59)
  O 20; (60) Ap 20.
The Magic Shirt: (59) N 2, 8.
The Magic Trumpet: (59) Ja 17.
Mahmoud the Robber, or Americans in Tripoli; *Hoare:* (04) My 31.
Mahomet, or The Imposter; *Payne:* (10) Ap 13, 25.
The Maid and the Magpie, or Which is the Thief?; *Payne:* (16) Mr 16,
  18, Ap 15, 20, 26, 27; (17) Ja 13, D 31; (21) My 12; (28) F 23;
  (32) Mr 29; (36) Mr 7, 10; (54) Ap 17.
The Maid of Artoris; *Balfe:* (48) Ja 24, 25.
The Maid of Bristol, or Lady of the Haystack; *Boaden:* (04) Ap 12.
The Maid of Croissey, or Theresa's Vow; *Gore:* (39) My 22; (40) Ap
  21, 24, 25, N 10; (42) D 29; (43) Ja 4; (58) Mr 23.
The Maid of Hungary, or The Rigid Father; *(Turnbull):* (06) Mr 26.
The Maid of Lodi, or Secret Marriage: (08) My 25; (09) F 27.
The Maid of Mariendorpt, or A Daughter's Love; *Knowles:* (50) Mr
  9, 15.
The Maid of the Mill; *Bickerstaff:* (02) Ap 26; (17) F 12; (18) Ap
  22, N 18.

The Maid of the Oaks; *Burgoyne:* (02) Ap 12; (04) Mr 13.
Maidens, Beware, or Ladies, Beware: (46) Ja 30.
The Maiden's Vow, or The Yankee in Time: (44) N 23, D 5.
Major Jones' Courtship, or Life in Georgia: (50) My 2, 3; (51) F 24; (58) Ap 27.
Make Your Wills: (42) Ja 7, 10, 13, 17, 31; (46) N 24, 26, D 10; (47) Ja 30; (51) My 3.
A Man about Town, or Cheap Boarding; *Bernard:* (39) N 30; (40) N 6; (41) Mr 6; (44) N 26, 30; (55) F 2, 3.
Man and Wife, or More Secrets Than One; *Arnold:* (10) Mr 12, 23; (11) My 2; (17) Ap 14; (18) Mr 14; (29) Mr 16; (30) Ja 13, Mr 15; (32) F 8; (33) Mr 6; (40) Mr 5, 7; (46) Ja 21, 27.
Man and Wife, or Shakespeare's Jubilee; *Coleman:* (00) Ap 14.
The Man of Fortitude, or The Knight's Adventure; *Hodgkinson:* (00) My 5.
The Man of Many Friends; *Coyne:* (56) F 9, 12.
Man of the World, or A Hint to Politicians: *Macklin:* (08) Ja 27, F 6, 18, My 13; (43) D 23, 27; (44) D 2, 12; (48) F 1, 5.
The Man with the Carpet Bag: (43) F 10.
The Man without a Head: (52) D 20; (55) Mr 17; (58) N 17.
Management; *Reynolds:* (05) My 9.
The Manager in Distress: (09) Ja 19, 23; (23) Ju 30, Jy 7; (24) My 10; (29) My 8; (40) My 20; (41) Mr 25.
The Manager's Daughter; *Lancaster:* (39) Ja 29.
The Maniac: (57) Ap 24.
The Maniac Lover: (60) Ja 4.
Marble Hearts, or The Sculptor's Dream: (57) Ja 1, 5; (59) F 12; (60) Mr 26.
March of Intellect: (33) Mr 11, 15.
Marco Bomba: (41) F 6, 25, Mr 4.
Margot, the Poultry Dealer: (58) D 24, 25; (59) Ja 6.
Marion, or The Carolina Swamp Fox (or His Merry Men of 1776); *(Paul):* (33) My 10.
Marion, or The Hero of Lake George; *Noah:* (22) Ap 8.
Maritana, or The Maid of Sargossa; *Wallace:* (52) D 6, 8.
Marmion, or The Battle of Flodden Field; *Barker:* (20) D 9; (24) F 13.
The Marriage of Figaro; *Mozart:* (29) N 30, D 2; (38) Ap 9, 10; (40) Mr 17, 26; (43) Mr 15.
The Marriage Promise; *Allingham:* (04) Mr 5, 9; (07) Ja 30, F 14, N 30, D 18.
Married and Settled: (52) D 13.
Married and Single; *Poole:* (25) Ja 5, Ap 8; (34) N 24.
The Married Bachelor, or Master and Man: (30) Mr 8; (32) Mr 29; (35) N 18, 30; (44) N 20; (45) F 15.
Married for Money: (58) Ap 12, 15.
Married Life; *Buckstone:* (40) Ap 6; (41) F 3; (43) F 27; (44) Mr 19; (55) O 27, 30, N 1, 2, 7, 10, 15; (56) Ja 4, F 5, N 7, 14.
The Married Rake: (39) N 19, 25, D 21; (40) F 21, Mr 17; (43) D 6; (44) F 12, Mr 12; (47) F 12, 17; (48) F 16; (53) N 11, 19; (54) F 22.
Married Yesterday, or My Wife and I: (18) My 2; (20) Ja 10, 26.
Marry in Haste, or An Hour in the Bastile; *(Byron):* (60) O 16, 17.
Mary of Mantua; *Hayne:* (56) Mr 6, 11.

Mary Stuart, Queen of Scotland; *Haynes:* (46) N 27.
Mary Tudor, or The Artigan and the Jew; *(Flagg):* (54) Ja 19.
Mary's Birthday; *Miles:* (59) Ja 28.
The Masked Ball: *See* Gustavus III.
Massaniello, or The Dumb Girl of Portici (or The Fisherman of Naples);
  Auber: (34) Ja 4, 6, F 24, 25, 26; (40) Ja 24, 27, 28, 29, F 1; (43)
  Mr 13, 16, Ap 12; (45) F 10; (47) Mr 5; (49) Ja 4.
Massaniello Tarentelle: (53) N 30, D 2.
Master Clark: (43) Ap 18.
The Master Key: (24) Ja 31.
The Master of Ravenswood; *Simmons:* (24) Ap 12, 21.
Master's Rival, or Peter and Paul (or A Day at Bologne): (30) F 24,
  Mr 1; (34) N 24.
A Match in the Dark: (53) F 5, 14; (55) Ap 21.
Match Making, or 'Tis a Wise Child that Knows His Own Father;
  Kemble: (24) Mr 19.
Mathilde: (57) F 11.
Matrimonial Squabbles: (55) Mr 3.
Matrimony, or The Test of Love (or The Castle of Linburg); *Kenney:*
  (07) Mr 9; (08) Ap 6; (17) F 19, Mr 5; (18) Ap 22; (20) Ja 21,
  Ap 7; (23) Ju 25, D 15; (24) Mr 6; (25) Ap 18; (26) Ap 12; (27)
  Mr 12, My 18; (28) Ap 14; (30) D 15; (33) Mr 29; (36) Mr 17;
  (43) My 11; (53) F 7.
Maurice, the Woodcutter: (44) Mr 18.
The Mayor of Garratt; *Foote:* (02) Ap 19; (12) D 9, 11, 30; (18)
  My 2; (21) D 11; (28) D 10; (44) F 24; (50) F 16.
Mazeppa, or The Wild Horse of Ukraine; *(Payne):* (34) Mr 25, 26,
  27, 28; (41) Ap 28, 29, 30, My 1, 4, 5, 8; (44) Mr 25, 27; (45) Ja
  20, 25, Mr 1.
Mazulme, or The Night Owl: (54) Ap 5, 6, 7; (59) F 15, 16, 17, 18,
  19, 21.
Medea: (57) Mr 28, 30, 31, D 9.
Medea and Jason, or The Golden Fleece: (07) Mr 9.
Medea Burlesque: (57) Ap 9, 10.
A Medley Olio, or New Brooms to Rub off the Rust of Care: (05)
  My 31.
Merchant and His Clerks: (43) N 7, 8, 10.
The Merchant of Smyrna: (01) My 20.
The Merchant of Venice; *Shakespeare:* (00) Ja 16; (02) Ap 28; (03)
  N 14; (11) Ap 22; (15) N 24; (18) Ja 16, O 29; (20) Mr 10; (21)
  Mr 26; (22) F 27; (25) Mr 29; (26) Mr 22, Ap 3; (27) Ap 6; (29)
  Mr 24, D 7; (32) F 11, D 15; (33) F 28; (34) N 27; (35) Ap 11,
  N 19; (38) Mr 24; (39) Ja 12, F 1; (40) F 12; (41) Ap 23; (43)
  My 4; (44) F 28; (45) Ja 22, N 11; (46) F 11; (48) Ja 1, Mr 16;
  (49) Ja 15; (51) F 21, Ap 30; (53) Ja 14, 18, 27, N 8, D 8; (55)
  F 8, N 21, 24; (56) D 3; (60) Ap 3.
The Merry Wives of Windsor; *Shakespeare:* (07) Mr 2; (20) F 28;
  (21) My 14, 18; (22) Ap 26; (23) Ju 4, 11; (42) F 21, 23, 25; (43)
  D 22; (55) D 8, 22.
Mesmerism, or Irish Sympathy: (52) N 20, 25, D 13; (53) F 11, N 1,
  D 23; (54) Mr 21; (55) F 10, 15, O 24; (56) Mr 7, 12, Ap 1; (57)
  Ja 27, 31, F 19.

Metamora, or The Last of the Wampanoags; *Stone:* (31) Mr 2, 5; (41) Ja 15, 20; (44) F 16; (47) Ja 30, F 1, 2.

The Metamorphoses; *Dibdin:* (28) Ap 16, 22, 26.

Michael Bonham, or The Fall of Bexar; *Simms:* (55) Mr 26, 27, 28.

Michael Earl, or The Maniac Lover: (52) Ja 3, 17, F 7.

Michel et Christine: (39) My 6.

Midas, or The Assembly of the Gods (or The Deities Assembled): (04) My 7, 21, D 17; (09) Ap 7; (10) Mr 6; (58) F 3.

Middy Ashore; *Bernard:* (38) D 21, 22; (39) F 8, Mr 20; (40) Ja 24, F 28.

Midnight Hour, or Ruse Contra Ruse; *Inchbald:* (01) Ap 18; (04) F 10; (08) Ja 29, F 3; (11) Ap 15; (12) F 27; (13) Ja 13; (17) Ap 25; (20) F 4, Ap 3, My 5; (21) Ap 30; (24) Ja 16, Ap 2; (25) Ja 31; (27) Mr 26; (28) D 18; (41) Ja 6, 8.

Militia Training: (32) F 4, 6, 16; (35) Ap 6; (38) Mr 10; (42) F 19; (43) D 23.

The Miller and His Men; *Pocock:* (15) D 20, 22, 26, 27; (16) Ja 6, 10, F 14, Mr 2; (17) Ja 18, Mr 12, 26; (25) Ap 22; (32) Mr 28; (35) D 5; (40) Ap 27.

The Miller, or Nocturnal Rendezvous: (04) Ju 7.

The Miller's Maid; *Waldron:* (26) F 20, 25; (28) Ap 16; (32) Mr 21, 30; (34) Ja 11, 22; (36) Mr 16; (48) F 18; (54) Ap 12.

The Milliners; *Harpley:* (00) Ap 4; (04) Ap 12; (05) Mr 15; (06) Mr 10; (10) F 26; (39) Ap 30.

The Millionaire; *(Leman):* (44) D 5, 10.

Milly, or Maid of the Milking Pail: (54) Ja 25, 28, F 25; (56) Mr 13, 15, 25; (58) Mr 26, D 21, 25; (59) Ja 8.

Mirza and Lindar: (06) Mr 12, Ap 28.

Mischief Making: (32) F 3, 10; (39) N 22, D 30; (40) F 18, 26, Mr 2, Ap 9, My 22; (42) Ja 11; (56) F 11, 13; (59) O 13.

Mischievous Annie; *Florence:* (58) F 23, 24, 26, Mr 8; (59) Mr 17.

The Miser; *(Wild):* (05) D 23.

The Miser of Marseilles: (41) Mr 17, My 7, 11.

Miseries of Human Life: (58) Mr 27.

Miss in Her Teens, or The Comical Lovers: (00) Ja 11, 13; (05) My 20; (10) Ap 30; (33) D 12.

Mob, the Outlaw, or Jemmy Twitcher: (53) D 10.

The Mock Doctor, or The Dumb Lady (or The Dumb Lady Cured); *(Fielding):* (03) F 12, 14, Mr 5; (06) Ap 16, D 23.

A Model of a Wife: (54) Ja 9; (56) Ap 7, 15.

Modern Antiques, or The Merry Mourners; *O'Keeffe;* (03) N 21; (12) F 26, Ap 17; (18) My 6; (20) F 16.

Modern Honor; *White:* (12) Mr 6, 9, 12.

The Mogul Tale, or The Cobbler's Descent in a Balloon; *Inchbald:* (06) Mr 12; (28) F 13, 23; (33) F 18; (35) Mr 12; (36) F 19, Mr 4.

Mohammed, or The Arabian Prophet; *Miles:* (51) My 8, 10; (53) F 10.

Momentous Question: (46) Ja 2, 3, 14; (48) N 27, 28; (53) N 25; (54) Mr 7; (57) N 14; (59) O 14, N 5.

Mona Lisa: (57) Ap 3, 4, D 8.

Money, or Duplicity Exposed; *Bulwer-Lytton:* (42) F 28, Mr 1, 2; (45) N 3; (46) N 25; (50) F 5; (52) Ja 19; (55) F 10, 16, Mr 7, 29; (56) Ja 21, 30; (57) N 5, 25; (58) D 16.

Monsieur Deschalumeau, or Master and Valet (or Village Holiday):
(51) O 16, 18; (53) N 23; (59) Ja 12, 18.

Monsieur Jacques; *Barnett:* (39) My 18, 21; (56) Mr 14, 15.

Monsieur Mallett, or My Daughter's Letter (or The Post-Office Mistake); *Moncrieff:* (35) Ap 6, 10; (38) Mr 9, 14; (42) F 15, 18, 21, 24; (43) D 23; (46) Ja 10.

Monsieur Molinet: (34) Ja 17, 22.

Monsieur Tonson; *Moncrieff:* (00) F 27; (02) Ap 12; (23) My 28, Ju 23, D 31; (24) F 23, Ap 26; (25) Mr 9; (28) Ja 14, 26, D 1, 15; (32) Ja 31, F 4, D 7; (35) N 19; (38) Mr 8, 15; (42) F 26; (43) D 28; (44) F 10.

More Blunders than One, or The Irish Valet: (57) Mr 10, 11.

Morning Call: (52) D 3, 4; (53) F 21, D 17; (54) N 4, D 16; (55) Mr 22, 24; (56) Ja 23, Mr 3, N 17; (57) Ja 30; (59) O 13; (60) Ap 20.

Mose in California; *Chapman:* (54) Ja 14; (56) Ap 10, 11, 19.

Mose, or New York as It Is: (54) Ja 9, 10, 11.

A Most Unwarrantable Intrusion; *Morton:* (57) F 4, 5, Mr 27, Ap 4.

Mother and Child Are Doing Well: (50) Mr 7, 13; (52) F 24, 26, 27, Mr 27.

Mother Bailey, or The Hero of Connecticut: (55) D 27.

Mother Goose, or The Golden Egg: (09) Mr 3; (33) My 4, 7.

The Mountain Maid: (57) N 11, D 9.

The Mountain Sylph, or The Magic Scarf: (40) F 3.

The Mountaineers, or Love and Madness; *Coleman:* (00) Ja 6, Mr 19, Ap 30; (01) F 14, N 13; (02) N 15; (03) Ap 21; (04) N 21; (05) F 23; (06) Ja 6, My 12, N 10; (07) N 13; (08) Mr 9, N 14; (10) Mr 28, Ap 27; (11) F 16, 27; (12) Mr 13; (15) N 13, 22, D 23; (16) Mr 29; (17) Ja 3, Mr 10, D 20; (18) F 14; (20) Mr 4; (21) Ap 11, N 30; (24) Ap 30; (25) Ap 16; (27) Mr 10, N 30; (28) N 26; (33) F 23; (39) Ja 18, Ap 13; (43) My 6; (47) D 30.

Moustache Mania: (54) N 13, 25, D 6, 22; (55) F 9; (56) D 9, 30; (59) O 21.

Mr. and Mrs. Dobson: (57) N 3, 14.

Mr. and Mrs. Peter White: (38) D 20, 26; (39) Ja 5, F 16, Mr 9, Ap 22, 24; (52) Mr 4; (54) Ap 10; (56) Ja 24, 30; (59) O 13; (60) Ap 16.

Mr. and Mrs. Pringle: (40) D 9, 17.

Mr. H!, or Beware a Bad Name: (07) Ju 3; (09) Mr 22.

Mrs. Wiggins; *Allingham:* (12) D 14, 21.

Much Ado about Nothing; *Shakespeare:* (04) F 25; (05) Mr 1; (07) My 27; (16) Ja 31, F 27; (17) Ja 29; (18) F 9; (19) Ap 21; (20) D 1; (24) Ja 26, N 29; (27) Ap 3, 21, 30; (29) Ap 3; (32) Mr 2; (35) Mr 18, 21; (38) Ja 4, 15, Ap 24; (39) My 15; (44) Mr 4, 15; (46) F 3, 13, D 9; (50) Mr 14; (52) D 29; (53) F 23; (54) F 20, N 22; (55) F 15; (56) D 2; (59) F 4; (60) Mr 23.

The Mummy, or The Liquor of Life; *Burton:* (39) N 29, D 2; (41) My 5; (58) D 3, 9.

Musical Festivity, or Mirth's Pinnacle: (09) Mr 20.

The Mutineer, or The South Sea Islander: (29) D 21, 24, 26; (30) Ja 2, F 12, 20, Mr 17.

Mutiny at the Nore: (43) Ap 18.

My Aunt, or My Aunt in Virginia (or Arrivals in New York); *(Galt):*

(33) F 4, 23; (34) D 8; (44) F 29, Mr 14; (45) F 13; (46) D 2; (48) Mr 28; (49) Ja 1; (55) Ja 31, F 1; (56) D 6, 10.

My Fellow Clerk: (38) Ja 3, 25, F 20, 23; (42) F 7, 23, Mr 12; (57) Ja 9, 12, 15.

My Grandmother; *Hoare:* (00) Ja 16; (02) F 19, Mr 1, Ap 28, N 24, D 20; (05) N 13; (06) Ap 14; (11) Mr 20; (12) F 14; (13) Ja 15; (15) N 25; (16) Ja 15, Ap 22; (19) F 8; (20) F 7, Ap 4.

My Handsome Husband: (39) Mr 14, Ap 15, 17, 23, D 16; (40) Ja 31; (43) N 13, 23; (46) Ja 1, F 12.

My King and I: (51) F 10, 15.

My Little Adopted; *Bayley:* (41) F 27, Mr 2; (42) Ja 6, 8; (54) N 2, 11, 22.

My Master's Rival: (39) Ja 17, 22; (43) D 29; (47) Ja 11.

My Neighbor's Wife: (39) Ja 14, 15, 16, 21, F 5, Ap 5, 25; (44) D 16; (51) F 13; (52) Ja 14, F 6, Mr 25.

My Old Woman, or Love and Wrinkles: (42) Ja 5, 7, 13.

My Precious Betsy, or Betsy Baker; *Morton:* (51) Ja 22; (52) Mr 3, 5, 24; (55) Mr 5, 19, Ap 18; (57) Ja 3, N 2; (58) Ja 7, F 20, D 13, 14, 18.

My Sister Kate: (43) Ja 24.

My Uncle Foozle, or My Wife's Mother: (43) F 20, 24, Mr 1, 3, 10, Ap 10, 26, My 8; (44) Mr 6, 15; (45) Mr 7, 14; (48) Mr 20; (55) D 6, 24, 28; (56) Ja 11; (59) F 7, 12.

My Unlucky Day: (39) Ap 1.

My Wife's Come; *Morton:* (44) D 9, 14, 23; (45) Ja 15, 23, 28, F 24.

My Wife's Husband: (39) F 13.

My Wife's Second Floor; *Morton:* (44) Ja 8, 11, F 8, 23, D 11, 24; (46) D 9, 17; (47) Ja 18.

My Young Wife and My Old Umbrella; *Webster:* (38) D 27, 28; (39) Ja 12; (40) N 12, 16; (58) Ap 28.

The Mysteries of Paris; *Wemyss, Gann* and *Sefton:* (45) Ja 22, 23, F 21.

The Mysteries of the Castle, or The Victim of Revenge; *White:* (06) D 26, 29; (07) F 19.

The Mysterious Stranger: (58) D 21; (59) Ja 4.

The Mysterious Visitor: (49) Ja 17.

The Mystery, or The Nocturnal Visitor: (56) Ja 21, F 5.

The Naiad Queen, or The Mysteries of Lurlei Berg (or Nymphs of the Rhine): (60) Ja 5, 6.

Nan, the Good for Nothing: (60) Ja 6.

Napoleon Bonaparte, or Emperor and Soldier; *Amherst:* (29) D 14; (33) My 7, 10; (35) D 1.

Napoleon, or Passage of Mt. St. Bernard: (38) Ap 12, 17; (51) Ja 24, F 7, Mr 3, My 14.

Napoleon's Old Guard: (47) Ja 14, 16; (50) Ap 27, My 4.

Nathalie, or A Wife's Secret (or The Frontier Maid); *Noah:* (41) Ja 1; (48) F 21, 24, Mr 24.

The National Guard, or Bride and No Bride; *Auber:* (54) Mr 15.

Native Land: (39) D 26, 27.

The Natural Son; *Cumberland:* (00) Ap 16, 17.

Nature and Philosophy, or The Youth Who Never Saw a Woman: (21) N 21, D 3, 10; (22) My 3; (23) D 22; (24) Ja 8, Mr 3, D 6; (27)

Ja 24, 31, Ap 30; (33) Ja 7, 11, Ap 1, D 9; (35) Mr 31, N 17, 23; (36) F 25, Mr 9; (43) N 4; (45) Mr 7, 15; (53) F 8, 16, 24, N 8, D 22.

Nature versus Art: (57) D 11, 17.

Naval Engagements, or the Freaks of Love; *Dance:* (43) F 16; (50) Ap 27; (53) N 23, 29; (54) Ja 17; (56) Ja 29.

The Nervous Man and the Man of Nerve; *Bernard:* (34) D 5; (41) F 13, 18; (46) D 24; (47) Ja 1; (57) Mr 14; (59) N 2.

Never Judge by Appearances: (60) O 18.

The New Footman: (44) N 22, D 2, 13; (45) Ja 15.

New Lovers: (53) Ja 1.

New Notions: (43) N 28.

New Way to Pay Old Debts; *Massinger:* (18) My 11; (21) D 5, 10; (24) My 8; (25) Mr 21; (26) Mr 17, 27; (32) F 10; (34) O 15; (38) F 12, Mr 13, 19; (40) F 14; (44) F 19, D 24; (46) Ja 16; (50) F 12; (52) Mr 24, 30; (58) F 19; (59) Mr 22; (60) Mr 20.

New Ways to Win Hearts: (04) My 17; (05) F 11.

The Next Door Neighbors; *Inchbald:* (03) Ap 14; (08) Mr 21.

The Nice Young Ladies: (58) Ja 16.

Nicholas Flam, Attorney-at-Law; *Buckstone:* (43) My 5; (48) F 14, 15.

Nicholas Nickleby, or Doings at Do-the-Boys-Hall; *(Boucicault):* (41) Ja 8, 9, 16; (58) Ap 19.

Nick of the Woods, or Kentucky in 1783 (or The Jibbenainosay): *Medina:* (42) D 24, 26, 31; (43) D 11; (44) D 7, 12; (54) F 14.

Nicodemus; *Ravel Family:* (51) Ja 31.

A Night in Venice: (53) N 28.

A Night with an Artist: (57) F 13, 18.

Nina, or The Love Distracted Maid (or Love and Madness); *Dunlap:* (05) Ap 3, My 14.

No, No, or The Glorious Minority: (32) Mr 7; (39) F 26; (41) Ja 12, 20, F 2, 12; (42) Mr 31; (44) Mr 19; (46) Ja 8, F 3, 14.

No Song, No Supper, or Lawyer in the Sack; *Hoare:* (00) Ja 24, 29; (01) F 10, N 16, 18; (02) F 24, D 6; (04) My 3, D 12; (05) D 2; (06) D 20; (07) My 25, N 27; (08) D 12; (10) F 7, My 11; (11) Mr 27; (12) Ap 16; (13) Ja 15; (17) Ja 29, 31, F 21, D 12; (19) Ap 16; (20) Ap 17, D 16; (22) F 13; (23) D 10; (24) D 9; (25) Ja 5, Mr 26; (27) Ja 6, F 27; (28) Mr 18; (29) D 11; (33) D 19; (34) N 15; (36) Mr 16; (39) F 25, Mr 23, Ap 2; (40) Ja 23; (41) D 28.

Nocturnal Visitor: (57) Ap 18, 20.

Norma; *Bellini:* (42) Mr 21, 22, 23, 29; (47) F 25, Mr 2, 6; (48) Ja 22, D 9, 13; (50) Mr 26, 27; (51) Ap 4, 5, 9, N 19, 22, 26, D 9; (60) F 22, 29, N 20.

Norman Leslie; *Wemyss:* (45) F 17, 18.

Not a Bad Judge: (58) N 16.

Nothing to Nurse; *Walcot:* (57) N 4, 5, 18.

Nothing Venture, Nothing Have: (60) O 20.

Notoriety: (03) F 4, 21; (05) Ap 19.

Novel Expedient: (53) Ja 18, 20, 24, 28, F 18.

Number One Round the Corner: (56) F 29.

An Object of Interest: (55) D 29; (56) Ja 16, 22; (58) Mr 27, D 28; (59) O 12, 14.

The Ocean Child: (56) Ap 14, 15.
Octavia Bragaldi; *Conner:* (38) Ja 17, 20; (40) F 8.
Of Age To-Morrow; *Dibdin:* (11) F 1, 20, Mr 1, My 7; (12) Mr 6, My
  6; (13) Ja 18; (16) Ap 26, N 6, 29; (17) F 7, D 24; (18) Ap 15;
  (19) F 3, D 24; (20) F 11, D 6; (21) Ap 2, My 28; (23) N 28;
  (25) Mr 25, 28; (26) D 20; (27) Ja 10, F 9; (29) F 28, D 14; (30)
  F 10, 25; (33) Ja 5, Mr 15; (35) Ap 9; (41) N 29, D 18, 23; (42)
  Ja 1.
O'Flannigan and the Fairies; *Power:* (56) Ap 19; (58) Mr 1, 12.
Oh! Hush, or The Verginny Cupids: (33) D 11, 13, 17, 20; (34) Ap
  10; (42) Ja 1.
Old and Young, or the Four Mowbrays: (06) Mr 14; (29) Mr 13, 25,
  Ap 4; (30) Mr 12; (32) Mr 21; (39) Ja 30; (40) N 21; (41) Ja
  5; (49) My 21; (53) Ja 18, 28; (59) Ja 11.
The Old Chateau [Homestead]; *(Aiken):* (56) N 8, 11.
The Old English Gentleman; *Dance:* (39) D 9; (40) N 16.
The Old Guard: (53) Ja 26; (56) Mr 25; (57) Ap 16.
Old Heads and Young Hearts; *Boucicault:* (45) N 14; (46) N 21; (55)
  O 25; (56) Ja 3.
The Old Maid, or Downfall of Vanity; *Murphy:* (02) Ap 23; (12) D 28.
The Old School and the New: (53) Ja 24, 26.
The Old Soldier: (04) Ap 19; (48) Ja 31.
Ole Bull; *Burke:* (52) Mr 9, 10.
Olympic Revels; *Dance:* (43) Mr 15, 17, Ap 21, 24, 29; (44) Mr 11;
  (47) Mr 6; (49) Ja 5, 6.
Omala, the Red Indian, or The First Settlers of America: (30) Ja 15,
  22.
Omnibus: (41) F 15, 18, D 6, 9, 11; (42) Ja 5, Mr 19; (52) N 19, D 1;
  (53) N 3; (54) Ja 27, Mr 24.
Ondine: (51) F 6, 8.
One Hour, or The Carnival Ball: (43) N 20.
102, or The Veteran and His Page (or Progeny, or The Centogenarian):
  (28) F 4; (32) Mr 9; (56) Ja 8, 9, 10.
The One Hundred Pound Note, or Two Billy Blacks: (27) N 21, 23,
  24, 28; (28) F 11; (29) Mr 4, 18, D 11; (30) F 19, N 29; (32) D
  21; (33) D 14; (34) O 23, N 27; (39) My 28.
One Hundred Years Old: (55) Ja 11.
1, 2, 3, 4, 5 by Advertisement: (40) My 15.
Oraloosa, or The Son of the Incas; *Bird:* (51) My 12.
The Orang-ou-tang, or The Monkey and His Double: (38) Ap 1, 2;
  (55) Ja 15, 22.
Origin of Harlequin: (20) Ap 19, 28.
The Orphan, or An Unhappy Marriage; *Otway:* (10) Ap 30.
Oscar and Melvina, or The Hall of Fingal: (03) Mr 31, Ap 18; (07)
  Ap 3, 24; (08) Mr 30; (26) Mr 1.
Othello; *Shakespeare:* (09) Ja 30, F 17; (10) F 16, Mr 2; (11) Mr 23;
  (12) F 10, Ap 8; (16) F 12, Mr 25, D 20; (18) F 13, Ap 10, N 9;
  (19) F 6, 26; (20) F 1; (22) Mr 1; (24) D 8; (25) Mr 26; (26)
  Mr 15, Ap 7; (27) F 12, 23, Mr 3; (30) F 5, 20; (31) Mr 7; (32)
  F 18; (34) O 23; (35) Mr 4, 6, 25, N 17; (36) Mr 14; (38) Ja 25,
  Mr 21; (40) D 29; (41) Ap 22; (42) F 8; (43) Mr 2, D 16; (44)
  Ja 15, F 17, D 27; (47) Ja 25; (48) F 8; (49) Ja 30; (50) Ja 29,
  F 15; (51) F 11, Ap 29; (52) Ja 13, Mr 23, D 18, 28; (53) N 10;

(55) Ja 30; (56) N 10, D 31; (57) D 21; (59) Mr 28, Ap 8; (60) Mr 21.

Othello Travestie: (57) Ap 18, 20, 21.

Our American Cousin: (59) O 24, 25, 26, 27, 28, 29, N 12.

Our Gal; *Johnson:* (54) F 2, 7.

Our Mary Anne; *Buckstone:* (39) Ja 7, 8, 11, F 7, 15, Mr 18; (41) Ja 1, 14, F 10, Ap 24; (43) Ja 9, 17, F 14, Mr 6, My 4; (44) N 26; (45) Ja 3, N 10; (46) F 16, N 11; (48) Mr 16.

Our Wife; *(Morton):* (59) O 22.

Ourselves: (12) Mr 16.

Out of Place, or The Lake of Lousanne; *Lemon:* (18) Ap 29, My 9; (42) Ja 4, 6.

Ovid and Obid: (34) N 21.

The Pacha's Pets; *Oxberry:* (38) D 31.

Paddy Carey, or The Boy of Clogheen; *Power:* (41) F 19.

Paddy Miles' Boy: (56) Ap 8; (58) Ja 16, Mr 24.

The Padlock; *Bickerstaff:* (00) Ja 31, F 14; (01) Mr 23; (02) F 8; (03) F 18; (04) N 19; (05) N 20, D 28; (07) My 22; (08) N 16; (11) F 9; (12) Ap 10; (17) Ap 21; (20) D 13.

Palo Alto: (47) Ja 13, 14.

Paquerette: (53) N 21.

Pas de Trois: (48) F 24.

Past Ten O'Clock, or A Rainy Night; *Dibdin:* (18) My 20, O 31; (23) Ju 2.

The Past! The Present!! The Future!!!: (61) N 27.

Patrician and Parvenu; *Poole:* (40) D 11; (41) Ja 25.

The Patrician's Daughter; *Marston:* (45) F 8.

The Patriot's Wife, or Emilia: (47) Ja 8, 9.

Patter versus Clatter; *Matthews:* (58) Ap 12, 13.

Paul and Alexis: *See* The Wandering Boys.

Paul and Virginia; *Cobb:* (05) Ap 25, My 2; (07) Mr 2; (08) Ap 22; (16) Ap 29, My 4; (17) Ap 9; (18) F 14; (20) My 1, D 9; (28) Mr 21.

Paul Jones, or The Pilot of the German Ocean; *Wallack:* (29) Ap 27; (33) D 17.

Paul Pry; *Brougham:* (27) Ja 17, 19, 22, F 27, My 2, N 26, D 22; (28) Ja 23; (29) Mr 25; (32) F 16; (33) Mr 8, 20, Ap 4, D 14; (34) N 25; (38) Mr 3, 15; (39) My 18; (41) N 22, D 4; (44) D 21; (45) D 3; (51) Ja 21, 28; (52) Ja 17; (53) Ja 17, 21; (56) Ja 31, F 1; (58) D 9.

Pauline; *Boucicault:* (56) N 17, 18, 28; (59) O 29.

Pavlo and Petrowna: (12) My 15.

Pay Me for My Eye, or Two Eyes between Two: (32) D 3; (33) Ap 2.

Peaceful Pelton, or The Vermonter: (45) N 28.

The Peacock and the Crow: (38) F 2.

The Peasant Boy; *Dimond:* (16) My 6, 11; (17) Mr 27; (18) F 23.

The Pedlar; *Davenport:* (01) Ap 27; (03) Mr 16; (04) My 11.

A Peep into Seraglia: (40) F 29.

Peeping in at Six P. M.: (52) Ja 15.

Peg Woffington, or Masks and Faces (or Before and Behind the Curtain): *Boucicault:* (55) O 15, 23; (57) Mr 23, 24, Ap 1, D 17, 18; (58) D 29.

The People's Lawyer, or Solomon Shingle; *Jones:* (43) D 2; (45) N
28; (52) Mr 8, 12; (56) Ap 8, 10.
Perfection, or The Maid of Munster; *Bayley:* (30) D 17, 20; (31) Mr
23; (32) F 22; (34) O 14, N 5, D 2; (35) Mr 28, Ap 8; (36) F 24,
Mr 21, 23, 31; (37) D 22; (38) Ja 11; (39) My 23; (41) Mr 10,
N 17, 30; (42) D 20; (43) F 23, My 12, D 20; (44) Ja 5, D 6; (45)
F 8, N 11, 27; (46) N 12; (48) F 24; (50) Ap 19; (51) O 17, 20,
29; (52) Mr 29, D 11; (53) Ja 14, N 7, 15; (54) D 24; (55) Ja 3,
F 6, 26; (57) N 25, D 8; (59) O 22.
The Persecuted Dutchman: (59) Ja 8.
Personation, or Fairly Taken in: (20) Ja 17; (32) D 1; (33) Mr 30.
Pet of the Petticoats, or The Convent: (42) Ja 17; (58) D 27; (59)
Ja 5.
Peter Wilkins, or The Flying Indians: (28) Ja 22, 23, 25, 26, 28.
A Petite Comedy: (48) Mr 17.
The Petite Savoyards: (06) Mr 21.
The Phantom; *Boucicault:* (56) D 20, 22, 25.
The Phantom Breakfast: (50) Ja 29, 31.
Phenomenon in a Smock Frock: (54) N 3, 7, 23, D 12; (55) Ja 17;
(57) Ja 7.
Phillip of France; *(Marston):* (59) F 2.
The Pickwick Club, or The Age We Live in: (40) Ja 15, 16, 18.
The Pioneer Patriot, or Maid of the War Path: (58) Mr 15.
Pizarro, or The Death of Rolla (or Spaniards in Peru); *Dunlap* or *Sheri-
dan* or *Smith:* (00) Ja 24, 27, 28, 29, F 5, 6, 13, 15, 21, Ap 2; (01) F 20,
Mr 9; (02) Ja 27, F 11, Mr 29, 31, N 22, D 3; (03) N 11; (04) F
17; (05) F 19; (06) My 5, N 28, D 8; (07) My 18, N 25; (08) My
9, N 16; (10) F 9, Mr 3, 5, Ap 9; (11) Ja 9, 12, Mr 29; (12) Mr 21,
My 1; (16) Mr 11, Ap 6, D 2; (17) Ja 10; (18) F 11; (19) Ap 16;
(20) Mr 1, 11, N 27; (22) My 10; (23) Ju 27; (24) F 21, 24, Mr
31; (25) Ap 15; (27) Ja 3, F 5, D 21; (28) N 20; (29) F 25; (31)
F 26; (32) Mr 14, D 7; (33) Ap 2, 27; (34) N 12; (35) N 20, D
10; (36) Mr 30; (38) F 13, 17; (39) Ja 11; (42) Mr 4, D 20; (44)
F 26, 29, Mr 26, D 14; (45) N 15; (46) D 1; (47) D 30; (49) F 1;
(51) F 14; (52) Mr 5, D 31; (53) F 17, N 12; (54) F 16; (55)
Ap 10; (57) Ja 31; (58) Ap 23.
Play, Plot and Passion; *(Taylor):* (55) Ja 9, 12; (57) Ap 21.
Pleasant Neighbors: (38) D 22, 26; (39) Ja 23, Ap 6; (41) F 13, D
8, 10; (42) F 16; (43) Ja 6, 10, N 15, D 21; (44) D 6; (45) F 20;
(46) D 31; (47) F 24, D 24; (54) Ja 9, 10.
Plot and Counterplot; *Kemble:* (10) F 14; (21) Mr 19.
The Poacher, or The Game Law: (01) F 9.
Pocahontas: *See* The Indian Princess.
The Point of Honor, or School for Soldiers; *Kemble:* (02) My 1; (06)
My 27, D 15; (08) Ja 21; (10) My 5; (12) F 12, D 23; (15) D 22;
(16) Ap 20; (17) Ap 12; (18) F 24; (23) Ju 3; (27) F 22; (30)
Ap 19; (38) Ap 26; (46) Ja 12.
The Poor Gentleman; *Coleman:* (02) Mr 3, 10, 15, Ap 2, My 14, N 24;
(03) F 11, N 26; (05) My 27, N 16; (06) N 24; (07) Ja 16, N 16;
(11) Mr 11; (12) Mr 30; (15) N 11; (16) Mr 8; (17) F 7, Mr 8,
D 26; (18) Ja 10; (19) My 1; (22) F 25; (24) F 11; (30) N 24;
(33) Mr 11; (38) Ja 22, Mr 1; (40) D 10; (41) N 15, 25; (44) D
16; (51) Ja 20, F 8; (52) Ja 3; (54) Ja 2, 11; (56) Ap 21; (57)
N 24; (59) N 12.

The Poor Lodger; *White:* (11) My 7.

Poor Pillicoddy; *Morton:* (50) F 15, Ap 22, 27; (51) Ja 31, F 12, My 5; (52) Ja 10, F 12, Mr 16; (55) F 3, O 22, D 5; (57) Ja 20, 22, 28, D 29; (58) Ja 5, 14, N 17; (59) N 1.

The Poor Soldier; *O'Keeffe:* (00) F 19, Mr 17; (01) F 18, My 18; (02) Ja 29, F 13, Mr 12, 29, 31, D 8; (03) D 7; (04) Mr 26; (05) D 18; (06) F 22; (07) F 19, My 16, N 16; (08) D 9; (09) F 25; (12) Mr 9; (15) D 4; (16) Ja 1, F 22, N 8, 23; (17) Mr 22, D 29; (18) F 11; (19) F 17, D 21; (20) Ja 31, N 29; (21) N 12, 29; (22) F 27, Ap 26; (24) Ja 23, Mr 18, Ap 12, D 8; (25) Ja 22, Mr 22; (27) Ja 15, 26, Mr 30; (28) Mr 19; (32) D 15; (33) Mr 13; (34) O 28.

Popping the Question; *Buckstone:* (35) Ap 15; (40) D 10, 12, 16.

Post of Honor: (45) Ja 4, 16, 29.

Postillion of Lonjumeau; *Adam:* (43) Mr 10, 14, Ap 11; (44) Mr 9; (45) F 7, 14; (47) F 23.

P. P., or The Man and the Tiger: (40) My 11; (55) Mr 22, 24; (56) Ja 31, F 7, Mr 13.

The Practical Man: (50) F 4, 14.

Preparations for Privateering, or The American Tars: (00) F 27, 28; (12) Ap 8.

Preparing for the Convention: (60) Ap 19.

Prescription for Happiness: (35) N 21.

Preservation, or The Hovel in the Rocks; *Williamson:* (00) Ap 14, 21.

The Press Gang, or Harlequin Aeronaut: (12) Mr 30, Ap 6.

Presumption: (26) Ap 13.

Presumptive Evidence, or The Munster Coast; *Buckstone:* (30) Ap 12.

The Pretty Bar Maid: (43) N 30.

A Pretty Piece of Business; *Morton:* (55) Ap 16; (58) N 16, 19.

The Pride of the Market, or The Flower Girl of Paris: (52) Ja 6; (54) D 29; (55) Ja 5; (57) Ap 11, 15.

The Prince and the Peasant: (43) Ja 10, 18.

The Prince and the Watchman: (57) N 14.

The Printer's Devil: (40) My 13, 14.

A Prior Claim: (08) Mr 2.

Prisoner at Large, or Humours of Killarney: (08) Ap 29, My 4, D 23; (09) F 14; (12) Mr 4; (15) D 15; (16) Ja 3, D 13, 27; (18) F 16, My 23, N 16; (19) Ap 17; (20) Ja 19, F 14; (21) Ap 16, My 29; (27) Ap 25.

The Prize, Ten Thousand Pounds, or 2, 5, 3, 8; *Hoare:* (05) Mr 21, 30, D 20; (06) F 3, D 19; (07) My 6; (09) Ja 19; (10) Mr 3; (11) Ja 14; (16) F 19, Mr 1, 16; (18) Ja 14; (19) D 22; (20) Ja 22, Mr 6; (22) My 13; (29) F 21, 24, Mr 2, D 7.

The Promissory Note, or The Effects of Endorsing: (21) Ap 6; (27) Ja 3, 8, 17, F 12; (28) Ja 16.

The Prophecy; *Fowler:* (47) Ja 15.

The Provoked Husband, or A Journey to London; *Cibber:* (01) My 22, N 11; (03) D 12; (16) Ja 8, F 10, D 6; (17) F 28, Mr 24; (20) Ap 24; (21) Mr 16; (25) Ap 22; (27) My 7.

The Provost of Bruges, or A Knight's Revenge; *Lovell:* (40) My 11, 14.

Punch's Festival, or Harlequin in Disguise: (18) Ja 30, F 3, 4, 5, 6, 7.

The Purse, or The Benevolent Tar (or The American Tar Returned from Tripoli, or The Generous Tar): (00) Ja 28, F 11, 12; (01) F 9, N 7; (02) N 22; (03) F 4; (04) F 20; (05) N 28; (06) Ap 23, My 27;

(07) Ap 20, N 28; (09) Ja 30; (10) F 21; (11) Ja 25; (12) Mr 18; (16) F 29, Mr 30; (18) Ja 24, Ap 1, 20; (19) F 5; (20) Ja 10, My 8.
Putnam, or The Iron Hand and the Vulture Steed (or The Eagle Eye and the Hand of Steel); *Bannister:* (45) Ja 15, 16, 17, 18, 20, 21, 24.

Quadrupeds, or A Tragedy of Warm Weather: (41) My 15.
The Quaker, or The May Day Dower; *Dibdin:* (01) Ja 26, My 22; (02) Ja 22, F 26, N 19; (03) F 9; (04) Mr 23; (05) Mr 23, N 27; (06) N 17; (08) D 30; (09) Ja 9, F 3; (10) Mr 12; (12) Ap 20; (18) Ap 13; (39) My 20; (60) N 21.
The Quartetti: (29) D 11, 16.
A Quiet Day; *Burton:* (43) F 2, 6, Mr 7, 8.

The Race Course, or Our Way at Fountainbleau (or Sporting Made Easy): (38) F 25.
Race for a Dinner, or Sponge Out of Town: (28) Ap 22; (30) Ja 11; (32) N 26; (39) N 22.
Rachel's Coming: (56) Mr 21, 27.
Raffael, the Reprobate; *Aiken:* (58) Mr 15.
Raising the Wind; *Kenney:* (04) N 16, 23, D 3, 14; (05) F 21; (06) N 14; (08) N 14, 23; (09) Ap 11; (10) Mr 5; (12) F 7, Mr 2; (16) Ja 16, 22, N 13, 27, D 28; (18) Ap 14; (23) N 26, D 13; (24) N 22, D 18, 31; (25) Ja 3; (26) Mr 27, Ap 7, D 23; (27) F 23; (28) Mr 24, N 21, D 18; (29) F 17; (30) N 26; (31) F 26; (34) N 6; (36) Ap 9; (39) My 25; (42) F 5; (43) Ja 10, 31, Mr 4; (45) D 3, 9, 13; (46) Ja 17, N 5, 23, D 8; (47) Ja 23; (48) Ja 19, 20, F 5; (50) Mr 6, 22; (51) F 11, 25; (54) F 16, 18, Mr 27; (58) Ap 23; (59) Mr 12.
The Rake's Progress, or Three Degrees of Loafing: (35) Ap 13; (56) Ja 23.
The Ransom, or A Father's Return from Slavery: (38) F 3.
Raoul, or The Magic Star: (59) Ja 20, 21, 22.
The Recruit, or Domestic Folly: (02) Ap 23; (07) My 30.
The Red Indian: (55) Ja 27.
The Red Man: (39) My 7.
Redowska: (51) O 23.
The Redwood; *Addams:* (44) N 29, 30.
Rehearsal Disappointed, or The Music Master in Distress: (12) Mr 18, Ap 4.
Release of the Captives of Tripoli: (08) Ap 13.
Removing the Deposits; *Finn:* (39) My 24.
The Rendezvous, or Love in All Corners (or All in the Dark): (20) N 27; (21) My 9, 18, D 7; (22) F 25; (24) Mr 13, 27, My 22, N 27; (26) D 26; (27) Ja 27, N 30, D 22; (28) Mr 4, N 27; (29) My 2; (30) Ja 25; (31) F 22, Mr 1, 2, 18; (32) F 2; (34) D 3; (35) Mr 21, 27; (36) Mr 18; (37) D 26, 30; (38) F 17, 22; (39) D 17; (43) F 2; (44) Ja 16, 18, F 15, N 29; (45) Ja 31, F 25; (46) Ja 9, N 9; (48) F 22, 24; (52) F 3; (53) Ja 13, 29.
The Rent Day; *Jerrold:* (33) F 4, 11, 21, Mr 21; (39) Mr 8; (41) F 22; (43) F 20; (44) F 27; (45) D 2; (46) D 3; (56) D 13.
The Reprobate, or The Death Token: (28) Ap 14, 22, 26.
The Restoration, or The Diamond Cross: (25) Ap 14, 19.
Retribution, or A Husband's Revenge; *(Bennett):* (57) Ja 7, 8.

The Revenge; (*Young*): (09) F 6; (10) F 23; (20) Ap 28, My 1; (21) My 30; (27) D 12; (30) F 19.

The Review, or The Wags of Windsor; *Coleman:* (04) D 5, 20; (05) F 16, 27; (06) Ja 17, 31, My 10; (07) Ja 21, F 23, N 30; (08) Ja 23, N 21, D 24; (09) Ja 21; (10) Mr 1; (11) Mr 6, My 20; (12) Mr 2; (15) D 8; (16) Ja 5, F 27, Mr 8, 25, N 4, 20; (17) F 22; (18) Ja 3, F 13, Mr 25; (20) D 14; (21) N 9; (22) Ap 10; (23) Ju 6; (24) F 13, Mr 24, Ap 20, N 26, D 27; (26) D 27; (27) Ap 3; (28) F 6, Ap 23; (33) Mr 2, 8, 29; (36) Mr 30; (38) Mr 23, 29; (40) N 20; (41) N 26; (43) D 18; (46) Ja 23; (52) Mr 26; (57) F 7, 10, D 21.

Richard: (58) D 25; (59) Ja 1.

Richard Coeur de Lion; *Burgoyne:* (01) My 11, 15.

Richard Number Three; *Durivage:* (43) D 29, 30.

Richard III on Horseback: (59) N 11.

Richard III, or The Battle of Bosworth Field; *Shakespeare:* (00) Ja 31; (04) F 10, 29; (06) Ja 29, Ap 21, N 17, D 20; (07) Ap 17; (08) My 23, D 2; (09) F 15; (10) Mr 1; (11) My 9; (15) N 27; (16) Mr 23; (18) Mr 2, O 30; (19) F 8; (20) Ap 26; (21) Ap 6, 14, N 29; (22) F 22; (23) Ju 18, D 27; (24) F 27; (25) F 9, Mr 18; (26) Mr 13, Ap 10; (27) My 9; (28) F 11; (29) Ap 10, My 2; (30) Ja 4, Mr 4; (32) F 13, Mr 5; (33) Mr 4; (35) N 18, 21, D 1; (38) F 23, Mr 7, 20, 28; (39) Ja 9, 16, 31, F 2; (40) F 13, 18; (41) Ja 21; (43) F 17, D 15; (44) F 21, Mr 13, D 23, 31; (45) N 18; (46) Ja 21, D 7; (47) D 22, 24; (49) F 2, My 28; (50) F 4, 13; (51) F 7, 20, My 7, 14; (52) Mr 22, 29; (53) Ja 11, 17, 22, 28, Mr 2, N 19, D 1; (55) D 27; (56) F 2; (57) N 7; (58) F 20; (59) Mr 25, Ap 2; (60) Ja 14, Mr 24, 29.

Richelieu, or The Conspiracy; *Bulwer-Lytton:* (40) Ap 7, 14; (41) Ja 13, 19, 23; (43) D 18; (44) Ja 11, F 15; (46) Ja 23; (49) Ja 10; (53) F 7, N 11; (54) F 17; (55) Mr 9, 13; (58) F 17, 18; (59) Mr 24, 30, Ap 9; (60) Mr 22, 28.

Riches, or The Wife and Brother: (22) My 6; (44) D 30.

Rienzi; *Mitford:* (29) N 23.

The Rifle Brigade: (43) N 13, 21, 29.

Rights and Wrongs of Women: (56) N 29.

Rights of Women: (44) D 3, 6.

Rigoletto; *Verdi:* (60) Mr 13.

Rinaldi and Armida, or The Assembly of Christians for the Conquest of Jerusalem: (00) Mr 31, Ap 21, 23.

Rip Van Winkle, or The Demons of the Catskill Mountains (or The Legend of the Catskill Mountains); *Kerr:* (30) Ap 2, 16; (32) F 2, 4; (35) Ap 4; (38) Mr 10; (43) D 21; (52) Mr 10.

Rival Pages: (45) Mr 5, 8; (53) F 9, 15.

The Rival Soldiers, or Huzza for Florida: (36) F 10, Mr 3.

The Rivals, or A Trip to Bath; *Sheridan:* (00) Mr 7, 8; (01) Ap 11; (08) Ap 18; (11) F 15; (12) F 14; (15) N 15; (16) Mr 4, N 13; (18) My 20; (20) My 8; (23) N 26; (24) My 7; (25) Ap 9; (28) Mr 18; (29) Mr 6; (38) Ja 19; (40) F 5, 6, N 11; (44) F 12; (47) Ja 13; (50) Ja 28, F 7; (51) F 5, Mr 1, Ap 14; (52) Ja 1, 21; (55) N 17, 20, 23; (57) Mr 7, 11; (59) F 7.

Rivers, or The East-Indian: (04) Mr 15, 21, Ap 9, N 26; (05) Ap 3; (08) Mr 28; (12) Mr 4, 7.

The Road to Ruin; *Holcroft:* (05) D 2; (08) F 1; (11) F 18; (12)

F 26; (15) N 25; (16) N 15; (20) Ap 19; (24) Ja 3, N 26; (25) Mr 1; (40) N 20; (54) Mr 18; (58) N 20.

Rob Roy MacGregor, or Auld Land Syne; *Pocock:* (19) My 3, 6; (21) Ap 2; (24) Mr 10; (27) D 10; (28) Mr 26; (29) D 2; (33) F 15; (36) Mr 9, 29; (38) Mr 30, Ap 7; (39) F 26, Ap 2, D 21; (41) N 24, 29, D 24; (43) Ap 22; (44) D 11; (46) F 23; (48) N 27, 28; (53) Ja 5, 6, 10; (54) F 15, D 2; (55) D 25, 28; (57) F 7; (58) Ja 9, Ap 21.

The Robbers, or The Forest of Bohemia; *Schiller:* (03) D 16; (04) F 15; (05) Mr 13; (07) Mr 4; (10) F 26; (19) Ap 20; (20) Mr 27; (29) N 21, D 30; (33) Mr 26, 30; (47) Ja 21; (55) Mr 17, 19, 21.

The Robber's Wife, or The Coiner's Cave; *Pocock:* (34) Ap 28.

Robert Emmett, the Irish Patriot, or The Hero of Ireland; *Bannister:* (44) Mr 21.

Robert le Diable; *Meyerbeer:* (41) F 27, Mr 2.

Robert Macaire, or The Auberge des Adrets: (40) N 9, 11, 13, 18; (45) Ja 14, D 15; (48) Mr 28, N 2; (52) D 11, 25; (53) Ja 7, D 3; (54) Ap 4; (55) Ap 13; (59) Ja 10, N 11.

Roberto Devereux: (51) D 10.

Robin Hood, or Sherwood Forest; *Hodgkinson:* (00) Mr 24; (01) N 20; (02) F 17; (04) F 21, Mr 3, 15, My 28, D 22; (05) F 18; (06) Mr 7; (07) Mr 4; (08) Mr 28; (09) Ja 7, 20.

Robinson Crusoe and His Good Man Friday: (33) D 31; (35) Ap 15; (40) Ja 4, 7.

Robinson Crusoe, or Bold Buccaneers: (27) Mr 21, 24, 31.

Robinson Crusoe, or Harlequin Friday: (03) Ap 25, D 16; (07) Ap 6.

Rochester, or King Charles Second's Merry Days: (21) My 5; (23) Ju 16.

Rogueries of Thomas: (57) Ap 24.

A Roland for an Oliver, or Tit for Tat; *Morton:* (21) N 17, D 1; (22) F 16; (26) Ap 6; (40) My 20, 23; (41) F 5, 16, N 24, 25; (44) N 18; (45) Ja 9, N 19; (50) Ap 30; (52) Ja 27; (53) N 24, D 20, 30; (59) F 11.

Roly Poly: (02) F 26, Mr 26.

The Roman Actor, or The Drama's Vindication; *Massinger:* (38) F 5, 7.

The Roman Father, or Deliverer of His Country; *Whitehead:* (00) Ja 18; (01) Ja 26; (50) Mr 16.

The Roman Gladiator: (59) Ja 19.

Romeo and Juliet; *Shakespeare:* (03) My 6; (04) N 19; (06) Ap 28, D 17; (07) My 2; (09) F 20; (10) Ap 4; (11) F 28; (16) Ap 8, N 25; (17) Ja 20, D 24; (18) F 4, Ap 14; (19) Ap 22; (20) Mr 6; (22) My 11; (23) Ju 20; (24) D 22; (27) F 26; (28) F 2, N 27; (29) Mr 2; (30) F 25, My 17, D 3; (32) F 29, N 28; (33) Mr 2; (35) Mr 7, 24; (36) F 11, Mr 3; (39) F 28; (40) N 14, 25, D 24; (42) F 24; (45) D 10, 17; (46) Ja 17, F 14, D 8; (47) D 29; (48) O 28, N 1; (50) F 1, Mr 7; (52) F 3, 25, D 2; (53) Ja 7, N 7; (54) Mr 2, N 3, D 8; (55) F 9, 22; (56) F 27; (57) Ja 19, My 11, D 4; (60) Ap 2.

The Romp, or A Cure for the Spleen; *Bickerstaff:* (00) Ja 4, F 4; (01) F 16; (02) Ja 21, Mr 3; (04) N 28; (05) Mr 13, D 13; (06) D 8; (07) N 25, D 7; (08) Ja 21, F 20; (09) F 6; (16) F 10, 21, Mr 4, N 22, D 23; (18) Ap 3; (20) Mr 22, D 23; (21) My 11; (27) F 2, 10, 14, 21; (29) Ap 1, 6.

Rory O'Moore; *Lover:* (42) Mr 31; (45) Mr 10; (57) Mr 14; (59) N 5, 10.

Rose and Colas; *Dibdin:* (05) My 1.

Rose de Mal: (57) D 3.

Rosina, or Love in a Cottage (or The Reapers); *Brooke:* (00) Ja 1, F 15, Ap 16, 17; (01) Ja 30, N 11; (02) Ja 23, 25, N 8, D 18, 24; (03) N 23; (04) N 14; (05) N 16, D 4; (06) My 9, D 29; (08) My 6, N 18, 25; (09) F 22; (10) My 12; (11) F 8; (12) F 20; (16) My 3; (17) F 5, 14; (18) Ja 28, Mr 14, Ap 8, 18; (20) F 1, D 4; (21) Ap 11; (23) D 8; (24) N 20; (25) Ja 29; (28) Mr 17; (29) F 26.

Rough Diamond, or Cousin Joe: (51) Ap 30, My 1, 6; (52) F 9, 13, D 6, 23; (53) Ja 10, 28, N 9, D 14, 24; (54) D 13, 15, 21; (56) F 15, 28, D 12; (57) Ja 9, 16, Mr 20; (59) F 4, O 21; (60) Ap 14.

The Ruffian Boy: (28) Ap 18.

Rugantino, or The Bravo of Venice: (23) Jy 2, 7, D 6; (25) Ap 16.

Rule a Wife and Have a Wife; *Beaumont* and *Fletcher:* (04) D 12; (05) F 21; (06) Ap 30; (07) Ap 20; (09) F 18; (10) Mr 6; (15) D 8, 26; (16) Ap 27; (17) Mr 3; (18) Ap 4; (19) F 27; (20) Mr 24; (24) D 9; (27) F 14, Mr 17; (30) F 15; (35) Mr 28.

The Rum Old Commodore: (41) Mr 18, 24.

Rumfustian: (29) Ap 29.

Rural Felicity, or Life in a Country Town; *Buckstone:* (40) My 4, 6, 12.

The Sailor's Daughter; *Cumberland:* (05) Mr 23, 27.

A Sailor's Hornpipe: (16) F 28; (23) Jy 4.

The Sailor's Joy, or Commerce Restored: (08) Ap 25.

The Sailor's Landlady, or Jack in Distress: (06) Ja 24, 27, F 17, 22, My 2; (07) Ja 21, Mr 2, Ap 28, D 16; (08) D 30.

St. George and the Dragon: (41) My 5.

St. Mary's Eve: (54) Ja 20; (59) O 22, N 10.

St. Patrick's Day, or The Scheming Lieutenant; *(Sheridan):* (00) Mr 14; (04) Mr 19; (16) Ap 19; (26) Mr 17; (35) Mr 17; (41) Mr 17; (54) Mr 17.

Sam Patch in France, or The Pesky Snake; *Addams:* (45) N 24, 29; (47) F 9.

Sam Patchieno, or The Perils of Love: (53) F 10, 11, 12.

Sam Slick, Esq., or Love in the Far, Far West: (44) N 27.

Sandy and Jenny: (26) F 27.

Sanguinary Bootjack, or The Murdered Lemon: (58) Mr 13.

Sarcophagus, or The Two Mummies: (41) D 30.

The Savage and the Maiden: (40) Mr 20, 23, 25, 26, 27.

Scan Mag, or The Village Gossip: (41) Ja 30.

The Scape Goat; *Poole:* (40) F 10.

The Scape Grace: (29) D 16.

The Scholar: (56) D 13.

The School for Citizens, or Choice, Love or Honor: (00) Mr 5.

The School for Friends: (07) Ja 19, 23, F 16.

The School for Greybeards, or the Mourning Bride; *Cowley:* (03) Mr 31.

The School for Prejudice, or Liberal Opinions; *Dibdin:* (03) F 2, 9, 23.

The School for Scandal; *Sheridan:* (01) Ap 24; (02) F 16; (05) F 26, D 9; (06) D 19; (07) N 27; (08) Ja 9; (10) F 6; (11) F 1, Mr 2; (12) F 29, My 12; (16) Ja 24, F 29, Ap 5; (17) F 5, 14; (18) Ja 12, 24, Ap 25, N 4; (19) Ap 14; (20) F 19, My 10; (21) Mr 21, N

9, 12; (24) Ja 5, N 24; (25) Mr 3; (27) Mr 30; (28) F 25, D 1;
(29) Mr 23, N 20; (30) Mr 3; (31) Mr 23; (32) F 27, 29, Mr 15;
(33) F 25, Mr 18; (35) Mr 10; (36) F 12, Mr 22; (38) Ja 12, 23;
(39) Ja 30, D 5; (40) F 4, D 9; (41) Ja 28; (43) F 17; (44) F 8,
Mr 16; (45) D 11, 24; (47) Ja 15; (48) F 7; (51) F 19, My 6;
(52) F 27, N 11, 17, D 20, 30; (53) N 18; (54) N 21, D 21; (55)
N 12, 16; (56) N 3, 19; (57) D 10.

A School for Tigers, or The Shilling Hop; *Lemon:* (51) O 22.

A School for Wives; *Kelly:* (00) Mr 14; (01) F 13, My 13; (05) F 16.

The School of Reform, or How to Rule a Husband; *Morton:* (06) F 3,
10, 22, N 14; (07) Ja 8, F 21, D 16; (15) N 29; (17) Ap 25; (18)
Ja 5, Mr 7, N 10; (22) Ap 20, 27; (24) My 24; (28) Ap 23, D 10;
(33) Ap 1; (40) N 18; (56) F 18.

A Scot's Pastoral: (08) Mr 30.

The Scottish Ghost, or Fanny's Love: (20) D 23.

The Sea Captain, or The Birthright; *Bulwer-Lytton:* (41) Mr 11, 15,
16, My 6.

Sea of Ice: (58) N 22, 23, 24, 25, 27, D 20; (60) Ja 9.

The Sea Serpent, or Gloucester Hoax; *Crafts:* (19) My 12; (21) My 2.

Second Love: (57) Ap 14, 15, 16, 17, D 2.

The Secret Marriage: (59) Ja 12.

The Secret Mine, or The Hindoos of the Cavern: (20) Ap 7, 8.

The Secret, or Hole in the Wall (or Natural Magic); *Morris:* (06) Mr
3; (28) D 8; (30) Mr 29; (32) F 29; (34) Ap 26, D 5; (35) Mr
18, 20, 25; (38) Mr 22; (40) Mr 14, 19, 24, Ap 7, N 25, D 12; (41)
F 17; (42) D 23; (44) Ja 19, Mr 26, D 5; (46) Ja 5, D 4; (47)
F 3, 23; (48) Ja 5; (51) O 24; (52) D 18, 21; (57) Ja 19, 26.

Secret Service; *Planché:* (40) D 15, 18; (41) Ja 25.

Secrets Worth Knowing, or The Young Auctioneer; *Morton:* (00) Mr
26; (06) Mr 12; (21) Mr 24.

Seeing Is Believing; *Joddrell:* (32) Mr 26, 30.

Self Immolation, or The Sacrifice of Love; *Neuman:* (01) F 2; (03)
Mr 18, Ap 4.

The Sergeant's Wife: (32) Mr 26; (43) Ja 28; (59) O 15.

The Serious Family; *Barnett:* (51) F 27, Mr 4, Ap 15, 23; (55) Mr 5,
8, 10, 23; (56) F 2, 6; (57) Ja 8, Mr 4; (58) Ap 24, 26, N 30, D 4;
(60) Ja 13.

The Serious Husband: (56) D 29.

Seth Slope, or Done for a Hundred: (43) N 29.

Shakespeare's Jubilee, or Stratford-on-Avon; *(Carey):* (04) Ap 30;
(12) Ap 28; (24) Ap 28.

Shandy Maguire, or The Bold Boy of the Mountain; *Pilgrim:* (54)
F 2, 3.

She Stoops to Conquer, or The Mistakes of a Night; *Goldsmith:* (02)
F 26; (03) Mr 9; (05) D 30; (08) Mr 25, D 26; (10) My 16; (11)
Ja 14; (12) Ap 11; (15) D 2, Mr 15; (17) Ap 19, D 31; (18) My
21; (25) Ap 7; (26) D 23; (27) D 1; (29) F 21, 24; (30) N 22;
(38) F 16, D 18; (39) Mr 4, 6; (40) N 17; (43) N 4; (50) F 2,
My 4; (51) F 25; (52) Ja 26; (54) Ja 25, 27; (56) N 29.

She Would and She Would Not, or The Kind Imposters; *Cibber:* (05)
My 2; (20) My 12; (29) Mr 20; (57) N 12.

She Would Be a Soldier, or The Battle of Chippewa; *Noah:* (20) Ja 10,
14; (21) My 12; (28) Ja 8.

Shelty's Frolic; *(Dunlap):* (20) Ja 12, 15, Ap 19.

Shin-de-Heela: (51) D 22, 23, 24, 25.

The Ship-Launch; *(Burton)*: (16) My 8.

The Shipwreck, or After the Storm; *Coleman:* (01) Ap 13; (04) Ap 19, My 14; (05) Ap 19; (06) F 5; (08) Ap 1, 21; (18) Ja 26, Mr 7; (19) My 7.

Shipwrecked, or The Sailor Boys: (09) Mr 8, 10.

The Shipwrecked Sailor: (34) Mr 20.

Shocking Events; *Buckstone:* (41) Ja 15, 19, F 2, 8, Mr 5, D 14, 15; (42) Ja 19.

The Siege of Belgrade; *Cobb:* (02) Mr 19, 24, Ap 9; (03) F 23; (09) Mr 16; (18) My 6, 15; (29) D 4.

The Siege of Charleston, or The Battle of Fort Moultrie: (43) F 22, 24, 28.

The Siege of Quebec, or The Death of General Wolfe: (01) My 4.

Sighs, or Poverty and Honor (or The Daughter); *Hoare:* (02) Ap 19, D 13, 22; (03) Mr 23; (09) Ap 3.

Simpson and Company: (24) D 13, 17, 23; (25) Ja 7, F 25; (28) Ja 22, F 2; (30) Mr 22; (34) N 4, 19; (35) D 3; (39) N 21; (40) Ja 14, D 16; (43) N 9; (44) Mr 20, 27; (45) Ja 17; (47) F 10; (48) F 1; (50) Ap 24, My 1; (55) Ap 10; (56) Ja 19; (58) Mr 22, 24.

Single Life; *Buckstone:* (55) N 3, 6, 10, 15, 28; (56) Ja 14.

The Sixty-third Letter; *Oulton:* (20) Ja 1, 14.

Skeleton Hand, or The Demon Statue: (47) F 8.

Sketches in India: (54) Mr 1; (55) Mr 6, 16; (57) O 21, 24; (58) F 17, 18; (59) Ja 27, 29; (60) Mr 19.

Slasher and Crasher; *Morton:* (52) Ja 9, F 2, Mr 2; (54) Ap 13, 17; (56) N 6, 11, 19, D 2; (59) F 1, 2; (60) Mr 19.

The Sleep Walker, or Village Phantom; *Oulton:* (15) N 11, 20; (16) F 9, 28, Ap 1, 15; (17) Ja 4, 22, Mr 1; (18) Ja 5, 21, Ap 15, N 7, 25; (20) Mr 7; (21) My 30; (23) My 30; (27) D 14; (33) Mr 18, Ap 4; (42) F 11, 12.

Sleeping Beauty, or The Enchanted Wood: (48) Mr 22, 23.

Sleeping Draught: (19) Ap 14, 22, 28; (20) F 10; (21) Ap 23; (24) Ja 9, Ap 8; (25) Mr 21; (27) D 8; (29) Ap 11; (32) D 1; (44) D 17.

Smiles and Tears, or The Widow's Stratagem (or A Mother's Prayer); *Kemble:* (25) F 28, Mr 9.

Smith and Fiske, or The Two Gay Deceivers: (58) Mr 27.

The Smoked Miser, or The Benefit of Hanging: (32) D 3.

Snapping Turtles, or Mr. and Mrs. T. T. Timms: (42) Ja 4, 14.

The Soldier and Boarder: (61) N 25.

The Soldier and the Peasant: (34) Ap 18; (41) F 20.

Soldier for Love: (59) Ja 18.

Soldier of Fortune, or The Irish Settler: (46) D 28, 31; (50) Mr 23; (59) N 3.

The Soldier, the Sailor, the Tinker and the Tailor: (54) Mr 9.

The Soldier's Courtship: (38) F 28.

The Soldier's Daughter: (04) D 24; (05) F 15, Mr 25; (07) F 4, 18, D 9; (08) F 24; (09) Mr 10; (11) Ja 7; (15) D 4; (16) F 17; (17) Ap 26; (19) D 29; (20) N 22; (24) My 19; (25) Ap 6; (27) Ja 20, 27; (28) F 15; (29) Mr 4, N 9; (30) D 1; (32) Mr 20; (34) Mr 6, O 16; (35) Mr 5; (36) F 9; (40) Mr 2, 6, Ap 8; (41) N 17; (42) Ja 11, F 24; (43) Ja 20; (44) Mr 8, 23; (45) Mr 26;

(46) N 18; (47) Ja 9, D 20; (48) Ja 19; (52) Ja 8; (54) N 20; (55) Ap 20.

Somebody Else; *Planché:* (46) F 18, 21; (52) Ja 12, F 4, N 13, 26, D 2; (53) Ja 27, F 23; (54) F 13, 24; (55) Mr 12, 15; (56) Mr 31; (57) Mr 30, Ap 8, 14; (59) Mr 9.

The Somnambulist, or The Phantom of the Village; *Moncrieff:* (28) D 8; (52) D 13; (53) Ja 15; (54) D 24; (55) Ja 6.

The Son-in-Law; *O'Keeffe:* (09) Ja 25, F 15.

Sonnambula, or There's a Silver Lining to Every Cloud: (60) O 17.

Sons of Erin, or Modern Sentiment: (16) Ja 1, 6, N 16; (20) Ja 12.

South Carolina's Contribution to the World's Fair; *Walcot:* (51) Ap 24.

Souvenir de Charleston: (54) D 2.

The Spanish Exile; *Requier:* (44) Mr 28, Ap 1.

The Spanish Fair: (06) F 21, My 14.

The Spectre Bridegroom, or A Ghost in Spite of Himself (or The Ghost): (22) Ap 13; (23) My 22, Ju 20, D 19; (24) F 21; (25) F 9; (27) Ap 9; (28) Ap 11; (29) Mr 5; (32) N 28; (33) D 27; (34) Mr 11, 20; (36) Mr 16, 23; (39) Mr 19, 26, Ap 4, 27; (40) Ap 14, N 7; (43) Ja 12, F 9; (47) F 1, 6, 16; (50) F 12, Mr 12; (51) Ja 25, F 20; (52) Ja 13, F 5; (55) N 17, D 1; (57) Ja 5; (58) Ap 21; (59) O 11; (60) Ja 12, Ap 10.

Speed the Plough; *Morton:* (01) F 27, Mr 4, 6, 13, N 23; (02) Ja 21; (03) Mr 7; (04) My 14; (06) F 5, D 6; (07) F 2; (08) Ja 6, F 29; (11) F 26; (15) N 18, 20; (16) Mr 5, My 4, N 23; (17) D 12; (28) Ap 18; (30) N 25; (33) Mr 13; (40) Ap 27, N 12; (44) D 18.

The Spirit of the Fountain, or The Student and the Sybil: (48) Mr 24.

Spirit Rappings and Table Movings: (53) D 10, 28.

The Spitfire, or The Cockney Afloat; *Morton:* (51) F 14, 18, Mr 1.

The Spoil'd Child; *Bickerstaff:* (00) Ja 6, 27, Mr 3, 26; (02) Ja 27, N 5; (04) Ap 4, D 1; (05) F 11, N 22; (07) N 24, D 9; (08) F 18; (09) F 1; (10) F 9, Mr 30; (11) Ja 30; (12) D 7; (15) N 27; (16) Mr 23, Ap 8, N 15, 30; (17) Mr 24; (18) F 9, Mr 27, My 21; (19) F 6, 13, Ap 13; (20) Ja 12, My 6, N 25; (24) Mr 31; (25) Ap 5; (27) Ja 1, 20, F 22, Mr 7; (28) Ap 14; (29) Mr 16, Ap 8; (30) Mr 15; (35) Ap 14; (36) Mr 23, Ap 1; (39) Ja 28, N 27, 29, D 13, 14; (40) Ja 8; (41) Ja 4, 13; (53) Ja 13, 29.

Sponge in Town, or Where Shall I Dine?: (25) F 14, 18, Mr 1, 12, 19, 23.

Sprigs of Laurel, or The Rival Soldiers; *O'Keeffe:* (05) D 16; (07) Ja 28; (08) Ja 18, My 28; (09) F 10; (15) N 15, D 6; (16) Ja 8, F 23; (18) Ja 9, 17, N 6; (19) F 12, 24, Ap 30; (20) F 2, My 10; (21) My 21; (22) Ap 19; (23) Ju 14; (24) Ap 21; (25) F 2; (28) F 15; (32) D 12; (33) Mr 4, 27, Ap 1, 3; (35) Mr 7; (38) Ja 17; (40) F 4.

Spring and Autumn, or The Bride of Fifty: (38) Ap 18.

The Spy, or A Tale of Neutral Ground; *Clinch:* (23) D 8, 13; (24) Ja 28, D 29; (46) Ja 29.

The Stage Struck Barber: (54) Ja 6, 7, 12; (56) Ap 7, 11, 15, 17.

The Stage Struck Yankee; *Durivage:* (43) N 2, 3.

Star Spangled Banner, or The American Tar's Fidelity: (43) D 8, 9.

Stars and Stripes in Mexico, or The Death of Davy Crockett: (60) Ap 5.

State Secrets, or The Taylor of Tamworth; *Wilks:* (39) D 4, 5; (41) My 8; (42) D 19; (43) Ja 5, 28, F 16, My 2; (44) F 20, Ap 2; (45) Ja 16, F 22; (55) O 31, N 2, D 25; (59) O 19.

The Steward, or Fashion and Feeling (or The Steward and the Deserted Daughter); *Holcroft:* (20) My 18; (21) Mr 19; (23) My 24; (25) F 14; (36) F 15.

Still Water Runs Deep; *Taylor:* (55) O 15, 20, 24, 26, N 7, 28, D 31; (56) N 6; (57) O 21, N 13; (58) Ap 28.

The Storm, or The American Tars on Shore: (26) Mr 6.

The Strange Adventure, or An Excursion to the Country: (00) Mr 7, 8.

The Stranger, or Misanthropy and Repentance; *Dunlap:* (00) Ja 9; (01) Mr 11, Ap 18; (02) Mr 12, My 5; (03) D 21; (06) My 16; (07) Mr 14, My 15, N 11; (11) Ap 3; (12) Mr 18; (16) F 23, N 22; (19) F 12; (20) N 24; (24) D 13; (27) Mr 9, D 8, 14; (28) Ap 9; (30) F 17; (31) Mr 21; (32) F 17; (33) D 9; (34) O 28; (35) N 25; (36) F 10, Mr 18; (38) F 15, 21; (39) Ja 22, 26, F 7, Mr 13; (40) F 21, Ap 2; (41) F 1; (42) D 30; (43) My 3; (44) N 19; (45) Ja 28, N 8, D 8; (46) F 2, N 19, D 18; (47) Ja 20, D 21; (49) Ja 11; (50) Ja 24, Ap 15; (51) Ja 23; (52) Ja 12, F 5, N 27, D 22, 30; (53) N 2, 5; (54) Ja 19, Mr 3, N 9, 30, D 16; (55) F 12, Ap 11, D 24; (56) D 5; (57) Mr 25.

Such Things Are; *Inchbald:* (07) Mr 30; (18) My 1.

Sudden Thoughts, or The Impulse: (38) Mr 23, 24, 27; (39) Mr 27, Ap 3; (44) N 27; (45) F 11; (51) Ja 21, 29, F 5; (52) Ja 1, 28, Mr 30; (56) F 27, Mr 4, 26.

The Sultan, or The American Captive (or A Peep into the Seraglio); *Bickerstaff:* (06) My 22; (11) Mr 13.

Sunshine through Clouds: (55) F 12, 21; (57) D 31; (58) Ja 1.

The Surrender of Calais; *Coleman:* (01) Ap 29; (08) My 11; (18) My 18.

The Suspicious Husband; *Hoadley:* (01) Ja 28; (03) F 26, N 9; (04) N 14; (05) F 22; (09) Ja 7, 23; (11) Ja 28, Mr 9; (20) D 8; (24) F 23.

The Swamp Steed: *See* Marion.

Swedish Nightingale: (58) Mr 25; (59) N 9.

Swedish Patriotism, or The Signal Fire; *Abbott:* (27) Ap 18; (41) Mr 11, 15.

Sweethearts and Wives; *Poole:* (27) Ap 18, 21, My 4, 11, N 19, 24; (28) F 13; (32) F 29, Mr 14; (34) F 20, 22; (36) F 18, Mr 15; (39) My 16, N 28; (42) D 24; (43) N 7; (45) Ja 11, D 2; (46) N 7; (48) F 9; (51) Ja 24, Ap 17; (52) Mr 11; (53) Ja 29; (56) Ap 2, 3; (58) D 3, 11.

Swiss Cottage, or Why Don't She Marry?: (37) D 19, 20, 30; (38) Ja 6, F 15, 21; (41) Ja 7, 11, F 9, Ap 23, N 20; (44) F 19; (45) N 13, 20, 28, D 18; (46) F 16; (47) D 28; (49) My 25; (53) Ja 12, 22, N 17, D 5; (55) Mr 7, 13, O 19, 20; (57) O 30, N 16, 30; (58) Ap 20.

Swiss Swains, or How to Make Love; *Webster:* (46) D 5, 11, 16; (52) F 23, 28, Mr 22; (55) O 17, N 9; (56) Mr 1; (58) Mr 22.

Sylvester Daggerwood, or The Mad Actor; *Coleman:* (07) Mr 6, N 18; (16) My 11; (17) Mr 24, 29, Ap 12, D 20; (18) Ja 8, Ap 13; (22) My 11; (24) Ja 3, 12; (27) Mr 10; (28) Ja 30; (32) F 6, 8; (35) Ap 8, D 8.

Take that Girl Away; *(Matthews):* (56) Ap 5; (58) Ap 19.

A Tale of Mystery, or The Dumb Man of Arpenay; *Holcroft:* (03) My 3, 6, D 19; (04) F 2, 14; (05) F 26, D 6; (06) My 7, N 12; (07)

Ap 30; (08) Ja 4, N 30; (16) My 1, 11; (17) Ja 15; (19) Ap 23; (23) Ju 28, D 3; (25) Mr 11; (27) Ja 6, Mr 2, Ap 4; (32) D 15; (38) Ap 26.

A Tale of Terror, or A Tale of Pleasure; *Siddons:* (05) Ap 15, 25.

Tam O'Shanter: (39) My 24, 30; (44) D 10.

The Taming of the Shrew; *Shakespeare:* (51) Ja 23, F 3, 21, My 1; (55) Ap 19.

Tancred and Sigismunda; *Thomson:* (10) Ap 6, 14.

Tancredi; *Rossini:* (48) Ja 21, 27.

Tartar Peasant in Crimea: (61) N 26.

Teddy, the Tiler: (34) O 16, 30, N 10, D 6; (41) F 13; (46) D 22, 25, 31; (48) Ja 10, D 30; (54) F 11; (59) O 31, N 3.

Tekeli, or The Siege of Montgatz; *Hook:* (08) Ja 23, 29, F 17, Mr 16, D 21, 30; (09) Ja 6; (10) Ap 2; (11) Mr 23; (12) My 8; (16) My 6; (17) Mr 31; (18) Mr 16; (20) Ap 22; (24) My 14; (28) Ap 7; (34) Mr 22; (43) Ap 28.

Telemachus (in the Isle of Calypso); *Graham:* (01) My 13; (04) Mr 9, 21; (08) My 21; (11) F 4, Ap 3.

The Tempest, or The Enchanted Isle; *Shakespeare:* (02) My 12; (06) Mr 31; (18) Ap 29; (39) Ap 8, 11.

Temptation, or The Irish Immigrant; *Brougham:* (57) Mr 2, 3, 6; (58) F 24, 27; (59) Mr 19.

The Ten Mowbrays: (30) Mr 26.

That Blessed Baby: (56) Ap 5.

Thelypthora, or The Blessings of Two Wives at Once; *Knight:* (00) F 27.

Therese, or The Orphan of Geneva; *Payne:* (21) N 19, 24, 28; (24) Ja 24, 26, 30; (27) Ap 16; (29) Ap 6; (30) D 6; (31) F 28; (32) F 1, D 5, 22; (33) Mr 20, D 24; (35) Ap 16, N 24, D 7; (36) F 20, Ap 12; (39) My 27; (43) F 25, My 16, D 9; (45) N 6; (48) F 23; (53) N 30; (55) F 14, Mr 10; (59) F 10.

Thomas and Sally; (02) My 14; (08) Ap 8, 21, My 25; (11) My 18.

Three and Deuce, or Which Is He?; *(Hoare):* (16) N 8, 18, D 16, 21; (17) F 25, Mr 21; (20) Mr 10, N 24, D 15; (21) N 23; (23) D 17; (24) F 25, D 22; (27) Ja 29, My 23; (28) D 16; (30) F 1.

The Three-faced Frenchman: (39) Ap 26, My 1, 6; (54) Ap 1, 8.

The Three Gladiators: (59) Ja 13, 14, 20.

Three Jack Sheppards: (58) Ap 22.

Three Weeks after Marriage; *Murphy:* (01) Mr 25; (03) F 11; (11) Mr 8, 9; (20) Ap 12, D 20; (25) Ja 24, Ap 18; (28) D 3; (30) N 24; (31) F 21; (32) F 1, 18, D 5; (36) Mr 11; (43) N 15.

The Three Wishes, or Harlequin, Puck and Puddings: (32) D 26.

The Three Witches: (26) Ap 14.

Thrice Married: (58) Mr 9, 12, 13.

Thumping Legacy; *Morton:* (59) O 18.

The Tiger Horde, or Dubar the Terrible: (20) Ap 10, 15.

Time Tries All: (54) D 20.

Time Works Wonders, or The Inconstant; *Jerrold:* (45) N 19, 21; (46) Ja 31; (55) Mr 12, 14, 20; (58) D 17.

Time's a Tell-Tale; *Siddons:* (08) N 25, 30; (09) Mr 18.

The Times, or Travelers in America (or Life in New York); *Hackett:* (32) F 1.

Timour the Tartar; *Lewis:* (18) My 23, N 21; (20) F 3, 4, 5, 7, 9, 10,

Ap 3, 4, 5; (25) Ap 19; (32) D 31; (33) Ja 1, 4, 5; (34) Ap 3, 7, 8, 9; (41) My 11; (45) F 27.

'Tis All a Farce; *Allingham:* (15) N 10, 22, D 18; (16) F 5, 26, Mr 11; (18) Ja 12, 23, F 26, N 9; (20) F 25; (23) Ju 9; (25) Ap 11; (27) D 10.

To Be or Not to Be: (39) F 11, 12.

To Marry or Not to Marry; *Inchbald:* (06) Mr 24; (08) Ja 18, F 15; (24) My 21; (27) My 18; (30) D 20.

To Oblige Benson: (54) D 5; (55) Ja 8, 16, F 7, D 4.

To Paris and Back for Five Pounds; *Morton:* (54) D 7, 8, 24.

Tom and Jerry, or Life in London; *Moncrieff:* (24) Mr 1, 2, 3, 5, 6, 8, 17, 18, Ap 3, 20, My 1, 22, 26, N 27, D 11, 15; (25) Ja 15, F 24; (27) Ap 20, 26, My 2; (28) F 4; (29) Ap 22; (32) D 21; (33) My 17, D 28; (34) Mr 5, N 29; (39) My 24; (43) F 15; (56) F 9, 12.

Tom Cringle, or Mat of the Iron Hand (or The Seaman's Log Book): (34) N 3, 4, 5, 6, 7, 8; (35) Ap 11; (45) Mr 7.

Tom Noddy's Secret; *Bayley:* (41) Ja 27; (50) F 2, 7, Ap 18.

Tom Thumb the Great, or The Lilliputian Hero; *Fielding:* (05) My 14, 20; (06) Ja 20, F 26, N 24; (08) My 11; (23) D 26; (24) Ja 1, 19; (25) Ap 13; (29) Ap 11, 24.

Tomar, the Corsair, or The Italian Nuptials: (05) My 23.

Too Many Cooks; *Kenney:* (07) D 23, 26; (08) Mr 18.

The Toodles; *Burton:* (52) Mr 9, 16; (54) Ja 2, 4, 5, 7, 14; (56) Ap 8, 9, 12, 19; (58) D 1, 4; (60) Ja 2, 4, 13.

Touch and Take, or The Singing Bailiff: (30) F 15; (39) My 4.

The Touchstone of Truth, or Harlequin Traveller; *Dibdin:* (04) Ap 2.

Towers of London, or The Queen and the Mechanic: (45) F 12, 21.

Town and Country, or Which Is Best?; *Morton:* (07) D 30; (08) Ja 4, F 16, Mr 11; (09) Mr 1; (11) Ap 26; (12) Ap 24, My 20; (17) Ap 9; (18) F 3; (20) My 6; (21) D 11; (24) My 3, N 20; (25) F 5, Mr 23; (26) D 26; (27) Mr 1, D 19; (29) F 18; (32) Mr 12; (33) F 18; (34) O 22; (39) Ja 15; (40) F 20; (44) Mr 2; (46) Ja 30; (57) O 23, 27.

Travellers in Turkey: (09) F 14.

The Travellers, or Music's Fascination; *Cherry:* (08) Mr 14, 18, 23, D 5.

Trial by Jury: (12) Ap 11.

Trick upon Trick, or Double Deception: (25) Ap 16.

Trip to Coney Island: (60) Ja 14.

Trisac, the Duelist: (53) N 25.

The Troubadour Soldier: (61) N 25.

The Trumpeter's Daughter: (46) D 14, 19.

Trust to Luck: (55) Ja 23.

Trying It On: (53) N 18, D 13; (54) F 17, N 1, 29; (56) N 25; (58) Ap 17; (59) Mr 11; (60) Ap 2.

Turn Out, or The Enraged Politician; *Kenney:* (16) F 2, 12, Mr 6, 15; (17) Ap 12, 28; (18) My 16; (19) My 1, D 29; (20) Ja 26; (21) Ap 25, N 10; (22) Ap 13; (24) My 12; (27) Mr 16, Ap 6, D 12; (28) Mr 12, 19; (29) My 8; (33) D 21; (34) Ja 15, Ap 28; (38) F 13; (41) N 19; (46) Ja 21, F 2, 19.

Turned Head: (41) Mr 18, Ap 22; (46) N 14, 25, D 24; (47) Ja 21.

Turning the Tables, or The Exciseman of Winchester: (39) D 7; (44) D 3.

The Turnpike Gate, or The New Road to Mirth: (02) My 3; (05) D 30; (20) My 13, N 22; (24) Ap 30; (26) F 13, 15, 22, Mr 13, 31;

(28) Ja 11, F 18, 20, Ap 25; (32) D 10, 22; (35) Mr 10; (36) F 13; (38) Ja 18.

'Twas I, or The Truth's a Lie; *Payne:* (27) My 7, 11; (30) F 8; (33) D 23; (38) D 27; (39) F 6; (45) D 4, 10; (46) F 5, 25; (58) N 20; (59) Mr 11, 14.

Twelfth Night; *Shakespeare:* (46) F 12; (55) N 26, 27.

The Two Bonny Castles; *Morton:* (57) Mr 16, 18, 19.

Two Buzzards; *(Morton):* (55) Ja 23, 24, F 5; (57) D 30; (58) Ja 4, 11, Mr 24.

Two Can Play at that Game: (58) Ap 19.

The Two Friends; *Holcroft:* (30) Ap 16; (32) Mr 21; (34) N 3, 11; (38) Ap 23; (42) D 28; (43) Ja 9, F 4, N 14; (44) Ja 4; (53) F 28.

The Two Greens: (41) My 10; (43) Ap 22.

The Two Gregories, or Luck in a Name (or Like Master Like Man, or Where's the Money Come From?): (28) Ap 16; (32) Mr 1; (34) D 3; (35) Ap 6; (36) Mr 10; (38) Ja 26, F 6, 12, D 26, 27; (39) Ap 18, 19; (41) My 3; (48) Mr 16; (51) Ap 29, My 7, 9; (54) Mr 20; (57) O 28, N 7, D 1.

The Two Hunters, or The Milkmaid: (01) Ja 28; (04) F 11.

Two Late for Dinner: (21) N 24, 30; (22) F 20; (24) Mr 13; (41) N 23, D 1.

Two Loves in a Life: (55) Ja 13.

The Two Murders, or Henri and Louise: (55) Ap 13.

The Two Pages of Frederick the Great; *Poole:* (23) D 5, 12; (24) Mr 13; (27) Ap 20, My 4.

The Two Philosophers, or The Merry Girl: (12) D 28.

The Two Quakers and the Merry Girl: (05) Ap 22.

The Two Queens; *Buckstone:* (41) Mr 4, 6; (45) N 18, 21; (46) Ja 13, F 13; (59) O 18.

Two Strings to Your Bow, or The Servant with Two Masters; *Jephson:* (03) Ap 12, D 20; (04) Mr 5; (08) My 13; (10) Mr 10; (11) Ap 17; (18) My 2; (21) Ap 27; (24) Ap 24, My 17; (26) F 20, 27; (32) D 21.

The Two Thompsons, or William Thompson: (32) Mr 30, N 30; (33) Mr 28, D 24; (36) F 27, Mr 17; (38) Ja 13, 20.

The Ugly Club: (07) Mr 4.

Uncle Ben: (32) Ja 31.

Uncle Foozle's Wedding Day: (47) F 10.

Uncle John, or The Cashmere Shawl: (38) D 31; (39) Ja 24; (40) D 8, 18; (41) Ja 27; (44) D 20; (45) D 29.

Uncle Pat's Cabin, or Lights and Shades of Lowly Life; *Conway:* (54) F 8, 9.

Uncle Sam, or A Nabob for an Hour: (40) N 14; (41) Ja 30, D 13, 21, 30; (42) Ja 12, F 14, Mr 15; (44) D 18; (45) D 30; (46) Ja 24, F 10, N 12, 28; (47) Ja 27.

Uncle Tom's Cabin, or Freedom at the North and Service at the South (or Life among the Lowly); *Aiken:* (53) O 24, 25, 26.

An Undescribable Something, or I'll Tell You What: (04) F 2, 6, Mr 19; (12) Ap 6.

Une Bonne Bouche Musicale: (40) Mr 27.

Une Fille Terrible!: (61) N 25.

The Unfinished Gentleman, or Billy Downey; *Selby:* (36) F 15, 16, Mr 18; (39) Ja 10, D 30.

The Unfortunate Man: (39) F 22.
The Unhappy Family: (02) My 7.
Union Oath, or Commemoration of American Independence: (03) Ap 21.
An Unprotected Female: (54) D 20; (55) Ja 1; (59) O 10, 11.
Uriel, or The Demon Lover: (58) Ap 5.
Used Up, or There's Nothing in It; *Boucicault:* (45) D 5, 6, 17; (46) Ja 19, 26; (48) F 11; (51) Ap 17, 30, My 5; (53) Ja 21; (56) Mr 19, 21, 27, D 27; (58) Ap 17.
The Useless Resolution, or The Lover Disguises: (04) F 11.

Valentine and Orson, or The Wild Man of the Woods; *Dibdin:* (06) Mr 21; (08) F 8; (18) My 19; (29) Ap 27, D 23; (44) N 25.
Valeria, or The Roman Sisters; (57) Mr 20, 21.
Valet de Sham, or Trick for Trick: (43) My 11, N 6; (44) Ja 10; (46) F 11.
The Vampire, or The Bride of the Isles: (20) D 15; (25) Ja 14.
Velasco, or Castilian Honor; *Sargent:* (39) Mr 14, Ap 9.
Venetian Carnival: (39) Ap 29; (59) Ja 15.
Venetian Models, or Living Models of Antiquity: (33) Ja 7.
Venetian Statues: (38) Ap 1.
Venice Preserved, or The Plot Discovered; *Otway:* (01) F 9, My 20; (04) N 12; (07) Ap 13, My 4; (08) Ja 25; (09) Ja 27; (11) Mr 19; (16) Ja 9, D 30; (18) Mr 25; (19) F 1; (20) Mr 18; (24) Mr 22, D 3; (27) F 24, Mr 7; (29) F 17; (30) Ja 20, F 24; (32) N 26; (33) D 11; (35) Mr 11; (38) Ja 10; (40) Mr 31, N 21; (43) F 28; (45) D 29; (48) N 29, D 1; (51) F 12; (54) D 1.
Vermont Wool Dealer; *Logan:* (48) O 26.
The Veteran Tar; *Arnold:* (07) Mr 20, Ap 11.
The Vicar of Wakefield; *Taylor:* (57) Ja 9.
The Victims: (59) N 11.
Victor and Hortense, or The Pride of Birth; *Boucicault:* (56) D 24, 27.
Victorine, or I'll Sleep on It; *Buckstone:* (33) Ja 7, 14; (39) Mr 12, 13; (40) Ap 3; (41) Mr 9; (45) Mr 10; (55) N 1, 5, 9.
Views in Tripoli: (09) Ja 25.
The Village Doctor; *Webster:* (41) Ja 30.
The Village Lawyer, or Ba! Ba! Ba!; *Macready:* (00) F 21, My 5; (01) F 23, N 13; (02) F 10, Ap 21, N 13; (03) Ja 31; (05) D 11; (06) N 26; (07) Ja 10, Ap 20, N 13; (10) F 16; (16) Ja 26, F 17; (17) F 10, Mr 8; (18) Ap 18; (21) Ap 28; (24) Mr 17; (28) Ja 7; (30) Ja 15; (41) Ja 22.
Village Sports: (00) F 4.
Violet, or The Career of an Actress; *Boucicault:* (56) Mr 17, 18, 20, D 15, 18.
The Virgin of the Sun; *Dunlap* or *Smith:* (00) Mr 3, Ap 4; (07) Mr 12; (22) Ap 15, 17, 24, My 3; (36) Mr 24.
Virgin Unmasked: (00) F 17.
Virginia; *(Parke):* (57) D 18.
Virginius, or The Roman Father (or The Liberation of Rome); *Knowles:* (20) D 26; (21) Mr 23, My 25, 29; (24) Ja 21, Ap 8; (26) D 29; (27) Ja 26, F 7, D 5; (28) Ja 4; (29) Ap 24, N 11; (30) F 3; (31) F 25; (35) Mr 16; (38) Ja 26, 30; (39) Ja 18; (41) Ja 11; (42) F 10; (43) Ja 19, D 13; (44) Ja 17; (45) Mr 13; (46) Ja 9; (51) F 4; (53) F 11, D 30; (57) F 13.
The Virginny Mummy: (38) Ja 27, 30; (45) Mr 1.

Visitandines: (05) Ap 6.
Vivandiere of Chapultepec: (56) F 18.
The Voice of Nature; *Boaden:* (04) F 14, 21, Mr 2; (05) My 14.
Vol-au-Vent, or A Night of Adventure: (37) Mr 10, 13, 14; (59) Ja
10, 19.
Votary of Wealth; *Holman:* (16) F 14, Mr 2; (20) Mr 15.
Vulcan and Cyclops: (34) Ap 25.
Vulcan's Gift, or Harlequin Humorist: (04) Ap 23, My 17, N 21; (05)
F 22; (06) F 14; (07) Ja 1; (08) Ja 1, 20, D 26; (10) Ap 23.

Waggeries at Wapping, or The Merry Monarch: (33) D 20.
Wallace, or The Hero of Scotland (or The Scottish Chief); *Barrymore:*
(21) N 21; (22) Ap 10; (24) Ap 26; (25) F 4; (36) F 29, Mr 4,
10; (41) Mr 10, 12.
The Wanderer, or The Rights of Hospitality; *Kemble:* (08) D 16; (09)
Ja 6, Mr 24.
The Wandering Boy(s), or The Castle of Olival (or Orphans of the
Rhine); *Noah:* (12) Ap 20, 22, My 20; (22) My 15, 17; (23) Ju 27,
D 20; (24) Ja 17; (25) Ap 12; (26) D 30; (27) Ja 12, F 17, Mr 1;
(29) Mr 9; (33) My 20, D 19; (39) D 28; (40) Ja 1; (55) N 29;
(59) Ja 1.
The Wandering Minstrel(s), or Mirth and Music: (18) Ap 28; (40)
Ap 1, 4; (43) F 27; (44) F 22; (47) Ja 4, 6; (56) F 26; (58) D
2, 6; (59) N 8; (60) Ja 10, 11.
Wanted—A Wife, or A Cheque on My Banker; *Moncrieff:* (20) Ja
19, 22.
Wanted, One Thousand Milliners: (53) Ja 11, 12; (58) N 30, D 2, 8, 11;
(59) Ja 17.
Warlock of the Glen, or The House of Glencairn: (21) My 14, 19, N 10,
D 5; (24) Ap 5; (30) D 21; (34) Ja 24, F 27; (35) Ap 15, N 30;
(36) Ap 11; (48) N 30, D 2.
Washington, or The Orphan of Pennsylvania (or The Spirit of '76):
(24) Ja 8, 14; (40) Ap 20, 22, 24, 25, 28, 30, My 20.
The Water Party: (41) Ja 7, 9, 26.
The Waterman, or The First of August; *(Dibdin):* (01) F 20; (03)
F 2, D 22; (09) Mr 22; (18) Ap 13; (37) D 15, 21; (38) F 20;
(40) D 5, 11; (43) N 2; (45) Ja 4; (49) My 21; (55) O 15, N 8.
The Way to Get Married, or The Affectionate Daughter; *Morton:* (02)
Ap 21, N 19; (06) Ja 15; (07) Ju 5; (08) Ap 1; (11) F 8, Mr 1;
(12) Ap 13; (17) D 15; (21) Ap 13; (24) Ja 7, F 26; (25) Ap 18;
(40) N 13.
The Way to Keep Him; *Murphy:* (24) My 10.
Ways and Means, or A Trip to Dover; *Coleman:* (03) Mr 16, 25; (04)
Ap 6; (08) F 20; (11) F 27; (13) Ja 18; (20) Ap 8, My 3; (21)
Mr 17.
We Fly by Night, or Long Stories; *Coleman:* (07) Ju 1, 5; (08) F 6,
10, 17, Mr 9, D 2; (28) Ap 12.
The Weathercock, or Love Alone Can Fix Him; *Allingham:* (06) N 10,
18; (07) Ja 6, Ap 9, N 11; (08) Ja 16; (09) Ja 27; (10) Ap 7;
(11) Ja 16; (16) Ja 24, 27; (17) F 27; (20) Ja 7, D 11; (21) Mr
23; (24) My 3; (26) D 30; (27) Ap 7; (30) Ja 6; (33) Mr 1, 7,
12, Ju 15; (40) Ja 17, F 19, My 21; (41) F 18; (45) D 22; (48)
F 18.

The Wedding Day; *(Inchbald):* (07) My 4; (08) Ap 27, My 11; (10) F 28; (18) My 4, 16; (24) My 21; (25) F 23, Ap 14; (27) Ja 22, Mr 24; (29) N 23; (30) Mr 26, D 15; (36) Mr 9; (52) D 22.

The Welsh Girl: (55) Ja 4.

The Wept of Wish-ton-wish, or The Indian Girl: (46) N 16, 20; (58) D 28; (59) Ja 5.

Werner, or The Inheritance: (44) Ja 12, 14, 18, D 13; (49) Ja 17; (51) F 28; (55) Mr 30.

The West End, or The Irish Heiress; *Boucicault:* (45) D 30; (47) Ja 16.

The West-Indian; *Cumberland:* (01) F 25; (02) Mr 5, N 8; (03) N 17; (04) N 16; (07) My 22; (11) Ja 21, Mr 8; (16) N 6; (18) Mr 11; (20) N 23; (23) Jy 2, N 28; (25) F 16; (31) Ap 4; (39) My 28.

West-Point Preserved, or The Death of Major André; *Brown:* (02) Ap 26.

What Is She?, or The Female Stranger: (06) Mr 10.

What Will the World Say?; *Lemon:* (43) F 6, 9, 22.

The Wheel of Fortune, or The Misanthrope; *Cumberland:* (05) F 7, Mr 11; (06) Ap 18; (07) Ap 15; (08) Ap 22; (09) Ja 2, F 22; (10) F 27; (18) Ap 6; (20) Ap 22; (27) Ja 1.

Where Shall I Dine?: (20) Ja 5, 17; (28) D 17.

Where There's a Will There's a Way; *Morton:* (52) D 25.

Which Is the Man?, or The Soldier of Honor; *Cowley:* (04) My 7; (05) Mr 15; (09) Mr 14.

Whim upon Whim, or Harlequin Skeleton (or Harlequin Pastry Cook): (04) F 8, 15; (05) D 26; (06) D 17; (07) Ja 19, D 22, 30; (08) F 24; (11) Ap 15.

Whims of a Comedian: (28) D 6, 9; (32) Mr 1.

Whirligig Hall: (33) F 27, Mr 6.

The White Horse of the Peppers, or Ireland in the Year 1690: (41) F 22, 23, 25; (45) Mr 26; (57) Mr 12, 13; (59) F 9, 11.

The White Milliner: (45) Ja 21.

The White Rose, or The Conspiracy: (40) My 13.

Who Do They Take Me For?: (48) D 27, 28.

Who Speaks First?; *Dance:* (51) Ap 14, 19; (52) F 11; (57) D 7; (59) Ap 11.

Who Wants a Guinea?; *Coleman:* (05) N 27, D 16; (06) F 17; (08) Mr 7; (15) N 17; (17) Ap 11; (21) My 7; (30) Ja 25.

Who's the Dupe?; *Cowley:* (06) Ja 27, F 28; (07) Ja 30; (08) F 29; (27) Mr 19, 31.

The Widow Slow, or Female Outwitted: (12) D 23.

The Widow Wiggins; *Buckstone:* (40) F 23, 25, Mr 2, 7, Ap 8, 13; (42) Ja 7, 13, 17, 31.

The Widow's Victim: (39) Ja 9, F 18; (45) Mr 12, 13, 15; (51) Ap 23; (59) N 3.

Wife for a Day: (43) N 27, 29, D 4, 13.

The Wife of Two Husbands; *Dunlap:* (05) N 20, 25; (06) F 20.

The Wife, or A Tale of Mantua; *Knowles:* (36) F 22, 23, Mr 10, 11, 12, 31; (37) D 21; (38) Ap 23; (40) N 5; (41) D 18; (43) F 7; (45) N 12, D 6; (46) Ja 24, D 2; (48) F 2, 3; (50) F 6, Mr 12; (51) My 9; (52) F 11, 26, D 4; (53) N 3; (56) D 12; (57) Ja 24, D 7; (59) Ja 27; (60) Ap 18.

The Wild Goose Chase; *Dunlap:* (04) Mr 2, 7; (05) F 15.

Wild Oats, or The Strolling Gentleman; *O'Keeffe:* (03) D 7, 20; (04) Mr 23; (11) Mr 4; (18) F 26, N 6; (20) My 15; (21) My 16; (24) Ja 9; (25) Mr 4; (34) D 6, 8; (40) N 9, 19; (44) Mr 6, 12; (56) N 22, 25.

Wilful Murder: (50) Ja 24, F 1, Mr 11.

Will for the Deed; *Dibdin:* (06) D 23; (07) Ja 16, F 20, Ap 13.

The Will, or A School for Daughters (or The Old Bachelor in the Straw, or A Lesson for Daughters, or The Benevolent Daughter) ; *(Reynolds):* (00) F 19; (03) Mr 11, Ap 28; (09) Ja 21; (16) My 8, N 4; (17) D 13; (20) Ja 1; (27) Ja 5, My 23; (29) Mr 13, N 13; (30) Mr 12; (32) F 22; (36) F 17; (40) F 25, Mr 3.

Will Watch, the Bold Smuggler: (35) D 8.

William Tell, or The Swiss Patriot (or The Hero of Switzerland); *Knowles:* (27) Ja 8, 10, 15, 29, Mr 19; (28) F 1; (29) Ap 8, 25; (39) Mr 15; (40) Ap 23, My 23; (41) Ja 6, 23; (43) Ja 27, N 24; (45) F 20, Mr 4; (46) Ja 8; (51) F 6; (55) Ja 31; (56) Ja 8, 9.

The Willow Copse; *Boucicault:* (56) Ja 8, 16; (57) O 29, 30, N 11; (60) Mr 19.

The Windmill: (55) F 19, 20, 28; (56) Ja 5, 7, Mr 6.

Wine Does Wonders, or The Way to Win Him: (24) Ja 12; (29) Ap 1.

Winning a Husband, or Seven's the Main: (30) Ja 20, Mr 31, D 13; (31) F 24.

A Winter's Tale; *Shakespeare:* (11) Ap 1, 17.

The Wise Man of the East, or Modern Magic; *Inchbald:* (02) Mr 17.

Wives as They Were and Maids as They Are; *Inchbald:* (00) Mr 28; (01) F 10; (04) My 11; (06) Ja 1; (09) Mr 3; (13) Ja 1; (16) F 7; (17) Ja 9, 15, 31; (18) F 28; (20) F 23, My 13; (21) My 19; (29) F 28; (30) F 10, D 6; (31) Mr 14; (35) Mr 80; (42) Mr 2; (43) F 15, N 8; (45) D 19; (46) F 24, D 21; (56) Ja 26, 28.

Wives Metamorphosed: (11) Ja 21.

The Wizard of the Wave, or The Mighty Man of Garth: (47) Ja 4, 5, 6, 12.

The Wolf and Lamb; *Matthews:* (33) F 11; (47) Ja 29, F 22.

The Wolf and the Fox: (40) D 28.

Woman—Her Love! Her Faith! Her Trials!: (50) My 3.

Woman's Wit; *Knowles:* (40) Ap 21.

The Wonder, or A Woman Keeps a Secret; *Centlivre:* (01) Ja 23, My 1; (02) N 12; (03) N 21, D 14; (04) N 23; (07) My 6; (08) Mr 4; (11) Ap 29; (16) Ja 15, 27, Mr 1, D 16; (18) F 16; (19) D 22; (20) Mr 7, D 23; (23) Ju 13; (24) F 4, 6; (25) Ja 29, F 21; (27) Mr 14, 26; (29) F 26, N 10; (32) Mr 16; (33) F 13; (37) D 22; (39) N 10; (41) Mr 9, N 27; (43) My 16; (44) F 27; (46) F 18, D 3; (48) Ja 5; (51) Ja 25, F 1, 26; (56) F 4, 7, D 11; (57) N 6.

The Wood Demon, or The Clock Has Struck; *Turnbull:* (09) Mr 27; (10) Mr 10, Ap 16; (25) F 23, 25, 28, Ap 15.

The Woodcutters: (09) Ja 16, F 22; (10) Ap 7; (11) Ap 26.

The Woodman's Hut, or The Forest of Bohemia: (21) Ap 23, 27, 30, N 23.

The Wool Dealer: (35) Mr 11; (44) N 28; (47) F 13, 16; (52) Mr 15, 17.

The Wool Pedlar: (44) Ap 3.

Working the Oracle: (58) F 26, 27, Mr 12.

The World: (08) D 9.

The World as It Goes, or A Touch at the Times; *Cowley:* (06) My 22.

The Wreck Ashore, or A Bridegroom from the Sea (or The Rover's Bride); *Buckstone:* (43) F 10, 11; (55) Ap 11, 17.
The Wrecker's Daughter; *Knowles:* (45) N 17; (46) N 24; (52) Mr 2, 6; (53) D 24; (54) Ja 21.

X. Y. Z., or The American Manager; *Coleman:* (29) F 19, 23; (41) Mr 1.

Yankee Doodle: (51) O 11.
The Yankee Gal: (58) F 22, 24.
The Yankee Housekeeper: (59) Mr 21.
Yankee Land, or The Foundling of an Apple Orchard: *Logan:* (44) Ap 2, N 25, 30.
The Yankee Pedlar, or Old Times in Virginia; *Barnett:* (34) N 17, 20; (43) N 30, D 5.
Yard Arm and Yard Yarm: (29) Mr 27.
The Yemassee; *(Simms):* (45) Ja 6, 7.
Yes and No: (11) Mr 11.
You Can't Marry Your Grandmother; *Bayley:* (39) My 30; (40) Ja 20, Mr 11; (46) F 25; (47) Ja 1.
The Young Actress; *Boucicault:* (56) Mr 13, 14, 15, 17, 25, 26, 29, D 15, 16, 17, 20, 25; (58) Mr 1, 10; (59) Mr 19.
The Young Ambassador: (46) D 29.
Young America: (45) N 4; (47) Ja 12; (50) F 13, Ap 23; (52) D 31; (53) Ja 5, 17; (54) F 28, Mr 22, Ap 8; (55) Mr 9, 14, 21.
The Young Couple: (53) Ja 12, 13, 14, 15, 17, 20, 21, 26, 29.
Young England: (50) F 6.
The Young Hussar; *Dimond:* (38) Mr 5, Ap 6; (41) D 29.
The Young Jockey: (53) F 3.
The Young Lovers, or The Daring Theft: (30) Mr 31.
The Young Quaker, or The Fair American; *O'Keeffe:* (03) My 10; (07) F 6; (19) My 10; (20) D 13; (22) My 8; (25) Mr 11.
Young Scamp, or My Grandmother's Pet: (53) Ja 24, 27; (54) D 23; (55) Mr 29.
The Young Widow, or Lessons for Lovers: (29) Ap 11, N 14, 28; (34) Ja 27; (35) Ap 20; (36) Mr 2, Ap 9; (38) Mr 21, 26; (43) Mr 13; (45) Ja 30, F 10; (47) F 8, 11; (48) F 23; (49) My 24; (59) N 7.
Your Life's in Danger; *Morton:* (54) N 6, 9, 16, 21; (55) Ja 19, F 22, Mr 1, 20; (57) N 4, 12, 26; (58) Ap 12.
Youth, Love and Folly; *Dimond:* (32) F 21.
Youth, Love, and Matrimony, or They Are Their Own Rivals; *Remoussin:* (08) My 4.
Youth of Frederick the Great: (58) D 24.
Youthful Days of Mr. Hyatt: (24) Ap 24.
The Youthful Queen, or Christine of Sweden; *Shannon:* (38) Ja 19, 22; (39) My 11; (40) F 5, D 3, 21; (44) F 9, Mr 14; (47) Ja 7; (49) Ja 11, 12.

Zembuca, or The Net Maker and His Wife; *Pocock:* (24) Mr 24, 29, Ap 24; (25) F 11, 16.
Zemire and Azor: (05) Mr 8, 25.
Zorinski, or Liberty in Poland (or Struggle for Liberty); *Morton:* (08) My 17; (18) My 8.

IX: THE PLAYER LIST

THE FOLLOWING PAGES contain a list of the players who appeared on the Charleston stages between 1800-1861. The numerals which follow each entry refer to the seasonal years in which the actor or company appeared. If the reader will look for that season in the Annual Chronological Records (Chapter VII), he will find the name, status, dates, or rôles played by that individual or the performances presented by that company.

Abbott, William, mgr., 37-38, 38-39, 39-40, 40-41.

A'Beckett, Thomas, 38-39, 39-40 (D 13-27, Ja 20–F 3), 43-44 (Mr 7-11).

A'Beckett, Mrs. Thomas, 39-40 (D 13-27, Ja 20–F 3), 43-44 (Mr 7-11).

Abella, 56-57 (My 11).

Adams, F. C., mgr., 49-50, 51-52.

Adams, J. J., 26-27; mgr., 28-29, 29-30.

Adamson, 16-17.

Adamson, Miss, 34-35.

Adeline, Miss, 54-55.

Aeolian Minstrels Company, 53-54 (Mr 7-10).

Aiken, F., 55-56.

Aiken, George L., 54-55, 57-58.

Alaimo, Carolina, 59-60 (F 20–Mr 14).

Albertine, Miss, 55-56 (Ap 7-21).

Alcedid, 47-48 (N 4-17).

Alexander, Herr, 48-49 (My 7-15).

Alinson, 59-60.

Allen, 19-20, 26-27.

Allen, A. J., 45-46, 48-49.

Allen, J. H., 51-52, 52-53.

Allen, Mrs. J. H., 52-53.

Amilee, Miss, 47-48, 49-50.

Amodio, A., 56-57 (F 16-17), 57-58 (Mr 2-6).

Anderson, Mrs., 20-21.

Anderson, D. C., 45-46.

Anderson, David (?), 35-36.

Anderson, James, 11-12, 12-13.

Anderson, James R., 46-47 (Ja 18-23).

Anderton, E. W., 45-46, 49-50.

Anderton, W. A., 53-54.

Andes, 24-25.

Andrews, 16-17.

Andrews, A., 44-45 (Ja 29–F 15), 47-48 (Ja 12-27), 48-49 (Mr 16-24).

Andrews, L. S., 37-38.

Ansell, 27-28.

Antonia, Il Diavolo, and Family, 35-36 (N 23–D 9).

Apparisso, 26-27.

Archbold, Mrs., 54-55.

Archer, Thomas, 42-43 (Mr 3-18, Ap 10-27).

Arditi, Luigi, 49-50 (Mr 26–Ap 2).

Arnold, G. J. (?), 45-46.

Arnold, James, 60-61 (N 19-26).

Arnold, M. A., 56-57.

Arnot, Louisa, 59-60 (Ja 2-14).

Arraline, Mrs., 40-41 (D 28–Ja 1).

Ashe, W. A., 54-55.

Ashley, Miss, 58-59.

Ashmer, Mr. and Mrs. J. G., 53-54.

Aspinall, Miss, 25-26.

Assoni, 57-58 (Mr 2-6).

Augusta, Madame, Ballet Troupe, 47-48 (F 14–Mr 28).

Austen, Mrs., 55-56.

Austin, 23-24.

Avogardo, L., 56-57 (F 16-17), 57-58 (Mr 2-6).

Ayling, Mr. and Mrs. W. L., 56-57.

Bachelier, 05-06.

Bailey, 07-08, 33-34, 34-35, 35-36.

Bailey, Mrs., 34-35.

Bailey, C. G., 04-05, 05-06, 06-07, 08-09.

Baralli, N., 59-60 (F 20–Mr 14).

Baratini, Timeoleon, 49-50 (Mr 26–Ap 2).

Barber, 38-39.

Barnes, Miss Charlotte M. S., 34-35, 35-36, 37-38, 39-40 (F 4-10), 41-42.

Barnes, John, 27-28 (F 13–Mr 18).

Barnes, J. (?), 34-35, 35-36, 37-38, 39-40, 41-42.

Barnes, Mrs. J. (?), 28-29, 34-35, 35-36, 37-38, 39-40, 41-42.

Barre, Miss Ducy, 54-55, 55-56.

Barrett, Master, 07-08.

Barrett, Mrs. G., 43-44.

Barrett, Mr. and Mrs. G. H., 23-24, 24-25, 52-53.

Barrett, G. L., 00-01, 01-02, 04-05, 07-08.

Barrett, Mrs. G. L., 00-01, 01-02, 04-05, 07-08, 15-16, 16-17, 17-18, 18-19, 19-20, 20-21, 22-23.

Barrett, J. H., 58-59.

Barry, Miss, 31-32.

Barry, John, 24-25, 29-30.

Barry, Mrs. John, 29-30.

Barry, M. E., 51-52.

Barrymore, 04-05.

Barton, 10-11, 11-12, 27-28, 31-32, 32-33.

Barton, Marie, 60-61.

Bass, Charles, 47-48.

Basson, Miss, 58-59.

Bateman Family (Mr. and Mrs. H. L., Kate, and Ellen), 52-53 Ja 12-29).

Bates, William, 05-06, 06-07.

Battersby, Mrs., 25-26.

Beaumont, 10-11 (Mr 29–Ap 22).

Beaumont, Mrs., 10-11 (Mr 13–Ap 22).

Beck, 39-40.

Beckwith, 32-33.

Bedouin Arabs Company, 38-39 (D 26–Ja 8, My 7), 48-49 (Ap 16-21).

Bellamy, William H., 40-41, 43-44, 49-50.

Belletti, 50-51 (D 26-28).

Bellini, Miss Louisa, 49-50 (Mr 26–Ap 2).

Benedetti, Sesto, 50-51 (Mr 21–Ap 9).

Benedetti, Signora Truffi, 50-51 (Mr 21–Ap 9).

Benedict, Julius, 50-51.

Bennett, Julia, 51-52 (Ja 26-31).

Bennetti, 47-48 (Ja 12-27), 48-49 (Mr 16-24).

Bennie, Mr. and Mrs., 42-43.

Benson, 34-35, 38-39.

Benton, 20-21.

Benventano, 51-52 (N 10-25).

Benvuevento, 50-51 (Mr 21–Ap 9).

Berger, 43-44.

Berger, Octavia, 43-44.

Bernard, Charles, 21-22, 24-25.

Bernard, Mrs. Charles, *See* Miss Tilden.

Bernard, John, 07-08.

Berry, 05-06, 10-11, 11-12.

Beverley, 57-58.

Biadiali, Frederico, 49-50 (Mr 26–Ap 2).

Bignall, 21-22.

Bihin, Mons., 54-55 (Ja 4-6).

Bishop, Madame Anna, Opera Troupe, 47-48 (Ja 12-27), 48-49 (Mr 16-24).

Bishop, R. R., 21-22.

Bishop, Thomas, 38-39 (F 11-23, Mr 18–Ap 6, My 2-10).

Blake, Miss Fanny, 56-57.

Blake, William Rufus, 29-30.

Blake, Mrs. William Rufus, *See* Caroline Placide.

Blakeley, Thomas, 25-26.

Bland, W. H., 55-56.

Blangy, Madame, Dance Troupe, 50-51 (Ja 27–F 8).

Blondeau, Mlle., 51-52 (O 28–N 8).

Blondin, M., 58-59 (Ja 10-22, F 15-24).

Bokee, Mr. and Miss, 52-53.

Booth, Edwin, 49-50 (F 16), 57-58 (F 17-20), 58-59 (Mr 22–Ap 11), 59-60 (Mr 20–Ap 4).

Booth, Junius Brutus, Sr., 21-22 (N 29–D 11, F 22–Mr 1), 24-25 Mr 18-30), 37-38 (Mr 13-29), 43-44 (F 19-24), 44-45 (D 23-31),

49-50 (F 12-16), 51-52 (Mr 22-30).

Boree, [99]-00.

Boscha, Robert N. Charles, 47-48 (Ja 12-27), 48-49 (Mr 16-24).

Bossio, Angelina, 49-50, 51-52.

Bottardi, Stecchi, 57-58 (Mr 2-6).

Bottesini, 49-50 (Mr 26–Ap 2).

Boucicault, Dion, 55-56 (Mr 17-29), 56-57 (D 15-27).

Boudinot, Mr. and Mrs. F. B., 60-61.

Boullan, 39-40 (D 13-27, Ja 20–F 6).

Bowler, Brookhouse, 60-61.

Boyle, 16-17.

Bradshaw, Mr. and Mrs. John J., 53-54.

Branthwaite, 01-02.

Brauer, 49-50.

Braun, 50-51 (D 26-28).

Bray, Mr. and Mrs. John, 09-10.

Brazier, 22-23.

Brennen, 21-22.

Brett, Mrs., 03-04.

Brignoli, F., 56-57, 57-58.

Bristow, 30-31.

Broadhurst, Miss, 01-02, 02-03.

Brock, Adam, *See* E. B. Williams.

Brooks, 18-19, 19-20.

Brooks, Mrs., 39-40.

Brosa, Juan, 21-22.

Brough, William Francis, 38-39, 39-40, 40-41, 47-48, 48-49.

Brougham, Mrs. John, 43-44 (Ja 13, F 8-14).

Brown, 32-33, 50-51.

Brown, C. M., 58-59.

Brown, Frederick, 16-17, 18-19, 19-20, 21-22, 22-23, 23-24, 24-25, 26-27, 30-31, 32-33.

Brown, Mrs. Frederick, 21-22, 22-23, 23-24, 24-25, 26-27, 27-28, 31-32, 32-33.

Brown, John Mills, 27-28 (Ap 9-26).

Brown, Mr. and Mrs. J. M., 28-29, 29-30.

Browne, James F., 57-58.

Browne, James S., 40-41 (N 9-20).

Bruno, 60-61 (N 19-26).

Buckley's Burlesque Opera Troupe, 59-60 (N 21-25).

Buckstone, John Baldwin, 41-42, (Ja 4-17, 31).

Bulan, Mlle., 51-52 (O 20–N 8).

Bunyie, Miss, 40-41.

Burd, 06-07.

Burke, Charles, 51-52 (Mr 8-20).

Burke, Master Joseph, 32-33 (F 26–Mr 15).

Burke, Thomas, 02-03, 11-12, 12-13, 20-21.

Burke, Mrs. Thomas, *See* Miss Thomas.

Burns, T. A., 56-57.

Burrie, Daniel, 26-27.

Burroughs, Watkins, 27-28 (Ap 9-26).

Burton, 38-39.

Burton, William E., 39-40 (N 28–D 9), 58-59 (N 29–D 11).

Butler, 36-37.

Butler, Samuel W., 41-42 (F 1, 7-12).

Byrne, J., 41-42, 45-46.

Byrne, Mrs. J., 45-46.

Cadwallader, 33-34.

Caldwell, J. H., 16-17; mgr., 20-21.

Camden, 34-35.

Campbell's Minstrels, 53-54 (S 26–O 2), 55-56 (F 19-25), 57-58 (F 8-13).

Cappell, Mrs., 54-55.

Cappell, Miss Cordelia, 54-55, 57-58.

Caresi, 50-51 (Mr 21–Ap 9).

Carey, Master, 22-23, 23-24.

Carpenter, 17-18.

Carpenter, Miss and Mrs., 49-50.

Carriere, Eugene, 47-48 (N 4-17).

Carter, Miss, 33-34.

Carter, Mrs., 34-35, 35-36.

Carter, James (?), 33-34.

Cassells, 55-56.

Catherine, Miss, 07-08 (F 15–Mr 25).

Caulfield, 09-10, 10-11, 11-12, 12-13.

Celeste, Miss, 44-45, 45-46.

Chalmers, [99]-00, 00-01, 02-03.

Chambers, [99]-00.

Chambers, Mrs., *See* Charlotte Sully.

Chanfrau, F. S., 53-54 (Ja 2-14), 55-56 (Ap 7-21).

Chapman, Mrs., 50-51.
Charles, Miss, 43-44.
Charles, Mr. and Mrs. J. S., 43-44, 44,45.
Charleston Volunteers, 61-[62] (N 28-30).
Charnock, 02-03, 03-04, 04-05.
Chatel, 52-53, 53-54.
Chekini, 52-53.
Chippendale, F., 57-58.
Chippendale, W., 49-50, 54-55.
Chippendale, Mrs. W., 44-45.
Chizzola, 37-38.
Christy's, George, Minstrels, 60-61 (D 17-20).
Church, 02-03.
Clairville, Mrs., 45-46.
Clarke, 05-06, 06-07, 07-08, 08-09, 09-10, 10-11, 11-12, 12-13, 17-18, 18-19, 19-20.
Clarke, Miss, 50-51.
Clarke, Mrs., 06-07, 07-08, 08-09, 09-10, 10-11, 11-12, 12-13, 17-18, 18-19, 19-20.
Clarke, Miss Caroline, 10-11, 11-12, 17-18, 18-19, 19-20, 20-21.
Clarke, Master Edward, 17-18, 20-21.
Clarke, Miss Emily, 34-35.
Clarke, Frederick, 50-51.
Clarke, N. B., 30-31.
Claude, John, 05-06, 06-07, 08-09.
Claude, Mrs. John, 05-06, 06-07, 08-09, 17-18.
Claveau, 33-34.
Cleary, 18-19 (F 6-26, Mr 3-Ap 30).
Clifford, 38-39, 39-40.
Clifford, J. W., 52-53.
Clifton, Miss, 57-58.
Clifton, Miss Josephine, 32-33 (N 26-D 17, F 15), 37-38 (Ja 11), 39-40 (Ap 15-17), 44-45 (Ja 27-F 8).
Cline, Mrs., 43-44.
Cline, Herr Andre, 29-30 (N 9-23), 44-45 (Ja 9-13).
Clinton, 57-58.
Clough, 08-09, 09-10.
Coad, Miss, 41-42 (D 7-16, Mr 12-29), 42-43 (Mr 3-18, Ap 10-27).
Codet, 41-42.
Coemans, 50-51 (Mr 21-Ap 9).
Colby, George W., 60-61.

Coleman, E. B., 58-59.
Collett, Master, 25-26.
Colletti, Dominico, 49-50 (Mr 26-Ap 2), 56-57 (F 16-17), 57-58 (Mr 2-6).
Collingbourne, 25-26.
Collins, 01-02, 10-11, 29-30, 44-45.
Collins, Mrs., 29-30.
Collins, Holywell, 60-61 (N 19-26).
Collins, John, 46-47 (D 22-Ja 2), 47-48 (Ja 6-11), 48-49 (D 30), 59-60 (O 31-N 10).
Colvin, 39-40.
Condi, Pietro, 49-50 (Mr 26-Ap 2).
Coney and Webb's Trained Dogs, 54-55 (Ja 22-27).
Conway, Mrs. E. L., 38-39 (My 30).
Conway, Mr. and Mrs. Fred, 54-55 (F 6-17).
Conway, H. J., 38-39, 44-45.
Conway, William A., 24-25 (D 1-Ja 3).
Cook, Aynsley, 60-61 (N 19-26).
Cook, F. C., 45-46.
Cooke, 24-25, 35-36.
Cooke, Henry, 58-59.
Coon, Zip (Hall), 33-34 (D 21-Ja 1).
Cooper, H. C., English Opera Troupe, 60-61 (N 19-26).
Cooper, Miss Priscilla, 34-35 (Mr 16-30), 37-38 (Ja 4-15).
Cooper, Thomas Apthorpe, 05-06 (Ap 14-My 16), 06-07 (Ap 9-My 27), 08-09 (Ja 27-F 27), 09-10 (F 12-Mr 7), 15-16 (Mr 20-Ap 8), 17-18 (Mr 25-Ap 20), 18-19 (F 1-Mr 1, Ap 13-28), 19-20 (F 2, 11-14, Mr 17-27, Ap 17-My 1), 20-21 (My 25-30), 26-27 (F 7-Mr 7), 28-29 (D 12-19), 29-30 (Ja 29-Mr 4), 30-31 (Mr 1-18), 31-32 (F 27-Mr 2), 34-35 (Mr 4-30), 37-38 (Ja 4-15).
Cooper Ballet Team, [99]-00.
Corby, Mlle., 51-52 (O 20-N 8).
Corrigan, J., 58-59, 59-60.
Coster, Miss, 28-29, 29-30.
Costini, Elisa, 49-50 (Mr 26-Ap 2).
Couldock, Charles Walter, 49-50 (Ap 15-24).
Coult, 33-34.
Cowell, Joe, mgr., 25-26.

Durivage, O. E. (?), 37-38, 43-44, 57-58.
Duvenelle, Mrs., 45-46.
Dwyer, 57-58.
Dwyer, John Hambury, 10-11 (Ja 19–F 16, 25–Mr 9), 17-18 (Ja 15, F 4-16, Mr 11).
Dyball, 22-23.
Dykes, 02-03, 03-04, 04-05, 05-06, 21-22, 33-34.
Dykes, Mrs., 02-03, 03-04, 04-05, 05-06, 33-34.
Dyott, John, mgr., 26-27.
Dyott, John (?), 57-58.

Eastcott, Mrs., 46-47.
Eberle, Henry, 30-31, 38-39.
Eberle, Mrs. Henry, 38-39.
Eckhardt, Mr. and Mrs. H., 58-59, 59-60.
Eckhardt, J., 05-06, 23-24.
Edwards, H. (?), 49-50, 53-54.
Edwin, 37-38.
Eichrenbach, 51-52 (O 8-18).
Eldred, G. N., mgr., 48-49.
Ellis, Clara, 45-46 (N 4-17), 46-47 (N 18–D 7).
Ellis, W. (?), 35-36, 45-46, 46-47.
Ellis, Mrs. W. (?), 46-47.
Ellsler, Fanny, 40-41 (D 28–Ja 1).
Ellsler, John, 50-51; mgr., 51-52.
Ellsler, Mrs. John, 51-52.
Elmore, Mr. and Mrs. Marcus, 58-59, 59-60.
Elton, 51-52.
Entwistle, Mr. and Mrs., 20-21.
Espinosa, Leon, 51-52 (O 8-18).
Essender, 26-27.
Estell, Miss Katy, 59-60.
Estelle, 26-27, 27-28.
Evain, W. H., 53-54.
Evans, George, 57-58.
Eveline, Miss, 51-52.
Everett, 51-52.

Farren, Miss, 35-36.
Farren, Henry, 54-55 (Ja 9-13).
Farren, Mrs. G. P., 53-54 (Ja 16-21).
Faulconbridge, 41-42.
Faulkner, Thomas, 17-18, 18-19, 19-20, 20-21, 21-22, 22-23, 23-24, 24-25; mgr., 29-30, 30-31.

Faulkner, Mrs. Thomas, 17-18, 18-19, 19-20, 20-21, 21-22, 22-23, 23-24.
Faulkrod, Emily Virginia, 52-53.
Felix, Mlles. Dinah, Lia, and Sarah, *See* Mlle. Rachel Dramatic Corps.
Fenelon, E., 55-56.
Fennell, James Jr., 16-17, 17-18, 18-19, 19-20.
Fenno, William A., 31-32.
Feron, Madame, 29-30 (N 25–D 14).
Ferrin, Louis, 47-48 (N 4-17).
Field, Miss, 03-04, 04-05, 08-09.
Field, J. M., 31-32, 32-33, 33-34, 34-35.
Field, J. R., 40-41.
Fielding, 20-21, 26-27, 28-29.
Finn, Henry J., 18-19, 19-20, 20-21, 34-35, 38-39.
Fiot, L., 51-52 (O 8-18).
Fisher, Clara, 28-29 (Mr 11–Ap 8), 29-30 (Mr 10-26), 31-32 (F 21-22, Mr 2, 15-21).
Fisher, G., 56-57.
Fisher, Miss Kate, 55-56.
Fiske, Moses W., 57-58.
Fitzjames, Mlle. Nathalie, 50-51 (Mr 21–Ap 9).
Fitzwilliam, Fanny, 39-40 (F 24–Mr 9, Ap 8-13), 41-42 (Ja 4-17, 31).
Fleming, William M., 42-43, 44-45, 49-50 (F 8-11).
Fletcher, 51-52.
Florence, Mr. and Mrs. W. J., 57-58 (F 22–Mr 1, 8-13), 58-59 (Mr 17-21).
Floyd, William Randolph, 35-36.
Flynn, Thomas, 32-33, 37-38.
Flynn, Mrs. Thomas, 32-33.
Forbes, W. C., 32-33, 34-35; mgr., 42-43, 43-44, 44-45, 45-46, 46-47.
Forbes, Mrs. W. C., 42-43, 43-44, 44-45, 45-46, 46-47.
Ford, John T., 53-54.
Forrest, Edwin, 30-31 (F 21–Mr 7), 40-41 (Ja 11-23), 43-44 (F 15-17), 46-47 (Ja 25–F 6).
Forti, 50-51 (Mr 21–Ap 9).
Foster, 09-10, 10-11.
Foucard, 17-18, 21-22.
Fournier, 03-04.

Harper, 06-07, 07-08, 24-25.
Harper, Mrs., 06-07, 24-25.
Harrington, W., mgr., 32-33, 33-34; 40-41.
Harris, Miss, 53-54.
Harrison, 37-38.
Harrison, Mr. and Mrs. C. B., 56-57, 57-58.
Hart, 31-32; mgr., 32-33, 33-34, 34-35, 35-36.
Hart, Mrs. 34-35, 35-36.
Hatch, Mrs., 26-27.
Hatton, 06-07, 23-24.
Hatton, Mrs., 06-07, 07-08.
Hautonville, Mr. and Mrs., 39-40.
Havana Italian Opera Company, 49-50 (Mr 26–Ap 2), 57-58 (Mr 2-6).
Haviland, 55-56.
Hayes, Mr. and Mrs., 19-20.
Hayman, 04-05, 06-07, 07-08, 08-09.
Hayne, Mrs., *See* Julia Dean.
Hedderley, 15-16.
Henkins, Harry, 37-38, 39-40, 49-50.
Henri, Miss, 53-54.
Henry, William, Mr. and Mrs., and Miss, 41-42.
Herbert, C., 56-57, 57-58.
Herbert, John, 26-27, 27-28, 37-38.
Herbert, Mrs. J., 37-38.
Heron Family, The (J., Agnes Heron and others), 48-49 (My 21-28).
Herz, Henry, 47-48 (N 4-17).
Heyward, Mrs., 57-58.
Hield, Mr. and Mrs. C. W., 48-49, 52-53.
Higgins, 20-21.
Hilariot, Antonio and Charles, 51-52 (O 8-18).
Hildreth, Miss Sarah, 40-41.
Hill, Mrs., 28-29.
Hill, Charles Barton, 53-54.
Hill, Frederick S. (?), 30-31.
Hill, G. H. ("Yankee"), 33-34 (Mr 21), 34-35 (N 14-24), 42-43, 43-44.
Hillyard, 38-39.
Hilson, Thomas, 15-16, 17-18, 18-19, 19-20, 20-21, 21-22, 22-23, 32-33.
Hilson, Mrs. Thomas, 32-33.
Hind, T. J., 53-54.
Hockney, 20-21.
Hodgkinson, Miss, 03-04.

Hodgkinson, John, 03-04, 04-05.
Hodson, George, and Miss Georgia, 57-58 (Ja 17–F 6), 58-59 (F 28–Mr 8).
Hogg, Mrs., 05-06, 06-07.
Holdridge, Miss, 56-57.
Holland, 08-09.
Holland, George, 28-29 (D 5-10), 31-32.
Holloway, 16-17.
Holman, Mrs., 16-17.
Holman, G., 46-47 (F 22–Mr 6), 48-49 (D 7-16, Ja 1-6).
Holman, Joseph G., 15-16, 16-17.
Holman, Mrs. Joseph G., *See* Miss Lattimer.
Holmes, 06-07, 08-09, 11-12, 15-16.
Homer, Miss, 46-47.
Hood, 34-35.
Hood, Miss, 43-44.
Hopkins, 17-18.
Horn, Miss, 38-39.
Horncastle, James Henry, 39-40 (Mr 11-28).
Horton, 15-16, 16-17, 18-19, 20-21, 21-22, 22-23, 23-24, 24-25, 26-27.
Horton, Mrs., 15-16, 16-17, 20-21, 21-22, 24-25, 26-27.
Hosack, 27-28.
Hosmer, Adele, 56-57.
Howard, Charles, 41-42, 54-55 (D 18–Ja 6).
Howard, Mrs. Charles, 54-55 (D 18–Ja 6).
Howard, James, 19-20, 24-25.
Howard, Louisa, 54-55 (Ja 9-13).
Hudson, James, 49-50 (Mr 18-23).
Huggins, 24-25.
Hughes, [99]-00, 03-04, 04-05, 22-23, 23-24, 31-32.
Hughes, Mrs., [99]-00, 22-23, 23-24, 26-27, 27-28, 31-32, 39-40, 40-41, 42-43.
Hughes, Mrs., 58-59 (N 29–D 11).
Humber, 21-22.
Hunt, Charles (?), 45-46.
Hunter, 24-25.
Huntingdon, 07-08.
Hurley, 60-61 (N 19-26).
Hutin, Mrs., 28-29.
Hutton, Mr. and Mrs., 20-21.
Hyatt, George, 17-18, 18-19, 20-21, 21-22, 23-24, 24-25, 32-33.

Ince, Annette, 54-55 (O 30–N 11), 56-57 (Ja 19–F 14).
Ince, Emma, 42-43.
Incledon, Benjamin Charles, 17-18 (Ap 13-24).
Ingersoll, Miss, 55-56.
Inverarity, Miss, 40-41 (F 20).
Irving, 54-55 (Ja 16-20).
Irving, John B., mgr., 27-28, 29-30.
Irving, R., 37-38.
Isherwood, H., 25-26, 41-42, 42-43.
Isherwood, Mrs. H., 42-43, 44-45.
Isherwood, W., 25-26.
Italian Opera Company, 50-51 (Mr 21–Ap 9), 59-60 (F 20–Mr 14).

Jackson, [99]-00, 00-01, 30-31, 53-54.
Jacobs, 07-08.
Jacobs, 59-60 (Ap 23-28).
James, Mrs., 45-46.
Jamie, 25-26.
Jamieson, George, 37-38.
Jeannette, Mlle., 51-52, (O 8-18).
Jefferson, Mrs. J. J., 50-51, 51-52.
Jefferson, Joseph J., 50-51; mgr., 51-52.
Jefferson, T., 20-21.
Jenny, Mlle., 51-52 (O 8-18).
Jenree, J., 51-52.
Johello, Mons., 51-52 (O 28–N 8).
John, 39-40 (F 11–My 10).
Johnson, 28-29, 36-37.
Johnson, T. B., 43-44.
Jones, [99]-00, 00-01, 01-02, 02-03, 04-05, 05-06, 07-08, 25-26.
Jones, Mrs., [99]-00, 00-01, 25-26.
Jones, Miss Avonia, 57-58 (N 30–D 5, Ja 4-13).
Jones, Mrs. Melinda, 53-54, 57-58.
Jones, Solomon I., 29-30.
Jones, W. G., 44-45.
Jones, William, 09-10, 10-11.
Josephs, 50-51.
Judah, 20-21.
Judah, Emanuel, 35-36.
Justis, Mrs., 30-31.

Kaiffer, Mons., 40-41 (F 6, 24–Mr 8).
Kames, 49-50.
Katen, 28-29.
Kean, Charles, 31-32 (F 10-18), Mr 5-12), 39-40 (F 11-22), 45-46 (F 2-20).

Kean, Mrs. Charles, 45-46 (F 2-20).
Kean, Edmund, 25-26 (Mr 13–Ap 10).
Keene, Arthur, 20-21, 21-22, 23-24, 27-28, 52-53.
Keller Ballet Troupe, 57-58 (Mr 29–Ap 10).
Kelly, Miss Lydia, 28-29.
Kelsey, 34-35.
Kemble, Mr. and Mrs., 43-44.
Kemp, Miss, 60-61 (N 19-26).
Kensler, 50-51 (Mr 21–Ap 9).
Kent, John, 26-27.
Kenyon, 19-20, 20-21, 21-22, 22-23, 23-24, 24-25, 27-28.
Keough, Emma, 53-54.
Kilmeste Family, The, 48-49 (F 25–Mr 5).
King, Miss Ada, 57-58 (Ja 18–F 6), 58-59 (F 28–Mr 8).
Kirby, Mr. and Mrs., 25-26.
Knight, Mrs. Adeline, 37-38, 38-39.
Knight, Mrs. Eliza Povey, 27-28 (F 29–Mr 28).
Knox, 11-12.
Korsinski, Madame M., 47-48 (Ja 12-27), 48-49 (Mr 16-24).
Kreutzer, 50-51 (Mr 21–Ap 9).
Kunkel's Nightingale Burlesque Opera Troupe, 53-54 (O 17-28, My 1-9).
Kyle, 50-51 (D 26-28).

La Combe, Mrs., 27-28.
La Compte Ballet Troupe, 40-41 (F 6, 24–Mr 8).
La Rose, Miss, 43-44.
Labotierre, J. K., 03-04.
Laidley, 25-26.
Lamb, 24-25, 26-27.
Lamb, J. C., 44-45, 45-46.
Langdon, G. C., 54-55.
Langton, 31-32, 33-34.
Lannagan, 55-56.
Lanning, W. M., mgr., 35-36.
Larkins, 41-42, 42-43.
Larousseliere, 57-58.
Latham, W. H., 37-38, 38-39, 39-40; mgr., 41-42.
Latte, [99]-00.
Lattimer, Miss (Mrs. J. G. Holman), 16-17, 17-18, 20-21.
Laws, 26-27, 27-28.
Lawton, Miss, 58-59.

Leach, Mrs. S., 48-49 (D 7-16, Ja 1-6).

Lear, 28-29.

Leati, Mr. and Mrs., 48-49 (D 30).

Leaumont, 04-05, 06-07, 07-08, 10-11, 11-12.

Lee, C., 25-26.

Lee, Miss Mary Annie, 43-44, 46-47.

Lege, [99]-00, 00-01.

Lege, Master Cherri, 10-11, 11-12, 12-13, 16-17.

Legg, 16-17, 20-21.

Lehman Family, The, 47-48 (N 4-17).

Lemoyne, 58-59.

Lennox, Mr. and Mrs. W., 58-59.

Leoval, [99]-00.

Lester, John Wallack (J. Lester Wallack), 56-57 (N 17-29).

Lettine, Miss, 16-17, 17-18.

Lewellen, 40-41.

Lewellen's Trained Horses, 40-41 (Ap 28–My 5, 8-15).

Lewin, Miss, 20-21, 21-22.

Lewis, 00-01.

Lewis, Miss E., 50-51, 55-56.

Lewis, Henry (?), 57-58, 58-59.

Lietti, 50-51 (Mr 21–Ap 9).

Lind, Jenny, 50-51 (D 26-28).

Linden, Miss, 53-54.

Linden, R., 50-51.

Lindsey, 04-05.

Lindsley, 15-16, 23-24, 24-25.

Lingard, Mrs., 59-60.

Lipman, Mrs., 09-10.

Littell, Mr. and Mrs., 54-55.

Locatelli, Vicenzo, 49-50 (Mr 26–Ap 2).

Logan, Eliza, 54-55 (F 19–Mr 3, Ap 10-23).

Logan, T. D., 34-35.

Lomas, 55-56.

Lorini, Dominico, 49-50 (Mr 26–Ap 2), 51-52 (N 10-29).

Love, 38-39 (F 28–Mr 6), 59-60 (Ja 16-22).

Loveday, 55-56.

Lovell, Mr. and Mrs., 49-50.

Lowry, 23-24.

Lozier, J. C., 31-32.

Ludlow, Miss Kate, 51-52.

Lyons, George, 21-22, 29-30, 33-34, 34-35.

Lyons, Mrs. George, 33-34, 34-35.

Lyster, Fred, 57-58 (Ja 18–F 6), 58-59 (F 28–Mr 8).

Macallister, A., mgr., 49-50.

Macready, Charles William, 43-44 (Ja 8-19), 48-49 (Ja 8-17).

Maddox, 29-30.

Maguire, 28-29.

Major, 17-18.

Mandeville, 60-61 (N 19-26).

Manfredi Family, 07-08 (F 15–Mr 25).

Manvers, Mr. and Mrs., 41-42 (D 7-16, Mr 12-29).

Manville, 39-40.

Marble, Dan, 45-46 (N 24–D 1), 46-47 (F 9-17).

Marchant, G. F., 53-54, 56-57; mgr., 57-58, 58-59, 59-60, 60-61, 61-[62].

Marchant, Mrs. G. F., 56-57, 57-58.

Maretzek's, Max, Opera Company, 51-52 (N 10-29), 56-57 (F 16-17).

Marini, Ignazio, 49-50 (Mr 26–Ap 2), 51-52 (N 10-29).

Marino, 38-39.

Marks, Henry, 22-23, 23-24, 37-38, 38-39, 39-40, 40-41, 41-42, 47-48.

Marsh, B. G., Juvenile Comedians, 59-60 (Ja 2-14).

Marshall, 20-21, 21-22, 53-54.

Marshall, Mrs., 04-05.

Marshall, G., [99]-00, 00-01, 01-02, 02-03, 03-04.

Marshall, Mrs. G., [99]-00, 00-01, 01-02, 02-03, 03-04, 04-05, 06-07.

Marshall, Miss Louisa, 59-60.

Marshall, Polly, 59-60 (O 11-21).

Martinelli, Luigi, 49-50 (Mr 26–Ap 2).

Martinetti Brothers, 53-54 (Mr 20–Ap 8, 24-26), 58-59 (Ja 10-22, F 15-24), 59-60 (Ja 25–F 15).

Martini, Mons., 51-52 (O 28–N 8).

Martyn Opera Troupe, 40-41 (F 20).

Marzetti, Joseph, 47-48 (N 4-17).

Marzetti, Louis, 33-34 (Ja 7–Ap 25), 36-37 (Mr 10–My 15).

Mason, 24-25.

Mason, Charles K., 35-36, 37-38 (Ja 12-23, Mr 7-30, Ap 23-28), 50-51.

Massett, Stephen C., *See* Stephens.
Mathias, Yrca, 53-54 (Mr 20–Ap 8, 24-26).
Matthewes, T., Mrs. Charles and Miss Helen, 45-46.
Matthews, Mr. and Mrs. Charles, 57-58 (Ap 12-19).
Mauroi, [99]-00.
Maxwell, Miss, 55-56.
Mayberry, [99]-00, 00-01, 07-08, 11-12, 15-16, 16-17.
Maywood, Mrs. Martha, 45-46.
Maywood, Robert Campbell, 42-43, 44-45.
McBride, 38-39.
McBride, Miss M. C., 38-39, 39-40.
M'Cafferty, 20-21.
McClure, Mr. and Mrs., 38-39.
M'Cluskey, 43-44.
M'Cullock, 16-17.
McCutcheon, Thomas, 40-41, 44-45.
McDonald, 06-07, 07-08, 10-11, 11-12, 16-17, 25-26.
McDougall, R. W. (?), 48-49, 49-50.
M'Duall, Miss, 43-44.
McGowan, Mrs., 46-47.
McGregor, Mlle., 51-52 (O 28–N 8).
M'Kenzie, 07-08.
McLean, Mrs., 46-47, 47-48.
Meadowcraft, Miss, 32-33.
Meeker, W. H., 45-46, 46-47.
Meholla, 17-18.
Melmoth, Mrs., 02-03.
Melton, Miss, 37-38, 40-41, 41-42.
Melton, Charles M., 39-40, 41-42.
Melville, Douglas, Mr. and Mrs., 51-52.
Merryfield, Jerry, 40-41.
Mertevais and Hinson, 35-36 (Ap 7-11).
Metkiff, 58-59.
Meyer, 46-47 (F 22–Mr 6).
Meyer, F., 55-56.
Meyers, 43-44.
Millar, 31-32.
Miller, 23-24, 26-27.
Miller, 60-61 (N 19-26).
Miller, Miss, 00-01, 01-02, 26-27.
Miller, D. J., 55-56.
Miller, Miss Mary, 58-59.
Milner, 43-44.
Milner, Miss Annie, 60-61 (N 19-26).
Milot, 45-46.

Minnigin, Miss, 07-08 (F 15–Mr 25).
Mitchell, Maggie, 58-59 (D 21–Ja 8).
Mitchell, William, 44-45.
Monier, Miss Virginia, 27-28, 37-38.
Montez, Lola, 52-53 (D 6-10).
Montgomery, Mrs., 49-50.
Montplasir, W. M., Ballet Troupe, 51-52 (O 20–N 8).
Moore, Miss, 16-17.
Moore, John, 28-29.
Morant, Fannie, 55-56, 56-57 (Ap 14-21).
Morden, 02-03.
Moreland, A. G., 57-58.
Moreland, Harry, 22-23, 25-26, 28-29.
Morris, 26-27.
Morse, 06-07, 07-08, 10-11.
Morton, 27-28.
Morton, A. T., 54-55.
Morton, Charles H., 51-52, 52-53, 58-59.
Moses, 27-28.
Moss, Miss, 44-45 (Ja 29–F 15).
Mossop, Mrs. George, 44-45.
Movray, Mrs., 06-07.
Mowatt, Anna Cora, 45-46 (D 4-30, Ja 17-28), 46-47 (D 8-21), 53-54 (F 20–Mr 6).
Mozart's Don Giovanni Opera Company, 51-52 (D 1-13).
Mude, 17-18, 18-19.
Muiller, 46-47.
Muller, L., 56-57 (F 16-17), 57-58 (Mr 2-6).
Murdoch, James E., 48-49 (O 25–N 1), 58-59 (D 13-18).
Myers, Mrs., 50-51.

Nagel, 42-43.
Nagle, Joseph E., 54-55.
Nau, Mlle., 54-55 (Ja 16-20).
Neafie, Andrew Jackson, 49-50 (Mr 4-16), 50-51 (My 7-12), 52-53 (Ja 31–F 12), 56-57 (Ja 12-17).
Neufville, Mrs., 24-25.
New Orleans Burlesque Opera Company, 51-52 (D 15-27).
New Orleans English Opera Troupe, 57-58 (Ja 18–F 6), 58-59 (F 28–Mr 8).

Newton, 43-44.
Niblo's English Opera Troupe, 54-55 (Ja 16-20).
Nichols, W., 16-17, 17-18, 18-19, 19-20, 20-21, 23-24.
Nickerson, 31-32.
Nicola, 23-24, 26-27.
Noah, Mrs. W. J., 54-55 (N 13-D 2).
Norton, Miss, 58-59.
Nugent, 00-01.

Oatland, 26-27.
Oldmixon, Mrs., 05-06.
Ole Bull Company, 52-53 (F 8), 53-54 (Ja 23-24).
Ollier, J., 48-49, 50-51.
O'Neil, 52-53.
Otto's, Madame, Opera Company, 38-39 (F 11-23, Mr 18-Ap 6, My 2-10), 39-40 (D 13-27, Ja 20-F 3).
Owens, T., 51-52.
Oxley, John, 45-46, 46-47, 52-53, 53-54.

Page, 17-18.
Palmer, 16-17; mgr., 33-34, 34-35. 61 (N 5-7, 12-13).
Palmer, Mrs., 33-34.
Palmer and Harrington's Circus, 33-34.
Palmer's Pavilion Circus, 36-37.
Parisian Ballet Troupe, 51-52 (O 8-18).
Parker, Miss Ada, 48-49.
Parker, John, 25-26.
Parks, 56-57.
Parodi, Madame Teresa, 59-60 (F 20-Mr 14).
Parozzi, 50-51 (Mr 21-Ap 9), 51-52 (N 10-29).
Parsloe, C. T., 39-40 (Ja 4-25), 40-41 (D 28-Ja 1).
Parsons, Charles Booth, 26-27, 27-28.
Patti, Adelina, 52-53 (F 8), 53-54 (Ja 23-24).
Patti, Adelina, and Company, 60-61 (N 5-7 ,12-13).
Paul, Mons., 42-43 (Ja 9-21).
Payne, Miss H., 60-61 (N 19-26).
Payne, Master John Howard, 09-10 (Mr 26-Ap 30).
Pearson, Henry, 40-41, 43-44.

Pebernard, Jean, 33-34 (Ja 7-Ap 25), 36-37 (Mr 10-My 15).
Peck, 47-48.
Pelby, William, 23-24 (Ap 6-9).
Pemberton, 20-21, 21-22.
Penistan, 58-59.
Penson, Mrs., 49-50.
Perkins, 00-01, 03-04.
Perkins, Mrs., 00-01.
Perkins, Granville, 53-54, 55-56.
Perry, H. A., 51-52.
Petrie, Robert P., 20-21.
Phillips, Miss, 43-44.
Phillips, Aaron J., 15-16 (Ap 19-24), 18-19 (N 16-27, F 2-22), 41-42.
Phillips, Adelaide, 46-47 (F 22-Mr 6), 57-58 (Mr 2-6).
Phillips, Mrs. H., 48-49 (D 7-16, Ja 1-6).
Phillips, H. B., 42-43; mgr., 43-44; 44-45, 59-60.
Phillips, Mrs. H. B., 42-43, 43-44, 59-60.
Phillips, J. B., 26-27.
Phillips, M.S., 48-49 (Ap 16-21).
Pico, Mlle. Rosina, 48-49 (Mr 14-15).
Pinder, Mr. and Mrs., 31-32.
Pitt, 26-27.
Pitt, Charles Dibden, 47-48 (D 13-30), 48-49 (Ja 29-F 2).
Pitt, Mrs. Charles Dibden, 48-49 (Ja 29-F 2).
Placide, Alexander, mgr., [99]-00, 00-01, 01-02, 02-03, 03-04, 04-05, 05-06, 06-07, 07-08, 08-09, 09-10, 10-11, 11-12.
Placide, Mrs. Alexander, [99]-00, 00-01, 01-02, 02-03, 03-04, 04-05, 05-06, 06-07, 07-08, 08-09, 09-10, 10-11, 11-12; mgr., 12-13.
Placide, Caroline (Mrs. Leigh Waring; Mrs. William Rufus Blake), 07-08, 09-10, 15-16, 16-17, 17-18, 18-19, 19-20, 20-21, 29-30.
Placide, Elizabeth, 02-03, 03-04, 04-05, 05-06, 06-07, 08-09, 10-11, 11-12, 12-13, 19-20, 20-21, 21-22.
Placide, Henry., 09-10, 10-11, 11-12, 12-13, 19-20, 20-21, 21-22, 22-23, 40-41 (D 8-23, Ja 25-F 3), 44-45 (D 16-21), 45-46 (D 24-30), 46-47 (Ja 13-16).

Placide, Jane, 08-09, 09-10, 10-11, 11-12, 12-13.
Plumer, Mr. and Mrs. Cramer, 29-30.
Poe, David, 03-04.
Poe, Mrs. David, 10-11.
Pougaud, Mlle., Leontine French Ballet Troupe, 53-54 (N 21–D 3).
Power, Tyrone, 34-35 (D 2-8), 40-41 (F 8-19).
Pozzesi, 50-51 (Mr 21–Ap 9).
Presto, 26-27.
Preston, Henry W., mgr., 47-48.
Preston, T., 32-33, 33-34; mgr., 35-36.
Preston, Mrs. T., 31-32, 32-33, 33-34, 35-36.
Prigmore, Mr. and Mrs., [99]-00.
Pritchard, James, 19-20.
Proctor, Joseph, 43-44.
Pullman, Miss S., 48-49.

Queen Sisters, The, *See* Thespian Family.
Quin, 17-18, 18-19, 19-20.
Quinto, L., 56-57 (F 16-17), 57-58 (Mr 2-6).

Rachel's, Mlle., Dramatic Corps (Elizabeth Rachel, Lia, Dinah, and Sarah Felix), 55-56 (D 10-17).
Radcliffe, Thomas, 44-45.
Ralton, D. E., 57-58, 59-60.
Raphael, 43-44.
Ravel Family, 33-34 (Ja 7–Ap 25), 36-37 (Mr 10–My 15), 38-39 (Ap 22–My 7), 39-40 (N 19-27), 48-49 (D 18-28), 53-54 (Mr 20–Ap 8, 24-26), 58-59 (Ja 10-22, F 15-24), 59-60 (Ja 25–F 15).
Raymond, Miss Adelaide, 58-59.
Raymond, John T., 49-50, 55-56, 56-57, 59-60.
Rea, Mr. and Mrs. Frank, 54-55, 57-58.
Read, 26-27.
Read, Mrs., 26-27, 27-28.
Reed, 53-54.
Reed, R., 38-39, 39-40, 40-41.
Reede, Miss, 52-53.
Reeves, Mrs., 23-24, 55-56.
Reeves, W. H., 47-48 (Ja 12-27), 48-49 (Mr 16-24, D 7-16, Ja 1-6).

Remoussin, 08-09, 09-10.
Reynolds, 55-56.
Rice, 06-07, 08-09.
Rice, Decius, 28-29, 29-30.
Rice, T. D. ("Jim Crow"), 33-34 (D 9-20).
Richards, 58-59.
Richards, Mr. and Mrs. Davis, 33-34.
Richardson, Miss, 50-51 (F 10–Mr 3, Ap 28–My 14).
Richings, 34-35.
Rickets, 01-02, 02-03.
Riddle, Mr. and Mrs. and Miss C., 30-31.
Riddle, Miss Eliza, 26-27, 30-31.
Riddle, Miss S., 26-27.
Rieff, Antoine, 57-58 (Ja 18–F 6), 58-59 (F 28–Mr 8).
Riggs, Mrs., 59-60.
Riley, Henry J., 30-31.
Ringwood, 06-07, 07-08, 08-09, 09-10, 19-20.
Rink, 42-43, 43-44.
Rivers, 15-16, 58-59.
Rivers, Mrs., 40-41.
Roberts, Miss, 52-53.
Roberts, James, 27-28.
Robertson, 01-02.
Robertson, Mrs., 27-28 (Ap 9-26).
Robertson, Agnes, 55-56 (Mr 13-29), 56-57 (D 15-27).
Robertson, Hopkins (?), 11-12.
Robertson, W., 19-20, 20-21, 21-22, 22-23, 23-24.
Robinson, 15-16.
Robinson, Alexander, 47-48; mgr., 48-49.
Robinson's, Alexander, Equestrian Company, 44-45 (F 24–Mr 1).
Rock, Mary, 30-31 (N 29–D 20, F 23, Mr 11-23).
Rodney, 38-39.
Rossi, 50-51 (Mr 21–Ap 9), 51-52 (N 10-29).
Rousset Sisters Dance Troupe, 52-53 (Ap 4-16).
Rowe, Mr. and Mrs. George, 25-26.
Russell, Miss, 22-23, 23-24.
Russell, Mr. and Mrs. R., 20-21.
Rutherford, 04-05, 09-10.
Rutley, Mr. and Mrs., 02-03.
Ryder, Mr. and Mrs., [99]-00.
Ryder, William, 43-44, 50-51.

Sage, Mrs., 26-27.
Salvi, Lorenzo, 49-50 (Mr 26–Ap 2).
Sandford, Samuel S., 51-52 (D 15-27).
Sandford, Samuel S., Opera Company, 59-60 (N 14-19).
Sandrue, 51-52.
Santford, 06-07, 07-08.
Sarzedas, David A., 26-27, 29-30.
Sathill, 41-42.
Saunders, 16-17.
Savage, S. S., 51-52.
Savannah Quartette Club, 61-[62] (O 15-16).
Saxon, Miss Kate, 54-55.
Sbriglia, G., 59-60 (F 20–Mr 14).
Schinotti, 17-18, 18-19, 19-20.
Schmidt, 35-36.
Scholes, 20-21.
Schreiber, Louis, 56-57 (My 11).
Scott, Mr. and Mrs. John, 29-30.
Scott, John R., 43-44 (D 12-20).
Scott, Robert J., 27-28, 42-43.
Sedley, Henry (?), 37-38.
Sefton, John, 43-44, 53-54 (D 5-10).
Seguin, Mr. and Mrs. Arthur E. S., Opera Company, 39-40 (Mr 11-28), 41-42 (D 7-16, Mr 12-29), 42-43 (Mr 3-18, Ap 10-27), 43-44 (Mr 7-11), 44-45 (Ja 29–F 15), 46-47 (F 22–Mr 6), 48-49 (D 7-16, Ja 1-6).
Sera, 24-25.
Seward, 17-18, 18-19.
Seymour, 00-01, 02-03.
Seymour, Mrs., 00-01, 01-02.
Sharp, Mrs., 34-35, 37-38.
Shaw, Mrs., 39-40, 40-41 (N 24–D 5, 21-24).
Shaw, Misses C. and J., 39-40.
Shaw, Miss Mary, 57-58.
Shelley, Walter, 47-48.
Shepherd, R. A., (?), 52-53.
Sherman, Henry, 39-40 (D 13-27, Ja 20–F 6).
Shirreff, Miss Jane, 38-39 (F 11-23, Mr 18–Ap 6, My 2-10), 39-40 (D 13-27, Ja 20–F 6).
Shrival, 42-43 (Mr 3-18, Ap 10-27), 43-44 (Mr 7-11).
Sierson, 05-06.
Silsbee, 56-57.

Silsbee, J. S., 43-44 (Ap 1-3), 44-45 (N 25-30).
Siminski, Madame, Musical Company, 53-54 (Ap 20).
Simms, William Gilmore, 54-55 (Mr 27).
Simpson, 27-28.
Simpson, Mrs., 02-03, 03-04, 04-05, 08-09, 27-28.
Sinclair,, Miss Anna, 50-51.
Sinclair, Mrs. C., 52-53 (D 20-30).
Sinclair, John, 41-42.
Singleton, 24-25.
Sissan, Mlle., 51-52 (O 20–N 8).
Sivori, Camillo, 47-48 (N 4-17).
Sloan, John, 52-53; mgr., 53-54, 54-55, 55-56, 56-57.
Sloan, Mrs. John, 52-53, 53-54, 54-55, 55-56.
Sloman, John, 29-30 (F 22–Mr 8), 34-35, 39-40 (Mr 30–Ap 6), 42-43 (F 24-27), 46-47 (Ja 4-13), 48-49; mgr., 52-53; 54-55.
Sloman, Mrs. John, 29-30 (F 22–Mr 8), 39-40 (Mr 30–Ap 6), 52-53.
Smith, 40-41, 42-43.
Smith, Miss, 16-17, 32-33.
Smith, Mrs., 16-17.
Smith, Master George Frederick (?), 20-21 (Ap 6-14).
Smith, G. H., 46-47.
Smith, G. W., 53-54 (Ap 10-15), 55-56.
Smith, H. S., mgr., 50-51.
Smith, James Sidney, 57-58.
Smith, T. R., 57-58.
Smith, Theodore I., 32-33.
Solomon, [99]-00, 01-02, 02-03.
Solomon, Miss, 02-03.
Somers, 52-53.
Somerville, 22-23.
Sothern, E. A., 59-60 (O 24-29).
Soto Dance Troupe, 53-54 (Ap 10-15).
Southwell, Henry, 29-30.
Sowerby, F., 29-30.
Spanoletti, 17-18.
Spear, 07-08, 08-09, 09-10.
Spencer, 53-54.
Spencer, Mrs., [99]-00.
Spiller, 16-17, 17-18, 21-22, 22-23, 23-24, 24,25.
Spiller, Mrs., 17-18, 21-22, 22-23.
Spinicuta, Mr. and Mrs., 07-08.

Valentine, 44-45.

Vallee, Miss Henrietta, 47-48.

Valtellina, Mons., 47-48 (Ja 12-27), 48-49 (Mr 16-24).

Vandenhoff, George, 47-48 (Ja 4-7), 52-53 (D 20-30).

Vandenhoff, John M., 37-38 (Ja 24-F 9).

Vegas, Mons., 51-52 (O 8-18).

Victorian, 07-08 (F 15-Mr 25).

Viennoise Children, The, 48-49 (N 13-25, D 2-5, Mr 28-Ap 3).

Vietti, Adelino, 48-49 (Mr 14-15).

Vietti, Carolina, 49-50 (Mr 26-Ap 2).

Viewig, Carl, 61-[62] (O 15-16).

Villalave Family, The, 27-28 (F 5-Mr 1).

Villiers, 01-02, 02-03.

Villiers, Mrs., *See* Miss E. A. Westray.

Vitto, de Carlo, 56-57.

Walcot, Charles Melton, Jr., 58-59 (N 16-20).

Walcot, Charles Melton, Sr., 50-51.

Waldgrave, 28-29.

Waldron, 30-31, 31-32.

Wallack, Henry, 19-20 (Mr 1-11), 23-24 (F 21-27, Mr 4-20, 31-Ap 5).

Wallack, J. Lester, *See* John Wallack Lester.

Wallack, James W., 32-33 (F 4-25), 43-44 (F 26-Mr 6, 12-16), 46-47 (D 1-7), 56-57 (D 1-13).

Wallis, Joseph L. (?), 58-59.

Walters, Miss, 52-53.

Ward, Thomas, 39-40, 46-47, 47-48.

Ward, Mrs. Thomas, 47-48.

Warden, Edward A., 52-53.

Waring, Leigh, 15-16.

Waring, Mrs. Leigh, *See* Caroline Placide.

Warrell, 19-20.

Warren, Miss, 39-40.

Warton, H., 57-58 (Ja 18-F 6), 58-59 (F 28-Mr 8).

Warwick, J. H., 53-54.

Waters, 30-31.

Watson, Mrs., 40-41.

Watson, C., 49-50.

Watt, 35-36.

Watts, 53-54.

Weaver, John H. (?), 50-51.

Webster, 08-09.

Weiss, Madame Josephine, 48-49 (N 13-25, D 2-5, Mr 28-Ap 3).

Wells, Master and Miss, 39-40 (D 30-Ja 17).

Wells, Mr. and Miss, 29-30.

Welsh, Mr. and Mrs., 43-44.

Wesley, 49-50.

West, 03-04, 27-28, 28-29, 31-32.

West, J., 03-04, 04-05, 06-07, 07-08, 08-09, 11-12, 15-16, 16-17, 17-18, 18-19, 19-20.

West, Mrs. J., 19-20.

West Horse Troupe, 19-20 (F 3-10, Ap 3-15).

Western, H., 00-01.

Weston, J. M., 37-38, 38-39, 39-40, 40-41, 54-55.

Westray, Miss E. A. (Mrs. Villiers), 02-03, 03-04, 04-05.

Wheatley, Mr. and Mrs. Frederick, 19-20, 20-21.

Wheatley, Mrs. S. and Master William, 19-20.

Whiting, Virginia, 50-51 (Mr 21-Ap 9), 51-52 (N 10-29).

Whitlock, Mr. and Mrs., 03-04, 04-05, 05-06.

Wickens, Miss, 60-61 (N 19-26).

Wiethoff, 51-52 (O 20-N 8).

Wilkins, 25-26.

Wilkinson, 25-26.

Willard, 29-30.

Williams, 17-18 (F 11-14).

Williams, Mrs. 20-21, 52-53.

Williams, Mr. and Mrs. Barney, 53-54 (Ja 30-F 11).

Williams, E. B., 54-55, 56-57.

Williams, Falvy, 43-44 (Ja 13, F 8-14).

Williams, H. A., 26-27.

Williams, T., 22-23.

Williamson, 27-28.

Williamson, J. Brown, [99]-00, 00-01, 01-02.

Williamson, Mrs. J. Brown, 01-02.

Wilmot, 04-05.

Wilson, 05-06, 19-20.

Wilson, A., 38-39 (Ja 9-18).

Wilson, John, 39-40 (D 13-27, Ja 20-F 6).

Wilton, Miss Emma, 55-56.

Winson, Mrs., 01-02.

Winther, Charles, 47-48 (N 4-17).

Wood, Mr. and Mrs. C., 48-49.
Wood, J. S., 48-49.
Woodham, Mrs., 07-08.
Woodhull, Mr. and Mrs. J., 29-30.
Woodville, Mrs., 04-05.
Wray, Mrs., 45-46, 46-47, 51-52.
Yates, 48-49.
Young, Mr. and Mrs., 06-07, 07-08, 08-09, 10-11, 11-12.

Young, Charles, 17-18, 18-19, 31-32, 35-36.
Young, Edward, 15-16, 16-17, 17-18, 18-19, 19-20, 21-22, 31-32.
Young, Mrs. Edward, 15-16, 16-17, 17-18, 18-19, 19-20, 21-22.

Zouaves, The, French Soldiers of the Crimea, 61-[62] (N 25-30).

X: THE PLAYWRIGHT LIST

THE FOLLOWING LIST includes approximately three hundred writers whose plays were presented on the Charleston stages between 1800 and 1861. Parentheses are used to enclose titles of doubtful authorship.

Abbott, William: *Swedish Patriotism.*

A'Beckett, Gilbert: *Don Caesar de Bazan.*

Adam, Adolph: *The Brewer of Preston; The Postillion of Lonjumeau.*

Addams, J. P.: *The Redwood; Sam Patch in France.*

Addison, Joseph: *Cato.*

Aiken, G. L.: *(The Old Chateau [Homestead]); Raffael, the Reprobate; Uncle Tom's Cabin.*

Allingham, J. T.: *Fortune's Frolic; Hearts of Oak; The Marriage Promise; Mrs. Wiggins; 'Tis All a Farce; The Weathercock.*

Almar, George: *Crossing the Line.*

Amherst, H. J.: *Napoleon Bonaparte.*

Arnold, S. J.: *The Devil's Bridge; Man and Wife; The Veteran Tar.*

Auber, D. F.: *The Crown Diamonds; Fra Diavolo; Gustavus III; La Bayadere; Massaniello; The National Guard.*

Baker, B. A.: *A Glance at New York.*

Balfe, M. W.: *The Bohemian Girl; The Maid of Artoris.*

Banim, John: *Damon and Pythias.*

Bannister, N. H.: *Putnam; Robert Emmett.*

Barker, J. N.: *The Embargo; The Indian Princess; Marmion.*

Barnes, Charlotte M. S.: *(The Captive); (Charlotte Corday); La Fitte; Octavia Bragaldi.*

Barnes, William: *Bombastes Furioso.*

Barnett, C. Z.: *The Dream of Fate.*

Barnett, Morris: *Monsieur Jacques; The Serious Family; The Yankee Pedlar.*

Barrymore, William: *El Hyder; Gilderoy; Wallace.*

Bayley, T. Haynes: *The Barrack Room; The Culprit; A Gentlemen in Difficulties; The Ladder of Love; My Little Adopted; Perfection; Tom Noddy's Secret; You Can't Marry Your Grandmother.*

Beaumont and Fletcher: *Rule a Wife and Have a Wife.*

Beazley, Sam: *(The Boarding House); Fire and Water; Gretna Green; Is He Jealous?; The Lottery Ticket.*

Bellini, Vincenzo: *Il Puritani; La Somnambula; Norma.*

Bennett, George: *(Retribution).*

Bernard, W. Bayle: *The Dumb Belle; His Last Legs; Job Fox, the Yankee Pedlar; Man about Town; Middy Ashore; The Nervous Man and the Man of Nerve.*

Bickerstaff, Isaac: *The Absent Man; The Hypocrite; Love in a Village; The Maid of the Mill; The Padlock; The Romp; The Spoil'd Child; The Sultan.*

Birch, Samuel: *The Adopted Child.*

Bird, R. M.: *The Gladiator; Oraloosa.*

Blake, W. R.: *The Last Man.*

Boaden, James: *Fountainville Forest; The Italian Monk; The Maid of Bristol; The Voice of Nature.*

Boucicault, Dion: *Alma Mater; Andy Blake; Bluebelle; The Corsican Brothers; The Knight of Arva; London Assurance; Love and Money; (Nicholas Nickleby); Old Heads and Young Hearts; Pauline; Peg Woffington; The Phantom; Used Up; Victor and Hortense; Violet; The West End; The Willow Copse; The Young Actress.*

Brooke, Mrs. Francis: *Rosina.*

Brooke, Henry: *The Earl of Essex; Gustavus Vasa.*

Brough, William: *The Comical Countess.*

Brougham, John: *(Bachelor of Arts); (David Copperfield); Dombey and Son; (The Game of Love [Life]); The Gun Maker of Moscow; Love and Murder; Paul Pry; Temptation.*

Brown, Alfred: *The Crusaders.*

Brown, William: *West-Point Preserved.*

Browne, John: *Barbarossa.*

Buckstone, J. B.: *An Alarming Sacrifice; The Banished Star; The Bear Hunters; The Breach of Promise; The Dead Shot; The Dream at Sea; The Duchess de la Vaubaliere; Flowers of the Forest; Good for Nothing; Green Bushes; The Happiest Day of My Life; Husband at Sight; The Irish Lion; Leap Year; Married Life; Nicholas Flam; Our Mary Anne; Popping the Question; Presumptive Evidence; Rural Felicity; Shocking Events; Single Life; Two Queens; Victorine; The Widow Wiggins; The Wreck Ashore.*

Bulwer-Lytton, Edward: *The Lady of Lyons; Money; Richelieu; The Sea Captain.*

Burgoyne, John: *(The Lord of the Manor); The Maid of the Oaks; Richard Coeur de Lion.*

Burke, Charles: *Ole Bull.*

Burke, J. D.: *The Battle of Bunker Hill; The Inn-keeper of Abbeville.*

Burton, W. E.: *Forty Winks; The Ladies' Man; The Mummy; A Quiet Day; (The Ship-Launch); The Toodles.*

Butler, Mrs. Fanny K.: *The Duke's Wager.*

Butler, Richard: *Irish Tutor.*

Byron, H. J.: *(Marry in Haste).*

Calcraft, J. W.: *The Bride of Lammermoor.*

Carey, George S.: *(Shakespeare's Jubilee).*

Carey, Henry: *Chrononhotonthologos.*

Centlivre, Mrs. Susanna: *The Busy Body; The Wonder.*

Chapman, W. B.: *Mose in California.*

Cherry, Andrew: *The Travellers.*

Cibber, Colley: *The Provoked Husband; She Would and She Would Not.*

Clark, Stephen: *The Kiss.*

Clinch, C. P.: *The Spy.*

Cobb, James: *The Haunted Tower; A House to Be Sold; Paul and Virginia; The Siege of Belgrade.*

Coffey, Charles: *The Devil to Pay.*

Coleman, Benjamin: *The Hero of the North.*

Coleman, George (the Elder): *The Clandestine Marriage; The Jealous Wife; The Poor Gentleman; We Fly by Night.*

Coleman, George (the Younger): *Actor of All Work; The Battle of Hexham; Blue Devils; The Heir at Law; Inkle and Yarico; The Iron Chest; John Bull; (The Law of Java); Love Laughs at Locksmiths; Man and Wife; The Mountaineers; The Review; The Shipwreck; The Surrender of Calais; Sylvester Daggerwood; Ways and Means; Who Wants a Guinea?; X. Y. Z.*

Conner, Mrs. C. B.: See Charlotte M. S. Barnes.

Conrad, R. T.: *Jack Cade.*

Conway, H. J.: *(Charlotte Corday); Uncle Pat's Cabin.*

Cowley, Mrs. Hannah: *The Belle's Stratagem; A Bold Stroke for a Husband; The School for Greybeards; Which Is the Man?; Who's the Dupe?; The World as It Goes.*

Coyne, J. S.: *Done Brown; How to Settle Accounts with Your Laundress; (Lola Montez); The Man of Many Friends.*

Crafts, William: *The Sea Serpent.*

Cruikshank, George: *The Battle.*

Cumberland, Richard: *The Carmelite; The Jew; The Natural Son; The Sailor's Daughter; The West-Indian; Wheel of Fortune.*

Custis, G. W. P.: *The Indian Princess.*

Dance, Charles: *Bengal Tiger; Beulah Spa; Naval Engagements; The Old English Gentleman; Olympic Revels; Who Speaks First?*

Danvers, H.: *A Conjugal Lesson.*

Davenport, Fannie: *Adrienne, the Actress.*

Davenport, Robert: *The Pedlar.*

Dean, Julia: *Mary of Mantua.*

Delpini: *(Don Juan).*

Dibdin, Charles, Sr.: *The Birthday; The Deserter; The Metamorphoses; The Quaker; Rose and Colas; The Touchstone of Truth; The Waterman.*

Dibdin, Charles Isaac: *The Farmer's Wife.*

Dibdin, T. J.: *Alonzo and Imogene; The Cabinet; Guilty or Not Guilty; The Horse and the Widow; The Jew and the Doctor; Of Age Tomorrow; Past Ten O'Clock; The School for Prejudice; Valentine and Orson; The Will for the Deed.*

Dimond, William: *Adrian and Orilla; The Aethiop; The Bride of Abydos; The Broken Sword; Brother and Sister; The Conquest of Taranto; The Doubtful Son; Englishmen in India; The Foundling of the Forest; The Hunter of the Alps; The Lady and the Devil; The Peasant Boy; The Young Hussar; Youth, Love and Folly.*

Donizetti, Gaetano: *Anna Bolena; Don Pasquale; L'Elisir d'Amore; La Favorita; Lucia di Lammermoor; Lucrezia Borgia.*

Dudley, H. B.: *The Flitch of Bacon.*

Dunlap, William: *Abaellino; The Blind Boy; Bluebeard; Deaf and Dumb; False Shame; The Flying Dutchman; (Fraternal Discord); The Glory of Columbia; (Lovers' Vows); Nina; (Pizarro); (Shelty's Frolic); The Stranger; (The Virgin of the Sun); The Wife of Two Husbands; The Wild Goose Chase.*

Durivage, O. E.: *The Lady of the Lions; Richard Number Three; The Stage Struck Yankee.*

Farquhar, George: *The Beaux's Stratagem; The Inconstant.*

Farren, Percy: *The Field of Forty Footsteps.*

Field, J. M.: *The Artful Dodger; Family Ties; Griseldis.*

Fielding, Henry: *(The Mock Doctor); Tom Thumb the Great.*

Finn, H. J.: *Removing the Deposits.*

Fitzball, Edward: *The Daughter of the Regiment; Esmeralda; (Home Again).*

Flagg, E.: *(Mary Tudor).*

Fletcher, John: *The Elder Brother.*

Florence, W. T.: *Mischievous Annie.*

Foote, Samuel: *The Liar; The Mayor of Garratt.*

Fowler, M. B.: *The Prophecy.*

Galt, John: *(My Aunt).*

Gann, James: *The Mysteries of Paris.*

Garrick, David: *Catherine and Petruchio; The Clandestine Marriage; The Country Girl; Cymon and Sylvia; High Life below Stairs; The Irish Widow; The Lying Valet.*

Gautier, Theophile: *Giselle.*

Gay, John: *Beggar's Opera.*

Glover, S. E.: *The Last of the Mohicans.*

Goldsmith, Oliver: *She Stoops to Conquer.*

Gore, Mrs. Catherine: *King O'Neill; The Maid of Croissey.*

Graham, George: *Telemachus (in the Isle of Calypso).*

Greffuhle: *A Budget of Blunders.*

Grice, C. E.: *The Battle of New Orleans.*

Hackett, J. H.: *Jonathan in England; (The Times).*

Haines, J. T.: *Amilie.*

Harby, Isaac: *Alberti; The Gordian Knot.*

Harpley, T.: *The Milliners.*

Hatton: *(The American Brothers).*

Hayne, Mrs.: *See* Julia Dean.

Haynes, T. J.: *Mary Stuart, Queen of Scotland.*

Hoadley, Benjamin: *The Suspicious Husband.*

Hoare, Prince: *Lock and Key; Mahmoud the Robber; My Grandmother; No Song, No Supper; The Prize, Ten Thousand Pounds; Sighs; (Three and Deuce).*

Hodgkinson, John: *The Man of Fortitude; Robin Hood.*

Holcroft, Thomas: *The Deserted Daughter; Follies of a Day; Hear Both Sides; The Lady of the Rock; The Road to Ruin; The Steward; A Tale of Mystery; The Two Friends.*

Holland, Edwin C.: *The Corsair.*

Holman, J. G.: *Votary of Wealth.*

Home, John: *Douglas.*

Hook, Theodore E.: *Catch Him Who Can; Killing No Murder; Tekeli.*

Horncastle, James H.: *Buy It Dear, 'Tis Made of Cashmere.*

Inchbald, Mrs. Elizabeth: *Animal Magnetism; Everyone Has His Fault; Midnight Hour; The Mogul Tale; The Next Door Neighbors; Such Things Are; To Marry or Not to Marry; The Wedding Day; The Wise Man of the East; Wives as They Were and Maids as They Are.*

Ioor, William: *The Battle of Eutaw Springs and the Evacuation of Charleston; Independence.*

Jackman, Isaac: *All the World's a Stage.*

Jephson, Robert: *Julia; Two Strings to Your Bow.*

Jerrold, Blanchard: *Cool as a Cucumber.*

Jerrold, D. W.: *Ambrose Gwinnett; Black Eyed Susan; Hazard of the Die; The Rent Day; Time Works Wonders.*

Joddrell, Paul: *Seeing Is Believing.*

Johnson, S. D.: *Brian O'Lynn; In and Out of Place; Our Gal.*

Johnstone, J. B.: *Ben Bolt.*

Jones, J. S.: *The Carpenter of Rouen; The Green Mountain Boy; The People's Lawyer.*

Jones, Richard: *The Green Man.*

Kelly, Hugh: *A School for Wives.*

Kemble, Charles: *Plot and Counterplot; The Point of Honor; The Wanderer.*

Kemble, Mrs. Charles: *A Day after the Wedding; Match Making; Smiles and Tears.*

Kemble, J. P.: *Lodoiska.*

Kenney, James: *Count Benyowski; Ella Rosenberg; (The Illustrious Stranger); Love, Law and Physic; Matrimony; Raising the Wind; Too Many Cooks; Turn Out.*

Kerr, John: *Rip Van Winkle.*

Killigrew, Thomas: *Chit Chat.*

Knight, Thomas: *The Honest Thieves; Thelypthora.*

Knowles, J. S.: *Brian Boroihme; The Bridal; Caius Gracchus; The Hunchback; John of Procida; Love; The Love Chase; The Maid of Mariendorpt; Virginius; The Wife; William Tell; Woman's Wit; The Wrecker's Daughter.*

Lancaster, Edward: *The Manager's Daughter.*

Lee, Nathaniel: *Alexander the Great.*

Lee, Sophia: *A Chapter of Accidents.*

Leigh, Richard: *Grieving's a Folly.*

Leman, Walter: *(The Millionaire).*

Lemon, Mark: *Don Caesar de Bazan; Grandfather Whitehead; The Ladies' Club; Out of Place; A School for Tigers; What Will the World Say?*

Lewis, M. G.: *Adelgitha; Adelmorn; Alfonso of Castile; The Castle Spectre; Timour the Tartar.*

Lillo, George: *George Barnwell.*

Logan, C. A.: *Vermont Wool Dealer; Yankee Land.*

Lovell, G. W.: *Love's Sacrifice; The Provost of Bruges.*

Lovell, Mrs. Maria Anne: *Ingomar.*

Lover, Samuel: *The Happy Man; Rory O'More.*

Lunn, Joseph: *Family Jars; A Fish Out of Water.*

Macklin, Charles: *Love a la Mode; Man of the World.*

Macready, William: *The Irishman in London; The Village Lawyer.*

Marston, J. W.: *Ann(ie) Blake; The Patrician's Daughter; (Phillip of France).*

Massinger, Phillip: *The Fatal Dowry; New Way to Pay Old Debts; The Roman Actor.*

Matthews, Charles: *The Dowager; Patter versus Clatter; (Take that Girl Away); The Wolf and the Lamb.*

Maturin, C. R.: *Bertram.*

Medina, L. H.: *Ernest Maltravers; The Last Days of Pompey; Nick of the Woods.*

Mercadante: *Il Guiramento.*

Meyerbeer, Giacomo: *Robert le Diable.*

Miles, G. H.: *Mary's Birthday; Mohammed.*

Milman, H. H.: *Fazio.*

Milne, William: *(The Comet).*

Milner, H. M.: *Alonzo the Brave; (The Gambler's Fate).*

Milton, John: *Comus.*

Mitford, Mary R.: *Rienzi.*

Molière, Jean: *Le Tartuffe.*

Moncrieff, W. T.: *(The Bashful Man); The Cataract of the Ganges; Foreign Airs and Native Graces; Giovanni in London; Monsieur Mallett; Monsieur Tonson; The Somnambulist; Tom and Jerry; Wanted—A Wife.*

Moore, Edward: *The Gamester; Gil Blas.*

Morris, Edward: *The Secret.*

Morton, J. M.: *(Aladdin); All that Glitters Is Not Gold; Box and Cox; The Double Bedded Room; Friend Waggles; Grimshaw, Bagshaw, and Bradshaw; The King and I; Lend Me Five Shillings; A Most Unwarrantable Intrusion; My Precious Betsy; My Wife's Come; My Wife's Second Floor; (Our Wife); Poor Pillicoddy; A Roland for an Oliver; Slasher and Crasher; The Spitfire; Thumping Legacy; To Paris and Back for Five Pounds; The Two Bonny Castles; (Two Buzzards); Where There's a Will There's a Way; Your Life's in Danger.*

Morton, Thomas: *The Angel of the Attic; The Children in the Wood; Columbus; A Cure for the Heartache; Education; Go-to-Bed-Tom; Henry Quatre; The Invincibles; A Pretty Piece of Business; The School of Reform; Secrets Worth Knowing; Speed the Plough; Town and Country; The Way to Get Married; Zorinski.*

Mowatt, Mrs. Anna C.: *Armand; Fashion.*

Mozart, Wolfgang: *Don Giovanni; The Marriage of Figaro.*

Murphy, Arthur: *All in the Wrong; The Apprentice; The Citizen; The Grecian Daughter; Know Your Own Mind; The Old Maid; Three Weeks after Marriage; The Way to Keep Him.*

Murray, W. H.: *Cramond Brig.*

Neuman, Henry: *Self Immolation.*

Noah, M. M.: *Marion; Nathalie; She Would Be a Soldier; The Wandering Boy(s).*

O'Keeffe, John: *The Agreeable Surprise; The Castle of Andalusia; The Farmer; The Highland Reel; The Lie of the Day; Modern Antiques; The Poor Soldier; The Son-in-Law; Sprigs of Laurel; Wild Oats; The Young Quaker.*

Otway, Thomas: *The Orphan; Venice Preserved.*

Oulton, W. C.: *Botheration; Frightened to Death; The Sixty-Third Letter; The Sleep Walker.*

Oxberry, W. H.: *Actress of All Work; The Pacha's Pets.*

Oxenford, John: *Dr. Dilworth.*

Parke, John: *(Virginia).*

Parry, Tom: *The First Night.*

Paul, H. H.: *(Marion).*

Paulding, James K.: *The Kentuckian.*

Payne, J. H.: *Accusation; Adeline; Ali Pa(s)cha; Brutus; Charles II; Clari; Love in Humble Life; (Lovers' Vows); Mahomet; The Maid and the Magpie; (Mazeppa); Therese; 'Twas I.*

Peake, R. B.: *Amateurs and Actors; Blanche of Jersey; The Bottle Imp.*

Phillips, Ambrose: *The Distressed Mother.*

Pilgrim, James: *(Ireland and America); (Irish Assurance and Yankee Modesty); Kathy O'Sheal; The Limerick Boy; Shandy Maguire.*

Placide, Alexander: *Birth, Death and Renovation of Harlequin.*

Planché, J. R.: *The Brigand; Captain of the Watch; Charles XII; Faint Heart Ne'er Won Fair Lady; Follies of a Night; Fortunio; Grist to the Mill; Irish Post; The Jacobite; The Knights of the Round Table; The Loan of a Lover; Secret Service; Somebody Else.*

Pocock, Isaac: *For Freedom! Ho!; Hit or Miss; John of Paris; The Miller and His Men; Rob Roy MacGregor; The Robber's Wife; Zembuca.*

Pocock, John: *The Green-Eyed Monster.*

Poole, John: *Hamlet Travestie; Intrigue; John Buzzby; Married and Single; Patrician and Parvenu; The Scape Goat; Sweethearts and Wives; The Two Pages of Frederick the Great.*

Power, Tyrone: *Born to Good Luck; How to Pay the Rent; The Irish Ambassador; The Irish Attorney; O'Flannigan and the Fairies; Paddy Carey.*

Ranger: *Father and Daughter.*

Ravel Family: *The Bedouin Arabs; The Green Monster; Nicodemus.*

Ravenscroft, Edward: *The Anatomist.*

Raymond, R. J.: *Cherry Bounce.*

Reade, Charles: *The Courier of Lyons.*

Rede, W. L.: *Faith and Falsehood.*

Reed, Leman: *(The Backwoodsman); (Hue and Cry).*

Rees, James: *Lucretia Borgia.*

Remoussin, A.: *Youth, Love, and Matrimony.*

Requier, A. J.: *The Spanish Exile.*

Reynolds, Frederick: *Arbitration; Begone Dull Care; Blind Bargain; (The Bridal Ring); Cheap Living; Delays and Blunders; The Delinquent; The Dramatist; The Exile; Folly as It Flies; How to Grow Rich; Laugh when You Can; Life; Management; (The Will).*

Rook, W. M.: *Amilie.*

Rossi, Gaetano: *Il Guiramento.*

Rossini, Giacomo: *The Barber of Seville; La Gazza Ladra; Tancredi.*

Rowe, Nicholas: *The Fair Penitent; Jane Shore.*

Sargent, Epes: *Velasco.*

Sawyer, Lemuel: *(Black Beard, the Pirate).*

Schiller, Johann: *The Robbers.*

Schomberg, Ralph: *(The Judgment of Paris).*

Sefton, John: *The Mysteries of Paris.*

Selby, Charles: *Boots at the Swan; Catching an Heiress; A Day in Paris; The Fire Eater; Frank Fox Phipps, Esq.; The Unfinished Gentleman.*

Shakespeare, William: *Antony and Cleopatra; As You Like It; A Comedy of Errors; Coriolanus; Cymbeline; Hamlet; Henry IV; Henry VIII; Julius Caesar; King John; King Lear; Love's Labor Lost; Macbeth; The Merchant of Venice; The Merry Wives of Windsor; Much Ado about Nothing; Othello; Richard III; Romeo and Juliet; The Taming of the Shrew; The Tempest; Twelfth Night; A Winter's Tale.*

Shannon, Charles: *The Youthful Queen.*

Sheil, R. L.: *The Apostate; Evadne.*

Sheridan, R. B.: *The Critic; The Duenna; (Pizarro); The Rivals; (St. Patrick's Day); The School for Scandal.*

Siddons, Henry: *A Tale of Terror; Time's a Tell-Tale.*

Simmons, J. W.: *De Montalt; The Master of Ravenswood.*

Simms, W. G.: *Michael Bonham; (The Yemassee).*

Smith, Albert: *The Cricket on the Hearth.*

Smith, Charles: *(Fraternal Discord); The Happy Family; (La Pe(y)rouse); (Pizarro); (The Virgin of the Sun).*

Smith, W. H.: *The Drunkard.*

Soane, George: *The Falls of Clyde.*

Somerset, C. A.: *The Day after the Fair.*

Southerne, Thomas: *Isabella.*

Stirling, Edward: *Bachelor's Buttons; Blue Jackets.*

Stokes, J.: *The Forest of Rosenwald.*

Stone, J. A.: *Fauntleroy; The Knight of the Golden Fleece; Laroque, the Regicide; Metamora.*

Talfourd, Sergeant: *Glencoe; Ion.*

Taylor, Tom: *(Play, Plot and Passion); Still Water Runs Deep; The Vicar of Wakefield.*

Terry, Daniel; *Guy Mannering.*

Thomson, James: *Tancred and Sigismunda.*

Tobin, John: *The Curfew; The Honeymoon.*

Turnbull, J. D.: *(The Maid of Hungary); The Wood Demon.*

Verdi, Guiseppe: *Ernani; Il Trovatore; La Traviata; Rigoletto.*

Walcot, C. M.: *The Custom of the Country; Nothing to Nurse; South Carolina's Contribution to the World's Fair.*

Waldron, F. G.: *The Miller's Maid.*

Wallace, Vincent: *Maritana.*

Wallack, W. H.: *Paul Jones.*

Ware, C. P.: *Azael.*

Weber, Carl von: *Der Freischutz.*

Webster, Benjamin: *The Golden Farmer; My Young Wife and My Old Umbrella; Swiss Swains; The Village Doctor.*

Wemyss, F. C.: *The Mysteries of Paris; Norman Leslie.*

White, J. B.: *Foscari; Modern Honor; The Mysteries of the Castle.*

White, James: *The King of the Commoners.*

White, William C.: *The Clergyman's Daughter; The Poor Lodger.*

Whitehead, William: *The Roman Father.*

Wild, James: *(The Miser).*

Wilkins, John: *Camille.*

Wilks, T. E.: *Bamboozling; Ben, the Boatswain; The Devil's in It; State Secrets.*

Williamson, J. B.: *Preservation.*

Woodward, Henry: *Harlequin Dr. Faustus.*

Woodworth, Samuel: *The Forest Rose; Lafayette.*

Workman, James: *Liberty in Louisiana.*

Young, Edward: *(The Revenge).*